SOLIDARITY AND SCHISM

SOLIDARITY AND SCHISM

*'The Problem of Disorder' in
Durkheimian and Marxist Sociology*

DAVID LOCKWOOD

CLARENDON PRESS · OXFORD

1992

Oxford University Press, Walton Street, Oxford OX2 6DP
Oxford New York Toronto
Delhi Bombay Calcutta Madras Karachi
Petaling Jaya Singapore Hong Kong Tokyo
Nairobi Dar es Salaam Cape Town
Melbourne Auckland
and associated companies in
Berlin Ibadan

Oxford is a trade mark of Oxford University Press

Published in the United States
by Oxford University Press, New York

British Library Cataloguing in Publication Data
Data available

Library of Congress Cataloging in Publication Data
Lockwood, David, 1929–
Solidarity and schism : 'the problem of disorder' in Durkheimian and
Marxist sociology / David Lockwood.
p. cm.
Includes bibliographical references and index.
1. Sociology—Philosophy. 2. Durkheimian school of sociology.
3. Marxian school of sociology. 4. Social conflict. 5. Order
I. Title.
HM24.L76 1992 303.6'01—dc20 91-26810
ISBN 0–19–827717–2

Typeset by Cambridge Composing (UK) Ltd
Printed and bound in
Great Britain by Bookcraft (Bath) Ltd,
Midsomer Norton, Avon

For Leonore

PREFACE

The work that follows is an attempt to extend and clarify a line of argument which was first stated, highly schematically, in a critique of Talcott Parsons's book, *The Social System*.[1] The fact that the essay was extensively reprinted and referred to during the following years encouraged me to think that the themes it pursued might be worth treating in more detail. It was written at a time when its viewpoint was less than fashionable, and its target the most influential social theory of the day. This might explain both why the essay's lease of life was prolonged and why it is almost invariably cited as an early contribution to 'conflict' as opposed to 'consensus' theory—even though its main purpose was to argue that the distinction is an artificial and unproductive one. This is also a major theme of the present work.

The subject of that essay, and of this book, is one that Parsons, above all, kept in the forefront of the conception of what sociology is about: namely, 'the problem of order'. His efforts to establish this problem as the central focus of sociological theory—against the tendency of the subject to fragment into more or less fortuitously proliferating specialisms—provided for a long time the closest approximation to what may be considered a genuine paradigm. In the intervening years, of course, sociology has not stood still. Parsons's solution of the problem of order (almost entirely Durkheimian in its derivation), and the conceptual edifice he built upon it, no longer command the authority they once had for his followers and critics alike. It is also easy to have considerable sympathy with the judgement that the work which developed in opposition to Parsons's system, and which contrasted a conflict to a consensus model of society, has outlived its usefulness. Indeed, it might be supposed that this whole debate is a chapter in the history of the subject which is best closed, in order that the serious work of studying less grandiose and more exigent problems can proceed unhindered by such metasociological confrontation.

[1] D. Lockwood, 'Some Remarks on "The Social System"', *British Journal of Sociology* (1956).

Yet this would be to ignore the fact that the specific form of the arguments centering on Parsons's social theory represented only one phase of an intellectual tradition that is far older than sociology as the latter is usually understood. And it is unlikely that sociology, which—like any other activity—has a need to discover and adhere to its own centre, will readily abandon the theoretical legacy that has provided it with whatever fragile coherence it possesses. More importantly, the rejection of these concerns as purely metasociological is a view that greatly underestimates the extent to which more specific, substantive theories of the middle range are of necessity formulated in terms that imply some kind of solution of the problem of order. For these reasons, it may be supposed that, although the form of the debate will alter, its significance will not diminish. At different ends of the theoretical spectrum, the evident shortcomings of the structureless world of ethnomethodology and the actorless world of structural Marxism have attested to the fact that the key problems of the Parsonian schema have not been removed from the agenda but have merely been reproduced in different and arguably much less adequate terms. Moreover, within mainstream social theory, the renewal of interest in the writings of the classical founders of modern sociology has resulted in several notable works of exposition and interpretation which have contributed directly or indirectly to what might be regarded as the beginnings of a post-Parsonian formulation of the problem of order. Marxian and Marxist social theory found no real place in Parsons's work, and this is an omission that those working within and without his problematic have sought to remedy.[2]

It is to this continuing debate that the present work seeks to contribute. Its title indicates the scope of the study, namely, the analysis of order and disorder at the level of social rather than system integration,[3] the limiting cases being denoted by the terms 'solidarity' and 'schism'. Because Durkheim and Marx are the thinkers whose insights into the nature of order and conflict have

---

[2] G. Poggi, *Images of Society* (Stanford, 1972), was an important early contribution to this revision, and J. C. Alexander, *Theoretical Logic in Sociology*, ii (London, 1982), is unquestionably the most authoritative.

[3] For this distinction, see D. Lockwood, 'Social Integration and System Integration', in G. K. Zollschan and W. Hirsch (eds.), *Explorations in Social Change* (New York, 1963). This essay is reproduced in the Appendix below.

had the most profound influence on the general and particular treatment of these issues in modern sociology, their theories were the natural starting-point. And because the basic flaws of both theories can be revealed most clearly by examining the assumptions underlying their explanations of social conflict (anomic declassification and class polarization respectively), the problem of disorder is the main subject of the following discussion.

In addition to this bald statement, some inkling of how the work began and unfolded may be appropriate. At the inception, the fact that Durkheim's work deals only marginally with the nature of social disorder suggested that a remedy might be sought in the implications of his explanation of social solidarity. By contrast, in the case of Marx, the explanation of order seemed entirely subordinated to the question of the conditions making for class conflict, although this had more to do with the economic theory of capitalist-system contradiction than with any systematically worked out political sociology of revolution. From these considerations, several problems emerged.

To begin with, Durkheim's limiting case of disorder, anomie, appeared in several ways to be inconsistent with the assumptions underlying his limiting case of order, solidarity. First of all, it seemed that an alternative conception of disorder was available. Instead of a society lapsing into the unstructured chaos suggested by his idea of anomie, there was entailed by the notion of solidarity a state of affairs in which the polarization of society into two totally opposed moral communities presented itself as an equally logical possibility. This implicit, limiting case of disorder came eventually to be described as schism. Secondly, it seemed that an alternative conception of order could be derived from Durkheim's frequent reference to the 'utilitarian' or economic factors which he considered to be the prime causes of anomic disorder. This led to a re-examination of his obscure concept of 'fatalism', and to the discovery that this contained a hidden theory of order (conditional fatalism)—although an alternative concept of 'ethical fatalism' would have been more in keeping with the centrality he accorded to shared values and beliefs in his theory of social solidarity. Conversely, these normative elements were strikingly absent in the explanation of anomie, whose most general cause was a sudden change in the distribution of 'power and wealth'. But this, like the other terms Durkheim used to describe the utilitarian or profane sphere of society, was patently peripheral to his social theory and very uncertain in its connotation; most especially since it seemed to refer to what in another place he calls 'the distribution of men and things', rather than to any definite set of social relationships. Nevertheless, some notion of class structure seemed to be at least nascent in this shifting and uncertain terminology.[4]

At a certain stage, not immediately, the incongruity between status and power then suggested itself as a conceptual means of elucidating these basic contradictions in the analysis of order and disorder. The idea of a status system, or what Durkheim refers to occasionally as 'social classification', turned out to be indispensable in bridging the gap between his fairly explicit theory of solidarity and his sketchy account of anomic disorder, whose general form he describes as social declassification. The notion of a status system as the major structural embodiment of common values and beliefs and, more particularly, as a major determinant of wants or interests, was also a concept which eventually proved to have an important bearing on many of the problems raised by the Marxist problem of disorder. The latter presented itself first and foremost as that of why proletarian revolution had not occurred in the most advanced capitalist societies. It is safe to say that this question has been decisive for the course of Marxist theory almost from the beginning. Less obvious were the manifold ways in which the presentation and solution of this problem were founded on a utilitarian theory of action[5] whose assumptions were the exact opposite of the predominantly normative ones which had caused greatest difficulty in making sense of the inconsistencies between Durkheim's overt theory of order and his covert theory of disorder.

At this point, the line of enquiry that appeared most intriguing was to consider the implications of ideological class polarization as a limiting case of disorder. And, since Durkheim had thought of society as basically a religious entity, it seemed at least worth trying to pose and reconsider the Marxian problematic of revolu-

---

[4] In particular, E. Durkheim, *Suicide: A Study in Sociology*, trans. J. A. Spaulding and G. Simpson with an introduction by G. Simpson (London, 1952), 252–4.

[5] On the utilitarian theory of action, see T. Parsons, *The Structure of Social Action* (New York, 1937), 51–60.

tionary conflict in terms of schism, that is as 'a state of disunion, dissension, or mutual hostility', or as 'a division into mutually opposing parties of a body of persons that have previously acted in concert; the division of a church into mutually hostile organizations'.[6] As a result of this way of looking at the problem of class polarization, several things fell into place, the principal clue being found in the residual, but indispensable, role of normative factors within Marxism's basically utilitarian action schema, with all the implications this had for the troublesome notion of class interest.

The assumption of rational egoists pursuing their system-determined interests was one that seemed to predominate in explanations of both why proletarian revolt is imminent and yet why it is indefinitely postponed. In the former case, the normative determination of wants played an insignificant role in theories of the awakening of proletarian consciousness which dwelt on such conditions as material and moral impoverishment, and on the exigencies of revolutionary practice. Such elements were also at first equally residual in theories of ideological domination, which became increasingly the principal means of explaining the absence of class polarization. In this type of theory, it is notions of ignorance and error (the only sources of deviation from rational action) which are called on to account for putative false consciousness, whether this is seen as the product of deliberate indoctrination or as an unintended system effect: that is, as the indirect result of rational, self-interested action. Within this action schema, then, there appeared to be little room for normative or value elements, for an understanding of how they are grounded in social action: in short, a lack of appreciation of the significance of the category of nonrational as opposed to irrational action.

Normative factors were either subsumed under an all-embracing notion of ideology at the societal level, or else they were drawn on *ad hoc* at the situational level by invoking an undefined notion such as 'tradition'. Value elements therefore remained analytically undifferentiated from other ideological components, which meant in turn that they were most usually assimilated into the category of the rational or the irrational, depending on whether they were seen as means of action on the part of the indoctrinator or as

---

[6] *The Shorter Oxford English Dictionary.*

conditions of action on the part of the indoctrinated. One consequence of this was to exclude consideration of how norms are embodied in status systems, and thereby of how nonrational evaluations enter into the definition of class interest. Most importantly, however, this action schema resulted in chronic theoretical instability, marked by the oscillation between highly positivistic and idealistic explanations of revolutionary consciousness or the lack of it. In this way, proletarian revolt or passivity could equally well be accounted for—the former being seen as the fairly direct outcome of some unspecified kind and degree of economic deprivation; and the latter as due to an equally indeterminate, because global, ideological domination.

These then appeared to be the basic features of the Marxist action schema, which, once explicated, served to elucidate not only many of the problems faced by specific theories of class formation but also the direction in which these theories have developed. Perhaps the most important example of this is provided by revisions of the theory of ideology. As the need to explain the lack of revolutionary consciousness became more exigent, the kind of indoctrination theory whose utilitarian underpinnings are probably most pronounced in the work of Lenin gave way to a theory of 'hegemonic' domination, in which class-neutral, or common, values became quite central, and in which there was explicit recognition of the extent to which class interests are determined not so much by irrational, scientifically corrigible, beliefs as by the kind of moral, nonrational commitments to ultimate values that had hitherto occupied a small space within the Marxist action schema. In this way, the theory of class polarization appeared to return full circle to the problem of disorder entailed by Durkheim's notion of social solidarity—not least because, for Gramsci, the exemplar of hegemony was the Church.

The general results of the investigation just outlined can be stated summarily as follows, though naturally not in the order in which they gradually emerged. The chief conclusion is that, although deriving from apparently very different conceptions of society, the explanations of disorder demanded of Durkheimian and Marxist sociology entail remarkably similar assumptions about the structuring of social action. Reduced to its essentials, the thesis is that:

1. Each body of theory has a dominant conception of structure, that is a concept of society as a system, and, associated with this, a dominant conception of the determinants of social action. In relation to these, other concepts of structure and action remain residual or inchoate.

2. Given these assumptions, each theory generates for itself a 'problem of disorder' (actually a set of discrete but interrelated problems) for the solution of which its dominant concepts of structure and action prove inadequate.

3. As a result, in the explanations of their respective problems of disorder, both theories are marked by a necessary, but more or less *ad hoc*, recourse to, or promotion of, their residual concepts of structure and action.

4. In turn these auxiliary hypotheses serve to show that the concepts of social structure and social action characterizing the two bodies of theory are at once antithetical and complementary, in that the residual concepts of the one theory are those which enjoy analytical priority in the other.

This said, it is important to point out what the work does not seek to accomplish. First of all, it is not intended to be a balanced and comprehensive exposition of the work of Durkheim and Marx. Given the concentration on the problem of disorder, the use of their writings is inevitably selective, and surely tendentious. Assaying the authentic Durkheim and Marx is therefore not part of the purpose. Secondly, it is not only their writings that are taken into account, but also those of other scholars who can be placed within the Durkheimian and Marxist traditions. This is done analytically rather than chronologically. For example, since Smelser's analysis of 'value oriented movements' is the most highly elaborated theory of disorder of Durkheimian provenance, it is introduced as, so to speak, independent evidence in testing criticisms that can be made of Durkheim's own rudimentary theory of moral innovation. Thirdly, whilst at several points the thesis is buttressed by reference to a broad range of social and historical research, its subject matter is mainly conceptual and the evidence adduced in favour of particular arguments is more often than not intended to be illustrative rather than conclusive. Finally, the study does not seek to propound a new system of sociology. Although highly critical of both Durkheimian and Marxist explanations of disorder, and more especially of their underlying assumptions about the structuring of social action, it is far from the intention to replace them by some abstract, anodyne synthesis. There are firm grounds for thinking that would be a futile exercise. What might be hoped for is that the demonstration of the weaknesses and strengths of both bodies of theory, and above all of their complementarity, will contribute to a better sociological practice.

D.L.

Wivenhoe,
May 1991

ACKNOWLEDGEMENTS

I have worked on this book intermittently over a good many years, during which time the basic line of argument has undergone several substantial shifts in emphasis. As a result, some of those who offered comments on various parts and versions of the manuscript, or on publications arising from it, could well be forgiven if by now they have forgotten that they ever made them. If they do remember, they might well wonder what effect their views have had on the final result. However this may be, I am very grateful to the following for their detailed criticisms of my writings: André Béteille, Ernest Gellner, John H. Goldthorpe, Geoffrey Hawthorn, Michael Mann, Gordon Marshall, and Frank Parkin.

At one stage, my work was generously supported by a Personal Research Grant (HR 6268/2) from the then Social Science Research Council.

To Mary Girling I am very much indebted for her unstinting secretarial assistance whilst performing what I always think of as her chief role—holding together the Department of Sociology at the University of Essex.

The book is dedicated to my wife, Leonore Davidoff, for her support, encouragement, and example.

Parts of this book have been previously published as follows: Chapter 3, 'The Ethics of Fatalism', is a virtually unamended version of an article entitled 'Fatalism: Durkheim's Hidden Theory of Order', which appeared in A. Giddens and G. Mackenzie (eds.), *Class and the Division of Labour: Essays in Honour of Ilya Neustadt* (Cambridge, 1983). Chapter 5, 'Anomic Declassification', includes slightly amended passages from an article entitled 'On The Incongruity of Power and Status in Industrial Society', which appeared in *Status Inconsistency in Modern Societies* (Proceedings of the ISA Reseach Committee on Social Stratification; H. Strasser and R. W. Hodge (eds.), Duisburg, 1986). Chapter 10, 'The Theory of Action', and Chapter 16, 'The Problem of Class Action', include revised passages from an article entitled 'The Weakest Link in the Chain? Some Comments on the Marxist Theory of Action', which originally appeared in G. and I. Simpson (eds.), *Research in the Sociology of Work* (Connecticut, 1981).

The Appendix reproduces 'Social Integration and System Integration', which appeared in G. K. Zollschan and W. Hirsch (eds.), *Explorations in Social Change* (New York, 1963), in its original form—a decision that may be justified by the fact that subsequent interest in the article has centred more on the conceptual distinction it seeks to make rather than on the few historical details on which it rests.

CONTENTS

PART ONE
SOLIDARITY

I.

THE DURKHEIMIAN DILEMMA

I

To the extent that societies may be thought of as systems, they are surely distinguished by their peculiar need for solidarity and their occasional liablity to schism. And because consensus is the unique constitutive property of societies, as opposed to other kinds of systems, it is primarily as the study of the causes of solidarity and schism that sociology (as opposed to the hundred and one sociologies of this, that, and the other) has its *raison d'être* as an autonomous discipline. More than anyone else, Durkheim is the founder of the subject in this sense, the incomparable theoretician of the bases of social order. The ideas he fashioned for this purpose have the power and simplicity of extraordinary intuition; and it is no exaggeration to say that, where contemporary social theory is not a refinement and revision of Durkheim's ideas, any rival interpretation of social order and social conflict that wishes to be taken at all seriously must address itself to his formulation and solution of this problem. But, since the insights of Durkheim's theory are profound, its deficiencies are also in every sense outstanding and equally worthy of note. This chapter introduces one of them. It is an important, enlightening flaw which also faults the neo-Durkheimian school of normative functionalism.[1]

The main source of this problem is to be found in Durkheim's ambiguous and contradictory explanation of disorder or anomie. But it is more than just a problem. It poses a dilemma, which can be stated most briefly by asserting that his basic concepts of the structuring of social action force a choice between two limiting states of social disorder which are within these suppositions equally unthinkable and untenable. This is of considerable import-

---

[1] The assumptions which distinguish normative, from general functionalist analysis are set out in the Appendix, 'Social Integration and System Integration'.

ance, mainly because Durkheim is credited with a solution of 'the problem of order' on which Parsons and his school of normative functionalism have based a whole system of sociology which, despite much criticism, remains a major reference point in contemporary debates on the sense in which societies may be said to possess or lack social integration. It is as well, therefore, to begin by saying something in general terms about Durkheim's concept of order and the notion of solidarity which designates its limiting case.

II

Reduced to its essentials, Durkheim's explanation of social order rests on two ideas which are expressed most generally by his distinction between the individual's 'need for discipline' and his 'need for attachment to groups'.[2] Moderation in the regulation of human wants and in the attachment of individuals to social groups is the precondition of psychological and social stability alike. This fundamental distinction between regulation and attachment appears in a variety of forms throughout his work: the moral community of the church is integrated by both shared beliefs and a common ritual; social solidarity is built upon both a society's collective conscience and the spontaneous attachments between individuals and groups that result from the division of labour; and, again, in the context of his study of suicide, the under- and over-regulation of wants results in the pathologies of anomie and fatalism just as the under- and over-attachment to groups leads to correspondingly extreme forms of egoistic and altruistic modes of behaviour. Groups no less than individuals are in need of moral discipline and of membership in larger social entities than themselves if a society is to achieve stability.

Just as private conflicts can be only contained by the regulatory action of a society that embraces all individuals, so inter-social conflicts can only be contained by the regulatory action of a society that embraces all societies. The only power which can serve to moderate individual egoism

---

[2] E. Durkheim, *Moral Education*, trans. E. K. Wilson and H. Schnurer, foreword by Paul Fauconnet, edited, with an introduction by E. K. Wilson (New York, 1961).

is that of the group; the only one that can serve to moderate the egoism of groups is that of another group that embraces them all.[3]

Those who argue that the distinction between regulation and attachment is invalid because the two concepts are inseparable[4] fail to understand that, when sociologists refer to the individual's reference groups and his membership groups, they are making exactly the same kind of distinction. The case where the individual takes his norms from the same group which satisfies his need for group attachment[5] is only a limiting one. The fact that Durkheim, unlike Simmel, did not concern himself with the social fact of 'multiple group affiliations' may be surprising. But once this notion is introduced it only serves to show the validity and importance of the distinction between regulation and attachment. For example, if for whatever reason an individual comes to take his norms from outside his membership group, then this is likely to weaken his attachment to the latter. Conversely, people whose attachment to their membership group is for some reason weakened will be more likely to take their norms from another group. In these cases, it is both possible and useful to distinguish between regulation and attachment. The same applies to relationships between groups and the wider society. For example, a revolution-

[3] E. Durkheim, *The Division of Labour in Society*, with an introduction by L. Coser, trans. W. D. Halls (London, 1984), 336–7.

[4] See B. D. Johnson, 'Durkheim's One Cause of Suicide', *American Sociological Review*, 30 (1965). A sharper appreciation of the relevance of the distinction between egoism and anomie is to be found in the paper by A. R. Mawson, 'Durkheim and Contemporary Social Pathology', *British Journal of Sociology*, 21/3 (1970).

[5] 'When individuals who share the same interests come together, their purpose is not simply to safeguard those interests or to secure their development in face of rival associations. It is rather, just to associate, for the sole pleasure of mixing with their fellows and of no longer feeling lost in the midst of adversaries, as well as for the pleasure of communing together.' (*Professional Ethics and Civic Morals*, trans. C. Brookfield (London, 1957), 25.) Marx makes the same point in strikingly similar terms in his characterization of communist society: 'When communist *artisans* form associations, teaching and propaganda are their first aims. But their association itself creates a new need—the need for society—and what appeared to be a means has become an end. The most striking results of this practical development are to be seen when French socialist workers meet together. Smoking, eating and drinking are no longer a means of bringing people together. Society, association, entertainment which also has society as its aim, is sufficient for them; the brotherhood of man is no empty phrase but a reality, and the nobility of man shines forth upon us from their toil-worn bodies.' (*Karl Marx: Early Writings*, trans. and ed. T. B. Bottomore (New York, 1963), 176.)

ary sect, whether religious or secular, would rank high in terms of group integration and the 'altruism' of its members, but its goals would have to be thought of as extremely 'anomic'.[6] Conversely, some 'parish' groups may be said to be well regulated, perhaps even 'fatalistic', in accepting or acquiescing in ideological definitions of their derogation, yet at the same time they remain isolated from the wider society, but in this case by exclusion rather than choice. The various permutations of individual and group regulation and attachment are not of central concern here and enough has been said to demonstrate the possibility and utility of Durkheim's distinction.

Regulation and attachment refer to quite general features of social relationships, and their contribution to social solidarity is highly variable. It is impossible to make an exclusive distinction between social integration based on a primordial sense of attachment between individuals who are related to one another by ascriptive properties (such as age, sex, kinship, ethnicity, and linguistic or territorial affinities) and group integration based on shared values and beliefs. But it is indisputable that groups and societies do differ greatly in the extent to which their integration is due to ascriptive as opposed to consensual solidarity.[7] However, it is solidarity based on shared values and beliefs which will be of principal concern from now on, since this is the aspect of social integration that is given greatest emphasis in Durkheimian and normative functionalist sociology. It is also the more controversial aspect, because the way in which ascriptive solidarities enter into the determination of conflict and order can be dealt with to a large extent by the theory of multiple-group affiliations or cross-pressures, which is accepted by sociologists of all persuasions.

[6] The dynamics of attachment and regulation in such groups is of course complicated by the fact that they not only tend to attract already socially isolated or marginal individuals but cultivate their members' sense of detachment from the wider society by rituals of incorporation, tests of loyalty, promotion within steep hierarchies of authority and status as well as by time-consuming indoctrination and privileged acquisition of esoteric knowledge. A less extreme example is provided by the kind of working-class community that industrial sociologists have called an 'isolated mass', which is typically both highly solidary and refractory in the face of public opinion. See C. Kerr and A. Siegel, 'The Inter-industry Propensity to Strike: An International Comparison', in A. Kornhauser, R. Dubin, and A. M. Ross (eds.), *Industrial Conflict* (New York, 1954).

[7] On ascriptive solidarities, see T. Parsons, E. A. Shils, K. D. Naegele and J. R. Pitts (eds.), *Theories of Society* (New York, 1961), i.

III

With only that degree of simplification necessary to provide an initial definition of normative functionalism, it could be said that its trademark is Durkheim's view that society is ultimately a religious entity. His claim has two grounds. Historically, all major social institutions can be shown to have had their origin in religion. Sociologically, the integration of society has its basis in shared values, which, though not necessarily religious in origin, enjoy a sanctity similar to sacred beliefs proper. Durkheim's definition of a church is that it is 'a society whose members are united by the fact that they think in the same way in regard to the sacred world and its relation with the profane world, and by the fact that they translate these common ideas into a common practice'.[8] This could equally well represent his understanding of the fundamental constitution of society in general. The idea that society is a moral and ultimately a religious entity whose intrinsic feature is a set of commonly held values and beliefs[9] is, as Parsons has shown, not only Durkheim's main contribution to the theory of the integration of social systems, but one that is not fundamentally qualified by his untenable distinction between 'mechanical' and 'organic' types of solidarity.[10] Indeed, in arguing that the

[8] E. Durkheim, *The Elementary Forms of the Religious Life*, trans. E. K. Wilson and H. Schnurer (London, 1964), 44; see also p. 419; and, esp., p. 427: 'There can be no society which does not feel the need of upholding and reaffirming at regular intervals the collective sentiments and the collective ideas which make its unity and its personality. Now this moral remaking cannot be achieved except by the means of reunions, assemblies and meetings where the individuals, being closely unified to one another, reaffirm in common their common sentiments: Hence come ceremonies which do not differ from regular religious ceremonies, either in their object, the results which they produce, or the processes employed to attain these results.'

[9] 'Once a goal is pursued by a whole people, it acquires, as a result of this unanimous adherence, a sort of moral supremacy which raises it far above private goals and thereby gives it a religious character' (S. Lukes, 'Durkheim's "Individualism and the Intellectuals"', *Political Studies*, 17 (1969), 25 and 23 respectively).

[10] T. Parsons, 'Durkheim's Contribution to the Theory of Integration of Social Systems', in his *Sociological Theory and Modern Society* (London, 1967). Durkheim's notion of organic solidarity is unacceptable, because the fact of the interdependence of functions, from which the moral rules regulating this interdependence are supposed spontaneously to arise, is in itself just as likely to eventuate in conflict as in solidarity. This is partially recognized in Durkheim's introduction to the second edition of *The Division of Labour*; but only partially, because he still persists in thinking that the lack of spontaneous regulation is due to the rapidity of social change.

former type of solidarity refers to the higher level of ultimate values and the latter to the lower level of differentiated norms, Parsons has conveniently made explicit the premiss which he and other normative functionalists share with Durkheim. This is that, in so far as a society may be said to have a structure, it is most fundamentally a moral order, a system of shared values and derivative norms, in which those values and norms legitimating the allocation of facilities and rewards are especially crucial. The distinctiveness of normative functionalism, like any other social theory, consists in its selective conceptual emphasis. Few sociologists of whatever persuasion would disagree with Shils's ecumenical statement that 'the stability of institutions, and the corporate bodies which define their boundaries, is fostered through power, through expectations of advantage, through the consensual legitimacy of the rules and authority in the institution, and through the attachments of members towards each other'.[11] It is, however, the relative importance attributed to moral consensus, expediency, or coercion which distinguishes one social theory from another. This emphasis takes the form of the development of a certain set of analytically differentiated concepts in relation to which another set remains inchoate and thus residual in its degree of systematization. Normative functionalism is distinguished by the analytical priority which it accords to the normative structuring of social action, and more particularly by the assumption that social order is based on a widespread consensus on values and norms. It is not a Lockean order created by rational egoists who are also 'reasonable' enough to recognize that their self-interest is best realized by adhering to common rules.[12] It is rather a consensus resulting from processes of socialization and ritual through which individuals

[11] E. A. Shils, *Centre and Periphery: Essays in Macrosociology* (Chicago, 1975), 30. For a concise account of these three classical solutions of the problem of order, see P. S. Cohen, *Modern Social Theory* (London, 1968), ch. 2; and D. P. Ellis, 'The Hobbesian Problem of Order: A Critical Appraisal of the Normative Solution', *American Sociological Review*, 36 (1971).

[12] The distinction between 'rationality' (the efficient or economic adaptation of means to a given end or ends) and 'reason' (the capacity to understand the unintended consequences of rational action and to adjust one's ends and means accordingly) not only distinguishes Locke's theory of order from that of Hobbes, but is crucial to an understanding of Marx's theory of class action, which assumes that, while capitalists act rationally, the proletariat possess the additional capacity of 'reason'. On this, see below, ch. 16.

acquire and renew the need to conform to the norms defining their roles in the institutions which make up the structure of social systems.

More specifically, this school of sociology has a marked tendency to conflate the descriptive and explanatory uses of the notion of 'norms'. In its most innocuous sense, normative structure denotes the institutional patterns of a society which can be taken as a major point of reference for identifiying stability and change. While this concept of structure obviously differs from that of Marxism and is not, as normative functionalists would have it, the only or major systematic property of a society, it is nevertheless an important, indeed an indispensable, way of defining one meaning of social structure. But although normative structure is equatable with institutions, the latter are not equivalent to actual regularities of social action. They are patterns of normative expectations which constitute only one element governing the relationships between actors. The distinction between actions and expectations is crucial because the use of the term 'institution' often implicitly includes the notion that social actions are indeed 'institutionalized' in the sense that their regularity is principally attributable to the constraint of normative expectations. A representative statement by Parsons brings this out clearly: 'A role may be defined as the structured, i.e., normatively regulated, participation of a person in a concrete process of social interaction with specified role-partners.'[13] Or again, 'A social system consists of a plurality of individual actors, interacting with each other in a situation . . . and whose relations . . . are defined and mediated in terms of a system of culturally structured and shared symbols.'[14] Even though Parsons would not wish to equate concrete social interaction with normatively governed action, this tendency occurs by default, since there is no other equally wide-ranging conception of how the totality of interactions making up a social system is 'structured', 'defined', or 'regulated'.

[13] Introduction to Parsons *et al.* (eds.), *Theories of Society*, p. 42. Full documentation of the point made above is provided by W. Mitchell, *Sociological Analysis and Politics: The Theories of Talcott Parsons* (Englewood Cliffs, NJ, 1967), 68–70, and by A. W. Gouldner, 'Some Observations on Systematic Theory, 1945–55', in H. L. Zetterberg (ed.), *Sociology in the United States of America* (Paris, 1956). On Durkheim, see Poggi, *Images of Society*, ch. 7, 'The Primacy of Norms'.

[14] T. Parsons, *The Social System* (London, 1952), 5–6.

A further difficulty of this approach is that it confuses a way of describing structure with a way of explaining social order. As Merton points out,

> it is not enough to refer to the 'institutions' as though they were all uniformly supported by all groups and strata in the society. Unless systematic consideration is given to the *degree* of support of particular 'institutions' by *specific* groups, we shall overlook the important place of power in society.[15]

The point is well taken, but it would be wrong to conclude from it that the only alternative to the normative functionalist explanation of order is to revert to equally over-simplified solutions in terms of coercion and advantage, of fear and cupidity. For one thing, that would lead directly to the opposite, but no less erroneous assumption, apparently favoured by 'conflict' theorists, that the structure of values and norms is of neglible importance in accounting for social disorder. But at this stage such issues are best set aside, since they raise highly complicated problems to which there can be only facile general answers. For the time being, it is more profitable to concentrate on particular theories of order and disorder as these arise, and to reserve comment on their more general implications until much later. It is, therefore, sufficient to note that Merton's criticism is the quite elementary one that institutions engender variable support. For this reason, the notion of institutionalization may be preferable to that of institutions *per se*. But, like the latter, it can serve no more than a descriptive purpose, its main use being to denote a state of solidarity—that is, to provide a measure of the degree to which order is consensual. The following statement by Williams expands on this idea and provides a useful definition of solidarity as a limiting concept of order.

> In the fully developed case, institutional norms are (1) widely known, accepted and applied; (2) widely enforced by strong sanctions continuously applied; (3) based on revered sources of authority; (4) internalized in individual personalities; (5) inculcated and strongly reinforced early in life; (6) and are objects of consistent and prevalent conformity.[16]

---

[15] R. K. Merton, *Social Theory and Social Structure* (Glencoe, Ill., 1957), 122.
[16] R. Williams, *American Society: A Sociological Interpretation* (New York, 1960), 31.

Provided that institutions are taken to refer to the backbone of normative structure, and that solidarity is defined as the limiting case where there is widespread conformity with, and internalization of, the normative expectations attaching to the roles making up institutions, these terms are unexceptionable. However, the idea that norms constitute the structure of a social system may, and also often does, carry with it two further and highly questionable propositions. The first is that normative regulation, operating through the mechanisms of socialization, ritual, and the morally unifying effects of deviance and punishment, is the only society-wide medium through which actions and interests are determined or 'structured'. The second is that this normative regulation is the basis of social order, if not social solidarity. These two theses of the integrative and systematic nature of the normative structuring of actions and interests are the most distinctive and contentious characteristics of normative functionalism.

The use of the term 'systematic' as applied to the normative determination of interests deserves some further comment. While it is certainly the case that the concept of structure as consisting of norms is the distinguishing feature of neo-Durkheimian sociology, no adherent of this school of thought would wish to deny that, at the level of concrete social interaction, interests are determined not only by normative expectations but also by what Parsons refers to as the 'realistic' aspects of the situation: that is, the means actors have at their disposal and the conditions that they have to take as given. For this reason, it is impossible for institutional norms to be other than imperfectly embodied in social action. But the distinction between what is taken to be the structure of a society as a whole, namely institutions, and the 'realistic' features of particular situations of action is all important.[17] The latter have not been generally understood as adding up

[17] It is important not only analytically but also from the point of view of Parsons's intellectual biography. The distinction between the 'situation of action' and the 'social system' levels of analysis marks the important transition in Parsons's work from *The Structure of Social Action* (New York, 1937) to *The Social System*. In the former book, the splendid critique of the positivistic and particularly of the utilitarian theory of action results in the formulation of a 'voluntaristic theory of action' in which the normative determination of ends and means is introduced as one important, but not overdetermining element of the 'unit act'. 'Positively a voluntaristic system involves elements of a normative character. Radical positivism eliminates all such elements completely from empirical relevance. A utilitarian

to some kind of equivalent, non-normative, macro-social 'structure', that is, as a system of social relationships arising from the unequal distribution of resources. Most significantly, the conceptual apparatus of neo-Durkheimian sociology excludes any notion of class structure. For example, autonomy is an important feature of the work situation, which is, in turn, one aspect of a broader category of class situation. From this it may safely be assumed that a worker's interests will be jointly determined by his normative expectations of autonomy and by the degree to which the technical and organizational conditions of his work actually provide him with autonomy. But it is characteristic of normative functionalism that, while normative expectations of autonomy would be located within a wider complex of institutions (and ultimately of values) which make up the social structure, the realistic structure of autonomy would have merely a situational relevance and would not be conceptualized as part of the class structure of the society.

This concept of structure as both normative and systematic, by contrast with the notion of structure as 'realistic' and 'situational', is merely a reformulation in a slightly more sophisticated manner of the classical Durkheimian polarity between the ordering nature of shared values and beliefs and the random egoistic interests of unsocialized individuals. In the same vein for example, Smelser proposes a hierarchy of the 'components of action' which has four levels: values, norms, roles, and facilities.[18] The lower levels of the hierarchy are held to be less 'central to the integration of social systems' and more specific in the determination of action. Thus, values stand at the top of the hierarchy because they have an integrative relevance for the society as a whole as well as for all the components lower in the hierarchy, but facilities (means)

---

system admits them, but only in the status of random ends which are thus only data for the empirical application of the theoretical system. In the voluntaristic theory they become integral with the system itself, positively interdependent with the other elements in specifically determinate ways. The voluntaristic system does not in the least deny an important role to conditional and other non-normative elements, but considers them as interdependent with the normative.' (pp. 81–2.) In *The Social System*, the transition to an analysis in which the structure of a system is to all intents and purposes equated with the normative is complete.

[18] N. J. Smelser, *Theory of Collective Behaviour* (London, 1962), ch. 2; see also below, ch. 6, s. II.

are lowest in the hierarchy because they are defined as having only a situational relevance. Therefore, by simply attributing systematic significance to the higher level components of values and norms, the question of whether situational facilities might usefully be considered to be part of a structure which is non-normative, but nevertheless also an identifiable property of the total society, is never raised. *Vis-à-vis* the normative system, situational facilities are demoted to the same *ad hoc* conceptual status as that which Durkheim accorded to individual self-interest. The defining property of normative functionalism, then, is its assumption that normative factors are the sole, systematic determinants of the interests of actors.

From its modern starting-point in the work of Durkheim, normative functionalism has been committed to that solution of the 'problem of order' which attributes greatest importance to consensus on ultimate values and beliefs.[19] This consensus is achieved principally by the socialization of individuals into an identification with values and beliefs which provide standards of legitimacy and which regulate wants in such a manner that the moral cohesion of the society is regularly reproduced. Contrariwise, when consensus is lacking, order is replaced by disorder. This theory of order is, of course, an extension of the idea of normative structure as the systematic determinant of interests. It is a short step from the conception of solidarity as consensual order to the thesis that value consensus is a necessary, if not a sufficient,[20] condition of order. But this involves turning a particular definition of order (since order could be defined simply as conformity with institutional rules without specifying the degree of moral commitment involved) into a general explanation of order.

---

[19] Giddens has argued that Parsons has presented a highly selective interpretation of Durkheim's social theory, even to the extent of having invented the 'problem of order' as a central concern of Durkheim's work. Even if this argument were convincing, and the latter part is certainly not, what is important is that Parsons's interpretation has been extremely influential. As a result, the only real sociological purpose of rediscovering the 'original' Durkheim would be to dismantle Parsons's interpretation and replace it by a comparably cogent one. See *Emile Durkheim: Selected Writings*, ed. with an introduction by A. Giddens (Cambridge, 1972), 39–41.

[20] For instance, according to Durkheim, 'All that societies require to hold together is that their members fix their eyes on the same end and come together in a single faith.' In Lukes, 'Durkheim's "Individualism and the Intellectuals"', p. 23.

This theoretical approach has not been underpinned by any systematic enquiry into the correlation between order and consensus. This is perhaps not surprising, since neither is a common or garden variable. It is, however, not difficult to point to some instances of outwardly fairly orderly societies in which widespread adherence to common values appears to be lacking.[21] In the face of this objection it is, of course, possible to argue that the orderliness of such societies is inherently fragile. But to sustain this argument, it would be necessary to specify for how long, and with what degree of consensus on which particular values and beliefs, an inherently disorderly society can remain stable; and no normative functionalist has provided the formula. Nevertheless, the instancing of putative anomalies need not lead to a complete abandonment of the principle that a major consideration in the analysis of order and disorder is the extent to which actions are normatively structured and are in turn integrated through some degree of consensus on the values and beliefs from which these norms derive.

Even so, this position can serve only as a preliminary characterization of normative functionalism, as a convenient simplification which will provide a reference point for introducing more complex considerations, particularly the important qualifications that arise from the explication of the theory's residual categories. The tendency to ignore these complicating features, and to construct an easily demolishable straw man of normative functionalism, has been most evident among those whose main purpose is to promote some other, equally general, theory of social action. The latter has usually been some version of what Parsons called the 'utilitarian action schema'—now known principally as 'rational choice' theory—the very form of explanation in reaction to which normative functionalism originated, signally with Durkheim's critique of Herbert Spencer.[22] To a very great extent, however, these two vying perspectives have continued to elucidate very different sorts of issues, which correspond fairly well with Durkheim's archetypal distinction between the 'religious' and the 'economic' life. To

---

[21] See, e.g., P. van den Berghe, *South Africa: A Study in Conflict* (Berkeley, Calif., 1970), esp. chs. 9, 11; A. Lipjhart, *The Politics of Accommodation* (Berkeley, Calif., 1968); and B. Barry, *Sociologists, Economists and Democracy* (London, 1970), 86–7.

[22] Parsons, *The Structure of Social Action*, pt. I.

enter into the debate on the respective strengths and weaknesses of these two types of sociological explanation is not the main purpose of the present work. Nevertheless, issues bearing on this subject are raised at many points, because the distinction between rational and nonrational[23] action is the most useful way of identifying the residual categories of Durkheimian and Marxist theory alike.

To complete the preliminary survey of normative functionalism, one further and rather surprising feature of this school of thought may be noted. This is that a theory focusing on the consensual nature of social order should be conceptually so ill-equipped to deal with the variability of values and beliefs. At any rate, if it is assumed that the nature of particular beliefs is at least as significant for the understanding of order and conflict as the extent to which beliefs are shared, then it is quite remarkable that this line of argument is not at all salient in Durkheim's theory of solidarity and anomie, or in normative functionalism more generally. Durkheim's discussion of the subject is limited to the identification of highly formal properties of the 'collective conscience' (its volume, intensity, and determinateness) and of the very general aspects of the beliefs associated with mechanical and organic solidarity. But neither set of concepts is of much assistance in explaining variations in order and disorder. In the case of normative functionalism the omission is even more striking, given that the structure of values and beliefs is held to be the single most important factor in explaining long-run social change.[24] The reason for this theoretical hiatus would seem to be that, whereas normative functionalism takes its theory of social integration from the work of Durkheim, its theory of structural change stems mainly from the work of Weber. While Durkheim's main interest was in what all societies have in common, in what a society *is*, Weber's was in how societies

[23] The term 'nonrational' was coined by Parsons, ibid. 713, to emphasize the point that 'deviations' from purely rational action have to be understood not simply negatively in terms of 'ignorance and error', but also positively in the sense of action oriented to ultimate values and beliefs of which ritual action is prototypical. This is the principal respect in which Parsons's usage differs from Pareto's idea of 'nonlogical' action, which is the basis of the most important critique of utilitarian theory from within.

[24] The shortest, clearest and most emphatic statement is to be found in T. Parsons, *Societies: Evolutionary and Comparative Perspectives* (Englewood Cliffs, NJ, 1966).

differ. In particular, his comparative studies of the social ethics of religions, which remain unsurpassed in their scope and depth, provide an analysis of the structure of belief systems in contrast with which Durkheim's writings on religion and morality stand out as starkly deficient. Yet Weber, unlike Durkheim, offered no general theory of society that could found a distinctive school of thought. Thus normative functionalism, in basing itself on Durkheim's theory of society, and yet at the same time seeking to appropriate the substance of Weber's sociology of religion, has, as it were, kept two different sets of books. On the one hand, its general theory is derived almost entirely from Durkheim and oriented to the problem of order, whose conceptual limits are set by the ideas of solidarity and anomie. This is a problematic into which Weber's sociology does not easily fit. He was chiefly interested in the question of how different kinds of beliefs promote or hinder social change, particularly that which took the form of a movement from 'traditionalist' to 'rationalistic' economic activity. As such his theories have no ready-made applicability to the problem of order (which is not at all the same thing as saying that they do not have the most important potential relevance). Certain aspects of Weber's work were, nevertheless, particularly congenial to normative functionalism. To say that they were torn out of their context may be too strong an expression, but that they were most uncomfortably fitted into a basically Durkheimian model of society is undeniable. Weber's sociology of religion stands at some considerable distance from neo-Durkheimian 'social-system' theorizing. The appeal of his work seems to have been that it can be construed as providing the sufficient empirical basis of a sociology that attributes to values and beliefs a 'long-run' primacy in the structuring of social action; as providing a *cordon sanitaire* against Marxism.[25]

[25] Apart from his exposition of Weber's studies of religion in *The Structure of Social Action*, Parsons's introduction Weber's *The Sociology of Religion*, trans. and ed. E. Fischoff (London, 1965), is the major source, and it reveals very clearly the difficulties of accommodating Weberian categories to the main body of Parsonian theory. What is conspicuously absent from Parsons's interpretation is any reference to Weber's extremely crucial hypotheses about the determination of theodicies by the politico-economic structure. Weber's most explicit and unqualified statement of this kind is to be found in *The Sociology of Religion*, pp. 56–8.

IV

The foregoing introductory remarks can now be brought together by a statement of the thesis that will be pursued in chapters 2 to 6. It concerns what will be called the 'Durkheimian dilemma' because it is most clearly evident in his work, although it is a theoretical impasse typical of normative functionalism in general. The problem arises because the terms by which Durkheim sought a solution of the problem of order unavoidably posed a 'problem of disorder' which was insoluble within those same terms. Put alternatively, the concepts he used to define and explain order or solidarity entail two quite different conceptions of disorder, neither of which is tenable given his basic assumptions. These assumptions are twofold. The first is that order or disorder is defined by the degree of moral consensus, solidarity and anomie being the limiting cases. The second key assumption is that shared values are ultimately the only major source of the stable regulation of social interaction and of the structuring of wants or interests. Both assumptions enter into his idea of solidarity. But what limiting case of disorder is implied by solidarity? There are in fact two, and only two, possibilities. One is where consensus and moral regulation of social interaction are totally lacking. An approximation to this Hobbesian scenario is suggested by Durkheim's account of anomie. There is, however, another possibility that he does not seem to recognize, but which is equally conceivable, given the benchmark of solidarity. It is a form of disorder in which society becomes polarized around two opposing value and belief systems. This is most appropriately described as schism, a concept in keeping with his tendency to identify society as a basically religious entity. And following his broad usage of the term religion, schism may also be understood in a general rather than in a strictly ecclesiastical sense.[26] Schism also refers to a

[26] The general definition given by *The Shorter Oxford English Dictionary* is 'A state of disunion, dissension, or mutual hostility. Now, a division into mutually opposing parties of a body of persons that have previously acted in concert.' That such a disunion is defined primarily by reference to values and beliefs is basic to the sense in which the term schism is used here, even though this meaning is one which, in the ecclesiastical context, has been reserved for heresy in explicit contradistinction to schism. In practice, however, it has never been easy to draw a hard and fast line between groups adhering to 'false doctrine' and 'orthodox sects' which have broken from the church. See S. L. Greenslade, *Schism in the Early Church* (London, 1953).

disunion of the moral community which is endogenous; and thereby raises the question of what Mannheim called the utopian potentialities of ideologies, and more generally the exploitability of 'common values and beliefs'.[27]

Solidarity, therefore, yields two antithetical, extreme states of disorder: the amoral war of all against all; and the moral polarization of society into two irreconcilably opposed but internally solidary communities. These implications are the horns of the Durkheimian dilemma, since neither is compatible with his basic sociological assumptions. They are indeed unthinkable. If disorder means a complete lack of moral regulation it is tantamount to the termination of society. Conflict is socially unstructured. If it is not, what gives it any kind of form? This question is raised most acutely by Durkheim's further claim that anomie is an interregnum in the course of which society reconstitutes itself around a new system of values and beliefs. But it is impossible to explain how this occurs except by assuming that disorder is somehow socially structured. Schism is equally impossible to explain since it must mean that, instead of being the only source of social regulation, the common value system characterizing the state of solidarity is itself systematically disunited by some other social force, which again is unidentifiable within Durkheim's basic analytical scheme.[28]

This is the sense then in which Durkheim's sociology presents a 'problem of disorder'. The conceptions of disorder that can be derived from his solution of the problem of order force a choice between two equally unacceptable limiting cases of conflict. One is an unstructured, completely random, and interminable state of disorder, the cause of which remains obscure. The other is schism, or moral polarization, a form of structured conflict which is equally impossible to explain. This highly compressed statement of the Durkheimian dilemma naturally requires detailed substantiation. But its main purpose will be to show that the residual

[27] Karl Mannheim, *Ideology and Utopia* (London, 1952).
[28] Even if it were assumed that systems of values and beliefs vary in their degree of logical closure and hence in their inherent tendency to polarization, schismatic conflict would still pose the (for Durkheim) insoluble problem of the basis of differential adhesion to one or other of the rival 'churches'. Reference to degree of 'regulation' and 'attachment' would be useful only as a way of specifying what requires to be explained.

categories of his sociology point the way to a much more interesting theory of disorder in which the problems just delineated become, if not resolvable, at least more productively explicit. For the time being, it is sufficient to indicate this line of argument by noting that there are only two main ways of dealing with the Durkheimian dilemma. The less satisfactory one is to avoid or leave unstated the implications of the concept of disorder, whether this refers to moral deregulation or moral polarization. This tendency is certainly evident in the work of Durkheim and his successors, and has necessarily led to highly ambiguous interpretations of the concept of anomie. The other possibility is to abandon the assumption that the structuring of wants or interests is mainly a matter of moral regulation, and to recognize that interests are also shaped by a system of social relationships which has no necessary correspondence with the normative or institutional order. This way out of the Durkheimian dilemma has tended to take the form of referring to 'realistic' or 'non-normative' factors in a more or less *ad hoc* manner. They have not been treated as aspects of a wider system of social relationships which has to be included as part of what can be called the structure of a society.[29]

These considerations raise issues that are by no means narrowly confined to the explication of Durkheim's theory of disorder. Indeed, the overall argument will be strengthened if it can be shown that the selfsame problems are generated by his theory of order. For this reason, the discussion in chapter 2 focuses on the latter by raising the question of whether his account of the temporal alternation between the sacred and profane moments of social interaction provides an adequate explanation of what might be called 'normal' variations in solidarity. It will be argued that his account of how adherence to collective beliefs is first weakened by the pursuit of 'utilitarian' interests, and then strengthened through the act of ritual, is unconvincing, and that the major respects in which his explanation is deficient prefigure the main

---

[29] Indeed, in the case of Parsons, there is in his later work a quite clear and deliberate attempt to assimilate the concept of power to normative structure. The interesting aspect of this move (apart from the intrinsic merits and limitations of the concept of power he adopts) is that it is the only definition of power which is consistent with the normative conception of structure. For an incisive exposition and critique, see A. Giddens, '"Power" in the Recent Writings of Talcott Parsons', *Sociology*, 2 (1968).

inconstitencies of his theory of anomie. Approaching the same general problem from a rather different angle, Chapter 3 raises the question of whether there is implicit in Durkheim's theory of disorder a concept of order other than that of solidarity. It will be argued that a 'hidden' theory of fatalistic order can be derived from his explanation of anomie, and that the distinction between solidarity and fatalism serves to bring out the instructive ambiguity of the limiting case of anomie, and especially that form of it which Durkheim calls 'social declassification'.

It should be said, however, that although the following discussion centres on these key Durkheimian concepts, it is by no means exclusively concerned with his work, and is certainly not intended as a comprehensive and balanced exposition of his sociology. Since it focuses on the problem of disorder, a considerable amount of extrapolation will be necessary, simply because his treatment of this subject is so sparse and incomplete. Moreoever, since the wider aim of the present work is to find a common ground between Durkheimian and Marxist theories of disorder, the arguments that follow are in this respect quite openly tendentious.

2.

RITUALS AND
HYPER-RITUALS

I

Durkheim's theory of solidarity presupposes that a 'collective conscience', or a system of shared values and beliefs, is a necessary condition of order.[1] Most of his work is concerned with those institutions which he considered vital for the production of solidarity: religion, law, education, and the division of labour. The attention devoted to the collective conscience itself is by comparison negligible. While Durkheim was aware that consensus is a variable, he made no systematic study of its variability, and on the question of the effects on solidarity and conflict of particular values and beliefs he is almost completely silent.

It is true that he identifies three formal properties of the collective conscience: volume, intensity, and determinateness. By volume is meant the extent to which members of society have their individual consciences filled by the collective one, the degree to which they share beliefs in common; by intensity he refers to the strength with which these beliefs are held; and by determinateness he denotes the degree of generality and specificity of the beliefs in question. The first thing to note about these concepts is that they relate to highly formal aspects of the collective conscience and avoid consideration of the question of the extent to which consensus might be affected by differences in the content of particular values and beliefs. One consequence of this is that his theory of disorder has, paradoxically, to invoke a form of explanation which is, if anything, more materialistic than the Marxist interpretation of ideology which he rejected.[2] His highly formal

---

[1] However, as will be seen in ch. 4, s. V, the implication of his account of anomic declassification is that a stable distribution of power is a precondition of the existence of moral consensus.

[2] See below, ch. 5.

conception of the structure of collective morality is characteristic of his propensity to think of social and moral forces in quantitative rather than qualitative terms. Volume, intensity, and determinateness are concepts that refer to matters of extent, and strength, and degree of definition, and principally to the question of how far beliefs are shared. They are not designed to address the question of whether some types of beliefs are more likely than others to contribute to solidarity or conflict. This is not to say that Durkheim never considers particular belief systems. That of the Australian aborigines is described in great detail in his treatise on the 'elementary' religious life. But these particulars serve the purpose of identifying the integrative functions of all religions, and not as a preliminary to the comparative study of religious beliefs from this viewpoint.[3] Indeed, Durkheim ruled out this method on the ground that the 'confusing' array of particular beliefs and rites obscured what it was important to discover about the 'religious mentality in general'. But, considering the importance he attributes to the integrative function of the collective conscience, it is very odd that throughout his writings there is so little consideration of the possibility that values and beliefs might vary in their contribution to social solidarity. It is more understandable that his theory of order and conflict contains equally limited reference to variations in adherence to common values and beliefs that are associated with class division and status differentiation.

Volume, intensity and determinateness are nevertheless concepts that provide a useful measure of the degree of consensus.[4]

---

[3] His work on 'primitive classification' aims to show how beliefs vary according to social structure, not how social solidarity varies according to beliefs. E. Durkheim and M. Mauss, *Primitive Classification*, trans., ed., and with an introduction by R. Needham (London, 1963).

[4] Volume and intensity are clearly descriptive concepts. The degree to which collective beliefs shape the consciousness of individuals, and the strength with which individuals adhere to these beliefs may be a useful way of defining consensus. But it is not the basis of an explanation of variations in social solidarity that will command much attention. The concept of the determinateness of the collective conscience is less obviously merely descriptive. Durkheim's assumption that the more determinate or specific the beliefs shared by the group the more solidary it will be is questionable. If the concept refers to the determinateness of the beliefs held by individuals, this would seem to be simply one way of describing the degree of consensus in a group. But if determinateness is taken to refer to a property of the structure of the beliefs themselves, the concept has some possible explanatory relevance. Even so, is it necessarily the case that the more determinate the structure of beliefs, the more solidary the group? Here Durkheim's thinking would

Had Durkheim attempted its study by these means, he would probably have been forced to the conclusion that consensus is a very imperfect, uneven, and fragile thing. In contemporary industrial societies, at least, there is abundant evidence to show that, as far as one crucial area of central values and institutions is concerned, most citizens do not have 'either a clear understanding of, or intense or consistent attachment to, the values and principles of democratic procedures' and that the 'political concern of a large part of the population is intermittent and marginal at best'.[5] There is also much evidence that the volume, intensity, and determinateness of the collective conscience exhibit marked differences according to position in the system of stratification.

II

Durkheim's interest in consensus does not extend to include the question of whether the strength of commitment to collective beliefs is related to inequalities of power and status. This is undoubtedly due to his having worked out his theory of religion by reference to a society with only the most rudimentary division of labour.[6] However, he does consider the variation in social

---

have been helped by the distinction which Parsons makes between the levels of values and norms. For, while it may be true that the greater the ambiguity of norms the greater is the potential for dispute about their legitimate application, this normative conflict may not seriously impair the solidarity of the group if there is widespread consensus about the higher level values from which the norms derive their (disputed) legitimacy. On the other hand, extremely determinate norms may derive their legitimacy from values which are themselves highly ambiguous or exploitable. Determinateness is then a much more complex concept than Durkheim seems to recognize.

[5] P. H. Partridge, *Consent and Consensus* (London, 1971), 93, 112. This careful study of the subject also makes two further points which have a critical bearing on any simple consensus model of society. The first is that, far from a strong and widespread attachment to common values being a requisite of order, 'stability may be a consequence of the low intensity of involvement in the central value system'. The second, which is implicit in Durkheim's own theory of anomic declassification, is that, 'rather than consensus being needed to achieve stability, as long as conditions remain stable, consensus is not required and may only be important when these conditions fail to work'.

[6] Although, as was noted above, this was a deliberate choice which was made in order to examine religion in abstraction from (among other complicating factors) the uneven distribution of religious activities 'according to the men, the environment and the circumstances'.

solidarity through time for society as a whole, and his explanation of this leads fairly directly to the problem how adherence to collective beliefs varies according to class and status. For the moment, the terms class and status need not be precisely defined: they are discussed extensively below. Weber's concept of 'fortune' as covering 'all the "good" of honour, power, possessions, and pleasure' is sufficient to indicate the kinds of inequality that are referred to.

The idea of the temporal variation in individuals' degree of attachment to the collective conscience derives from the assumption that there is an attrition of social solidarity as a result of the pursuit of economic self-interest during 'profane' moments of the society's existence:

On ordinary days, it is the utilitarian and individual avocations which take up the greater part of the attention. Every one attends to his own personal business; for most men, this primarily consists in satisfying the exigencies of material life, and the principal incentive to economic activity has always been private interest. Of course, social sentiments could never be totally absent. We remain in relations with others; the habits, ideas and tendencies which education has impressed upon us and which ordinarily preside over our relations with others, continue to make their action felt. But they are constantly combated and held in check by the antagonistic tendencies aroused and supported by the necessities of the daily struggle. They resist more or less successfully, according to their intrinsic energy; but this energy is not renewed. They live upon their past, and consequently they would be used up in the course of time, if nothing returned to them a little of the force that they lose through these incessant conflicts and frictions.[7]

Therefore the intensity with which collective sentiments are held by the members of the society is subject to cyclical variation. Periods of moral enfeeblement alternate with periods of ritual unification and reaffirmation of the beliefs which symbolize the solidarity of the group. Durkheim thus postulates a process of social entropy and derives from this the need for a periodical ritual recharging of the moral energy of the society.[8] In the course of his argument he introduces fairly casually certain key but

---

[7] Durkheim, *Elementary Forms*, p. 348.

[8] This seems to be similar to what, on the level of 'ego-alter interaction', A. W. Gouldner calls the 'declining marginal utility of conformity' (*The Coming Crisis of Western Sociology* (London, 1970), 232 ff.).

vaguely defined concepts which also come to play an equally crucial role in his theory of anomic disorder: namely, 'utilitarian avocations'; 'exigencies of material life'; 'private interest'.

There is, however, no inherent reason why the weakening of a system of beliefs should be followed by their ritual reinforcement. In the first place, if social solidarity reaches a low point just before a new ritual is 'called for', why is it that the members of the society should feel compelled to join together in such a ritual at all? To say that it is necessary for social integration does not help; and to argue that the members of society are themselves conscious of this need of the role of ritual in meeting the functional requirements of an orderly society would violate Durkheim's key assumption that the function of ritual is a latent or unintended one from the viewpoint of the actor. This criticism does not, of course, imply that Durkheim was necessarily correct in his assumption, because to say that ritual has latent consequences as far as one group of individuals is concerned, but manifest ones for another group, is one way of defining manipulation. Finally, to suppose that it is something like 'tradition' which activates individuals to participate in a new ritual would imply that, for some unexplained reason, the only aspect of common beliefs which does not suffer attrition is the belief in the value of having periodic rituals.[9]

Durkheim does not appear to be able to explain why rituals of reinforcement take place at all, or why they should always lead to a reaffirmation of the existing collective morality. But quite apart from this flaw in his theory, an important class of facts remains completely outside its scope: namely, that, during periods in which the sway of the dominant morality is weakened, societies often experience not rituals of reinforcement but profound ideological innovations. The latter also raise the moral temperature of society, much more so than routine rituals; but they usually

---

[9] When the timing of ritual re-associations is accounted for by seasonal variations, Durkheim's explanation lapses into a radical positivistic theory of social action which is incompatible with his general theorem that social facts must be explained by reference to other social facts; see *Elementary Forms*, pp. 349–50. Moreover, shortly before this (p. 345), he writes: 'The intermittency of the physical life can affect religious beliefs only when religions are not yet detached from their cosmic basis. The intermittency of the social life, on the other hand, is inevitable: even the most idealistic religions cannot escape it.'

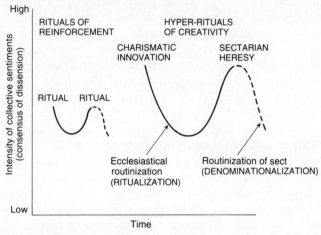

FIG 1.1. Rituals and hyper-rituals

produce this effect by division, not unification. The most familiar process of this kind is the emergence of heretical sects within the church: the church against the church. Just as Durkheim's conception of a church is not limited to the ecclesiastical variety proper, so too the idea of a sect can be broadened to include 'secular' movements whose aim is to regenerate quasi-religious institutions which claim to embody exclusively within themselves all that is sacred and charismatic in society and which bestow grace in accordance with their promise of wordly redemption.[10] The church-sect dynamic can be described in terms analogous to Durkheim's depiction of the cycle of the sacred and profane (see Fig 1.1), but it is a social fact which has no place in his theory of religion, and introduces a quite different concept of ritual. The routinization of charisma typically involves a weakening of the role of beliefs and a strengthening of the role of ritual in the integration of the religious community. But this process of ritualization, in demanding outward conformity rather than inner conviction, stands in sharpest contrast to the function attributed to

[10] Such an argument, based on Weber's concept of a *Gnadenanstalt*, is advanced by O. Rammstedt, *Sekte und Soziale Bewegung: Soziologische Analyze der Täufer in Münster* (Cologne, 1966), 9.

ritual by Durkheim.[11] The closest he comes to providing an explanation of the kind of moral innovation which is typified by sectarian movements is in his brief account of what might be called 'hyper-rituals of creativity'. These, as will be shown presently, are to be thought of as special cases, more 'morally dense' forms, of normal rituals of reinforcement.

If the concept of sect is understood in the sense that is in keeping with but in contradistinction to Durkheim's definition of a church, it would be hard to deny that sects are just as much an elementary form of the religious life as common beliefs and rituals. But, unlike the latter, sectarian movements of any scale are a manifestation of moral disunity; they reflect the uneven distribution of commitment to the common value system of a society. The imperfection of solidarity displayed by the antagonism between church and sect is a social fact of prime significance which a theory of religion with such a claim to generality as that advanced by Durkheim must account for. No one would wish to argue that purely doctrinal and liturgical issues do not lie at the root of sectarian challenges to orthodoxy. But it is also generally the case that the adherents of such movements are not drawn randomly from the population at large. Certain groups are, to adapt a Durkheimian phrase, more likely than others to be 'candidates for heresy'. And it is difficult to imagine how any explanation of the variation in adherence to dominant beliefs could proceed very far without consideration of the distribution of power and status. This is not to suggest that there exists a linear relationship between privilege and strength of attachment to the moral centre of the society. Disaffection with one's position, and still less the repudiation of its legitimation, are not simple matters of lack of privilege.[12] But the connection between social stratifica-

---

[11] For example, a large part of the appeal of the Protestant reformers was that they offered an escape from the ritualistic burden imposed upon the laity by the Catholic church ; see S. E. Ozment, *The Reformation in the Cities: The Appeal of Protestantism to Sixteenth-century Germany and Switzerland* (New Haven, Conn., 1975), chs. 2, 3.

[12] In one of the few contexts in which Durkheim deals with the function of religion in a stratified society, he appears to present a simple Marxist explanation of its pacifying effect on lowly social strata—and thus implicitly accepts that by reason of their position in the 'class structure' such groups are naturally less attached to major social institutions than more advantageously situated groups. 'What is needed if social order is to reign is that the mass of men be contented

tion and religious commitment in the Durkheimian sense is so well established that, even in the unlikely event that all groups in a society were equally affirmative of the values and beliefs that legitimated their differing rank and power, this would still be a fact which demanded explanation. Indeed, the extent to which such a state of affairs existed would be a most important criterion of social solidarity.[13]

Durkheim's theory is in one sense not inconsistent with the fact that identification with common values varies according to differences in power and status. If the function of membership in a church is to maintain and reinforce attachments to the existing social order, then it would follow that those who are more weakly attached to the church will be less likely to support the *status quo*. But this does not explain why different groups vary in the strength of their attachments in the first place. Instead of a low degree of involvement in the beliefs and rituals of a church resulting in antinomian tendencies, is it not more reasonable to suppose that the causal link runs in the opposite direction and that these tendencies are somehow bound up with the structure of inequality? But, if this is so, then it is necessary to ask what it is about different sections of society that leads them to be more or less receptive to one system of beliefs rather than another. This is the problem posed by the concept of the sect. To it Durkheim cannot provide an answer because his theory is only able to account for the structuring of interests in terms of common values and egoism.[14]

---

with their lot. But what is needed for them to be content is not that they have more or less, but that they be convinced that they have no right to more . . .' This is precisely the role played by religion: 'Religion instructed the humble to be content with their situation, at the same time it taught them that the social order is providential, and that it is God himself who has determined each one's share, and, giving them glimpses beyond this earth of another world where everything will be balanced, whose prospect made inequalities less noticeable, it stopped them feeling aggrieved.' (*Socialism*, ed., with an introduction, A. W. Gouldner (London, 1962), 242–3.)

[13] 'One might say that the extent to which a pattern (of social action) is supported by people who have no vested interests in it is an index of the degree to which that pattern is institutionalised' (H. Johnson, *Sociology* (London, 1961), 556).

[14] However, in so far as differential status is apportioned by reference to criteria based on common values; and in so far as those who suffer 'legitimate' derogation are more likely to feel ambivalent towards, or even more alienated from the

The source of the difficulty lies in his strict dichotomy between the collective conscience and private interest. This is a major reason why his theory of the cyclical disassociation and reunion of society through its profane and sacred phases is of small relevance when it comes to explaining the disunion of church and sect. In the former case the centrifugal forces of private interest which weaken the centre of moral gravity of the society presumably act uniformly upon all its members as they pursue their 'utilitarian and individual avocations'. But to explain why some groups of society are more affected than others by these centrifugal forces would necessitate a differentiation of the category of private interest. It would imply that there are, so to speak, 'collective' private interests of varying intensity. Durkheim does have a concept of this kind. He calls it 'corporate egoism'.[15] But the idea of corporate egoism is merely an extension of the idea of indiviual egoism. It involves recourse to the same utilitarian explanation of action which is already to be found in his account of the uniform weakening of the collective conscience in the profane phase of the social cycle. But the question of how interests are structured cannot be solved by compounding error. It is not simply that the introduction of the concept of corporate egoism still cannot explain why this form of egoism varies from one group to another. The main problem lies not in the lack of a concept of collective private interest but rather in the radical disjunction between any form of private interest and common values. Given this opposition there is an inherent tendency for Durkheim's explanation of order and conflict to swing between moral determinism and egoistic indeterminism. Corporate egoism leads to anarchy just as does individual egoism: it can no more explain the disunion of church and sect than individual egoism can explain why the church is reunited by ritual after a period of profane life.

This problem is not resolved when Durkheim turns his attention from the elementary religion of undifferentiated societies to the

---

common values than those who by the same criteria are entitled to greater amounts of deference; then it is possible to explain differences in attachment to the church and its belief system within the premises of Durkheim's theory. Further discussion of this (untenable) solution of the problem is postponed until ch. 4, s. V, which deals with the normative functionalist analysis of stratification.

[15] Durkheim, *Professional Ethics*, p. 20.

organic solidarity of the division of labour. It might be thought
that the concept of the division of labour provides some alternative
theory of the structuring of interests. But this is not so. As Parsons
has rightly pointed out, it is not possible to maintain the argument
that the division of labour itself spontaneously gives rise to a form
of organic solidarity which is then accorded moral recognition.
Durkheim himself, in the preface to the second edition of his
work on the subject, clearly recognized that the division of labour
had resulted in social conflict rather than a natural solidarity of
functional interdependence, and that, in order to counter its
disruptive tendencies, some moral regulation would have to be
imposed. Far from organic solidarity being an alternative to
mechanical solidarity, what was chiefly needed was that the
latter should be refashioned in such a way that the regulatory
power of a common morality should be accommodated to the
differentiation of groups. But behind all this the basic distinction
between moral regulation and private interest remains. It is
corporate egoism that undermines the solidarity of modern society, and the way of containing corporate egoism is through
'occupational morality' and 'professional ethics'. The common
morality of the church does not disappear. It continues as a matrix
of solidarity from which a new 'kind of moral polymorphism'
emerges.[16] It would not be inconsistent with Durkheim's general
line of argument to suggest that the collective conscience and
central institutions appropriate to this type of society are what
have been called 'civic culture' and 'citizenship'.[17] Certainly, for

[16] Durkheim, *Professional Ethics*, p. 7. 'Whilst common morality has the mass
of society as its sole sub-stratum and only organ, the organs of professional ethics
are manifold . . . Whilst public opinion, which lies at the base of common morality,
is diffused throughout society, without our being able to say exactly that it lies in
one place rather than another, the ethics of each profession are localized within a
limited region. Thus centres of a moral life are formed which, although bound
together, are distinct, and the differentiation in function amounts to a kind of
moral polymorphism.'

[17] See G. A. Almond and S. Verba, *The Civic Culture* (Princeton, 1963), *The
Civic Culture Revisited* (Boston, 1980); and T. H. Marshall, *Citizenship and Social
Class* (Cambridge, 1950). The ideology of citizenship might be regarded as the
chief expression of the 'cult of the individual', which is how Durkheim refers to
the principal feature of the collective conscience in modern societies. It is also the
case that the establishment and augmentation of civil, political, and social rights of
citizenship have had the effect of reducing grosser inequalities in the 'external
conditions of conflict', which for Durkheim were the cause of 'the forced division
of labour' and the major cause of social disorder. In both these senses, then,

most of the time people's sense of identification with these values will be even more feeble and intermittent than their sense of sharing the status of a common citizenship. Nevertheless, it is difficult to think that some even fragile sense of membership in this wider moral community is not a precondition of the polymorphism of occupational moralities and professional ethics. Morever, that there should appear to be two distinct yet related levels of morality is not inconsistent with Durkheim's portrayal of the effects of the division of labour. As Parsons has pointed out, one plausible interpretation of the distinction between mechanical and organic solidarity is that, whereas the former refers to ultimate values common to all members of society, the latter refers to those values which are specific to particular groups. If this interpretation is correct, Durkheim's conception of the normative structuring of interests undergoes no fundamental change as the weakened integrative function of the church is compensated for by the more vital integrative function of occupational or professional solidarity.

But this is not entirely in accord with Durkheim's much more negative view of the latter, which is that, although occupational groups have their own moral codes, these chiefly represent a corporative form of egoism which is essentially no different from the individual egoism which weakens social solidarity and has periodically to be counteracted through the act of ritual. However, this remedy is no longer available, since it presupposes that 'elementary form' of the religious life whose social substratum the division of labour has undermined. In the place of ritual Durkheim's substitute is the most un-Durkheimian *deus ex machina* of governmental regulation. Without this theoretically ungrounded intervention, the conflict resulting from the clash of corporate egoists persists and merely represents in a different form the same inexplicable problem of the sect.

---

citizenship qualifies as the normative and institutional framework of organic solidarity. Nevertheless, Durkheim's solution was corporatist. He thought that the natural unit of political representation was the 'corporation' or 'occupational' group and not a territorially and artificially defined aggregate of socially unrelated individuals. Such self-governing corporate groups, in collaboration with the state, would provide the regulation of economic life. See the Preface to the second edition of *The Division of Labour*, esp. p. lix, n. 34, which envisages something like 'co-determination'.

III

Durkheim's inability to explain how the disunion of the moral community might approximate the limit of schism should be distinguished from the general line of criticism which holds that his theory cannot account for the fact that religion, far from being always a source of social integration, is frequently the cause of the most intense dissension.[18] Durkheim's premiss that religion unites the members of a society into a single moral entity is by no means incompatible with the fact that religious divisions are often the source of internecine conflict. Indeed, his own theory would suggest that sacred conflict, by contrast with conflicts of profane or material interest, would be exceptionally disruptive because it relates to the ultimate values of the contending groups. In the extreme case, antagonistic religious groups would have to be regarded from a Durkheimian viewpoint as separate societies, even though they might continue to share a minimum common membership of a political corporate group which maintains a successful monopolization of the means of violence.

However, the criticism becomes more pertinent if a distinction is made between religious divisions that are exogenous and those that are endogenous in origin. In the first case, conflict may occur because, as the result of some historical 'accident', such as conquest, colonization, or migration, there is imported into the society a religion whose doctrines and practices are radically opposed to those of the indigenous church.[19] In such instances, Durkheim's equation of society and church is still relevant, because the understanding of this kind of religious conflict does not require an explanation of how a single church produces from within itself a counter-church and of how a common value system undergoes internal polarization into orthodoxy and heresy. The same is true of conflicts arising from 'historically given' cleavages

[18] See particularly Merton, *Social Theory and Social Structure*, pp. 28–30.

[19] However, a full explanation of this would once again require reference to macro-social factors outside the scope of Durkheim's theory, since it is generally accepted that the intensity of conflict in religiously or ethnically mixed soicieties is determined by the extent to which lines of religious or ethnic cleavage coincide with or cross-cut lines of socio-economic division. See, however, the important critique of this type of explanation by E. A. Nordlinger, *Conflict Regulation in Divided Societies* (Cambridge, Mass., 1972), ch. 6.

along the lines of ethnicity, race, and nationality. But in the case of religious dissension that arises from within what was formerly a homogenous religious community Durkheim's theory is incapable of providing a convincing explanation of how schismatic tendencies occur. The chief reasons for this have already been adduced, and it has been seen that the inadequacy of his theory is due above all to his decision to concentrate on 'elementary' religious life and to ignore the 'complicating' variety of religious doctrine and organization. In short, when Durkheim discusses the forms of religious life he does not consider the division of labour, and when he considers the division of labour he does not apply that concept to the form of religious life itself.

When all this is said and done, it would be incorrect to conclude that Durkheim offers no explanation whatsoever of endogenous change in collective beliefs. In spite of his disavowal of presenting a 'materialistic' theory of religion, [20] it is difficult to reconcile this with statements such as the following:

Religious conceptions are the products of the social environment, rather than its producers, and if they react, once formed upon their own original causes, the reaction cannot be very profound. If the essence of pantheism, then, is a more or less radical denial of all individuality, such a religion could be constituted only in a society where the individual really counts for nothing, that is, is almost wholly lost in the group. For men conceive of the world only in the image of the small social world in which they live. Religious pantheism is thus only a result and, as it were, a reflection of the pantheistic organisation of society. [21]

In view of this and similar observations, it is difficult to disagree with the view that Durkheim's account of the social determination of beliefs is at least as 'materialist' as that of Marx himself; and perhaps more so, since Durkheim's theory seeks to sociologize the most basic categories of thought. [22] From this it would seem to follow that changes in the collective conscience have to be understood largely as consequences of changes in social structure.

However, when Durkheim addresses himself directly to the

---

[20] Durkheim, *Elementary Forms*, p. 471.

[21] E. Durkheim, *Suicide*, trans. and ed. J. A. Spaulding and G. Simpson with an introduction by G. Simpson (London, 1952), 226–7.

[22] See E. E. Evans-Pritchard, *Theories of Primitive Religion* (Oxford, 1965), 77, and A. Giddens, *Capitalism and Modern Social Theory* (Cambridge, 1971), 219.

problem of moral change, there emerges a rather different line of argument: namely, that the conditions under which new ideals are created are only special instances of the more general conditions under which established beliefs are periodically reaffirmed. This is an extension of the idea that social solidarity is subject to cyclical change, alternating between a sacred or ritual phase in which collective sentiments are intensified and concentrated and a profane or utilitarian phase in which they are dissipated and diminished. Just as ordinary rituals serve to bring believers into a moral communion to counteract the force of self-interest, so moments of creativity in the moral life occur when, for some reason, these collective interactions become exceptionally powerful and intense. It might be said, therefore, that the creation of new social values takes place under conditions of *hyper*-ritual. The essentially quantitative difference between ordinary rituals and hyper-rituals is made evident in the following passage:

When individual minds are not isolated but enter into close relation with and work upon each other, from their synthesis arises a new kind of psychic life. It is, in fact, at such moments of collective ferment that are born the great ideals upon which civilizations rests. The periods of creation or renewal occur when men for various reasons are led into a *closer* relationship with each other, when reunions and assemblies are *most frequent*, relationships *better maintained* and the exchange of ideas *most active*. Such was the great crisis of Christendom, the movement of collective enthusiasm which, in the 12th and 13th centuries, bringing together in Paris the scholars of Europe, gave birth to Scholasticism. Such were the Reformation and the Renaissance, the revolutionary epoch and the Socialist upheavals of the nineteenth century. At such moments this higher form of life is lived with such an intensity and exclusiveness that it monopolises all minds to the more or less complete exclusion of egoism and the commonplace. (italics added)

But this state of collective ferment is too intense to last because 'the exaltation cannot maintain itself at such a pitch; it is too exhausting. Once the critical moment has passed, the social life relaxes, intellectual and emotional intercourse is subdued, and individuals fall back to their ordinary level.' However, the ideals that are created at these moments 'could not survive if they were not periodically revived. This revivification is the function of religious or secular feasts and ceremonies, all public addresses in churches and schools—in a word, whatever draws men together into an intellectual and moral communion. These movements are, as it were, *minor versions of the great creative movement.*[23]

It is not difficult to understand what Durkheim has in mind by moments of 'collective ferment', but his explanation of their origin is unsatisfactory.[24] To say that at these times society becomes more morally concentrated and active is to focus on the epiphenomena of ideological innovation and to ignore the underlying social forces which account for the timing and structural location of the 'creative' movements in question. Are these hyper-rituals randomly associated with other changes that are occurring in ecclesiastical organizations as well as in the wider society? Are those who enter into such movements with the greatest enthusiasm drawn representatively from all sections of the population? Such questions, which must undoubtedly be answered generally in the negative, are simply not raised by Durkheim. Moral creativity is not treated as a social fact whose variation must be related to other social facts. Yet, in Durkheim's scheme of thought, moral innovation would surely count as a class of 'deviant' social action.[25] It should, therefore, be subject to the same kind of analysis as that which he devoted to the study of suicide, a work which has

[23] E. Durkheim, *Sociology and Philosophy*, trans. D. F. Peacock, with an introduction by J. G. Peristiany (London, 1953), 91–2. See also Durkheim, *Elementary Forms*, pp. 213–14.

[24] An excellent study of ritual which exemplifies Durkheimian concepts without referring to them is M. K. Whyte, *Small Groups and Political Rituals in China* (Berkeley, Calif., 1974). This shows how the rituals of the primary political group (*hsiao tsu*), which are oriented to changing attitudes and not simply to the promotion of social integration, exhibit a tendency to routinization; that is, to become normal rituals of reinforcement. It is in this context that the extraordinary ritualism of the periodically mounted 'campaigns' (of which the 'Cultural Revolution' was only the most dramatic instance) has to be understood. The latter attempts to accelerate ideological innovation 'recur precisely because their effects tend to wear off in time', This form of induced or managed hyper-ritualism may also be seen as an élite strategy aimed at both the appropriation of potential sectarian movements and the prevention of the routinization of party charisma into a church. In contrast, the concept of 'spontaneous' hyper-ritual is similar to what some Marxist theorists call an 'explosion of consciousness', the process by which trade-union consciousness is, so to speak, sacralized into socialist consciousness. This is discussed at some length in ch. 12.

[25] This is not to argue that there is no difference between criminality and creativity or that theories of deviant behaviour can be applied without qualification to the phenomena of moral innovation. For brief statements of the problem, see Merton, *Social Theory and Social Structure*, pp. 357–68, and P. Rock, *Deviant Behaviour* (London, 1973), 100–10.

long stood as a model of sociological analysis. But once again it seems as if it is those social facts which are most central to Durkheim's concept of society that receive the least systematic attention.

Through the concept of hyper-ritual, Durkheim moves closer to the problem of sect and schism. But his explanation of moral innovation is no more adequate than the theory of ritual reunification from which it derives. Just as the latter offers no convincing reasons why periods of profane life should be succeeded by the moral concentration and renewal of the society through normal ritual, so too his theory of hyper-ritualism cannot satisfactorily account for moral disunion. At bottom, it rests on the assumption that there is a threshold effect in the act of ritual itself; that beyond a certain point the concentration of the moral life is such that collective beliefs are not merely strengthened but transformed. But the structure of beliefs, of the church itself, and of the religious interests of those who adhere to it, are social facts whose variability simply do not enter into the analysis.

IV

Durkheim's views on the function of rituals of reinforcement and on the nature of the 'great creative moments' of hyper-ritual provide a preliminary perspective on his conception of the sources of disorder. Both types of event signify something less than the complete moral consensus of social solidarity. In both cases social disequilibrium is brought about by forces that are located outside the region of society which Durkheim associates with sacred activities and collective beliefs. The social forces that weaken social solidarity and have to be counteracted by rituals of moral reunion clearly stem from the sphere of profane and utilitarian activity. They are centrifugal tendencies whose debilitating effects gradually increase over time to the point where, if unchecked, they would threaten social integration. This idea of quantitative change bringing about a change in the quality of the moral life is even more strikingly evident in the case of hyper-rituals, moments when an extraordinary heightening of social interaction leads to the creation of new beliefs. But the causes of this moral effervescence are not specified. In particular, Durkheim's conception of the religious life does not allow him to deal with causes of hyper-ritualism that are associated with the 'confusing details' of dogma and religious organization. As a result, there is nothing to rule out the conclusion that, as in the case of ordinary rituals, these causes originate solely in the profane sphere of society. Implausible as this may be, it is entirely consistent with what he has to say about the nature of anomic disorder.

It is also in keeping with what can be extracted from his very brief reference to fatalism, a concept that designates a state of social life just the opposite of anomie. In the following chapter it will be shown that the implications of the idea of fatalism do in fact corroborate the conclusions so far arrived at from the discussion of ritual and hyper-ritualism. On the way to this topic, however, there is a conceptual puzzle. Since anomie is how Durkheim conceives of disorder, it must follow that fatalism contains a theory of order. And, since anomie is a condition of society in which commonly held values and beliefs are in abeyance, fatalism should refer to a condition of society in which order is the consequence of an unquestioning adherence to the collective conscience. But, if these two principles hold, how does fatalism differ from solidarity? To what kind of social order does it refer?

3.

THE ETHICS OF FATALISM

I

The significance of Durkheim's concept of fatalism is wholly unappreciated. The idea is seldom discussed and then only in relation to the study of suicide.[1] Unlike anomie, it has had a most undistinguished sociological career. This is curious because, if anomie can serve to illuminate in a quite general way the nature of social disorder, why should fatalism not be regarded as having the capacity to provide an explanation of order that is of equally wide scope? The aim of this chapter is to show that, hidden in the concept of fatalism, there is indeed such a theory, though it bears little resemblance to what is taken to be Durkheim's major contribution to the analysis of social integration.

It is understandable that fatalism should have been neglected, because Durkheim devotes no more than a few lines to the concept, and then only, it would seem, out of a logical instinct for symmetry. It appears as the opposite social state to anomie, which is a condition in which normative rules suddenly lose their power of regulating the wants of individuals. Consequently, fatalism is defined as 'excessive regulation', 'excessive physical or moral despotism', as a situation in which the future is 'pitilessly blocked and passions choked by oppressive discipline'. At one pole then there is an extraordinarily weak social regulation of wants, at the other an unusually stringent limitation of them. If anomie means that horizons become abruptly widened so that aspirations know no bounds, fatalism refers to hopes so narrowed and diminished that even life itself becomes a matter of indifference. As examples of the latter, Durkheim refers to suicides committed by slaves,

[1] As in the case of Johnson, 'Durkheim's One Cause of Suicide', and B. Dohrenwend, 'Egoism, Altruism, Anomie and Fatalism', *American Sociological Review*, 24 (1959). A notable exception to the tendency to confine discussion of fatalism to the study of suicide is the paper by S. Sariola, 'Fatalism and Anomie: Components of Rural-Urban Differences', *Kansas Journal of Sociology*, 1 (1965).

and he concludes by saying that, in order to 'bring out the ineluctable and inflexible nature of a rule against which there is no appeal, and in contrast with the expression "anomy" which has just been used, we might call it *fatalistic suicide*'.[2]

As it stands, Durkheim's treatment of the concept hardly goes much beyond the dictionary definition of fatalism as 'submission to all that happens as inevitable',[3] and the possibility of deriving a theory of social order from it would appear to be small. Nevertheless, a start can be made by considering the two main assumptions of his account. The first is that fatalism, like anomie, is a matter of degree. In characteristic fashion, he uses the term 'excessive' to describe both the fatalistic over-regulation of wants and their anomie de-regulation. It is reasonable then to suppose that fatalism is to be understood as varying according to the amount of 'oppressive discipline' involved. The second point is that there are two kinds of discipline; fatalism results from either 'physical or moral despotism'. In seeking the meanings that can be attached to these terms it is convenient to begin with physical despotism. The most obvious instance of this is coercion, and social organizations in which order is maintained by excessive and oppressive discipline of a direct and personal kind are all too familiar. These extreme cases, however, are of little relevance to an understanding of the more general problem of order because the degree of coercion required to ensure the compliance of inmates of organizations such as prisons and concentration camps is incapable of being reproduced as the sole or even as the major means of securing enduring social stability in a society of any size and complexity. The various arguments against a 'coercion theory' of social order have been well rehearsed[4] and it is no part of the present argument to reiterate or to challenge them. Moreover, to identify fatalistic order with a coercive regimen of this kind would be completely out of keeping with Durkheim's view that the coerciveness of society lies in its supra-individual nature. It has been argued on good grounds that in the course of his work Durkheim's idea of

---

[2] *Suicide*, trans. and ed. J. A. Spaulding and G. Simpson (London, 1952), 276.
[3] *Concise Oxford Dictionary*.
[4] Cohen, *Modern Social Theory*, pp. 21–5. It should also be noted that, even in the case of what are considered to be purely coercive institutions, order depends in no small degree on informal exchange relationships between custodians and inmates; see, e.g., G. Sykes, *The Society of Captives* (Princeton, NJ, 1958).

social constraint changed from a view of social facts as things, or conditions of social action, to a notion of social facts as moral forces which exert their influence by becoming internalized needs of the individual.[5] This distinction between social condition and moral beliefs is indispensable to a closer understanding of fatalistic order.

The first conclusion that can be drawn from it is that 'despotism' presents itself most effectively not as direct personal oppression but in the form of impersonal social constraint. What are called the 'unintended consequences' or 'latent functions' of purposive social action belong to this category. These terms refer to the systematic effects of social interactions which appear not to be the outcome of human volition and which thus acquire the property of objective conditions. In this way, massive unemployment or abject poverty have very often been experienced as unavoidable 'facts of life', privations that are due to anonymous forces over which no one has control. These conditions have the effect of narrowing people's horizons and inuring them to what seems to be part of the natural order of things. Students of the 'culture of poverty' have shown in some detail how such fatalistic attitudes are engendered and how they contribute to the maintenance of life-styles which serve to accommodate people to conditions of adversity.[6] In a similar fashion the structure of social organization itself may take on the property of unalterability or inescapability. When Weber speaks of 'the iron cage' of bureaucracy, or Marx of the 'fetishism of commodities', it is presumably to this kind of social fact that they refer. In all these instances, what is especially conducive to a fatalistic attitude is not so much the degree of 'oppressive discipline' involved, but rather the fact that social constraint is experienced as an external, inevitable, and impersonal condition. For, however oppressive direct personal coercion may be, it can never produce the same kind of acquiescence as that which is born of social conditions that appear to be unattributable to, and thereby inconvertible by, human agency.

This kind of 'conditional fatalism' probably comes closer to

---

[5] See Parsons, *The Structure of Social Action*, pp. 378 ff.

[6] See, e.g., the summary of research in this field by H. J. Gans, 'Poverty and Culture: Some Basic Questions about Methods of Studying Life-styles of the Poor', in P. Townsend (ed.), *The Concept of Poverty* (London, 1970).

Durkheim's notion of 'moral despotism'. Indeed, it may be all that he means by the latter term. 'Moral' has such a wide and uncertain significance in Durkheim's vocabulary that any further discussion of its association with fatalism is bound to be fairly speculative. Nevertheless, it is worth pursuing the idea that the meaning of moral despotism is not exhausted by the concept of conditional fatalism. The clue to what might further be implied by it is to be found in Durkheim's distinction between 'the spirit of discipline' and 'attachment to social groups'. Throughout his writings, these two 'elements of morality', which are fundamental to his explanations of social order and disequilibrium, simply appear in different guises (anomie versus altruism, belief versus ritual, mechanical versus organic solidarity, and so on). Now fatalism, like anomie, has to do with the way in which wants are disciplined, and for Durkheim the principal source of this regula-tion is the system of values and beliefs which makes up the collective conscience.[7] One entirely consistent interpretation of moral despotism then is that it refers to some aspect of the collective conscience which has the capacity to make individuals accept their life situation as unquestionable, because any altern-ative dispensation is, by virtue of the beliefs they hold, unthink-able. Here, by contrast with conditional fatalism, it is the constraint of a system of beliefs, rather than sheer force of circumstances, which is the key to social order. But if this interpretation is correct, it follows that moral despotism has its origin in precisely that aspect of the collective conscience which Durkheim deliberately excluded from his study of the religious life: namely, the 'confusing details' of the creeds and doctrines themselves. His silence on this subject is most remarkable. It is true that at one point in his writings, and in a manner not distinct from that of vulgar Marxism, he does appear to attribute to

---

[7] It seems unlikely that moral despotism can be equated with the loss of autonomy that occurs when individuals are 'over-attached' to social groups, since Durkheim identifies this state of 'excessive' social subordination as 'altruism' in contrast with 'egoism', and quite deliberately places fatalism at the opposite pole to anomie. Moreover, there is no reason to suppose that, simply because individuals are strongly attached to a social group, their wants and aspirations will be fatalistic in the sense that they present no challenge to the existing social order. Revolutionary sects (of the political as well as the religious kind) are a case in point: in Durkheimian terms, their internal bonds are in a high degree altruistic, but their ends are plainly anomic.

religious beliefs in general the capacity to induce a fatalistic ethos among believers.[8] But this passing remark goes very much against the grain of his conception of sociology as a subject concerned with the co-variation of social facts; and the assumption that all religions and ideologies have the same social consequences affords no basis for the serious examination of moral despotism.[9] If fatalism and anomie are the limiting cases of moral discipline, and if the chief source of the latter is 'religious' (in the widest, that is to say Durkheimian, sense of the term), then moral despotism must vary according to differences in the structure of religious beliefs. In short, certain types of beliefs must be assumed to be more conducive than others to what Mannheim has called the 'ethics of fatalism'.[10]

Before attempting to substantiate this point, two further general implications of the concept of fatalism need to be brought out. The first concerns its consequences for the Durkheimian, and therefore for the normative functionalist, solution of the problem of order. The second has to do with the connection between fatalism and ritual, which for Durkheim is the core of the 'religious life'.

II

There can be no more firmly established canon of sociological orthodoxy than the belief that Durkheim's major contribution to the understanding of social integration consists in his discovery and elaboration of the concept of the collective conscience. Renamed the 'common value system', this idea became the linchpin of normative functionalism, which, as the most influential school of neo-Durkheimian thought, took it as axiomatic that widespread consensus on ultimate values is not only a normal

[8] Durkheim, *Socialism*, p. 243.

[9] Or, for that matter, of anomie. The closest Durkheim comes to a consideration of the way in which specific belief systems exacerbate social conflict is in his discussion of the 'forced division of labour', and again, on the same theme, in *Professional Ethics*, ch. 18. But, in general, there is nothing in his work that suggests any systematic connection between the content of the collective conscience and the level of social integration. The subject is first rigorously attended to by R. K. Merton in his celebrated essay on 'Social Structure and Anomie', in his *Social Theory and Social Structure*.

[10] K. Mannheim, *Ideology and Utopia* (London, 1952), 170.

feature of stable societies but the single most important precondition of social order. From these assumptions it follows that the basic point of reference in the analysis of social integration are the processes by which values become internalized in actors, and that the conformity of actors with institutional norms must be understood first and foremost as the outcome of this commitment to values legitimating specific role obligations.[11] In this perspective, there is little room for explanations of order that emphasize the significance of either coerced compliance or the 'natural identity of interests'—explanations that are commonly believed to be the only possible alternatives to a 'consensus' theory of society. The last, as represented by normative functionalism, has been subject to much condign criticism, but attempts to displace it have resulted in little more than a regression towards some kind of equally unacceptable 'coercion' model of society. In this whole controversy, however, it has not been recognized that what is conventionally taken to be Durkheim's classical solution of the problem of order is not the only one that can be derived from his conceptual scheme. In the idea of fatalism there are the makings of an alternative explanation that depends neither on the assumptions of consensus theory nor on those of the latter's two chief rivals. Most importantly in the present context, the concept of fatalistic order can dispense with the view that widespread agreement on the ultimate values legitimating institutions is a prerequisite of social stability. A sufficient condition of order is simply that the structure of power, wealth, and status is believed to be inevitable, or, as Durkheim says, ineluctable. The general point has been well made by Tumin in his review of the evidence concerning the characteristic modes of response of lower strata to their position in the social hierarchy:

---

[11] For example, Parsons: 'There is a range of possible modes of orientation in the motivational sense to a value standard. Perhaps the most important distinction is between the attitude of "expediency" at one pole, where conformity or nonconformity is a function of the instrumental interests of the actor, and at the other pole the "introjection" or internalization of the standard so that to act in conformity with it becomes a need-disposition in the actor's own personality structure, relatively independently of any instrumentally significant consequences of that conformity. The latter is to be treated here as the basic type of integration of motivation with a normative pattern-structure of values.' (*The Social System*, p. 37.)

The fact is that we have tended to infer, from the relative stability of caste positions and arrangements over time, that the denigrated and deprecated castes accept as legitimate and appropriate a status of denigration and depreciation. But this inference, taken from the absence of significant action designed to alter the situation, neglects the numerous other reasons for such inactivity by lower caste members or relatively deprived peoples all over the world. In the more general case, it is probably true that subordinate people's failure to improve their situation is as much due to their inability to conceive of a possible alternative, and/ or when they do conceive and desire alternatives, to contrive ways to carry out these ideas. Only in a very restricted sense of the word can people under such circumstances be said to 'accept' their positions. And this degree of acceptance is a far cry from any acceptance of the legitimacy of the situation under which they live, if by legitimacy we mean more than nominal conformity to the dominant norms.[12]

This formulation, however, still leaves open the question of how the inability to conceive of an alternative state of affairs arises. For there is after all an important difference between fatalistic beliefs that stem from the individual's realization that he is personally in the grip of circumstances over which he has no control and fatalistic beliefs that are the result of his socialization into an ideology that provides a comprehensive account of why circumstances are beyond his (or anyone else's) control. The distinction is important if only because equally adverse conditions do not always produce equally fatalistic beliefs or the same degree of acquiescence to adversity. This is another reason for thinking that it might be useful to view moral despotism as a system of 'oppressive' beliefs. But in this case, how does the explanation of order differ from that advanced by normative functionalism? Does it not also presuppose the existence of a common value system, or a moral consensus?

The difficulty here lies in a further ambiguity of the term 'moral', which Durkheim uses to refer not only to values or ethical

---

[12] S. M. Tumin, *Social Class and Social Change in Puerto Rico* (Princeton, 1961), 478. See also G. D. Berreman, 'Caste in India and the United States', *American Journal of Sociology*, 64 (1960). Compare the distinction made by M. H. Mann between 'pragmatic acceptance, where the individual complies because he perceives no realistic alternative, and normative acceptance, where the individual internalises the moral expectations of the ruling class and views his own inferior position as legitimate' ('The Social Cohesion of Liberal Democracy', *American Sociological Review*, 35 (1970), 425).

standards but also to beliefs about the nature of the physical and social world. To speak of moral despotism is therefore to conflate two distinct elements that enter into any ideology and to treat as unproblematic the very connection between them which the idea of fatalism would seem to make questionable. The chief social fact that ideologies seek both to explain and to legitimate is human fortune and misfortune, and in particular inequalities of power, wealth, and status. But they do so more or less successfully, depending on the extent to which the existential and moral beliefs of which they are composed are in harmony with one another; in this respect ideologies differ markedly in their 'closure' or 'exploitability'. They differ also in the degree to which it is the existential or the moral element which has the more extensive hold over the various groupings of society and, most importantly, over its lowest strata.

These facts have not been sufficiently well recognized by normative functionalism, which has tended to treat values and beliefs as an integrated whole as far as the motivation of actors is concerned.[13] The main advantage of the concept of fatalism would seem to be that it leaves open the question of whether, and to what extent, beliefs in the inevitability of social structures are associated with beliefs in their justness and legitimacy. Indeed, by making it possible to ask whether institutions would continue to be supported in the event of the collapse of beliefs about their inevitability, the concept helps to provide a closer definition of solidarity. For it could hardly be denied that a society in which people continue to support central values and institutions, even though they can conceive of realistic alternatives to them, is in a real sense more solidary than a society whose members cannot make this comparison. Finally, the concept of fatalism has the merit of being able to explain those fairly common cases of societies undergoing

---

[13] See, e.g., Parsons, *The Social System*, esp. 349 ff. 'Since there must be relative consistency in the value orientation patterns of a collectivity—though perfect consistency is not possible—this consistency must extend to the system of beliefs which give cognitive meaning to these value-orientations, again imperfectly to be sure. If ideological beliefs and value-patterns are, as assumed, interdependent, relative stability and consistency of the belief system has the same order of functional significance as do stability and consistency of the value-orientation patterns. Hence there must be a set of beliefs, subscription to which is in some sense an obligation of collectivity membership roles, where the cognitive conviction of truth and the "moral" conviction of rightness are merged.' (p. 351)

a sudden discontinuity from order to disorder as a result of their members' exposure to new beliefs: for example, so-called 'revolutions of rising expectations'. The only way in which the value consensus theory of order could attempt to explain this kind of discontinuity would be to assume that the pre-existing orderliness of such societies was really a condition of potential instability characterized by weak attachments to, or even alienation from, common values and beliefs. But, since this type of theory rejects the argument that societies can be held together by expediency or coercion, it would still leave unexplained the sources of orderliness of a potentially unstable society. The concept of ideological fatalism involves no such dilemma.

III

The extent to which subordinate strata regard their position as legitimate, as opposed to simply accepting them as unalterable, is a matter that is closely bound up with the question of whether social cohesion is based principally on beliefs or ritual. For, while Durkheim defines a religious community by its adherents' shared beliefs and their participation in a common ritual, it is a frequently noted aspect of the variability of religious institutions that the strict observance of ritual practice is by no means always associated with a strong commitment to the beliefs the ritual symbolizes; indeed, very often the beliefs in question are no more than superficially understood. Robertson Smith, to whom Durkheim owed a great deal in forming his theory of the elementary religious life, drew a firm distinction between the external constraints of ritual in ancient religions and the internal constraints of conviction in modern religions:

It is of the first importance to realise clearly from the outset that ritual and practical usage were, strictly speaking, the sum-total of ancient religions. Religion in primitive times was not a fixed system of belief with practical applications; it was a body of fixed traditional practices, to which every member of the society conformed as a matter of course. To us moderns, religion is above all a matter of conviction and reasoned belief, but to the ancients it was part of the citizen's public life, reduced to fixed forms, which he was not bound to understand and was not at liberty to criticise or neglect. Religious nonconformity was an offence against the state; for if sacred tradition was tampered with the bases of society were undermined, and the favour of the gods was forfeited. But so long as the prescribed forms were duly observed, a man was recognised as truly pious, and no one asked how his religion was rooted in his heart or affected his reason. Like political duty, of which it was indeed a part, religion was entirely comprehended in the observance of certain fixed rules of outward conduct.[14]

Although the difference is certainly overdrawn, the point is an important one. It is exaggerated because the relative salience of ritual and belief varies with the rhythm of routinization and renovation common to all sacerdotal institutions. Even so, societies can be graded according to the extent to which ritualization is the predominant mode of religious integration, a tendency that is the more apparent the greater the intellectual gulf between the beliefs of dominant and subordinate strata. This is a line of analysis that Durkheim's theory excludes; or at least directs attention away from. It is true that he thought of ritual as the more fundamental aspect of the religious life, but it was also a mode of action that he considered to be inseparably connected with the reaffirmation and reinforcement of a common belief system. Ritualization, which term may be used to refer to Robertson Smith's emphasis on the routinization of religious conduct, thus differs markedly from the Durkheimian notion of ritual as an extraordinary moment of collective 'effervescence' in which a society undergoes a periodic act of moral communion and remaking. By concentrating on the 'elementary' case of a socially unstratified 'church', Durkheim was not led to consider the nature of religious integration in those far more numerous instances in which the refined soteriologies of the *Lehrstand* have at best only the most feeble and tenuous links with the substratum of folk magic. In such societies, the elementary fact of religious life is the chasm between élite and mass religiosity; and as a result the applicability of Durkheim's concept of the church as a morally unified community is severely limited. Under these conditions, ritualization acquires its significance as the chief means by which the rudiments of the dominant belief system can be infused into the plebian collective consciousness. But this superficial appropriation of popular beliefs is obtained only at the cost of the deformation and degeneration of élite ideology, through its

---

[14] W. Robertson Smith, *The Religion of the Semites* (New York, 1956), 20–1.

embodiment in rituals whose symbolism has to accommodate
religious needs that remain primarily oriented to magical solutions
of everyday exigencies.

It is perhaps profitable then to think of ritual and belief as
alternative and inversely related modes of religions, and hence, in
Durkheim's understanding, of social integration. Ritual, or rather
ritualization, is likely to be the principal agency when the cultural
stratification of society is profound. But it will be especially
prominent if, in addition, widespread heterodoxy is freely tolerated
or (and this might amount to the same thing) less easily manageable. Indian religion, for example, is characterized by just such an
extensive ritualization of conduct and by a correspondingly weak
dogmatism.[15] At the opposite extreme (the case from which
normative functionalism seems to have generalized its peculiar
ethnocentric idea of social solidarity) is the kind of society in which
dominant values and beliefs, principally those of 'secular' religions,
are much more accessible to the masses; and in which therefore the
problem of consensus, the legitimation and delegitimation of the
centre, becomes of much more crucial importance. In this case, the
need to secure social integration through pervasive ritualization is
less imperative, and the resort to manufactured ritual of a quasi-
Durkheimian kind is occasioned less by the lack of a common value
system than by the tension between an overly articulate ideological
promise and the evident faultiness of the reality it enshrines.[16]

The question of whether the mass of the population is integrated
into a religious community through ritual rather than belief has a

[15] This point is made very well by R. Kothari, *Politics in India* (Boston, 1970),
259–60. 'Any system that is wide open and flexible develops rigidities in some
sphere, which imparts a sense of confidence and manœuverability. In India we find
this in the social and institutional sphere. Ideologically, Indian society has faced
many challenges and this has produced a high degree of ideological tolerance and
flexibility. Institutionally, however, Indian society has been traditionally very rigid,
working out a precise and clearly identifiable hierarchy, formalised rules, and
conventions, conformity with which was mandatory and defined by birth, and a
system of substantive and symbolic distances which articulated the hierarchy in a
definitive and predictable manner. Thus developed a peculiar combination of a
high tolerance of ambiguity and diversity in thought and value patterns on the one
hand and a deep concern with formal rituals and compliance with "rules of the
system" on the other.'

[16] For a thorough consideration of this issue, see C. Lane, *The Rites of the
Rulers: Ritual in Industrial Society, The Soviet Case* (Cambridge, 1981) . See also
Whyte, *Small Groups and Political Rituals in China*.

direct bearing on fatalism. The crux of the matter is that the concept of fatalism forces a distinction between a social order that is based on a commitment to ultimate values that legitimate it, and one that rests on the rather less secure foundation of beliefs in its unalterability. Ritualization clearly approximates the latter case. For if the value and belief system communicated to the masses through ritual is remote from their understanding, then the question of its function in legitimating their life situation is otiose. Plamenatz makes this point well when he write that

In the Middle Ages, most people who were called or who called themselves Christians were ignorant and illiterate; and it is impossible that many of them understood what the religion they adhered to was all about. They were churchgoers and participants in ceremonies rather than persons having definite beliefs. We ought to say of them, as of the illiterate peasants in the Balkans and the southern parts of Italy as late as our own century, that they did not challenge the doctrines of the Church, and not that they accepted them. Where orthodoxy is unchallenged nothing more is required of most people than outward conformity, and orthodoxy is never less challenged than when the vast majority are illiterate, or almost so, and are incapable of either accepting or rejecting the doctrines which are orthodox.[17]

Ritualization has then a close affinity to fatalism—and there are several reasons why this should be so. When ritual symbolism provides the bridge between the disparate beliefs of higher and lower strata, it is in the nature of this syncretization that the dominant belief system remains cognitively remote from the masses and is just as likely to be regarded as part of the same unalterable order of things as are the institutions it seeks to legitimate. Moreover, in having to meet the exigent, relatively crude, redemptory interests of the masses, this symbolism tends to reinforce fatalistic attitudes by parochializing the sense of injury, injustice, and discontent, the more so when it is charged with magical significance. Fatalistic beliefs in chance and luck are very generally held by people who perceive their lives to be subject to supernatural forces that are only marginally within their

---

[17] J. Plamenatz, *Man and Society*, ii (London, 1969), 341. The emphasis on literacy is perhaps exaggerated, since religious teachings can be transmitted orally; e.g., for many centuries the *Vedas* were handed down by recitation alone. What is fundamental is the division of sacred from profane labour and the formation of a class of religious specialists.

control. And, since magic operates within the interstices of the soteriology of the ruling stratum, far from weakening the ideological sanctioning of the existing social order, it buttresses it.[18]

Ritualization is not, however, the cause of fatalism. Rather, the causes are respectively practices and beliefs whose mutually reinforcing and socially stabilizing effects are most evident in those societies in which the lower strata stand at such a great distance from the ideological centre that its constraint over them consists chiefly in its inscrutability.

But, while this is perhaps one sense in which Durkheim's notion of moral despotism may be understood, it is very much a conceptual point of reference, a limiting case. In one form or another, the rudiments of the dominant ideology are conveyed to the masses through ritual symbolism and stand in varying degrees of integration with popular beliefs. Because of this, it is important to return to the problem of what Mannheim has called the ethics of fatalism. For there is clearly a difference between the more general case of fatalism that is augmented by people's inability to question a remote and largely incomprehensible ideology, and fatalism that is grounded in their acceptance of a system of beliefs which, however imperfectly it is understood, is, by virtue of its particular soteriology, an ideology *of* fatalism.

IV

Probably the most thoroughgoing attempt to explain social order in terms of ideological fatalism is Weber's account of the Hindu doctrine of *karma*, which is part of his wider thesis that the theodicies of 'Asiatic religion' precluded the development of an ethical interest in radical social transformation. A major starting-point of his work on Indian religions is the problem of why rebellion against the caste system had not been more frequent and widespread.[19] In seeking to provide a solution to this problem

---

[18] On these points, see, e.g., K. Thomas, *Religion and the Decline of Magic* (London, 1971), ch. 2.

[19] M. Weber, *The Religion of India*, trans. and ed. H. H. Gerth and D. Martindale (Glencoe, Ill., 1958), 17: 'Rebellions by lower castes undoubtedly occurred. The question is: why were there not more of them, and most important, why did the great, historically significant, religious revolutions against the Hindu order stem from altogether different, relatively privileged strata and retain their roots in these?'

primarily by reference to the basic presuppositions of Hindu soteriology, Weber was, it may be assumed, not oblivious of the political and economic conditions that would have placed obstacles in the path of any concerted 'class' action on the part of the most disadvantaged, and thus potentially revolutionary, castes. What he wished to prove was that the goal of social revolution was unthinkable in the first place. His most categorical statement of this view is as follows: 'That these religions lack virtually any kind of social–revolutionary ethics can be explained by reference to their theodicy of "rebirth" according to which the caste system is eternal and absolutely just.'[20] The logic of *karma-samsara-moksha* did not, however, prevent inter-caste hostility; what Weber has to say about this brings out once again the highly questionable sense in which a social order based on a system of fatalistic beliefs may be said to be 'legitimate'.

Estranged castes [he writes] might stand beside one another with bitter hatred—for the idea that everyone had 'deserved' his own fate did not make the good fortune of the privileged more enjoyable to the under-privileged. So long as *karma* doctrine was unshaken, revolutionary ideas or progressivism were inconceivable. The lowest castes, furthermore, had the most to win through ritual correctness and were least tempted to innovations.[21]

Furthermore, this doctrine, 'the most consistent theodicy ever produced by history' and shared by all Hindus[22] not only acted as an infallible prophylactic against lower-caste revolt, but decisively determined the other-worldly religious interests of the many sectarian movements that challenged Brahminical orthodoxy and found their adherents mainly among the middle and higher castes. As Weber puts it, 'An absolute presupposition of Hindu philo-sophy after the full development of the *karma* and *samsara*

---

[20] Weber, *The Sociology of Religion*, p. 113.
[21] Weber, *The Religion of India*, pp. 122–3.
[22] 'All Hindus accept two basic principles: the *samsara* belief in the transmigra-tion of souls and the related *karma* doctrine of compensation. These alone are the truly "dogmatic" doctrines of all Hinduism' (Ibid. 118). See, however, M. N. Srinivas, *Social Change in Modern India* (Berkeley, Calif., 1966), 3: 'Certain Hindu theological ideas such as *samsara*, *karma* and *dharma* are woven into the caste system, but it is not known whether awareness of these concepts is universal or confined only to certain sections of the hierarchy. This depends on the degree to which an area is Sanskritized.'

doctrines, was that escape from the wheel of rebirth could be the one and only conceivable function of a "salvation".'[23]

Since Brahmins awarded themselves the exclusive privilege of being able to seek release from the *karma* mechanism, it is understandable that there was a strong incentive to doctrinal innovation among those less fortunately placed. For example, heterodox sects, and in particular the Jains, appealed especially to relatively privileged groups whose position in the secular and ritual hierarchies were incongruous,[24] just as the *bhakti* movements, promising redemption through ecstatic devotion to a saviour deity, recruited extensively from lower castes who were, according to orthodoxy, condemned to the torment of a virtually endless cycle of reincarnations.[25] In general, the states and stages of salvation envisaged by Hindu philosophies were as myriad as the methods by which it was believed that they could be achieved. Weber's basic contention, however, is that, although their specific goals and means might vary, all indigenous soteriologies were oriented to the same ultimate end, which Mrs Stevenson epitomizes in the opening sentence of her book on Jainism: 'The desire of India is to be freed from the cycle of rebirths, and the dread of India is reincarnation.'[26] Whatever the preferred salvation technology (meditation, asceticism, orgiasticism, *bhakti*), a radical denial of the purpose of worldly redemption was common to both orthodoxy and heterodoxy. There were many movements that rejected Brahminical authority, it was not unusual that caste was regarded as irrelevant to salvation, and some sects, most notably the Lingayats, even dispensed with the doctrine of transmigration. Yet, given the direction of the basic religious interest, the goal of protest could not be to reconstitute society in accordance with

---

[23] Weber, *The Religion of India*, p. 167.

[24] K. Burridge, *New Heaven, New Earth* (Oxford, 1971), pp. 86–95, provides a succinct and cogent account of the socio-economic context of the development of Jainism. Another noteworthy analysis of the process of innovation is to be found in G. Obeyesekere, 'Theodicy, Sin and Salvation in a Sociology of Buddhism', in E. R. Leach (ed.), *Dialectic in Practical Religion* (Cambridge, 1968). See also K. Malalgoda, 'Millennialism in Relation to Buddhism', *Comparative Studies in Society and History*, 12 (1970).

[25] Weber probably underestimated the mass appeal of the *bhakti* movements. See Srinivas, *Social Change in Modern India*, pp. 25–6, and esp. p. 76; R. C. Zaehner, *Hinduism* (London, 1972), ch. 6, and pp. 147–8; *Speaking of Siva*, trans. and with an introduction by A. K. Ramanujan (London, 1973).

[26] S. Stevenson, *The Heart of Jainism* (New Delhi, 1915; repr. 1970), 1.

some external ethical commandment, to replace caste by another form of social organization. It was constrained rather to assume some form of what Dumont has called 'renunciation'.[27]

On this point, Weber is unequivocal. As regards 'open-door castes', namely 'Jainism, Buddhism, some of the revivals of Vishnu faith in a redeemer, and the Shiva sect of Lingayat, all of which are considered absolutely heretical', his claim is that 'there is no basic difference between their sacred paths and those of orthodox Hinduism' and that none of them undermined the prestige of mystic contemplation as the highest holy path.[28] Finally, in Weber's estimation, these higher ethical currents scarcely touched the mass of the population, who for the most part, as always, relied on what were essentially magical remedies against immediate distress.[29]

Although Weber's thesis of *karma*-induced fatalism has not excaped criticism, much of which concerns issues that he himself considered problematic, it is not easily dismissed as a major element in the explanation of the stability of the traditional caste system.[30] While it is possible that the system was in certain respects more fluid than Weber thought, the results of recent anthropol-

[27] L. Dumont, *Homo Hierarchicus: The Caste System and its Implications* (London, 1970), ch. 9.

[28] Weber, *The Religion of India*, pp. 23, 326.

[29] 'Allowance must always be made for the thinness, past and present, of the Indian intellectual strata proper and in general the strata interested in 'salvation' in some sort of rational sense. The masses, at least, of the contemporary Hindus know nothing about "salvation" (*moksha, mukti*). They hardly know the expression, let alone its meaning. Except for short periods, it must always have been so. Quite crude and purely this-worldly interest, gross magic, along with the betterment of rebirth chances were the values for which they did and do strive.' (Ibid. 326.) L. S. S. O'Malley, *Popular Hinduism: The Religion of the Masses* (Cambridge, 1935), is still the best general work on the subject.

[30] See, especially, the review of Weber's *Religion of India* by Milton Singer in *American Anthropologist*, 63 (1961), 143–50. Also M. S. A. Rao, who, in his *Tradition, Rationality and Change* (Bombay, 1972), provides a useful summary of the principal objections to Weber's thesis. Many of these are misdirected: namely, that he ignored reformatory sects within Hinduism, that he believed that it was possible to deduce concrete motives from the study of sacred texts, and that he was unaware of the variety of interpretations of such notions as *karma* and *moksha*. The empirical study of fatalism in contemporary India is sparse. See, however, C. F. Keyes and E. V. Daniel (eds.), *Karma: An Anthropological Inquiry* (Berkeley, Calif., 1983); J. W. Elder, 'Fatalism in India', *Anthropological Quarterly*, 39 (1966), and 'Political Attitudes', in D. E. Smith (ed.), *South Asian Politics and Religion* (New York, 1969); and E. M. Rogers, *Modernization among Peasants* (New York, 1969), ch. 12.

ogical and historical studies of social mobility have not removed
the need to find an answer to his basic question of why the caste
order remained so remarkably immune to rebellion. These studies
show that, far from accepting their positions as unalterable,
individuals and subcastes at most levels of the hierarchy consistently strove to elevate their ritual status, and that, where they
achieved a dominant influence in terms of economic or other
forms of power, such as numerical preponderance in a locality,
they were generally successful in this endeavour. Although strict
karma doctrines might have demanded undeviating conformity to
the duties of immutable caste position, it is clear that aspirations
for upward mobility were by no means limited to those that might
legitimately be fulfilled in the next cycle of rebirth. Despite the
spiritual penalty of demotion attaching to such conduct, it appears
that status usurpation was endemic in the traditional caste order
and, as in other systems of stratification, it was closely bound up
with status incongruities stemming from shifts in the distribution
of power.[31] Nevertheless, the fact remains that this mobility
involved positional rather than structural change; it left the caste
system intact, and was indeed a means of stabilizing it.[32]

The same was true of radical sectarian protest movements that
challenged orthodox beliefs and treated caste as irrelevant to
salvation. Yet, in this case, the way in which Weber seeks to
explain how such movements were contained introduces an
important qualification into his basic thesis that the stability of the
social order was guaranteed by the fatalistic implications of *karma*
doctrine alone. Virtually without exception, sects that sought to
dissociate themselves from the caste system were, in one way or
another, forced to accommodate to its boundary-maintaining
ritual. Even movements that denied Brahmanical authority altogether and some of its most basic tenets ended up by acquiring a
quasi-caste status and undergoing internal differentiation that

[31] See Srinivas, *Social Change in Modern India*, ch. 1, and J. Silverberg (ed.),
Social Mobility in the Caste System in India (The Hague, 1968). These writings,
together with A. Béteille, *Caste, Class and Power* (Berkeley, Calif., 1965), F. G.
Bailey, *Caste and the Economic Frontier* (Manchester, 1957), and A. and J. de
Knight (eds.), *Caste and Race: Comparative Approaches* (London, 1967), seriously
weaken the claim made, above all by Dumont, that the Indian caste system cannot
be analysed in terms applicable to other forms of social stratification.

[32] Srinivas, *Social Change in Modern India*, p. 30. See also Weber, *The Religion
of India*, iii. 2, 'Caste Schism'.

reproduced the main features of the wider ritual hierarchy. Of the Lingayat, which 'represented a type of particularly sharp and principled "protest" reaction to the Brahmans and the caste order', Weber notes tersely that it was 'pressed back into the caste order by the power of the environment. It did not escape again.'[33] Here Weber refers to constraints of a very different kind than those imposed by fatalistic beliefs.

When a principled anti-caste sect recruits former members of various Hindu castes and tears them away from the context of their former ritualistic duties, the caste responds by excommunicating all the sect's proselytes. Unless the sect is able to abolish the caste system altogether, instead of simply tearing away some of its members, it becomes, from the standpoint of the caste system, a quasi-guest folk, a kind of confessional guest community in an ambiguous position in the prevailing Hindu order.[34]

Generally speaking, this ambiguity was resolved, and the position of the sect determined, by the way in which its style of life accorded with orthodox ritual observances of the host society.

This line of argument raises certain doubts about the validity of Weber's basic thesis. First of all inability 'to abolish the caste system altogether' is a very different matter from the inability to conceive of its rejection as a religiously meaningful objective. There are many reasons why the abolition of caste was not feasible, a major one being that the high degree of internal differentiation of the lower castes, together with their geographical dispersion and isolation in a myriad of what Bailey has called 'village microcosms', was a powerful obstacle to any concerted action.[35] In posing the problem of why lower-caste rebellion was

---

[33] Weber. *The Religion of India*, p. 305. On this sect, see R. E. Enthoven, 'Lingayats', *Encyclopaedia of Religion and Ethics*, viii (New York, 1915), 75; W. McCormack, 'Lingayats as a Sect', *Journal of the Royal Anthropological Institute*, 93 (1963); and Dumont, *Homo Hierarchicus*, pp. 187–90.

[34] Weber, *The Religion of India*, p. 19.

[35] Moreover, the extent to which objective conditions were in themselves conducive to fatalism should not be ignored. The tremendous economic burden imposed on the mass of the population by the governing and landowning classes, which is demonstrated by I. Habib, *The Agrarian Structure of the Mughal State* (Bombay, 1963), meant, as Lannoy has noted, that the lack of a 'stimulus to cultivate a surplus' was due to 'the certainty of its appropriation by landlords' rather than to 'any sense of religious fatalism'. See R. Lannoy, *The Speaking Tree* (Oxford, 1971), 223.

ostensibly so limited, and in seeking to explain this mainly by reference to religious factors, Weber must have assumed that the social and economic conditions impeding rebellion were not essentially different from those obtaining in other comparable societies that did experience frequent and widespread peasant revolt. But he never attempts to substantiate this very large assumption; and this omission is a serious weakness in his argument.

Another difficulty arises in connection with his claim, which is undeniable, that anti-caste movements were generally neutralized by the 'power of the environment', that is to say, by the constraint of ritual, which was the core of the religous order.[36] It is, however, essential to Weber's thesis that the observance of ritual duty was guaranteed principally through spiritual sanctions, by the beliefs in *karma* and *samsara*, 'the truly "dogmatic" doctrines of all Hinduism'.[37]

But whether radical secular protest by lower castes was stifled mainly because of their indoctrination into these beliefs is a question that is highly debatable and unlikely ever to be settled by appeal to historical evidence. To begin with, while Weber was aware that caste discipline was enforced by a whole range of material sanctions, it is possible that he underestimated the extent of their deployment, especially against the untouchables, who were in fact, if not in theory, integral to the system, and who must have formed a substantial part of those whom he considered as potentially rebellious. He probably also underestimated the extent to which economic and other forms of power not only decided ritual ranking but helped to maintain the caste system as a whole.[38]

---

[36] Weber, *The Religion of India*, p. 24. 'Hinduism is primarily ritualism, a fact implied when modern authors state that *mata* (doctrine) and *marga* (holy end) are transitory and "ephemeral"—they mean freely elected—while *dharma* is "eternal"—that is, unconditionally valid.'

[37] His argument on this score is well summarized by R. Bendix, *Max Weber: An Intellectual Portrait* (New York, 1960), 207–8: 'Certain common denominators of Indian religion—the belief in reincarnation, the idea of retribution (*karma*), and the identification of virtue with ritual observance—influenced the masses through the social pressures of the caste system. Caste was the "transmission belt" between the speculative ideas of an intellectual elite and the mundane orientation of religious observance among the people at large.'

[38] The untouchables do not appear in Weber's depiction of the caste system which appears to be based on the *varna* model. Scrinivas, among many modern authorities, holds this to be a quite inadequate representation of the historical

Quite apart from these considerations, it is quite impossible to know how far down the caste system the ideology of fatalism reached and with what practical effects. What slight evidence there is does not always sit easily with Weber's thesis. For example, it is by no means clear that the stability and rigidity of caste was always regularly associated with widespread belief in *karma* doctrine.[39] More importantly, the fact that anti-caste sects and movements recruited extensively from among lower castes shows that, even if *karma* doctrine was implanted in the minds of the masses, this did not make egalitarian ideas unattractive to them or prevent them from seeking to abandon their ritual duties.[40]

This last point, however, leads back once again to the strand of

---

reality, in that it does not take account of the innumerable *jatis* who were for the most part difficult to locate with an exactitude within the *varna* scheme, and who were engaged in constant local rivalry with one another over ritual precedence. 'One wonders', he writes, 'how many dominant peasant castes in rural India had even heard of the rules governing different *varnas*, or, having heard of them, paid heed to them. One is also at a loss to understand how people living in villages were made to obey the rules, or punished for violating them. Even today, with all the facilities and resources at the disposal of the Government of India, it has been found very difficult to ensure that the rights which the Indian constitution confers on the Harijans are actually translated into practice in India's 560,000 villages. The situation in ancient or medieval India can be left to the reader's own inferences.' (*Social Change in Modern India*, pp. 6–7.) Others who emphasize the role of relative power between castes as the stabilizing factor in the caste system include Berreman, 'Caste in India and the United States', pp. 120–7, and M. Marriott, 'Little Communities in an Indigenous Civilization', in M. Marriott (ed.), *Village India* (Chicago, 1955), 131.

[39] It is believed that a caste system existed in southern India before the infiltration of Verdic culture from the north; moreover, caste remained stronger in the south, even though it has been claimed that, in certain regions at any rate, belief in *karma* was not prevalent among lower castes. On caste, see J. H. Hutton, *Caste in India* (Cambridge, 1946), 136, 144, 152; and on beliefs, O'Malley, *Popular Hinduism*, p. 31, and G. L. Hart III, *The Poems of Ancient Tamil* (Berkeley, Calif., 1975), 119–33, and 'The Theory of Reincarnation among the Tamils', in W. D. O'Flaherty (ed.), *Karma and Rebirth in Classical Indian Traditions* (Berkeley, Calif., 1980). On the other hand, contemporary anthropological studies of caste tend not only to support Weber's portrayal of popular Hinduism, but to strengthen it, in that they show that the masses have a better understanding of Sanskritic Hinduism than he allowed for. See Singer, review of *The Religion of India*, p. 149.

[40] The Jains, Buddhists, Lingayats, and Sikhs, not to mention Islam, all attracted many recruits from the lower castes. See R. Thapar, *A History of India*, i (Harmondsworth, 1974), 67, 216, 311, and A. Béteille, *Castes Olds and New* (Bombay, 1969), 96.

Weber's argument that is at once most crucial and most difficult to disprove. For if, as many experts believe, the *bhakti* movements were the major expression of lower-caste 'rebellion' against the Brahminical order, what was it that prevented them from carrying their anti-caste ideology into practice outside their own religious communities? Weber's answer is clear. What impeded them was not mainly their inability to mount a frontal attack on the caste system as a whole, or the 'power of the environment' which ritually encapsulated them. What was decisive was that, especially in so far as these movements were anchored in, and constituted a reaction to, indigenous Hindu soteriology,[41] the nature of their rejection of caste had to be passive and accommodative, rather than active and social-revolutionary. In the last analysis, these movements were directed to the same kinds of other-wordly goals as those of the multi-faceted orthodoxy they attacked.

This then is Weber's 'anti-critical final word' on the Hindu ethic. From a social-scientific point of view it may be less than satisfactory. In the end his thesis is not open to empirical refutation and is hedged in by many refined qualifications. Nevertheless, in its range and power, it is at the very least a theory of ideological fatalism that has no rival. That is why so much attention has been devoted to it here.

V

While Weber's attempt to explain the lack of revolutionary movements in traditional India must be regarded as inconclusive, it is necessary to recognize that his views on the fatalistic implications of 'Asiatic religion' relate also to China. It is also possible that the interpretations that have been put upon the significance of the Taiping rebellion provide much firmer support of his thesis than any evidence that is likely to be forthcoming in the case of India. In Weber's estimation, the Taipings represented 'the most powerful and thoroughly hierocratic, politico-ethical rebellion against the Confucian administration and ethic which China had

---

[41] On the more radical, less easily containable, movements that were influenced by Islamic doctrine—of which the Sikhs are the most notable—see Thapar, *A History of India*, pp. 305–12.

ever experienced'.[42] His opinion is shared by many contemporary Sinologists, and most emphatically by Levenson,[43] who consider that the Taipings represented a decisive break with the previous pattern of inveterate, though intra-systemic rebelliousness.

The significance of the Taiping rebellion for Weber's thesis can only be appreciated in the context of his theory of the general nature of 'Asiastic' soteriology, the distinctive feature of which was that 'knowledge, be it literary knowledge or mystical gnosis, is finally the single absolute path to the highest holiness here and in the world beyond'.[44] The aim of this knowledge was the comprehension of an immanent and impersonal sacred order, and it generated a type of religious orientation that stood in fundamental contrast to the one that derived from the conception of a personal, transcendental god whose ethical demands were in tension with the world and who had created man as his tool for fulfilling these demands. As Weber puts it,

None of these mass religions of Asia, however, provided the motives or orientations for a rationalized ethical patterning of the creaturely world in accordance with divine commandments. Rather, they all accepted the world as eternally given, and so the best of all possible worlds. The only choice open to the sages, who possessed the highest type of piety, was whether to accommodate themselves to the Tao, the impersonal order of the world and the only thing specifically divine, or to save themselves from the inexorable chain of causality by passing into the only eternal being, the dreamless sleep of Nirvana.[45]

This distinction is not only vital to the way in which Weber seeks to discriminate between Occidental and Asiatic soteriologies, which find their respective limits in inner-worldly asceticism and other-worldly mysticism; it also has a direct bearing upon the difference between rebellion and revolution. The usual distinction between revolutionary and rebellious movements (irrespective of their success) is that, whereas the former seek to change the entire structure of authority, the latter seek only to replace particular

[42] M. Weber, *The Religion of China*, trans. and ed. H. Gerth (Glencoe, Ill., 1951), 219.
[43] J. R. Levenson, *Confucian China and its Modern Fate*, ii (London, 1964).
[44] Weber, *The Religion of India*, p. 330.
[45] Weber, *The Sociology of Religion*, p. 269.

occupants of positions of authority.[46] If this distinction is accepted, then it is easy to see that there is a close relationship between fatalism, rebellion, and the conception of the divine as an immanent principle of order. One way of defining an ideology of fatalism is to say that those who share it will be constrained to limit their social protest to rebellion. It is precisely this type of ideological constraint which Weber saw as inherent in the religions of India and China. There were differences, the most important one being that secular rebellion had a legitimate purpose within the Confucian world view, whereas in Hindu theodicy it was utterly meaningless and futile. But the revolutionary transformation of society was in both cases ruled out; it was, given the presuppositions of the belief systems, unthinkable.

The Chinese experience supports Weber's argument remarkably well.

The Chinese have been called the most rebellious but the least revolutionary of peoples [writes Marsh]; even the overthrow of a dynasty did not legitimise a basic, revolutionary change in the system of stratification. It signalled, rather, a return to a traditional, ideal *status quo*, which had been outraged in the downward swing of the dynastic cycle.[47]

Moreoever, what was crucial in legitimating, directing, and limiting the traditional pattern of protest was the Confucian concept of 'Heaven', the impersonal and immanent cosmic order. According to Confucian orthodoxy, disturbances in this order were attributable to the rulers' ritual impropriety, and their loss of the 'mandate' of Heaven was a legitimate ground for rebellion, through which the intrinsically harmonious order could be restored. It is against this background that the Taiping revolt stands out as distinctive in its aims, and the explanation of their novelty is one that adds considerably to the credibility of Weber's thesis.

There is fairly general agreement that, in contrast with previous movements, which had pursued restorationary goals, the Taiping uprising was revolutionary. Even though it failed to put its ideas

---

[46] A useful summary of the literature is to be found in Chalmers Johnson, *Revolutionary Change* (Boston, 1966), ch. 7.

[47] R. M. Marsh, *The Mandarins* (New York, 1961), 43. For similar characterizations of the traditional pattern of rebellion, see V. Purcell, *The Boxer Uprising* (Cambridge, 1963), ch. 7, E. Balazs, *Chinese Civilization and Bureaucracy* (New Haven, Conn., 1964), ch. 2, C. K. Yang, *Religion in Chinese Society* (Berkeley, Calif., 1961), ch. 9.

into practice, it is considered to have had a lasting and shattering effect on the structure of Confucian authority. As Levenson puts it: 'Proto-revolutionary Taiping rebels took the Confucian-imperial order out of the path of rebellions, and set it up for the unmistakable revolutionaries who were still to come.'[48] Whereas earlier rebellions had sought to replace emperors and ruling cliques through whose derelictions of ritual duty the natural social equilibrium had been disturbed, the Taipings envisaged a far-reaching transformation of social institutions, including the abolition of emperorship itself. In this way, they directly challenged the central Confucian doctrine of immanence,[49] which had hitherto survived any challenge from Taoist and Buddhist ideas that had provided fuel for rebelliousness. The source of the new, utopian element in Taiping ideology was undoubtedly exogenous, deriving from Christianity, with its conception of a personal, transcendental god and its millenary promise. Taiping ideology was naturally a syncretization of indigenous and 'imported' Christian beliefs; but it was the latter which appear to have been decisive in switching the movement from a rebellious to a revolutionary track.[50]

This is all that Weber's thesis would require in the way of confirmation. It is, therefore, arguable that the nature of the entry of the Taipings into Chinese history provides much firmer evi-

[48] Levenson, *Confucian China and its Modern Fate*, p. 86. S. Y. Teng (in *The Taiping Rebellion and the Western Powers* (Oxford, 1971), p. 6), agrees that 'the movement had a clear-cut revolutionary and anti-traditional character', but then argues that it should none the less be classed as a rebellion on the rather weak ground that 'the Taipings did not make any "permanent change of a good kind" or "progress"'.

[49] Levenson, *Confucian China and its Modern Fate*, ch. 7, sec. 2, and F. Wakeman, 'Rebellion and Revolution: The Study of Popular Movements in Chinese History', *Journal of Asian Studies*, 36 (1977).

[50] Levenson, *Confucian China and its Modern Fate*, ch. 7, 8. See also E. P. Boardman, 'Millenary Aspects of the Taiping Rebellion, 1851–64', *Comparative Studies in Society and History*, supplement II (1962). The most detailed account of the movement's ideology is to be found in V. Y. C. Shin, *The Taiping Ideology: Its Source, Interpretations and Influences* (Seattle, 1972). Although Shin stresses the inability of the Taipings to adopt Christian beliefs except by anchoring them in traditional Chinese thought, he acknowledges the 'catalystic influence' of the former and argues that 'without this new ideology, it would have been nearly impossible to break the hold that orthodoxy had on the mind of the people ' (p. xviii), and that these ideas 'held a genuine possibility of bringing about a real revolution' (p. xv). Moreover, he explicitly contrasts the revolutionary potential of Christian beliefs with 'the traditional attitude of fatalism' (pp. xiii, 472).

dence in support of his general theory of the religious determination of interests than any that is likely to emerge from the
historical study of the caste system, or indeed from the protracted
controversy over the 'protestant ethic' and the 'spirit of capitalism'.[51] For what distinguished the Taiping uprising from previous
ones was not so much a fundamental change in the social and
economic setting of the movement as the extent of its ideological
discontinuity. History is not a laboratory. It is, nevertheless, fairly
safe to say that the social conditions that gave rise to the Taiping
revolt were not basically different from those that were the
occasion of previous rebellions.[52] And the obstacles to revolutionary change remained largely the same. Among them, probably
the most important was the well-nigh invincible position of the
Confucian ruling class, who, as landlords, officials, and scholars
linked by extensive kinship networks, virtually monopolized major
power resources.[53] In this respect, the fate of the Taipings was no

[51] The impact of protestant theology on peasant rebellion is another matter. In
the hands of Zwingli and his disciples, the opposition of 'godly' to 'old' law
supplied the rebellion of 1525 with a revolutionary force and legitimacy (epitomized in the Twelve Articles) which marked it off from previous rebellions whose
appeal to 'ancient tradition' was never proof against 'old law'. See P. Blickle, *The
Revolution of 1525: The Peasants' War from a New Perspective* (London, 1985),
esp. ch. 9, 'Reformation Theology and Revolutionary Doctrine'.

[52] See F. Michael, *The Taiping Rebellion* (Seattle, 1966). 'If the Taiping
Rebellion was a new beginning in Chinese history, it arose in a setting that still
contained the familiar elements characteristic of periods of dynastic decline and
rebellious uprisings in the past. Grave corruption in government, heavy over-
taxation of the farmers, high rent, desertion of the land by the peasants, the
increase in a roaming population, banditry and general insecurity, the increasing
importance of secret societies, the formation of local self-defence units that took
matters into their own hands, and frequent small-scale warfare which led to
uprisings against government authority—these had been the conditions for dynastic
changes by rebellion or foreign conquest throughout imperial history . . . While
the setting was familiar to that of earlier rebellions, the Taiping Rebellion itself
and its goals were basically different from former dynastic upheavals. The Taipings
attacked not only the ruling dynasty—they attacked the traditional order itself.
And this wider attack gave their rebellion a character totally different from that of
rebellious movements of the past.' (p. 4) It is undeniable that the Western military
and economic impact on China was a new element in the setting of the rebellion.
But, since China had been subject to foreign conquest before without its having
had any marked effect on the nature of rebellion, it would seem unlikely that the
distinctive ideological character of the Taiping movement is attributable to the
military and economic effects of the Western encroachment.

[53] See, e.g., O. Lattimore, *The Inner Asian Frontiers of China* (New York,
1940), ch. 17, and J. Chesneaux, *Peasant Revolts in China, 1840–1949* (London,
1973).

different from that of any preceding rebellion. All of this, however, adds to the credibility of Weber's thesis. He concluded that the Taiping revolt showed that 'it was not an insurmountable "natural disposition" that hindered the Chinese from producing religious structures comparable to those of the Occident'.[54] In the light of subsequent work, he might have concluded that, until the Taipings, what hindered the Chinese from producing revolutionary movements was an insurmountable system of fatalistic beliefs.

VI

Weber's studies of Indian and Chinese religions come nowhere near providing incontrovertible proof that beliefs in the immanent nature of the sacred are sufficient to account for the peculiar structural stability of these societies and the distinctive forms of social protest they experienced. Such a conclusion would anyway be completely out of keeping with his general observations on the determination and effects of religious interests.[55] Nevertheless, his work still stands as the most thoroughgoing analysis of the 'ethics of fatalism'. It is ironic then that, although his studies of comparative religion are so highly esteemed by normative functionalists, their relevance to the Durkheimian theory of order has largely been ignored. For, if the foregoing arguments have any substance, Weber's studies of 'Asiatic' religion provide grounds for thinking that the concept of fatalism, far from being an obscure afterthought deserving of no more than its relegation to a footnote of *Suicide*, is in fact the key to a completely different solution of the problem of order than the one Durkheim has been credited with. Most importantly, Weber's work shows that if any precise meaning is to be attached to the idea of moral despotism, this can only be discovered through an analysis of the ideological constraints

---

[54] Weber, *The Religion of China*, p. 219.

[55] At the same time, Weber's hypotheses do raise problems of the weighting of causal factors to which historical evidence seems unlikely to provide unequivocal answers. On this, see his parting shot at the critics of his protestant ethic thesis: 'That no "numerical" scale of importance exists in historical accounting is something I cannot control' ('Anticritical Last Word on *The Spirit of Capitalism*', trans. with an introduction by W. M. Davis, *American Journal of Sociology*, 83 (1978), 1129). The difficulties encountered in testing Weber's thesis against historical data are clearly demonstrated by Gordon Marshall's admirable study, *Presbyteries and Profits* (Oxford, 1981).

inherent in the structure of specific systems of belief. This kind of enquiry has not been central in the theory of order and conflict propounded by Durkheim and elaborated by his successors. The neglect of it is one main reason why fatalism remains Durkheim's hidden theory of order.

It is arguable that the only formulation of fatalistic order Durkheim could consistently have arrived at from the idea of anomie is what has been called conditional fatalism. This judgement is based on a fact yet to be established: namely, that his theory of anomie locates the causes of this most severe disorder in very vaguely defined structural factors of a non-normative kind which are entirely residual to his conceptual scheme. This fault is remarkably the opposite of his failure to incorporate into his explanation of solidarity any systematic consideration of the structure of values and beliefs; and both would appear to be due to his very pronounced tendency to conceive of social forces, whether sacred or profane, in quantitative rather than qualitative terms. At any rate, the chronic form of anomie has its ultimate cause in what Durkheim refers to cryptically as an 'abrupt' change in 'power and wealth'. This couple is just one of the terms he uses to describe those socially disruptive forces which he generally sees as originating in the 'economic' or 'utilitarian' region of society, that dark and threatening Hobbesian realm existing only on the margin of his analytical vision. It must be concluded then that, since anomie results from sudden changes in these sorts of material conditions, fatalism must somehow be explained by reference to the extraordinary stability of the selfsame class of social facts. The form such an explanation might take has been indicated above. What is indisputable is that, whether fatalism is conceived of as conditional or ideological, it represents a state of imperfect solidarity whose elucidation necessitates reference to precisely those variations in beliefs and in social (class or status) differentiation that Durkheim deliberately ignored in his search for the primordial 'religious' basis of social order.

If this thesis is correct, it is perhaps unsurprising that such factors should also play no systematic role in the theory of anomie. But since the latter quite clearly refers to a society with a division of labour, and even, in some sense yet to be determined, to 'classes' and 'social hierarchy', it is worth asking why Durkheim's concept of class, and especially that of status, remains so shadowy.

The beginnings of an answer may be found by expanding on a previously noted point: namely, that the opposition of mechanical to organic solidarity serves an analytical rather than an historical purpose. In other words, the contrast relates less to two different kinds of solidarity than to the form of the values and beliefs appropriate to the type of society in question. From this perspective, there is no radical difference between the theories of order presented in *The Elementary Forms of the Religious Life* and *The Division of Labour in Society*. In both, the problem of social integration is above all one of moral integration—a 'moral task', as Durkheim says in the latter work. The differentiation of functions that distinguishes modern societies makes people and occupational groups dependent on one another, but this in itself is insufficient to produce organic solidarity. Occupational moralities do not spontaneously emerge from such relations: and even if they did, there would still be a need for overarching common values which would regulate the relations between corporate groups and between them and the state. Durkheim does not specify the beliefs that would be required beyond passing references to 'the cult of individual'. And he says relatively little about the ways in which the values and beliefs appropriate to organic solidarity are institutionalized; that is, how they come to determine the interests of specific social groups. Thus, whilst the normative order remains the central reference point in Durkheim's theory of organic solidarity, the values that constitute such an order and the institutional mechanisms that 'ground' values in action are not subjects that are pursued in any depth. This would seem to be the main reason why, in Durkheim's sociology, there is no explicit account of status-group stratification, the principal set of social relations incarnating a society's central values and beliefs. It is only through his idea of 'social hierarchy' or 'moral classification' that the importance of status receives the slightest recognition. Even then, these concepts are introduced, not by way of elucidating the meaning of solidarity, but as as a means of explaining anomie.

That Durkheim's theory of solidarity lacks a concept of class structure is less surprising. His occasional references to 'classes' place these entities in the profane region of society; but their relation to occupational groups is not made clear; indeed it is uncertain whether 'class' actually signifies social relationships at all, and not just categories of individuals distinguished by different amounts of power and wealth. Here again, then, there is a close identity between the forces that are seen as disruptive of both mechanical and organic solidarity. Mechanical solidarity knows nothing of anomie; the only corrosive force is egoism.[56] 'Corporate egoism', its modern counterpart, is likewise the principal source of conflict, this time the consequence of sectional interests lacking moral regulation through norms of organic solidarity. And an extreme form of corporate egoism, which extends to include even something like class conflict, is one, though not the only, interpretation that can be put on anomie.

In turning from discussion of imperfections in social solidarity to Durkheim's account of the most chronic form of disorder, there are few conceptual guide-lines. From now on, even more than before, exegesis will have to give way to conjecture. But it is hoped that the relevance of the foregoing preliminary comments on class and status will become apparent as the discussion proceeds, and will at least help to clarify the major issues at stake. Conveniently enough, Durkheim's account of anomie includes the only substantial reference to status ('social hierarchy') which is to be found in all his writings. How much weight should be placed on such an isolated passage is debatable. All that can be said at this stage is that without the concept of a status system, there would not be much in the way of a theory, as opposed to a definition, of anomie. De Grazia is therefore perfectly correct in introducing the idea of status into his definition of solidarity when he writes that anomie 'stands in contrast to *solidarité*, the expression Durkheim used to designate the perfect integration of a society with clear-cut values that define the status of each member of the community'.[57] This state of 'perfect integration' is the starting-point of Durkheim's account of anomie; and its most interesting feature is what he calls an 'established classification'.

[56] Which means self-interest, and is not to be confused with institutionalized individualism, or what Durkheim calls the 'cult of the individual'—a core element of the value system of modern societies. On the distinction, see Lukes, 'Durkheim's "Individualism and the Intellectuals"'. Durkheim often uses the term 'egoism' to signify an insufficiency of moral regulation as well as of group attachment (as in *Professional Ethics*, pp. 20 ff.), a usage that departs from that of *Suicide*.

[57] S. de Grazia, *The Political Community: A Study of Anomie* (Chicago, 1948), 4.

PART TWO
DECLASSIFICATION

4.

SOCIAL CLASSIFICATION

I

If solidarity is the state of order characterized by the integration of the ends of actors through a common value system, then disorder is a state in which this moral consensus loses its regulatory power. Just as value consensus may be more usefully taken as a measure rather than a cause of order, so too value dissensus can be regarded as an index of the severity rather than a direct cause of conflict. This is not to say that certain types of values and beliefs are not more productive of disorder than others or that religious divisions of labour do not differ in their propensity to doctrinal disunion. But these are not matters with which Durkheim concerned himself either in his theory of order or in his theory of disorder.

Anomie is the general term by which he denotes the lapse of moral regulation, and it refers to both individual and social disorder. Individual wants become anomic when, for whatever reason, they are no longer subject to moral discipline. But when Durkheim uses the concept to refer to widespread social deregulation he speaks of 'declassification'; and this, in turn, presupposes a prior state of social order which is described as a 'social hierarchy' or an 'established classification'. But both terms refer to a normative structure. Anomic declassification means the breakdown of the moral discipline which is transmitted through the legitimation of the social hierarchy; and this may or may not be associated with personal deregulation. In view of the very marked tendency for the concept of anomie to be interpreted as a state of personal deregulation and to be used to explain patterns of individual deviance, it is necessary to establish the significance of anomic declassification as a state of social disorder which, in the last analysis, is characterized by systematic group conflict rather than by situationally determined individual deviance.[1]

[1] Mainly because of the influence of Merton's celebrated essay on the anomic

Durkheim's description of social classification is as follows:

As a matter of fact, at every moment of history there is a dim perception, in the moral consciousness of societies, of the respective value of different social services, the relative reward due to each, and the consequent degree of comfort appropriate on the average to workers in each occupation. The different functions are graded in public opinion and a certain coefficient of well-being assigned to each, according to its place in the social hierarchy . . . a genuine regimen exists, therefore, although not always legally formulated, which fixes with relative precision the maximum degree of ease of living to which each social class may legitimately aspire.[2]

This hierarchy of aspirations and rewards is normally 'regarded as just by the great majority of persons' but 'when society is passing through some abnormal crisis' the moral classification becomes deregulated. Here is Durkheim's description of declassification in full:

But when society is disturbed by some painful crisis or by beneficient but abrupt transitions, it is momentarily incapable of exercising this influence; thence come the sudden rises in the curve of suicides which we have pointed out above.

In the case of economic disasters, indeed, something like a declassification occurs which suddenly casts certain individuals into a lower state than their previous one. Then they must reduce their requirements, restrain their needs, learn greater self-control. All the advantages of social influence are lost so far as they are concerned; their moral education has to be recommenced. But society cannot adjust them instantaneously to this new life and teach them to practice the increased self-repression to which they are unaccustomed. So they are not adjusted to the condition forced on them, and its very prospect is intolerable; hence the suffering which detaches them from a reduced existence even before they have made a trial of it.

It is the same if the source of the crisis is an abrupt growth of power and wealth. Then, truly, as the conditions of life are changed, the standard according to which needs are regulated can no longer remain the same; for it varies with social resources, since it largely determines

---

effects of the American value system, the whole discussion of Durkheim's theory of disorder has been side-tracked into the study of what is both analytically and comparatively a very special, if none the less illuminating, class of problems. For an account of this line of enquiry, see M. B. Clinard (ed.), *Anomie and Deviant Behaviour* (Glencoe, Ill, 1964). Mertonian anomie is discussed below, ch. 6, s. I.

[2] Durkheim, *Suicide*, p. 249.

the share of each class of producers. The scale is upset; but a new scale cannot be immediately improvised. Time is required for the public conscience to reclassify men and things. So long as the social forces thus freed have not regained equilibrium, their respective values are unknown and so all regulation is lacking for a time. The limits are unknown between the possible and the impossible, what is just and what is unjust, legitimate claims and those which are immoderate. Consequently, there is no restraint upon aspirations. If the disturbance is profound, it affects even the principles controlling the distribution of men among various occupations. Since the relations between various parts of society are necessarily modified, the ideas expressing these relations must change. Some particular class especially favoured by the crisis is no longer resigned to its former lot, and, on the other hand, the examples of its greater good fortune arouses all sorts of jealousy below and around it. Appetites, not being controlled by a public opinion, become disoriented, no longer recognize the limits proper to them. Besides, they are at the same time seized by a sort of natural erethism simply by the greater intensity of public life. With increased prosperity desires increase. At the very moment when traditional rules have lost their authority, the richer prize offered these appetites stimulates them and makes them more exigent and impatient of control. The state of de-regulation or anomy is thus further heightened by passions being less disciplined, precisely when they need more disciplining . . . All classes contend among themselves because no established classification any longer exists.[3]

The importance of this passage can hardly be overestimated. It is Durkheim's fullest statement of the nature and causes of anomic disorder.[4] The ambiguity and inconsistency of which it is full reflect the Durkheimian dilemma in its most acute form. In order to show this, it is necessary to begin by examining the two concepts which declassification presupposes: anomie and classification.

---

[3] Ibid. 252–3.

[4] In *The Division of Labour*, anomie has two distinct meanings. In one context, it refers to a lack of social integration which results from excessively rapid economic change and manifests itself in the absence, or weak development, of the system of occupational ethics which is needed to regulate the interests of the various groups thrown up by the division of labour. In this first sense of the term, there is a close connection with the concept of declassification noted above. The second sense of anomie relates not to social, but to system integration: it is a type of disorder which results from a lack of functional reciprocity between the various parts of a complex economic system. On this, see M. E. Olsen, 'Durkheim's Two Concepts of Anomie', *Sociological Quarterly*, 6 (1965), in which he distinguishes between anomie as a lack of 'normative integration' and anomie as a lack of 'functional integration'.

How does anomic declassification differ from Durkheim's general notion of anomie? And what exactly is the system of moral classification that undergoes deregulation?

II

Durkheim developed his theory of anomie in greatest detail to explain a particular form of suicide. Although his discussion centres on the causes of individual, rather than social, deregulation, the two phenomena tend to be treated as concomitant: thus, economic crises are seen as leading both to an increase in anomic suicides and to social declassification. But it is important to recognize that the two processes are analytically and empirically distinguishable. For example, if someone unexpectedly inherits (or loses) a vast fortune, or experiences long-range upward (or downward) social mobility, he or she may be subject to personal deregulation in the way that Durkheim suggests. But it is perfectly possible for such sudden alterations in individual circumstances to occur within a system of moral classification which itself remains undisturbed. It is only when this wider framework of moral discipline is subject to deregulation that Durkheim speaks of declassification.

Nevertheless, the basic assumptions entering into the explanation of personal and social deregulation are the same. The two forms of anomie differ only in their consequences for social solidarity. The idea of declassification builds on the elementary notions entering into the theory of anomic suicide; and the novelty of the latter lies mainly in the deduction that sudden good fortune is just as disastrous for the moral equilibrium of the individual as is bad fortune.[5] This in turn rests on the assumption that the wants of the individual are, so to speak, highly elastic in relation to what he gets if he suddenly gets much more, whereas they are highly inelastic if he suddenly gets much less than before. The latter situation is the more immediately comprehensible. Individuals who are suddenly cast down cannot immediately adjust their

---

[5] That this insight is entirely original to Durkheim may be questioned. One of the authors cited *en masse* in *Suicide*, pp. 52–3 n., T. G. Masaryk, puts forward essentially the same ideas in his book, *Der Selbstmord als sociale Massenerscheinung der modernen Civilisation* (Vienna, 1881), 56–62.

customary wants to a lower level; as Durkheim says, time is required for their moral re-education. In the case of a sudden increase in rewards, personal deregulation is once again due to the fact that pre-established expectations are no longer relevant. No new normative restraint is immediately available to curb the appetites which have been stimulated by the sudden over-indulgence of the previous level of wants. As a result, the individual's aspirations are momentarily unbounded, and exceed even those new goals which his good fortune allows him to realize. These two 'pathological' states stand in contrast to the 'healthy' moral condition which is conducive to personal and social equilibrium. In the latter case, wants are moderately in excess of what the individual is getting, just sufficiently distant to spur him to realize them, but not too remote to be beyond reach and to lead to chronic discontent.

The relevance of the anomic discontents of sudden bad or good fortune to the problem of social order depends entirely on whether they are perceived as legitimate discontents. This question cannot be answered except by reference to the wider system of moral classification; and this is another reason for distinguishing clearly between personal and social deregulation. In the case of the individual who is faced with the necessity of reducing his level of wants to meet adverse circumstances, it is possible that he will regard this as at least unfair, in that he has to give up a style of life to which he has become accustomed and which he has come to regard as right and appropriate to his status. This feeling may persist, even though his status has declined and his previous aspirations are no longer socially recognized as appropriate to his new position. Similarly, in the case of a sudden increase in fortune, the wants that 'run ahead' of the individual's new level of reward might seem to him to be very proper and acceptable aspirations, even though, according to the wider system of classification, they may be deemed excessive and illegitimate. Thus, as far as social order is concerned, the question of whether anomically dislocated individuals regard their aspirations as legitimate is subordinate to the question of whether the causes of individual dislocation also bring about a deregulation of the social classification as a whole. For, even if many individuals suffered from anomic dissatisfaction, this would not necessarily impair social solidarity unless there simultaneously occurred a delegitimation of the existing moral hierarchy which allowed these individual discontents to be aggregated and legitimated by moral innovation. Otherwise they would remain isolated grievances likely to be dissipated in some form of personal pathology. As far as Durkheim's explanation of disorder is concerned, then, the crucial problem is not whether his particular theory of anomic suicide is correct but rather whether the assumptions on which this theory is based are adequate to elucidate his concept and explanation of anomic declassification.

Whether anomie takes the form of personal deregulation or social declassification, its most basic feature is the existence of an intolerable gap between the wants of individuals and the actual level of satisfaction of those wants. In the case of personal deregulation, the wants in question are not necessarily regarded as legitimate entitlements by those who seek to realize them. But in the case of declassification the deregulation of legitimate expectations is the defining characteristic of disorder. That the disorder of anomic declassification centres on the legitimacy of conflicting wants is entailed by the notion of a pre-existing moral classification. The most elementary notion underlying Durkheim's theory of disorder is, therefore, what is now referred to as relative deprivation. This has been defined as follows: 'When an individual or a group has a particular expectation, and furthermore when this expectation is considered to be a proper state of affairs, and where something less than that expectation is fulfilled, we may speak of relative deprivation.'[6] Although it invented the label, modern sociology did not discover the idea. Goethe's dictum 'that no one is more eaten up with envy than he who considers all men to be his equals' is a succinct formulation of a basic principle of Aristotle's politics; and, before Aristotle, Lao Tzu held that 'man's greatest need is contentment; his greatest curse the desire for possessions; he who learns to adjust to his niche shall always be content'. Clearly the venerable ancestry of this truism about human nature attests to its importance.[7]

---

[6] D. Aberle, 'A Note on Relative Deprivation as Applied to Millenarian and other Cult Movements', in S. L. Thrupp (ed.), *Millenial Dreams in Action* (The Hague, 1962), 209. The most incisive discussion of the use of the concept in research into social stratification is by W. G. Runciman, *Relative Deprivation and Social Justice* (London, 1972), pt. I and postscript.

[7] The concept has played a central role in many theories which attempt to explain revolutionary conflict. An article of seminal importance is that by J. C.

But when Durkheim speaks of declassification, he is not simply assuming that conflict is most likely to occur under conditions of intense and widespread relative deprivation or that a sense of relative deprivation is just as likely to be experienced when people's circumstances are improving as when they are at their worst. These kinds of observations have been made by students of revolution from de Tocqueville to Trotsky. Anomic declassification refers to a form of systematic disorder. Its structure is determined by the hierarchical interdependency of the legitimate expectations which make up the moral classification. The kind of deregulation Durkheim seems to have in mind can perhaps best be described as a chain reaction of relative deprivations running through the system of social classification when the latter loses its power of legitimating the unequal distribution of power and wealth. The condition of declassification is, furthermore, a phase of disorder which presupposes not only a preceding stable classification of men and things but also a subsequent reconstitution of the society in which men and things are once again stably reclassified in a new moral hierarchy. This sequence of classification–declassification–reclassification is remarkably similar to the stages of 'crystallized ruling classes', 'renovation', and 're-crystallization' as set out by Mosca:

there comes a period of renovation, or, if one prefers, revolution, during which individual energies have free play and certain individuals, more passionate, more energetic, more intrepid or merely shrewder than others, force their way from the bottom of the social ladder to its topmost rungs. Once such a movement has set in, it cannot be stopped immediately. The example of individuals who have started from nowhere and reached prominent positions fires new ambitions, new greeds, new energies, and this molecular rejuvenation of the ruling class continues vigorously until a long period of social stability slows it down again . . . then, at last, the force that is essentially conservative appears—the force of habit. Many people become resigned to a lowly station, while members of certain privileged families or classes grow convinced that they have an absolute right to high station and command.[8]

Davies, 'Towards a Theory of Revolution', *American Sociological Review*, 27 (1962). T. R. Gurr, *Why Men Rebel* (Princeton, 1970), has explored most of the possible permutations of the assumptions implicit in Davies's original 'J-curve' hypothesis about the causes of revolutionary outbreaks.

[8] G. Mosca, *The Ruling Class* (New York, 1939), 67–8.

What Mosca calls 'renovation' not only resembles declassification but involves the same essential ingredient of disorder; namely, the demonstration effect of the shift in the fortunes of one group of individuals or class upon the aspirations of others. Similarly, the deregulation of aspirations only makes sense when contrasted with a stable or 'crystallized' set of class relations, the equivalent of which is clearly Durkheim's concept of social or moral classification. Before turning to the questions of the nature and causes of declassification, then, it is necessary to gain some more exact idea of the social hierarchy itself.

III

Durkheim's basic idea of the exclusively normative structuring of interests is not contradicted by his concept of social classification, since the latter refers not to class, in the Marxist or Weberian sense, but to a hierarchy of status. Classification is a moral order which legitimates social, and particularly economic, inequalities, and which limits the aspirations of the different 'social classes'. In other words, it is the key social institution through which the solidarity of an homogeneous, church-like moral community is reproduced in a functionally differentiated society. In societies ordered in terms of mechanical solidarity, of which the society described in *The Elementary Forms of the Religious Life* is archetypal, the collective consciousness is an homogenizing moral force. In societies characterized by the division of labour, this common value element is not lacking, but its function is to integrate the community by justifying inequalities of resources and rewards: 'The different social functions are graded in public opinion and a certain coefficient of well-being assigned to each, according to its place in the social hierarchy.' In these societies it is the status order which comes to play the central integrative role; as the institutional embodiment of the collective conscience, a stable classification is the precondition of organic solidarity. Durkheim takes it for granted that in normal circumstances the status hierarchy is generally regarded as legitimate because it is based on a broad consensus about the 'respective value of different social services'. His full account of this condition is as follows:

A genuine regimen exists, therefore, although not always legally formulated, which fixes with relative precision the maximum degree of ease of
living to which each social class may legitimately aspire . . . Under this
pressure, each in his sphere vaguely realizes the extreme limit set to his
ambitions and aspires to nothing beyond. At least if he respects regula-
tions and is docile to collective authority, that is, has a wholesome moral
constitution, he feels that it is not well to ask for more. Thus an end and
goal are set to the passions . . . This relative limitation and the moderation it involves, make men contented with their lot while stimulating
them moderately to improve it; and this average contentment causes the
feeling of calm, active happiness, the pleasure of existing and living which
characterises health for societies as well as for individuals.[9]

The system of classification has two distinct aspects. First, it
legitimates the hierarchy of status as a whole, and, secondly, it
legitimates the allocation of individuals to the various statuses
within it:

It would be of little use for everyone to recognize the justice of the
hierarchy of functions established by public opinion if he did not also
consider the distribution of these functions just. The workman is not in
harmony with his social position if he is not convinced that he has had his
desserts. If he feels justified in occupying another, what he has would not
satisfy him. So it is not enough for the average level of needs for each
position to be regulated by public opinion, but another, more precise
rule, must fix the way in which these conditions are open to individuals.[10]

The main significance of this distinction is that it enters into the
definition of the degree of disorderliness of anomic declassification, and further discussion of it will be postponed until that point
in the exposition. At this stage it merely needs to be noted that,
according to Durkheim, both the hierarchy of functions and the
distribution of functions are normally regarded as legitimate; and
that their being so regarded is a precondition of order. If the
social classification is

maintained only by custom and force, peace and harmony are illusory;
the spirit of unrest and discontent is latent; appetites superficially
restrained are ready to revolt. But this state of upheaval is exceptional; it
occurs only when a society is passing through some abnormal crisis. In

---

[9] Durkheim, *Suicide*, pp. 249–50.
[10] Ibid. 250.

normal conditions the collective order is regarded as just by the great majority of persons.[11]

It may be said, then, that, while the moral classification takes something like class inequality as the object of its regulation, it is itself a structure of status. It is true that the notion of 'class' in an economic sense does occasionally intrude into Durkheim's work. But it is always treated, like the whole area of economic life, as a generally threatening and unruly element of society which is in greatest need of moral regulation: it is the very antithesis of the religious life.[12] More importantly, 'class' and 'economic life' are concepts in Durkheim's sociology which remain almost entirely unexplicated. They refer to forces whose disordering effects are always analysed by reference to the normative structure; they themselves are not conceived of as having a structure which is worthy of detailed consideration. This is most clearly evident in Durkheim's treatise on the institutions of property and contract, which deals much more fully with the norms of organic solidarity than his account of this subject in *The Division of Labour in Society*. At one point in the former work, he notes that the 'supreme obstacle' to the legitimation of contractual relations is 'the institution of inheritance. It is obvious that inheritance, by creating inequalities amongst men from birth, that are unrelated to merit or services, invalidates the whole contractual system at its very roots.' He then goes on to introduce the notion of class in a non-normative sense:

Now inheritance as an institution results in men being born either rich or poor: that is to say, there are two main classes in society, linked by all sorts of intermediate classes; the one which in order to live has to make its services acceptable to the other at whatever the cost; the other class which can do without these services, because it can call on certain resources, which may, however, not be equal to the services rendered by those who have them to offer. Therefore as long as such sharp class differences exist in society, fairly effective palliatives may lessen the

[11] Ibid. 251.

[12] Consider only the following typical statements in *Socialism*: 'It is easy to understand that in any social organisation, however skilfully ordered, economic functions cannot co-operate harmoniously nor be maintained in a state of equilibrium unless subjected to moral forces which surpass, contain and regulate them' (p. 239); 'one of the functions of religion has always been to place a rein on economic appetites' (p. 275).

injustice of contracts; but in principle, the system operates in conditions which do not allow of justice.[13]

Now there is no doubt whatsoever that Durkheim is here dealing with something like the Marxian notion of class. But the passage just quoted is one isolated observation in a work which is given over entirely to the discussion of civic morals, the rights of property, and the morality of contract. Moreover, the major part of his argument is devoted to showing the religious origins of contract and property, and to demonstrating the need for new moral principles which can provide the appropriate quasi-religious foundations of these two institutions in contemporary societies.[14] Furthermore, it is not simply the division of society into 'rich and poor' which is the ultimate cause of discontent. This is to be found rather in the 'scale of values' which is part and parcel of the moral classification.

We know of course that in every society and in all ages, there exists a vague but lively sense of the value of various services used in society, and of the values, too, of the things that are the subject of exchange. Although neither of these factors is regulated by tariff, there is, however, in every social group a state of opinion that fixes its normal value at least roughly.

It is this scale of social values 'that is the touchstone by which the equity of the exchanges is to be judged'.[15] What causes discontent in modern society is not the fact of there being rich and poor,

[13] Durkheim, *Professional Ethics*, p. 213. See also the discussion of the 'forced' division of labour in *The Division of Labour*.

[14] 'Property is property only if it is respected, that is to say, held sacred' (*Professional Ethics*, p. 159); 'The juridical formula is only a substitute for sacred formalities and rites' (ibid. 182, repeated p. 187). From ch. 13 onwards, Durkheim's discussion is replete with statements of this kind and the whole argument is that the weakening of the specifically religious foundation of legal institutions must be counteracted by their reform in accordance with a new and no less 'sacred' morality. See esp. p. 172: 'We have, however, seen that although religious beliefs are not based on fact, they do nevertheless express the social realities, even when they interpret them by symbol and metaphor. We know indeed that the sacred character which still marks the individual today is founded in reality; it is no more than the expression of the very high value that has accrued to individual personality through the conscience and dignity it is invested with; we know too how closely this regard for the individual is bound up with our whole social structure. Now it is inevitable that this sacred virtue which invests the individual should be extended to the things he is closely and lawfully connected with. The sentiments of respect for him cannot be limited to the physical person alone; the objects considered as his own must certainly have a share in them.'

[15] Ibid. 209–10.

which has always been the case, but rather the fact that the values
have changed, so that something like equality of opportunity is
more and more the appropriate standard of distributive justice.

The inherited fortune loads the scales and upsets the balance. It is in
opposition to this inequitable assessment and to a whole state of society
that allows it to happen, that we get the growing revolt of men's
consciences. It is true that over the centuries, the injustice could be
accepted without revolt because the demand for equality was less. Today,
however, it conflicts only too obviously with the attitude which is to be
found underlying our morality.[16]

It is fairly clear, then, that, although some notion of class, in a
non-normative sense, is indispensable to Durkheim's argument, it
remains very much an *ad hoc* concept, lacking sociological definition. Neither 'class' nor 'economic life' is seen as possessing a
structure other than that which is given to it by the institutional
system. His exposition of the sociology of economic order is
almost exclusively devoted to distinguishing the various norms
that govern economic activity and to showing their interrelations.[17]

This conclusion is reinforced by considering his account of the
'forced' division of labour. In modern society, the 'eminent' form
of organic solidarity is 'contractual solidarity', which the law of

---

[16] Ibid. 214.

[17] This is also a distinctive feature of later normative functionalist theorization
of the economy, the definitive statement being T. Parsons and N. J. Smelser,
Economy and Society (New York, 1965), ch. 3, 'The Institutional Structure of the
Economy'. In fact, this work recognizes no other structure of the economy than
the institutional; there is only one specific reference to 'class structure', and this
has to do with Schumpeter's idea that the maintenance of capitalism in Europe
depended on entrepreneurs being able to acquire an 'élite status' through their
amalgamation with aristocratic strata. Institutions are defined as 'the ways in which
the value patterns of the common culture of a social system are integrated in the
concrete action of its units in their interaction with each other through the
definition of role expectations and the organization of motivation' (p. 102). Some
idea of how this concept is applied to the economy may be obtained from what is
said about the contract of employment. Its function is to 'integrate three partially
independent systems of action: (1) the organization in which ego is employed; (2)
the household of which ego is a member, and (3) the personality of ego'. The
values uniting the three through the employment contract are described as follows:
'A "good" organization recognizes an obligation to pay "good" wages and salaries;
furthermore, it is proud of its prestige position and the prestige that its personnel
derive from this position. Conversely, a "good" family in our society recognizes
the obligation of its employed members (especially the husband-father) to be
"good" at his job and to consider his job "important" above and beyond the
remuneration level.' (p. 117)

contract is not in itself sufficient to bring about as long as contracts are not fully consented to. Ideally, contractual law presupposes that individuals have the right to enter into free and equal exchange and thereby to develop their potentialities in a way that meets the requirements of the 'spontaneous division of labour', which is in turn the main condition of organic solidarity. But Durkheim argues that these rights lack full legitimacy and fail to serve their real social function as long as the formal equality of opportunity they enshrine coexists with gross inequalities in the 'external conditions of conflict'. The inheritance of wealth and position are the chief obstacles to a spontaneous or meritocratic division of labour in which the hierarchy of positions and the allocation of persons to them express the exchange of services of an 'equivalent social value', and in which 'social inequalities express precisely natural inequalities'.[18] This recipe for organic solidarity is quite radical in its implications for the redistribution of resources. It also leads once again into what was for Durkheim the conceptually uncharted territory of class relations. Yet, characteristically, he is not at all concerned with the structure and dynamics of the economic system which produces inequalities of power and wealth. His interest centres on the pattern of inequality which would enjoy legitimacy, that is, on the kind of classification or hierarchy prerequisite to organic solidarity.

In contemporary sociology, and especially the branch that draws its inspiration from Durkheim, there is a tendency to treat status merely as prestige-ranking or at best as a relation of informal social interaction. It is, therefore, surely important to note that, for Durkheim, the modern social classification found its chief

---

[18] Durkheim's use of 'social value' is not to be confused with the labour theory of value. He writes that 'In any given society, every object of exchange has, at any moment, a fixed value that might be called its social value. It represents the amount of useful labour intrinsic to it. By this must be understood, not the total labour that it may have cost, but the part of that effort capable of producing socially useful effects, that is, effects that correspond to normal needs. Although such a quantum cannot be calculated mathematically, it is none the less real. The principal conditions as a function of which it varies can even be grasped without difficulty. These are, especially, the sum total of the effort needed for the production of the object, the intensity of the need it satisfies, and finally the extent of the satisfaction it affords. Moreover, in fact, it is around this level that the average value fluctuates. It only diverges from it under the influence of abnormal factors. In that case the public consciousness generally more or less perceives this deviation.' (*The Division of Labour*, p. 317.)

institutional expression in the law of contract, that is, in one of
the basic civil rights attaching to the status of a common citizenship. And it is difficult to think that his idea of classification would
not also have included the social rights of citizenship, and rights
to collective bargaining, which have served to mitigate some of
the grosser inequalities in the 'external conditions of conflict'.[19]
When he writes that 'in a contract not everything is contractual',
he refers to legal and customary limitation on the exercise of
economic power, which Weber sees as the most general effect of
status orders: that is, 'the hindrance of the free development of
the market'.[20] But unlike Weber, for whom status, especially legal
status, was basically another form of power, antithetical to that of
the market, Durkheim saw legal rights as embodying beliefs and
values which were in turn expressive of a certain state of social
solidarity. In modern societies, the central belief was that of
equality, or, more exactly, equality of opportunity;[21] and the force
of law, resting on consensus, was measured by the extent to which
society brought about an approximation to this ideal. That is why
'the task of the most advanced societies may be said to be a
mission for justice';[22] and why contractual law is not the same as
contractual solidarity. Moreover, contractual solidarity is not the
same as organic solidarity, which must surely require not only
justice in the allocation of individuals to social functions but also
another kind of 'non-contractual', extra legal, consensus: namely,
a generally acceptable social hierarchy or grading of social functions by public opinon.[23]

---

[19] Durkheim's insight into the forces that have led to the supplementation of the
status of civil by social citizenship was remarkable. In one way or another, and
from different ends of the political spectrum, public debate has continued to centre
on the same basic issues of distributive justice which are to be found in his contrast
between the 'forced' and 'spontaneous' division of labour.

[20] M. Weber, *Economy and Society* (New York, 1968), ii. 937.

[21] Society 'recognizes as unjust an inferiority that is personally not merited ' and
'what manifests even more clearly this tendency is the belief, nowadays very
widespread, that equality between citizens is becoming ever greater, and that it is
right that this should continue to grow. So general a sentiment cannot be a pure
illusion, but must express, in some obscure way, an aspect of reality' (Durkheim,
The Division of Labour), p. 314).   [22] Ibid. 321.

[23] Except perhaps in the purely hypothetical case of a society in which relations
of socially divided labour are exclusively contractual and truly 'spontaneous'; then,
presumably, the social hierarchy of rewards would be a function of, and simultaneously legitimated by, the free exchange of the respective 'social values' of
individual services.

IV

It is in this context that Durkheim's fleeting references to the idea of classification should be understood. For, although his treatment of it may appear rudimentary, it is a concept which is anchored in the most basic presuppositions of his sociology. The idea that the status system legitimates inequalities of power and wealth and serves to integrate the ends of actors by grading their respective levels of legitimate aspiration is also characteristic of neo-Durkheimian sociology. Indeed, in normative functionalism this concept of status has arrogated to itself the entire meaning of stratification as a structural property of a society.[24] The importance of this perspective is as undeniable as its Durkheimian provenance is unmistakable. The propensity to rank is ineradicable because it has its basis in the fact that social action is inherently norm-governed. Of course, this proposition explains nothing about the structure of any particular status hierarchy. Furthermore, the normative functionalist elaboration of this truth does not exactly bring into prominence the equally important consideration that status orders are maintained by other than purely moral sanctions. In all major historical societies, the rights and obligations of status groups have been legally instituted; that is to say, in the last resort, they have been guaranteed by force. On this ground alone, then, status cannot be understood simply as a normative system. Nevertheless, the sense in which status differentiation is inherently normative is worth emphasizing, especially since its significance is likely to be underestimated by those who are prone to think of societies as riven by irreconcilable conflict and possessing a highly fragile order maintained principally by threats of force and expectations of advantage. From such a viewpoint, status hierarchies will be understood merely as means of ideological domination, as systems of normative sanctions that facilitate the manipulation of subordinates by the allocation of honorific rewards; or, as Napoleon had it, 'the baubles' by which men are led. This is not a point of view that is entirely without

---

[24] See, e.g., T. Parsons, 'An Analytical Approach to the Theory of Social Stratification', in his *Essays in Sociological Theory: Pure and Applied* (Glencoe, Ill., 1949), and B. Barber, *Social Stratification* (New York, 1957). The chapter entitled 'Class' in Shils, *Centre and Periphery*, is of especial interest as an instance of the attempt to reduce the concept of class to that of status.

substance, but it does not exhaust all that can be said about the nature of status. In particular, it is often associated with the belief that, given an appropriate redistribution of power, status differentiation is eradicable. But it requires no more than a brief consideration of the normative foundation of status to show that this belief is illusory.

In Durkheim's account of the social hierarchy there is a surprising omission: this is the connection of status with the sacred. It is surprising, because of his untiring insistence on the religious origins of all social institutions and on the religious nature of the ultimate beliefs which hold societies together. The sacred is the moral core of a society. Therefore, to know what is held most sacred by society is to know, as Durkheim might say, the differential coefficient of social worth. It is Shils who has essayed the formula. His argument is that status is grounded in the charisma of authority, by which is meant 'authorship' in the sense of creativity. This status-conferring quality attaches most intensely to activities which have to do with the exercise of political authority, the guardianship of ultimate beliefs, and the scientific mastery of nature. Shils's thesis goes beyond the elementary idea that status differentiation expresses the common values of society by arguing that all societies give highest value to the same broad set of order-creating functions.[25] Although his essay is Weberian in its terminology, its substance is essentially Durkheimian. The sacredness of charisma which emanates from what Shils calls the 'centre' of a society towards its 'periphery' may be more or less concentrated, but there is no known society in which such a central religious zone is indiscernible; and it seems unlikely that any society will lack one. Appreciation of the charisma of the centre is unevenly distributed among the members of a society; relatively few have an intense awareness of it, whether positive or negative; but there are equally few who lack some sense, however dim, of the extraordinary realm of the sacred. The significance of this argument lies in the fact that the charisma of the centre is independent of the particular groups of individuals who carry out

[25] E. A. Shils, 'Order, Charisma and Status', *American Sociological Review*, 30 (1965). This article can be read as a splendid Weberian gloss on Durkheim which dispenses with practically everything in Weber's writings on social stratification that is incompatible with normative functionalist assumptions.

these central activities and of the particular values and beliefs by which they seek to legitimate their activities. This means that the source of 'ultimate value' inheres not in any particular type of common value system or dominant ideology but in the constitution of a society *per se*. In particular, revolutionary change does not, and cannot, destroy the centre in this sense; on the contrary, a revolution involves a heightened consciousness of and reaffirmation of the charisma or sacredness of the centre.

But it is not only in the sacred, but in the morality of everyday life that the ineradicability of status consists. If the sacred or charismatic emanates a quality of extraordinariness that is perceived to be of great social worth, the moral standards that regulate social interactions in more mundane milieux easily congeal into conceptions of status whose lesser authority is more than compensated for by the fact that their influence is much more continuous and direct. As Durkheim says,

it is not only in exceptional circumstances that this stimulating action of society makes itself felt; there is not, so to speak, a moment of our lives when some current of energy does not come to us from without. The man who has done his duty finds, in the manifestations of every sort expressing the sympathy, esteem or affection which his fellows have for him, a feeling of comfort, of which he does not ordinarily take account, but which sustains him, nonetheless.[26]

The necessary and sufficient conditions of spontaneous status ranking are to be found, on the one hand, in the fact that action is norm-governed and, on the other, in the effect of the size of the social group.

Given that there are norms and that individuals live up to them in differing degrees, it is inevitable that persons will be ranked according to their particular merits and demerits. If the group is small, the norms which are relevant to ranking will be multifarious, because many aspects of individual conduct are open to inspection. In this circumstance it is unlikely that the sum of the various virtues and vices attaching to the conduct of an individual will be sufficiently consistent to enable him to be judged unequivocally as wholly deserving or undeserving relative to others. That is to say, if the group is small, status will be based on

---

[26] Durkheim, *Elementary Forms*, p. 211.

interaction, on a knowledge of the many-sided qualities of individuals, and will be unlikely to yield completely consistent status profiles that permit one set of persons to be ranked as wholly more or less worthy than another set. Things are different when social relations become so extensive that such face-to-face interaction can no longer be the basis of evaluation. Then the determination of social standing depends less and less on a knowledge of the many-sided instrinsic qualities of an individual, and is replaced by ranking according to a few, easily recognizable, extrinsic marks of status. There is, in other words, a threshold of anonymity at which 'interactional status' gives way to, or has superimposed upon it, 'attributional status'.[27] In formal and public contexts, the impersonal and generally applicable criteria of status tend to override the manifold and more subtle characteristics of individuals which are taken into account in allocating status in primary groups. For most people, most of the time, primary-group memberships continue to fulfil their need for attachment and to sustain their sense of identity and social worth. Moreover, the values that are prominent in primary group status-ranking often represent a defence, or a form of protest, against the derogations of the wider status system. Finally, since attributional status depends on a relatively few, closely related, criteria of social worth, it is likely to result in far less 'status inconsistency' than is the case in interactional status.[28] But such considerations are no more than elaborations of the general point that the social hierarchy proper subsists on the propensity to rank which is

[27] These terms were coined by D. E. G. Plowman *et al.*, 'Local Social Status in England and Wales', *Sociological Review*, 10 (1962).

[28] The tendency for metropolitan, attributional status to be characterized by highly consistent rankings (according to occupation, education, income, etc.) is what makes doubtful Steven Lukes's argument that there is 'an empirical possibility of a society containing a plurality of norms, each conferring and withholding status and prestige without themselves being ranked within a single system of inequality or stratification'. See his essay 'Socialism and Equality', in L. Kolakowski and S. Hampshire (eds.), *The Socialist Idea* (London, 1977), esp. pp. 93–4. For evidence on this subject, see W. Wesołowski and K. Słomczyński, 'Reduction of Social Inequalities and Status Inconsistency', in *Social Structure: Polish Sociology* (Wrocław, 1977), and P. Machonin, 'Social Stratification in Contemporary Czechoslovakia', *American Journal of Sociology*, 75 (1970). In state socialist societies, status inconsistency appears to be limited mostly to the relative ranking of lower white-collar and skilled-working occupations; in this respect their stratification systems are fairly similar to those of capitalist societies.

inseparable from norm-governed action and which is also the source of the elementary status distinctions that pervade every sphere of social interaction.

At the same time, it is always the case that the dominant status order, even though it may not expressly devalue, must of necessity exclude from its moral calculus, those standards whose application depends on the close appraisal of particular individuals in local settings. In this way it excludes not only those values which are peculiar to a vast number of primary groups, but also those qualities which are held to be most distinctively human and which are given great prominence in the most sublime, religious beliefs of a society. When the status honour of bureaucrats, warriors, prelates, entrepreneurs, or commissars fixes the coefficient of social worth, there is little room for the ethics of the Sermon on the Mount or of the Enlightenment under the *bodhi* tree. It is perhaps because of this that there is usually a certain affinity between the most central and the most peripheral spheres of value in a society, both of which stand in some degree of tension and incongruity with the system of institutionalized status. Among the highest ideals are values that are not and cannot be embodied in the dominant social hierarchy which nevertheless seeks its legitimacy by reference to this same realm of ultimate values and beliefs. The virtues that are set on one side by the system of institutionalized status very generally appertain to qualities such as charity, compassion, and humility, the possession of which may embellish already high status but which will not in themselves ensure it.[29] Even though an exemplary life based on unswerving dedication to such virtues can seldom be accomplished in the ordinary dealings which most people have with one another, it is nevertheless these kinds of values which do continually reassert themselves in the ranking of individuals within primary groups. The difficulty of living up to such values is also commonly accorded macro-social recognition in the ethical dualism of lay and virtuoso religiosity, such as the distinction between *praecepta* and *consilia*.

This affinity between the most elevated and the most everyday

---

[29] This is not to say that they are not widely regarded as deserving public recognition. See, e.g., 'Charity Workers Head Honours Poll', *The Times*, 30 Dec. 1983.

conceptions of human worth is not the only way in which the derogations of the dominant status order are diminished. Other standards than those set by the institionalized social hierarchy are of great importance in any comprehensive view of the effects of social comparisons on order and disorder. To begin with, the most immediate reference point an individual can take in evaluating his present situation is that of either his past or his expected future condition. In so far as these self-centred comparisons yield randomly distributed satisfactions and dissatisfactions which cancel each other out their consequences for social order will be negligible. It is a different matter if individuals severally make the same comparisons because they share some common experience or expectation. An example might be a set of individuals who are now comfortably well off, but who happen to have experienced some past adversity, such as long-run employment, at the same stage in their life cycle. In this case, the aggregate of their purely personal relative satisfactions will constitute a generational bloc of support for the existing social order, just as a negative comparison would produce a bloc of potential opposition. An equally important and lively reference point is another individual. This type of inter-personal comparison is the predominant feature of interactional status-ranking in primary groups. Its archetype is probably sibling rivalry. From the viewpoint of macro-social order, the significance of these highly particular, often dyadic, comparisons is that they absorb individuals into the highly restricted invidious comparisons of their immediate social milieux, from which the vast majority of significant others will be drawn. Any content analysis of the morality of everyday life would surely demonstrate, not only the large amount of time which is taken up in making evaluations of the conduct of kin, workmates, and neighbours, but also their emotional significance for the individual, not least as a means of meeting his need for self-esteem, which impulse, normally demanding the maximization of favourable comparisons, has greatest scope for fulfilment at this level of the social system where there is greatest discretion in the choice of comfortable peers as well as candidates for derogation. The importance for social order of this kind of inter-personal comparison can hardly be exaggerated, since most people most of the time are much more concerned with proximate and particular individuals in their local milieux than with more remote and abstract social categories. Only exceptionally does an extension of social horizons occur on such a scale and with such an intensity that it is sufficient to diminish the concern with parochial social standing and situational justice and to mobilize sentiments around wider collectivities based on class, or ethnic or religious membership. Even then, strong and widespread adhesion to these larger social units is normally of short duration and it is only a small minority who participate in their corporate actions. Moreover, intense personal status rivalries are a very characteristic feature of the leadership of these movements. All in all, it is possible that the contribution to social order of what may be called 'primary moral classification' is as important, if not more so, than that of the status hierarchy proper. This is because its influence is more direct, pervasive, and continuous, and because its effect is to particularize feelings of injustice and disaffection. But for the latter reason, and unlike the dominant status order, situational stratification offers no possibility of the systematic extension of social comparisons. The moral standards of primary classification are either peculiar to some small group, or else they refer to universal virtues whose authentication depends on an equally close appraisal of personal conduct.

Primary classification is subordinate and interstitial to the status hierarchy proper, taking interpersonal rather than inter-group comparisons as its point of reference. There is, however, a further source of social comparison which lies above the status order proper: this is the realm of ultimate values and beliefs. Naturally, it is here that the rationale of institutionalized status is to be found; but so also are conceptions of alternative societies by reference to which the established status order may be revealed as illegitimate and contingent. Since the ultimate values and beliefs of a society have utopian as well as ideological potentialities, they may be said to be the source of inter-societal comparisons. The same sort of comparison can also be afforded by a knowledge of other societies, and an external model of this kind has often led to 'revolutions of rising expectations', especially when people are suddenly made aware of the possibility of improvements in conditions of life they had hitherto thought of as unalterable and unexceptional. Naturally, other societies may provide just the opposite kind of 'demonstration effect'. In recent history, a most important example of this has been the reduction of the aspirations and public credibility of Western Communist parties against the background of post-Stalinist state socialism. Finally, in some degree, the indigenous values and beliefs of a society always provide 'external' bench-marks, by reference to which any prevailing ideological account of the existing social order may be brought into question. This is partly because it is in the nature of ideologies that they too appeal to ideal states of affairs of which institutionalized practices are necessarily an imperfect realization. It is also because it is in the nature of ideologies that they are selective of and never exhaust the full range of ultimate values and beliefs that are available to members of a society.[30] Any ideological interpretation is thus doubly unsafe, in that the inevitable lack of fit between its promise and the social reality it seeks to encompass is capable of being magnified and exploited by reference to an alternative ideal state of affairs. No matter what success professional ideologists may have in meeting these exigencies, no ideology can ever guarantee the cognitive and moral preconditions of a complete social *immobilisme*. Admittedly, ideologies vary greatly in their capacity to provide a consistent legitimation of the status hierarchy, and thus in their exploitability by counter-ideologies. But, quite apart from this, there are usually certain elements of ultimate values and beliefs which an ideology will naturally tend to play down or try to eliminate from its own system.[31] Past or future utopias are to be found in all religious or

[30] The best short statement of the need to distinguish ideologies from ultimate values and beliefs is by Parsons, 'An Approach to the Sociology of Knowledge', in *Sociological Theory and Modern Society*. This is also recognized in post-Gramscian Marxism through the distinction between 'popular democratic' beliefs and class ideologies proper. See Ernesto Laclau, *Politics and Ideology in Marxist Theory* (London, 1979), esp. ch. 3.

[31] Namely, what Mannheim calls utopias. Utopias are not distinguished from ideologies by the fact that they 'transcend the social situation', since ideologies are also 'situationally transcendent ideas which never succeed *de facto* in the realization of their projected contents'. It is rather that 'the representatives of a given order will label as utopian all conceptions of existence which *from their point of view* can in principle never be realized', and 'it is always the dominant group which is in full accord with the existing order that determines what is to be regarded as utopian, while the ascendant group which is in conflict with things as they are is the one that determines what is regarded as ideological'. Mannheim notes, however, that the difficulty 'in defining precisely what, at a given period, is to be regarded as ideology, and what as utopia, results from the fact that the utopian and ideological elements do not occur separately in the historical process. The utopias of ascendant classes are often, to a large extent, permeated with ideological elements.' See his *Ideology and Utopia*, pp. 175-7, 183.

quasi-religious theodicies that carry promises of salvation. The alternative society envisaged may involve a complete transformation of the existing social order or its restoration to a pristine state. In both cases, utopian beliefs are very commonly associated with expectations of the regeneration of the world and of human nature, and with some kind of messianic redemption.[32] The degree of exploitability of ideologies, the availability of utopian conceptions, and differences in the nature of these utopias are all matters relating to the variability of the structure of ultimate values and beliefs which are of great significance for the explanation of order and conflict. It has already been shown, for example, that one general condition of fatalistic order is a lack of inter-societal comparisons. Another important question is whether utopian bench-marks which are located in the remote historical past— golden ages—are likely to be less conducive to social disorder than those which are located in the future.[33] It should be said, once again, that, although these sorts of problems are of particular relevance to Durkheimian and normative functionalism, this school of sociology has not been much concerned with them.

In drawing attention to inter-societal, as well as to intra- and inter-individual comparisons, the object has been to show that what Durkheim calls the social hierarchy or classification is only one aspect of a wider system of moral regulation. In defining legitimate inter-group comparisons, by establishing the respective levels of wants appropriate to different ranks, the status system plays a strategic role in social integration. But it does not function in isolation from the levels of comparison which exist below and above it. Primary status classification is in part a reaction to, and serves to alleviate the harshness of, the derogations inflicted by the dominant social hierarchy. Since primary classification promotes values which are either peculiar to or only applicable in the

---

[32] Y. Talmon, 'Pursuit of the Millenium', *European Journal of Sociology*, 3 (1962), provides an admirable short review of the literature of this subject. She tends, however, to de-emphasize the 'millenarian' aspects of Hinduism and Buddhism. On this, see E. Abegg, *Der Messiasglaube in Indien und Iran* (Leipzig, 1928), and Yang, *Religion in Chinese Society*, ch. 9.

[33] This is a proposition advanced by C. A. Dreckmeier, *Kingship and Community in Early India* (Stanford, Calif., 1962), 104–5: 'It is not uncommon for men, in protecting themselves against disillusion, to put their Utopia in the past. A Utopia of this sort has weak critical potential and generally constitutes no threat to the established order.'

context of groups sufficiently small and enduring to permit of the emergence of interactional ranking, its general effect is to particularize the sense of injustice and thereby to strengthen the regulatory power of the larger status system. At the same time, some of the moral standards which enter into primary classification are primary in the sense that they emanate from the ultimate values and beliefs which lie above the dominant status order and by reference to which it both derives its ideological legitimation and is open to utopian deregulation.

V

It would be to take a very limited, and, so to speak, 'idealistic', view of the status system to conclude that it merely operates to restrict the range of legitimate inter-group comparisons. That it does operate in this fashion is indubitable. But it is not always successful in its objective. It has disordering effects as well. In the first place, considered purely as a normative structure, the status hierarchy is inherently conducive to attempts to modify the invidious distinctions of social worth which it establishes. The unavoidable derogations associated with status-ranking are always painful to those subject to them, however much they subscribe to the general values which legitimate the acts of deference they owe to their superiors.[34] And it is by no means always the case that it is those who stand lowest in the status hierarchy who feel these deprivations most intensely. There is, in consequence, even in the most stably founded status order, some pressure towards the amelioration of the indignities which it imposes, and the innovation very commonly takes the form of the development of subcultural status norms. Groups may seek to insulate themselves from status interactions which are damaging to their self-esteem by giving prominence to more parochial standards of social worth which, while mitigating the impact of the more inclusive status system, do not represent any fundamental challenge to it.[35] Or

---

[34] For a graphic account, see R. Sennett and J. Cobb, *The Hidden Injuries of Class* (Cambridge, 1972). The title is misleading, because the book is about status not class.

[35] Those on the margins or boundaries of status groups are especially sensitive to deference and derogation. A general consequence of the fear of disrespect from associating with those 'above' and of loss of respect from associating with those

again, innovation may take the form of the reinterpretation of dominant status criteria: for example, 'success' and 'achievement' in the way of the accumulation of consumer durables may be substituted for success as measured by upward occupational mobility.[36] A further very common mode of defensive status innovation is the proliferation of status distinctions within or around the boundaries of a status group. There must be few instances of lower status groups who, by some small inventiveness, are unable to alleviate their own derogation by discovering yet other groups that they in turn can look down upon. These and other types of innovation occur as a normal aspect of institutionalized status orders and they are possible because the values from which the status hierarchy derives its legitimacy are always in some degree exploitable. The pressure to innovation is, of course, not constant and uniform through the status system. But it is in some form and degree intrinsic to status-ranking, and, because of this, the exploitability of values is an important variable affecting the stability of the status order as a whole. If values are highly exploitable, extensive subcultural innovation will be possible, and this, in turn, will permit status groups to alleviate in various ways the deprivations which a more rigid and intractable hierarchy would impose upon them. As a result, a status order based on an exploitable ideology is less unequivocally punitive and at the same time possesses greater stability, because the subcultural deviations from the dominant criteria of rank variously express, and therefore sustain, a 'common' system of values and beliefs.

But the working of a status order cannot properly be understood if it is considered merely as a normative phenomenon. It is subject to innovation for other reasons than those connected with honorific discrimination *per se*. Unequal and never wholly stable

---

'below' is the avoidance of both kinds of interaction. The resultant isolation of status groups from one another is of considerable importance in its contribution to social cohesion. Not only are social frictions arising from ambivalent status interactions minimized, but inequalities of wealth and privilege are probably less apparent, and the amount of envy and relative deprivation correspondingly reduced. The significance for social order of such spontaneous social segregation (which can of course occur on other grounds than status and which is also determined by the material conditions of different life styles) has been stressed by Williams, *American Society*, i. 550–3.

[36] See E. Chinoy, *Automobile Workers and the American Dream* (New York, 1955).

distributions of goods and power are the source of an ever-present potential for conflict, the actualization of which is contrary to the nature of a status hierarchy, which seeks to justify privilege and disadvantage and to generate wants in accordance with its own moral matrix. This regulation is, however, always imperfect, because the accumulation and dissolution of power has a momentum of its own which is inconsiderate of established expectancies of status. Newly emergent power has a hunger for legitimation in a status order that is congruent with its own structure, just as status, once formed, endeavours to appropriate nascent power which might threaten its authorization of inequality. All status systems therefore have the further important function of establishing 'rates of exchange' by which spontaneous changes in the distribution of power can be legitimately translated into status.[37] The most basic aspect of this process is the transformation of power into institutional authority, because the latter is the most enduring and tangible form of status, the backbone of any status hierarchy, to which purely honorific recognition is secondary. The norms and rituals of status reallocation are thus an essential and normal part of the integrative mechanism of all status systems. However rigid status boundaries may appear to be, some degree of normatively regularized exchange of power and status is always present. There is, nevertheless, a limit to the capacity of a status order to accommodate itself to the redistribution of power and wealth. This limitation is, as will be seen, implicit in the notion of anomic declassification and provides a measure of its severity.

The more elementary point which needs to be made at this stage is that the determination of status aspirations, and the limitation of invidious comparisons which this involves, is not something which can be understood simply as the product of the moral classification of 'men and things'. The realistic conditions in which people act, the means available to them to realize their goals, and changes in these means and conditions, also affect their aspirations and the range of their social horizons. Although Durkheim does not give much emphasis to this side of the equation, he does recognize that resources as well as moral forces play a role in the determination of wants. After noting that

[37] P. M. Blau, *Exchange and Power in Social Life* (New York, 1964).

'poverty protects against suicide because it is a restraint in itself', he goes on to say:

> No matter how one acts, desires have to depend upon resources to some extent; actual possessions are partly the criterion of those aspired to. So the less one has the less he is tempted to extend the range of his needs indefinitely. Lack of power, compelling moderation, accustoms men to it, while nothing excites envy if no one has superfluity. Wealth, on the other hand, by the power it bestows, deceives us into believing that we depend on ourselves only. Reducing the resistance we encounter from objects, it suggests the possibility of unlimited success against them.[38]

Here Durkheim makes explicit what is already contained in his idea of anomie. If resources had no effect on people's aspirations, then the stability of the status system would simply be a function of the success with which people were socialized into the legitimate expectations appropriate to their respective ranks within it. If lack of proper socialization were a purely random occurrence, the process postulated by the concept of anomic declassification could not take place. But if failure of socialization, or rather something more like desocialization, is a systematic aspect of the deregulation of the aspirations of status groups, then its variability must be accounted for in part by some other structuring factor than the hierarchy of expectations making up the status order. This is not to say that the latter is irrelevant to the explanation of the determination of aspirations, but rather that its effect is always contingent upon the distribution of what Durkheim calls 'resources'. That is to say, if the distribution of resources is such as to limit aspirations in a manner that is congruent with the expectations of reward legitimated by the status hierarchy, then the social classification will be stable. Declassification, on the other hand, entails a state of affairs in which there is a marked incongruity between realistic conditions and legitimate expectations. Exactly what this incongruity consists of is a question which is most conveniently dealt with later on in the discussion of the nature and causes of declassification.

The most general conclusion that can be drawn from this interpretation of Durkheim's idea of classification is by now probably all too familiar. It is that the concepts of 'resources',

---

[38] Durkheim, *Suicide*, p. 254.

'possessions', 'power', and 'wealth' are, by contrast with those of hierarchy and classification, *ad hoc* and residual in nature. These concepts are necessary to a full explanation of how wants are determined and thus to an understanding of how the system of classification is stabilized as well as deregulated. But they remain peripheral to Durkheim's central concern. It is the social hierarchy, classification, or status order which is treated as the major structure of society, and it is through this that wants are seen to be systematically and normatively determined. At the same time, however, the effect upon the formation of wants of the distribution of resources and power is not a factor whose significance can be limited to the explanation of the 'abnormal' condition of anomic declassification. It is certainly the case that Durkheim invokes these residual concepts when dealing with the problem of disorder, whether in the general form of the attrition of the force of collective sentiments or in the particular form of the collapse of the system of moral classification. But if abrupt changes in the distribution of power and wealth lead to a deregulation of the status hierarchy, then it follows that a stable distribution of power and wealth must be a necessary condition of order, and even of the limiting case of order: solidarity. Thus the distribution of resources is not only a residual though necessary element in Durkheim's theory of disorder, but it is an equally important, though more obscure, presupposition of his theory of order as well.

Furthermore, it is difficult to avoid the conclusion that the ordering and disordering effects of the distribution and redistribution of 'men and things' or 'power and wealth' are to be thought of as systematic rather than random. When Durkheim deals with the general case of disorder in the context of 'elementary' religious life, or mechanical solidarity, he seems to assume that the 'conflicts' and 'frictions' which arise from the exigencies of everyday life and which enfeeble the collective conscience impinge upon it in an accidental manner. But in the case of declassification their effect must by systematic. How could the social hierarchy classify 'men and things' at all unless these men and things were distributed in some definite order? How could the social hierarchy regulate the wants of different 'social classes' if the latter did not already stand in some definite relationship to one another by virtue of their command over varying amounts of resources? And, if moral classification takes as its object some determinate distribution of things that is not in itself normative, then it would be strange if the redistribution of these things which leads to declassification did not also exhibit some regularity. This much is fairly clearly indicated by Durkheim when he says that, 'as the conditions of life are changed, the standard according to which needs are regulated can no longer remain the same; for it varies with social resources, since it largely determines the share of each class of producers'. And again, 'since the relations between various parts of society are necessarily modified, the ideas expressing these relations must change'.

Since classification and declassification imply some systematic distribution and redistribution of material resources that have no place in Durkheim's conceptual scheme, it is not surprising that the nature of these resources, never mind the causes of their variation, remains unclear. The distribution of resources is ambiguous because it might refer simply to an abstract, statistical distribution (for example, of income); on the other hand, since one person's means of action are often another's conditions of action, it might imply a pattern of social relationships. This ambiguity is nicely displayed in Durkheim's reference to the distribution of 'power and wealth'; power being necessarily, but wealth contingently, relational. There are then good grounds for supposing that the object of moral classification includes patterns of social relationships as well as the patterns of wants that are generated by a given distribution of resources. In other words, there is, in Durkheim's theory, another concept of structure *in statu nascendi*. It has to be there, because otherwise Durkheim could not begin to explain disorder; but it also has to remain inchoate, because otherwise the key assumption of the normative structuring of action would be brought into question. This problem is, however, merely indicative of a more basic difficulty in Durkheim's treatment of declassification. It is not simply that he has to introduce a residual concept of structure to explain disorder. His very conception of disorder contains a fundamental ambiguity which cannot be resolved in a way that is consistent with the implications of his notion of order as solidarity. This is the Durkheimian dilemma proper. His idea of disorder is flawed irredeemably from the outset and the unsatisfactory explanation of disorder is merely a consequence of this initial fault.

5.

ANOMIC DECLASSIFICATION

I

The major problem presented by Durkheim's account of declassification is that of determining the kind of disorder it entails. It is clear that once the social classification is disturbed its regulatory influence cannot immediately be re-established. 'The moral re-education of individuals must be recommenced, but they cannot be readjusted instanteously to their new circumstances,' and 'time is required for the public conscience to reclassify men and things'. The state of declassification is some sort of interregnum: one classification has broken down, but a new one will be, has to be, institutionalized. The crucial question then concerns the form of disorder during this interregnum.

Durkheim's answer is highly ambiguous. At certain points he seems to imply that all moral regulation is in abeyance and that individual wants become completely unruled: 'All the advantages of social influence are lost;' 'All regulation is lacking for a time;' 'There is no restraint upon aspirations.' Yet in other places he seems to suggest that declassification is associated with some kind of structured conflict: 'Some particular class especially favoured by the crisis is no longer resigned to its former lot;' 'the example of its greater good fortune arouses all sorts of jealousy below and around it'; and 'all classes contend among themselves'. How then is declassification to be understood? Does it mean the collapse of the common value system and a complete reversion to pure egoism and random conflict? Or does it signify a state of class conflict? And in that case what are the bases of class cohesion and class conflict? This ambiguity in the conceptualization of disorder is not resolved by Durkheim. It is necessary, therefore, to examine the two alternatives more closely.

The first alternative, a complete lack of moral regulation, finds its limit in the Hobbesian state of disorder. It is a society made up of rational egoists, each one pursuing his own self-determined ultimate ends, none recognizing that another's ends are more worthy than his own. All are locked in an incessant struggle over scarce means (or, what is the same thing, proximate ends which are in turn generalized means for the attainment of idiosyncratic ultimate ends), of which the inherently most scarce—power over other men—is no sooner gained than it is lost. This state of conflict presupposes that the society is made up of individuals who are more or less equal in their physical and mental capacities and in their hopes of realizing their ends. The ensuing disorder is a random and interminable conflict which has been well described by Poggi as follows:

What is ultimately in question is the nature of the units to be ordered. From Hobbes on, these units are taken to be individuals; and order is a problem because of the inherent tendency for social interaction to degenerate into a war of all against all. Just as Descartes addresses himself to ratiocinating units endowed with roughly the same capacities for forming clear and distinct ideas, so Hobbes contemplates warring units with roughly the same ability to exercise fraud and coercion. As Hobbes poses it, the problem of order arises from the fact that no one of the units to be ordered is much stronger than any other. Such a condition, given Hobbes' assumption about man's lust for power and wealth, would indeed engender a war of all against all—a random conflict going on all the time and everywhere, presupposing or bringing about no stable alignments and no pooling of resources. No unit could ever overpower the others and impose even a temporary order.[1]

If Durkheim does indeed mean that anomic declassification involves a complete lack of moral regulation, then this must be the type of disorder towards which the society moves.

But this concept of disorder contradicts the most basic principle of Durkheim's sociology. For underlying the postulated outcome of 'random conflict' is the assumption which Parsons has identified as one of the two defining characteristics of the utilitarian theory of action: namely, the 'randomness of ends'. Although his use of this term varies, the chief meaning he attaches to it derives from what he takes to be the basic assumption of the utilitarian action schema.[2] This is that the only 'norm' governing an actor's choice

---

[1] Poggi, *Images of Society*, p. 148.
[2] See *The Structure of Social Action*, pp. 59–60, 344–5, and 464–5. Crucial to Parsons's argument is the distinction between 'ultimate' and 'intermediate' ends: between ends (such as, presumably, taking pleasure in playing pushpin or reading

of ultimate ends is the same as that governing the means–ends relationship: namely, rationality, or a correct scientific understanding of the means and conditions of action. Deviations from rational action are therefore explicable only in terms of 'ignorance' (the actor's lack of an appropriate empirical understanding of his situation) and 'error' (his failure to apply this knowledge correctly, that is, logically). From this it follows that, although each individual actor is capable of ordering his own ends, and rationally using whatever means he has to satisfy whichever combination of ends he prefers, there is nothing to guarantee that the ends chosen by one actor will be the same as those chosen by other actors. In this sense, 'random' means that ultimate ends, such as taking pleasure in poetry rather than pushpin, are unpredictable. From the assumption that actors are more or less rational, nothing can be concluded about the nature of the ultimate ends each one is likely to prefer. As Parsons puts it:

wants are assumed to be subjective in a double sense. On the one hand, each individual creates his wants on his own initiative—they are outside the range of 'natural' determinism; and on the other hand, they are private to each individual. What any one may want has no necessary relation to the wants of others. The relations of individuals to each other are thought of entirely on the level of the extent to which they are significant to each other as a means to and conditions of attaining each other's ends.

---

poetry) which are ends in themselves, and ends (such as the pursuit of power and wealth) which can be used as a means of attaining a whole variety of ultimate ends. On this ground, he refers to Hobbes's theory of social action as 'almost a pure case of utilitarianism'. Hobbes's statements that 'whatsoever is the object of any man's appetite or desire, that is it which he for his part calleth *good*', and that there is no 'common rule of good and evil to be taken from the nature of the objects themselves', are taken by Parsons to mean that 'the basis of human action lies in the "passions". These are discrete, randomly variant ends of actors' (ibid. 90). But the kinds of ends that Hobbes concentrates on are, in Parsons's terms, intermediate rather than ultimate, desired by all rather than 'randomly variant'. It is the lack of regulation in the pursuit of these intermediate ends or generalized means that causes internecine conflict; and regulation is lacking because there is not and cannot be consensus on ultimate ends. Moreover, in Hobbes's scheme, the assumption that 'man, whose joy consisteth in comparing himself with other men, can relish nothing but what is eminent' (which results from 'equality of ability and hope') means that there is inherent in human society a quite chronic source of relative deprivation. The quotations from Hobbes are in *Leviathan*, ed. M. Oakeshott (Oxford, n.d.), chs. 13 and 17.

From this, he goes on to argue that:

in positivistic terms to be outside the realm of natural determinism has a specific implication—that of exemption from 'law'. This, in turn, means that wants are thought of as varying at random in the strict statistical sense, since this is the negation of natural law—that is, of uniformities in the behaviour of things.[3]

But if reason is merely the servant of the passions, if rationality is no certain guide to the choice of ultimate ends, this analogy would seem redundant; an unnecessary empirical gloss on an argument of logical entailment. 'Lawlessness' in the 'strict statistical sense' would mean, for example, that there could be drawn no regression line associating a preference for say poetry rather than pushpin with increments of rationality or decrements of ignorance and error. There is, however, a more serious implication of this claim. This is that the only possible alternative to the assumption that ends are 'random' necessarily leads to some kind of positivistic action scheme, and, finally, to the explanation of the determination of ends in terms of either environmental or biological factors. Within utilitarian theorizing this has usually taken the form of either an appeal to some irreducible notion of 'human nature'[4] or, as with the idea of 'class interest', the replacement of individual self-interest by a collective or corporate egoism which is understood to be structured by differential resources. In the latter case,

---

[3] Parsons, *Structured Social Action*, p. 344.

[4] Within this tradition, the concept of 'sympathy' or 'fellow-feeling' has played an important role in attempts to account for the integration of the ends of a plurality of selfish actors. But, on inspection, it seems just as liable to the sort of reductionism Parsons predicts. For example, David Hume: 'It is needless to push our researches so far as to ask why we have humanity or a fellow-feeling with others. It is sufficient that it is experienced to be a principle of human nature. We must stop somewhere in our examination of causes.' (*An Enquiry Concerning the Principles of Morals* (New York, 1957), 47.) Even Adam Smith's exhaustive treatment of the same subject does not finally abandon the idea of 'human nature'. And, to the extent that 'sympathy' remains a basic human disposition, it reduces the independence of the actor's choice of ends from his conditions of action. See especially A. L. Macfie, *The Individual and Society: Papers on Adam Smith* (London, 1967), chs. 3, 4. In any case, whatever its origins, 'sympathy', unlike moral commitment, can, as A. K. Sen points out, still be construed as 'egoistic, for one is oneself pleased at another's pleasure and pained at another's pain, and the pursuit of one's own utility may thus be helped by sympathetic action' ('Rational Fools: A Critique of the Behavioural Foundations of Economic Theory', in F. H. Hahn and R. Hollis (eds.), *Philosophy and Economic Theory* (Oxford, 1979)).

ends—or at least the only ends the theory needs to consider—become a function of the distribution of means, and more generally of the conditions of action.

The chief sociological implications of this type of action schema are well known. One very common consequence, especially within the economics branch of this intellectual tradition, is to treat the ends of actors as 'given', as lying outside the scope of the analysis. The ends that individuals find ultimately gratifying are from this viewpoint irrelevant, and attention is focused on the problem of how scarce means capable of alternative uses are allocated among competing ends. The actor is assumed to be capable of ordering his various ends in a hierarchy of their importance to him; but beyond this, changes in ends, or in matters of 'taste', are treated simply as exogenous changes in demand schedules.[5] This concept of action leaves entirely open two major questions. The first concerns the social determination of ends, and the second the nature of their integration.

In dealing with these issues, it is important to recognize the distinction between proximate and ultimate ends. It is undeniable that utilitarian theorists have perceived some sort of pattern in human wants and have thought of actors as being motivated not by randomly chosen ends, but rather by the same kinds of ends. From Hobbes to James Mill, the summary list is the same: power, wealth, and honour. But this typology of proximate ends, or generalized means—in fact, a quasi-sociological version of universal human wants—is not much help in understanding how, say, the *Weltanschauung* of the Confucian élite differed from that of the early protestant entrepreneurs. Equally, Bentham's exhaustive list of pleasures and pains—which again boil down to 'love of power, wealth and reputation'—is inadequate to account for the backward sloping supply curve of labour which Weber seized upon as the exemplar of the religious roots of economic motivation. The fact that utilitarian theory worked on the assumption of such general human wants precluded an understanding of how they are structured by ends that are ultimate in the sense that they are shaped by highly variable ultimate values and beliefs.

The same distinction has the utmost relevance to the problem

[5] Still the most succinct and lucid exposition of these assumptions is L. Robbins, *The Nature and Significance of Economic Science* (London, 1948), ch. 2.

of social integration. The assumption that all actors strive after the same scarce resources of power, wealth, and status is what poses, and makes insoluble, the Hobbesian problem of order. For Hobbes, it is 'Competition of riches, honour, command and other power' which 'inclineth to contention, enmity and war'. These are definitely intermediate ends 'All of which may be reduced to the first, that is, desire of means to obtain some future good. For riches, knowledge, and honour, are but several sorts of power.'[6] Given these motives, and a rough equality in human ability and hope, the state of war is inevitable. But so is the lack of any convincing explanation of its cessation. After considering the most plausible interpretations of Hobbes's solution—the 'covenant of mutual trust'—Oakeshott is led to the conclusion that the 'first performer' in this convenant must be 'a man, not "reasonable", but proudly careless of the consequences of being the first for peace'.[7] This notion of a 'first performer' is indistinguishable from the 'unconditional co-operator' invoked by Elster to explain collective class action in the face of the free-rider problem.[8]

According to Parsons, it was Durkheim who was first and foremost responsible for identifying these limitations of the utilitarian action schema, beginning with his critique of Spencer. This took the form of arguing that the explanation of social order as the outcome of ephemeral contractual relations mediating the self-interest of rational egoists was invalid, because it ignored (or was unable to explain) the fact that any particular contractual exchange depends on a 'non-contractual' set of shared norms which sets limits on the kinds of ends and means that can properly be sought and used by the parties involved. The critique of utilitarian theorizing is the relentless theme of Durkheim's work, and the integration of individual self-interest through common values and norms the principal feature of his sociology of order. It would therefore be ironic if his conceptualization of disorder led back to a Hobbesian state of individualistic, random conflict. But, given his strict dichotomization of the socially binding nature of the collective conscience and the socially disruptive effects of

---

[6] Hobbes, *Leviathan*, 46, 64.
[7] M. Oakeshott, 'The Moral Life in the Writings of Thomas Hobbes', in his *Hobbes on Civil Association* (Oxford, 1975), 129.
[8] J. Elster, *Making Sense of Marx* (Cambridge, 1985), 364.

individual egoism, the interpretation of anomie as the break-down of all moral regulation of wants seems to involve an unavoidable regression to the Hobbesian problem.

There is, however, an even more compelling reason for rejecting the interpretation of declassification as the complete absence of moral constraint. For if all the effects of 'moral education' were absent, it would be impossible for society to reconstitute itself around a new social classification. If 'all regulation is lacking for a time' and if there is 'no restraint upon aspirations', then everything that Durkheim considers to be most essential about society is absent, and, strictly speaking, a society can no longer be said to exist. Yet, at the same time, Durkheim wishes to argue that, 'since the relations between various parts of society are necessarily modified, the ideas expressing these relations must change', and that therefore moral regulation is only 'momentarily incapable of exercising its influence' and only 'time is required for the public conscience to re-classify men and things'. These two views are clearly incompatible. His cardinal assumption of normative integration leads to a concept of disorder which implies the termination of society, or, what is analytically the same thing, a state of random and interminable conflict. Yet the postulate of reclassification requires that disorder is not terminal. This problem is irresolvable.

The alternative form of disorder suggested by his account of declassification is some kind of class conflict. This interpretation can also be found in the definitions of anomie advanced by Parsons, and it will be noted that they replicate the same ambiguity that is evident in Durkheim's exposition. According to one definition, 'the polar antithesis of full institutionalization is, however, *anomie*, the absence of structured complementarity of the interaction process, or, what is the same thing, the complete breakdown of normative order'. Parsons goes on to say that 'this, however, is a limiting concept which is never descriptive of a concrete social system. Just as there are degrees of institutionalization so there are degrees of anomie.'[9] Another definition introduces the notion of class conflict: 'even societies ridden with anomie (for example, extreme class conflict to the point of civil war) still possess within themselves considerable zones of solidar-

[9] Parsons, *The Social System*, p. 204.

ity'.[10] It is not clear from this how closely 'societies ridden with anomie' approximate the limiting case of a 'complete breakdown of normative order'. But the example of societies riven by 'extreme class conflict to the point of civil war' does suggest that, rather than the limiting case of disorder being one in which normative elements are altogether absent, it is one in which these elements possess a completely different structure from the common value system that defines the limiting case of solidarity.

If anomie is characterized by class conflict, as both Durkheim and Parsons would have it, then two things follow. The first is that, if classes are sufficiently cohesive entities to engage in conflict with one another, there must be at least what Parsons calls a 'structured complementarity of the interaction process' within the contending classes. This raises the question of the sources of class solidarity. Secondly, if there is class war, disorder cannot be random and purely adventitious. The relationship between classes must be structured in some way, to some minimal extent. This raises the problem of the basis of such systematic conflict. In neither case is the solution of these issues compatible with a complete absence of moral constraint. On the contrary, so it will be argued, these casually introduced concepts of class solidarity and class conflict lead inevitably to a scenario of disorder that is best depicted by moral polarization which finds its limit in schism rather than a Hobbesian chaos.

Consider first the problem of class solidarity. What is it that gives contending classes their respective identities? One answer might be that they are held together by the coincidence of the self-interest of their members. There are, however, two objections to this line of argument. First, as Olson has shown, it can hardly be supposed that individuals sharing an objectively common class situation would decide to engage in concerted action if each one rationally pursued his self-interest.[11] This is the well-rehearsed free-rider problem. The second, and for Durkheimian theory more intractable, problem is that of why it should be assumed that there is in the first place a coincidence of individual interests. It is only possible to account for this by postulating a common class

---

[10] T. Parsons and E. A. Shils (eds.), *Towards a General Theory of Action* (Cambridge, Mass., 1951).

[11] M. Olson, *The Logic of Collective Action* (New York, 1968), 102–10.

situation; that is, by assuming that the conditions individuals find themselves in and the means by which they seek to achieve their interests under these conditions are sufficiently similar for them to recognize that they share the same life chances. Furthermore class situation implies the existence of class relations, and hence the idea of a societal class structure. Since this is exactly the kind of concept which is residual to Durkheimian and neo-Durkheimian sociology, the interpretation of declassification as a state of class conflict means abandoning the premiss that normative factors are the only systematic—as opposed to situational—determinants of social action.

Another difficulty of a rather different kind arises from this interpretation of declassification. For it is quite unrealistic to suppose that class solidarity, never mind class conflict, can be explained without reference to normative factors. As a matter of fact, class cohesion always depends on the existence in some degree of shared values and beliefs. Even in a model of purely rational, instrumental action, such as Olson's, these elements have to be brought in and subsumed under the category of 'selective incentives', without which action in concert is inexplicable. But it is unnecessary to labour the point, because Parsons readily acknowledges that the Marxist concept of class consciousness involves the idea of shared values. 'At the class-conscious level', he writes, 'another factor enters the situation, the organized concerted action of the proletariat to overthrow the existing order and establish socialism. This looks very much like a common value element.'[12] Now, since it could hardly be maintained that the definition of anomie as taking on the form of 'extreme class conflict to the point of civil war' excludes the notion of a high degree of class consciousness, it follows that anomic disorder must be characterized by 'common value elements' that are class specific.

It would seem then that neither of these two explanations of class cohesion is compatible with the key assumptions of the theory of anomie. If class cohesion involves shared values or a class specific morality, this seriously qualifies the idea of anomie as a complete lack of moral regulation. Alternatively, if class solidarity has to be explained in terms of some commonality of

---

[12] Parsons, *The Structure of Social Action*, p. 494.

individual self-interest, this leads to an indispensable but unavailable concept of class structure.

No less intractable problems arise in connection with the concept of class conflict. If anomie means lack of moral regulation, then, even if it were assumed that some kind of common interest accounts for class solidarity, classes so constituted would simply take on the character of what Durkheim calls 'corporate egoists'.[13] In this case, conflict would once again approximate the Hobbesian state of disorder, the only difference being that collective actors replace individuals. From this state it is difficult to see how social order could be established except through the subjection of one class by another. However, this solution is hardly compatible with Durkheim's notion of 'reclassification' as the reconstitution of social solidarity.

The only alternative to this model of declassification is one in which class conflict has to be thought of as a process of moral polarization, with schism representing the extreme opposite of a state of social solidarity. In the progression towards this hypothetical state of affairs social solidarity would vary inversely with class solidarity, and the limiting case of social disorder would be when class conflict, far from being morally unregulated, took on the form of a complete ideological opposition. Since the only remaining zones of consensual solidarity would be centred around irreconcilable class moralities, society would lack common values, but not normatively structured conflict. There would in effect be two moral communities within the same society, but related to one another through their antithetical values and beliefs.

For Durkheim this would be an anathema; the negation of a society as he understood it. But this is not a good reason for rejecting the idea of schism. The purpose is not to define any limiting case of disorder. If that were so, the Hobbesian state of nature would suffice just as well. The aim has to be to identify

---

[13] There is at least one passage in his work where he comes close to this position. This is in *The Division of Labour*, p. *xxxvi*. 'The sole groups that have a certain permanence are what today are called unions, either of employers or workers.' He then describes their relationship as follows: 'They lack a common organization to draw them together without causing them to lose their individuality, one within which they might work out a common set of rules and which, fixing their relationship to each other, would bear down with equal authority upon both. Consequently, it is always the law of the strongest that decides any disputes, and a state of out and out warfare prevails.'

that dimension and limit of disorder which is both the opposite of social solidarity (and therefore equally a moral phenomenon) and yet one that is consistent with the idea of declassification followed by reclassification. Of course, what Parsons says about anomie is equally relevant to schism: namely that 'it is a limiting concept which is never descriptive of a concrete social system'. Schism merely represents the pole towards which conflict moves but which it never reaches, just as solidarity represents the ideal but unrealizable limit of social integration. The important question is rather whether such a reference point is more useful in describing and explaining the kind of disorder which appears to be implicit in Durkheim's account of declassification and reclassification.

In attempting an answer, it must be said first of all that the concept of schism does not resolve the basic Durkheimian dilemma. If it is assumed that order is secured by common values and beliefs and that the systematic structuring of action is exclusively normative, then it is impossible to explain how a common value system undergoes polarization into opposing class moralities. A necessary part of the explanation is a concept of structure which is at best residual in Durkheimian theory. Secondly, it is not self-evident that polarization and schism are an improvement on the alternative notion of completely random, morally unregulated conflict when it comes to explaining how declassification can be understood as an interregnum through which society passes only to reconstitute itself around a new social classification or social hierarchy. The reason why this transition is inconceivable on the former assumption has already been stated. Given a Hobbesian situation of internecine conflict between amoral egoists, order can be restored only by some form of external coercion or by their rational calculation of a common interest in the cessation of conflict. But both of these classical and equally unsafe social-contract solutions are precluded by the tenets of Durkheimian and neo-Durkheimian sociology. At first sight, however, the concept of schism would seem to be no more useful. Is not the emergence of a new classification out of a state of complete moral polarization just as difficult to envisage? Is it not most likely that restoration of order would again result from one class being able to impose its values and beliefs upon another class or from some kind of *modus vivendi* arrived at through a balance of power between the classes?

Such solutions are not only hypothetically possible, but closely approximated in the real world, most clearly in the case of 'communal' conflicts centring on religious, ethnic, and linguistic divisions. But, as has already been argued, these types of communal conflicts, which arise from the historically 'given' and so to speak 'accidental' juxtaposition of radically opposed groups within the same territory have to be distinguished from the case of a disunion of an originally united moral community, of which the dissociation of a sect from a church is paradigmatic and of which class polarization may be taken as a secular form.[14] It is to the latter form of conflict that the terms schism and polarization will be taken to refer from now on, and it is also the kind of conflict which the Durkheimian schema has more difficulty in accounting for.

If polarization is understood in this way, it also involves a temporal as well as a structural dimension, which is absent from the alternative concept of anomie in which the transition from order to disorder must be more or less instantaneous, a total discontinuity without any shape or pattern to it. If the opposite of solidarity is the complete lack of moral regulation, it is difficult to imagine any intermediate stage of socially structured conflict. Once the integrative force of common values is in abeyance, it is impossible to speak of anomie as a matter of degree. This is not the case with polarization, and is the most important respect in which the limiting case of schism differs from and is preferable to that of anomie as complete moral deregulation.

Durkheim's concept of declassification as a period of social turmoil during which all traces of 'prior moral education' are lost must therefore be discarded in favour of a view of a society riven by sectarian or class conflict but in which there still exist, as Parsons would have it, 'considerable zones of solidarity', represented above all by inter-class values and beliefs without reference to which ideological polarization would have no meaning.[15] This conclusion is well in keeping with Durkheimian assumptions. If social solidarity is characterized by shared values and beliefs and their embodiment in a system of social classification which serves

[14] See above, ch. 2, s. III.
[15] Parsons, 'An Approach to the Sociology of Knowledge', in his *Sociological Theory and Modern Society*, esp. pp. 162–3.

to legitimate class inequality, it would be inconsistent to think of the dissolution of this form of social order, through class or other forms of social conflict, except in the context of some prior shared value system whose failure to accommodate these conflicts thereby gives them their socially destabilizing moral force. But what is it exactly that they destabilize?

II

One possible answer to this can be found in Durkheim's depiction of classification as involving a distinction between two kinds of justice. The first refers to the legitimacy of the relative rewards attaching to the hierarchy of social functions. The second refers to the legitimacy of the allocation of individuals to positions within this hierarchy. From this, it might be supposed that changes in the 'distribution of men and things' would lead first to conflict over the justice of the relative placement of individuals or groups within the existing status hierarchy rather than to a frontal attack on the values that legitimate the hierarchy *per se*. Yet, in describing declassification Durkheim holds that 'if the disturbance is profound, it affects even the principles of controlling the distribution of men among various occupations'. This is a curious statement, because it would surely be recognized that conflict involving the legitimacy of the status hierarchy is a more fundamental kind of disorder than conflict about the allocation of persons to positions within it. It is, of course, true that, if it is sufficiently intense, the latter type of conflict can lead to the former, just as the principle of equality of opportunity tends to lead fairly inexorably to the principle of equality. But the two aspects of classification are distinct. For example, in a status hierarchy of priests, warriors, and peasants, the criteria that determine who ends up as priest, warrior, or peasant are distinguishable from the values which legitimate the relative status of priests, warriors, and peasants. The fact that a peasant can become a priest by meeting the established criteria for admission to the priesthood does not necessarily affect the relative status of priests and peasants. Beyond a certain point of course it might. If too many people of lowly social origin enter a group of higher status, the status of the group tends to decline. But this only affects its relative position in the hierarchy—usually in the long run and without any conflict over the principles of the status order as a whole. Declassification is much more likely to occur if many people think they have a right to become members of a higher status group that rejects them, because this may lead to their attacking the values by which its higher status is legitimated. These considerations lead to the opposite of Durkheim's conclusion: namely, that disorder is more profound if it affects the principles defining the hierarchy of status than if it affects the principles 'controlling the distribution of men among various occupations'.

Nevertheless the distinction is important. From Durkheim's description of declassification it is clear that he conceives of a twofold deregulation of the status system. For this reason, the translation of *déclassement* as 'declassification' very well captures both types of deregulation, even though, strictly speaking, and in the particular context in which Durkheim introduces it, the term refers to neither, but simply to the fact that individuals are suddenly thrust 'into a situation inferior to the one they occupied hitherto'.[16] And despite his mistake in thinking that the justice of the hierarchy of functions is a less basic condition of order than the justice of the distribution of functions, these concepts provide a useful measure of the degree of disorder. In fact, they correspond to the distinction between rebellion, which seeks to remedy injustice by replacing those in authority, and revolution, which aims to change the structure of authority. In this way, Durkheim supplies a criterion for distinguishing approximations to the limiting state of schism which his idea of declassification has been shown to entail.

There is one final implication of Durkheim's account of declassification which lends further support to the conclusion that the extreme form of disorder is represented by ideological polariza-

[16] This use of 'declassification' to signify the status disequilibrating effects of changes in class structure accords with that to be found in Mancur Olson's eminently Durkheimian piece, 'Rapid Growth as a Destabilizing Force', *Journal of Economic History*, 23 (1963), 532: 'economic growth means vast changes in the distribution of income. The fact that some gain a lot and others lose a lot, in a rapidly growing economy, means that the bounds of class and caste are weakened. Some rise above the circumstances of their birth and others fall behind. Both groups are normally déclassé. Their economic status keeps them from belonging wholly to the class or caste into which they were born, and their social situation keeps them from belonging to the caste or class into which their income bracket should put them.'

tion. This stems from his observation that declassification is accompanied by an intensification of social interaction. It is a point that also helps to clarify his rather obscure and cursory explanation of changes in values and beliefs by reference to what has been called hyper-ritual. For, in the course of describing anomic deregulation, Durkheim argues that 'appetites, no longer being controlled by a public opinion', have their disruptive force increased by being 'seized by a sort of natural erethism simply by the greater intensity of public life'. This sounds very much like the condition under which normal rituals are transformed into hyper-rituals. And, since the latter designate an exceptional concentration of the moral community which supposedly leads to innovation rather than reinforcement of existing values and beliefs, might not declassification be thought to have the same effect? The sequence of classification–declassification–reclassification certainly bears a close resemblance to the cycle of the ritual and profane moments of social existence. But there is an important difference between them, and it is one that offers some elucidation of the causes of the increased moral 'effervescence' which, in the case of hyper-ritualism, remain indistinct. In contrast with the conditions giving rise to hyper-rituals, the intensification of moral life associated with declassification is the result of changes in the profane rather than the sacred region of society. Moreover, as the foregoing discussion has sought to show, these disruptive forces of the profane or 'utilitarian' life are not random but systematic in their origin. Here then there is an apparent contradiction that stands in the way of assimilating hyper-ritualism to declassification: the former seems to be caused by exceptionally intense social integration, whereas the latter is due to exceptionally intense social conflict.

Part of the difficulty lies in the fact that declassification is a more complicated process than hyper-ritualism, just as the organic solidarity or moral polymorphism of a society possessing a division of labour is more complicated than the mechanical solidarity or undifferentiated moral community of a segmental society. But the basic contradiction exists only if it is assumed that declassification is entirely unconnected with a concentration of the sacred life, and, conversely, that hyper-ritualism is entirely unconnected with conflicts in the profane sphere of society. If the argument of this section is accepted, then the first assumption must be rejected, since it has been found that declassification implies a limiting case of schism and thus just the opposite of a weakening of religious sentiment. The major difference is that hyper-ritualism in the form of ideological innovation is a function of the increasing polarization of a previously united moral community. The assumption that hyper-ritualism is divorced from conflicts in the profane or utilitarian sphere of social life must also be questioned. Durkheim's theory of changes in values and beliefs was criticized on the ground that it did not adequately account for the increase in the frequency and intensity of social interaction which he took to be the immediate cause of the moral effervescence from which new ideals are born. In particular, it was noted that the terms he used to describe changes in social interaction were of an exclusively quantitative kind. The significance of this is that such criteria in no way preclude the possibility that an increase in the frequency and intensity of social interaction might take the form of increasing class conflict and class cohesion. His account of hyper-ritualism and ideological change is therefore quite consistent with the argument that these phenomena have their basis in those 'antagonistic tendencies aroused and supported by the necessities of the daily struggle' which Durkheim generally regards as the quintessence of the profane.[17] Thus neither of the assumptions that seem to distance the theory of hyper-rituals from the theory of declassification is tenable. Moreover, this point of theoretical convergence greatly strengthens the interpretation of declassification as a process of moral polarization.

---

[17] There are, moreover, several passages in *Elementary Forms* that point to the same conclusion. For example, after describing the effects of ritual occasions, Durkheim writes: 'Besides these passing and intermittent states, there are other more durable ones, where this strengthening influence of society makes itself felt with greater consequences and frequently even with greater brilliancy. There are periods in history when, under the influence of some great collective shock, social interactions have become much more frequent and active. Men look for each other and assemble together more than ever. That general effervescence results which is characteristic of revolutionary or creative epochs.' (pp. 210–11) A little later on, he refers to the French Revolution and notes how, 'under the influence of the general enthusiasm, things purely laical by nature were transformed by public opinion into sacred things: these were the Fatherland, Liberty, Reason. A religion tended to become established which had its dogmas, symbols, altars and feasts' (p. 214).

III

Thus far it has been argued that the notion of declassification entails schism as the limiting case of disorder. This solution of the Durkheimian dilemma disposes of the alternative and wholly unacceptable interpretation of anomie as random and interminable conflict. At the same time, however, it brings to the fore a concept of structure that is residual to Durkheim's theory; and the promotion of this concept to the same analytical status as that of the privileged idea of normative constraint is indispensable to the explanation of the process of anomic declassification, which presupposes a systematic incongruity between these two aspects of structure. It is the nature of this incongruity that now deserves closer scrutiny.

The analytical dominance of the normative element consists in its being treated as the distinctive aspect of a system of social action, though not necessarily of any particular situation of action. Its major institutional expression is the social or status hierarchy. On the other hand, the residual element is more generally conceived of as having to do with 'utilitarian' activities and interests and as being bound up with the distribution of, and struggle over, resources. In the case of declassification, the tendency to locate this element in the sphere of economic life becomes explicit: 'an abrupt growth of power and wealth' produces the same effects as 'economic disaster'. Since Durkheim invariably associates order with the sacred, and disorder with the profane, region of society, it is not surprising that he concentrates his attention on the disruptive effects of discontinuities in economic life. Whether the residual element in his theory can be identified exclusively with this paradigmatic idea of economic power is not especially crucial for the present argument. The only assumptions that it is necessary to make are those that have already been established. The first is that concepts such as power, wealth, and resources imply definite social relationships that characterize not only situations but systems of social action. Secondly, it has also been shown that a subordinate, but equally important, theme of Durkheim's discussion is that wants or aspirations are determined by the distribution of power, wealth, and resources as well as by the normative expectations attaching to positions in the status hierarchy.

This latter point, incidentally, disposes of the conundrum that frequently crops up in theories of relative deprivation. A familiar form of it arises in connection with the hypothesis that subordinate groups accept their position because the range of their reference groups is restricted. This then leads to the question of whether such groups have modest expectations because of their restricted reference groups or whether the narrowness of their social comparisons is a result of their modest expectations, which are, in turn, accounted for by a realistic appraisal of their limited opportunities. Presumably Durkheim's answer would be that both factors are at work, and that the effects upon aspirations of limited resources and of socialization into norms legitimating inferior status are mutually reinforcing. Only when the two get out of joint does relative deprivation occur; and this can happen because of a shift in moral horizons, a change in resources, or both.

In Durkheim's theory of declassification, this disparity between normatively and factually generated expectations is brought about solely by a sudden change in the distribution of resources; it is socially structured; and it leads to systematic disorder. But what his theory needs, and yet lacks, is the conceptual means of expressing this structural and systematic incongruity. His idea of the social classification of a society is clear. But the related term, the object of classification—'men and things' or 'power and wealth'—is opaque. There is no reference here to any notion of structure apart from that imposed by the classification of men and things. But the fact is that the distribution of resources creates social relationships that are clearly distinguishable from the moral hierarchy in which they are encapsulated. These power relationships are implied by his theory of declassification. If they were not, the disorder of anomic declassification would be purely random.

The missing link is to be found in the idea of the incongruity of power and status relationships. This has been formulated in basically similar terms by many classifical social theorists; it has also been widely used in historical investigations. Since it appears to be indispensable to Durkheim's theory, it is a concept that deserves some comment. The first thing to be said is that this idea, which may be conveniently referred to as 'power incongruity', would seem to have a greater relevance to the understanding of social conflict and integration than the more familiar notion of 'status inconsistency', deriving from the work of Lenski—even though his original interest in the subject, focusing on explanations of the motivation of revolutionary cadres, was clearly located within the same classical tradition. The reasons for this judgement may be stated summarily as follows, by emphasizing, but not, it is hoped, exaggerating, the virtues of the former approach in contrast with the deficiencies of the latter:

1. Status refers to relationships between persons or groups, not to arbitrarily chosen attributes of individuals, such as income or 'educational status'. Status relationships are maintained by conventional, legal, or religious sanctions and express judgements of relative social worth.

2. Power is understood likewise as a form of social interaction, involving domination and subordination, rather than as the distribution of resources, such as wealth and credentials, which may or may not give rise to power relationships.

3. The relationship between power and status, as defined above, is contingent. So is the relationship between the various 'statuses' of the individual as these are defined in status inconsistency theory. The difference is that, in the former case, it is a social group's historically or sociologically ascertainable expectations of the legitimate trade-off between power and status that are significant in determining the existence of incongruity. By contrast, in the theory of status inconsistency, it is the attributes of abstract collectivities of individuals that are judged to be more or less consistent according to some arbitrarily chosen level of statistical significance, together with the observer's imputation of motives to the individuals in question.

4. Since power and status refer to systems of social relationships, their incongruity usually results in conflict between fairly well identifiable social groups. By contrast, status inconsistency theory merely predicts similar reactions on the part of categories of socially unrelated individuals, such as voting patterns; that is, what Weber termed 'mass actions' as opposed to communal or corporate actions.

5. Conflict arising from an incongruity of power and status is often not limited to the immediate antagonists: it ramifies and raises the aspirations, and thereby the relative deprivation, of other groups adjacent to them. This kind of demonstration effect

is unknown to status inconsistency theory which focuses on individuals in abstraction from their social setting.

6. Finally, an understanding of the incongruity of power and status can only be achieved by historical or anthropological investigation; that is, by whatever is recoverable by these methods about the emergence and accommodation of such incongruities over time, and within a definite social context. By contrast, status inconsistency theory favours (or perhaps adapts to) the methodology of the social survey, and thereby purchases precision at the expense of sociological relevance.

These points, and most importantly number five, can be amplified by considering their implications for Durkheim's theory of anomic declassification which posits a transition of the following kind:

1. A state of society in which the wants or aspirations of the constituent social groups are stably regulated through what Durkheim calls the system of 'social classification', or a 'moral regime', in which the distribution of wealth and power is regarded as legitimate because it is in accord with shared values defining the respective social worth of hierarchically differentiated social functions. In other words, Durkheim presupposes a stable status order, whether of a legal or conventional kind.

2. A state of interregnum, or anomie, whose primary cause is an abrupt and large-scale redistribution of 'men and things', or of 'power and wealth', which has the effect of unbalancing the existing status order. This stage, which Durkheim calls 'declassification', is marked by acute social conflict, partly because the status struggles arising from the changes in relative circumstances of contiguous social classes excite the aspirations of other groups and social classes not directly affected, and partly because 'moral re-education', or the reconstitution of the status hierarchy, cannot be instantaneously effected.

3. A stage of reclassification, during which the changes in the distribution of 'men and things' are accommodated within the moral matrix of a new social classification. Although Durkheim remains obscure on this point, it may be assumed that, in the first instance, status-incongruent groups have an interest in relocation within the existing status order rather than in its outright, ideological, transformation.

On the face of it, the concept of 'status inconsistency' would seem to provide the means of grasping the kind of structural incongruity that is implied by Durkheim's theory. There are, however, two significant features of the process of declassification which the idea of status inconsistency fails to capture, at least in the form in which it has been developed in modern sociological inquiry. The first is that declassification refers to a deregulation of the status hierarchy as a whole and not simply to the incongruity between the power and status of any one particular group or set of individuals. Earlier it was characterized as a chain reaction of relative deprivations running through the status system, a form of disorder in which a change in the resources and aspirations of one group affects the aspirations of other groups, either directly or indirectly. 'Some particular class especially favoured by the crisis is no longer resigned to its former lot,' Durkheim writes, 'and, on the other hand, the example of its greater good fortune arouses all sorts of jealousy below and around it.' Or, as Mosca puts it: 'the example of individuals who have started from nowhere and reached prominent positions fires new ambitions, new greeds, new energies, and this molecular rejuvenation of the ruling class continues vigorously until a long period of social stability slows it down again.' The second point is that the process of declassification is triggered off by a change in the condition of some particular group, whose members experience relative deprivation because of an increase or decrease in their power or wealth which is disproportionate to their position in the status hierarchy. It is to this form of incongruity that Scheler refers in his statement of 'the important sociological law that this psychological dynamite [*ressentiment*] will spread with the discrepancy between the political, constitutional or traditional status of a group and its factual power'.[18]

---

[18] M. Scheler, *Ressentiment*, trans. W. W. Holdheim (Glencoe, Ill., 1961), 49. Scheler elaborates as follows: 'It is the difference between these two factors which is decisive, not one of them alone. Social ressentiment, at least, would be slight in a democracy which is not only political, but also social and tends to equality of property. But the same would be the case—and *was* the case—in a caste society such as that of India, or in a society which sharply divided classes. Ressentiment must therefore be strongest in a society like ours, where approximately equal rights (political and otherwise) or formal social equality, publicly recognized, go hand in hand with wide factual differences in power, property and education. While each has the "right" to compare himself with everyone else, he cannot do

There are several respects in which sociological studies of 'status inconsistency' are of small relevance to these two essential aspects of declassification. Lenski's theory that status inconsistency leads to political radicalism[19] was the main impetus to a great deal of research, which, taken as a whole, has the following characteristic drawbacks. The use of the social survey as the chief means of research has concentrated attention on inconsistencies of status at a given time. This methodology may also be a reason why the selection of what counts as a 'status' dimension appears rather arbitrary, since the concentration on readily quantifiable criteria, such as the position of individuals in occupational, educational, and income hierarchies, has tended to neglect the close study of whether these statistical rank dimensions correspond to the demarcation of status groups *per se*, and of whether the objectively identifiable inconsistencies of status are experienced by the individuals concerned as socially significant ones and as grounds for a sense of injustice. As a result, the concept of status has come to have a very uncertain sociological meaning. These kinds of studies not only fail to throw light on the incongruity between power and status, but it is doubtful whether they are dealing with inconsistencies of status at all, if the term status means anything more than position on some potentially status-relevant rank order. The determination of what is and what is not status-relevant presupposes a knowledge of the structure of the status hierarchy as a whole in its specific historical context. Failing this, the finding that one status position is inconsistent with another status position is sociologically meaningless, whatever the level of its statistical significance. Moreover, the study of the structural context is indispensable to an understanding of the reaction of individuals or groups to their ostensibly anomalous position in the status hierarchy; and this in large part depends on the reaction to them of contiguous and unanomalous groups. Factors, such as the availability of institutionalized means of upward mobility and the

---

so in fact. Quite independently of the characters and experiences of individuals, a potent charge of ressentiment is here accumulated by the very structure of society.' In this passage Scheler anticipates the basic thesis of Merton's theory of anomie, which will be considered below, ch. 6, s. I.

[19] G. E. Lenski, 'Status Crystallization: A Non-Vertical Dimension of Social Status', *American Sociological Review*, 19 (1954).

exploitability of values legitimating the status hierarchy, will also affect the propensity to collective protest among those who feel that their status is no longer commensurate with their command over resources.

In all these respects, the great mass of research into 'status inconsistency' has added little to an understanding of the dynamics of social declassification. From this viewpoint, the work of sociologists compares unfavourably with that of historians and anthropologists, who, as a matter of course, locate incongruities of power and status within local or metropolitan status systems.[20] Moreover, the status inconsistencies studied by sociologists are rather minor ones that crop up within the relatively stable status systems of advanced industrial societies, which, even though not universally recognized as legitimate dispensations, are nowhere near a state of declassification. The main point, however, is that the concept of status inconsistency is ill suited to the understanding of declassification. The latter cannot be treated as if it consisted simply of a certain percentage of the population being subject individually to a variety of inconsistencies between their standing on one fairly arbitrarily chosen rank dimension and another. This abstract, statistical conception of status inconsistency may serve some purposes, but the explanation of declassification is not among them.[21] Declassification refers to social conflict that is structured by the disjunction between power and status relation-

[20] See e.g. E. G. Barber, *The Bourgeoisie in Eighteenth-century France* (Princeton, NJ, 1955); Bailey, *Caste and the Economic Frontier*; H. Rosenberg, *Bureaucracy, Aristocracy and Autocracy* (Cambridge, Mass., 1958); F. L. Ford, *Robe and Sword: The Regrouping of the French Aristocracy after Louis XIV* (New York, 1965); Béteille, *Caste, Class and Power*; L. Stone, *The Causes of the English Revolution, 1529–1642* (London, 1972).

[21] As is partly recognized by Lenski in his later work. For example: 'Research carried out during the last decade has suggested that all forms of status inconsistency do not have equally potent effects, and that some may not generate stress at all. The variables involved in the present study, it should be noted, include one element out of the nexus of achievable socio-economic variables (i.e. occupation, education, and income) and one out of the nexus of largely ascribed status variables (i.e. race, ethnicity and religion). On the basis of previous research, it appears that it is precisely this type of status inconsistency that is most likely to manifest itself politically.' (G. E. Lenski, 'Status Inconsistency and the Vote', *American Sociological Review*, 32/2 (1967), 300.) This finding is consistent with Durkheim's thesis of the 'forced division of labour'—a state of affairs which consists in the persistence of ascriptive norms in a society whose economic life is increasingly based on achievement.

ships. It has its origin in a change in the distribution of resources which is sufficiently sudden and extensive that the normal mechanism of institutionalized mobility cannot cope with it. As a result, the rank ordering of whole groups, and sometimes even the values legitimating this order, are brought into question.[22] From now on the term status incongruity will be used to refer to this chronic and systematic discrepancy between power and status.

Declassification, then, involves large-scale, uninstitutionalized mobility, which is conducive to conflict not only because of the status incongruity it creates but also because of certain other features which distinguish this form of mobility from that which is a normal part of the operation of any status system. First, the institutions that legitimate upward and downward mobility not only secure the renewal of higher status groups; their main integrative effect is to restrict the aspirations of the immobile, and to justify the sense of failure on the part of those whose ambitions to rise have been thwarted as well as of those who have been involuntarily demoted. Uninstitutionalized mobility has the opposite 'demonstration effect' of deregulating the traditionally established aspirations of immobile groups, especially those from whom the newly rich and powerful have arisen.[23] This is clearly one implication of Durkheim's theory of declassification and of Mosca's theory of ruling-class renovation. The second way in which the two kinds of mobility differ bears directly on the creation of status incongruity itself. Institutionalized mobility is not only a means by which persons are selected for promotion (and sometimes demotion); it is also a means by which they are socialized into the values and styles of life of the status groups into which they are recruited. But those who accumulate power and wealth

[22] See, e.g., G. Germani, 'Social and Political Consequences of Mobility', in N. J. Smelser and S. M. Lipset (eds.), *Social Structure and Mobility in Economic Development* (London, 1966); also Gurr, *Why Men Rebel*, ch. 4, and R. Williams, 'The Idea of Relative Deprivation', in L. Coser (ed.), *The Idea of Social Structure: Papers in Honor of Robert K. Merton* (New York, 1975). It may be noted that Mannheim attributes the shattering of legitimacy to vertical mobility: 'Only when horizontal mobility is accompanied by intensive vertical mobility . . . is the belief in the general and eternal validity of one's own thought-form shaken. Vertical mobility is the decisive factor in making persons uncertain and sceptical of their traditional view of the world' (*Ideology and Utopia*, p. 6).

[23] See Merton, *Social Theory and Social Structure*, pp. 267–8, and Gurr, *Why Men Rebel*, pp. 105–9.

outside this normal mode of social elevation are unlikely easily to acquire the attitudes and behaviour that make them acceptable as social equals to dominant status groups. The fact that one form of mobility is in its very nature a mode of status incorporation whereas the other is likely to lead to status rejection is essential to the explanation of why sudden changes in the distribution of power and wealth result in declassification. That an increase in resources will have the effect of raising status aspirations is implicit in the idea that the status order establishes, as Durkheim says, 'the coefficient of well being' appropriate to each group in the social hierarchy. But it is the blockage of the status aspirations thus engendered that creates status incongruity and the sense of relative deprivation associated with it. Therefore, the basic condition of declassification, which is a sudden change in resources, accounts for the likelihood of both the demand for an increase in status and the rejection of this demand. Of course, aristocracies have never had much difficulty in assimilating the occasional plutocrat, however uncultivated. But this fact leads directly to the third consideration, namely, the sheer magnitude of the mobility in question. In a system of institutionalized mobility, the amount of promotion is likely to be limited to what dominant status groups find tolerable. By contrast, declassification implies an upsurge of new power and wealth which is so rapid and widespread that it is unmanageable by any means of status incorporation and institutionalized mobility.[24] What is meant by manageable or tolerable in this context can be defined as that amount of incorporation, by whatever means, which is compatible with the maintenance of the distinctive privileges and style of life of the status group in

[24] An early exposition of this idea of declassification as applied to state socialist societies is R. A. Feldmesser, 'Equality and Inequality under Khrushchev', *Problems of Communism*, 9 (1960). Presented as an explanation of an earlier phase of Soviet 'restructuring', this essay is remarkable in having identified many of the problems now being addressed by perestroika, in that it locates such reforms in the context of a major system contradiction of state socialist societies. This is that the Communist party, which seeks to monopolize power and prevent the emergence of competing social forces, is at the same time the chief agency through which incipient bureaucratic and professional status groups seek to secure vested interests and transmit them to the next generation. For more generalized sociological accounts, see F. Parkin, 'System Contradiction and Political Transformation', *European Journal of Sociology*, 13 (1972), and M. Matthews, *Privilege in the Soviet Union* (London, 1978).

question.[25] This definition of tolerability is in turn one way of specifying what degree of uninstitutionalized mobility is likely to be 'anomic' in its effects.

III

The purpose of the discussion so far has been to explicate and exemplify what seem to be the most important assumptions entering into Durkheim's idea of declassification. At this point, it might be useful to try to draw together the various threads of the argument by presenting a model of the most elementary case of declassification imaginable.

1. Assume a society that is divided into two groups, Alpha and Beta. At a given moment of time, Alpha is superordinate to Beta in respect of both power and status. This order is defined as legitimate by Alpha and accepted by Beta. A stable classification exists. Then, as a result of an abrupt and profound transformation of economic life, there occurs a rapid increase in the power of a subgroup of Beta, which can be called Beta-plus. The remainder of the original subordinate group may be called Beta-minus. The increase in the power of Beta-plus may result from an increase in the sum total of power in the society (perhaps as a consequence of the exploitation of new resources), or it may be the outcome of a zero-sum relationship in which Beta-plus gains power at the expense of Alpha (or indeed Beta-minus). All that is necessary to produce an incongruity between the power and status of Beta-plus is that this group gains power that is incommensurate with its previously low status. But, since a zero-sum relationship between it and Alpha will intensify the potential for conflict, let it be assumed that this is the case: that the increase in the power of Beta-plus is directly related to a reduction in the power of Alpha, and that as a result the two classes are now roughly comparable in

---

[25] 'Style of life' is a Weberian rather than a Durkheimian concept. It connotes not simply the modes of behaviour by which the boundaries between status groups are maintained, but a whole range of prerogatives which characterize a 'status situation' and which determine the 'life-chances' of any particular status group: for example, rights appertaining to the ownership of specific kinds of property, the pursuit of specific occupations, the consumption of particular goods, the exercise of judicial and administrative rights, the use of weapons, the immunity to certain kinds of punishments, and so on.

respect of power. Under what conditions can this initial incongruity between the power and status of Beta-plus lead to a declassification of the status order?

2. The first relationship to be considered is that between Alpha and Beta-plus. Although Beta-plus is now roughly comparable in terms of power to Alpha, its status is lower. As a general rule, it may be assumed that Beta-plus will first attempt to resolve its incongruity by seeking status enhancement within the existing social hierarchy.[26] Whether this leads to conflict between Beta-plus and Alpha depends on the reaction of Alpha, which will be determined partly by the relative size of the two groups. Alpha will be unwilling to recognize the status claims of Beta-plus if Beta-plus is so numerous that its incorporation into Alpha would threaten the life-style and status privileges of Alpha. That the power mobility of Beta-plus does create an 'incorporation crisis' of this kind is a precondition of declassification. This crisis will be more or less severe depending on the internal differentiation of Beta-plus in respect of power. But this is a refinement of the argument that need not be pursued. It may simply be assumed that the conflict potential is increased because the relative status deprivation of Beta-plus cannot readily be resolved by the whole of the group being able to satisfy its aspiration for equality with Alpha.

3. Given the fact that the gain in power of Beta-plus involves a loss of power by Alpha (the zero-sum assumption), the status incongruity of the former group is necessarily matched by the inversely related status incongruity of the latter. That is to say, Alpha will also experience a sense of relative deprivation which is caused by the discrepancy between its high status and its reduced power. Alpha suffers from what has been called 'decremental' deprivation, and the fact that this is integrally linked to Beta-plus's experience of 'incremental' deprivation is likely to increase the potential for conflict between the two groups.[27] According to

[26] See A. Malewski, 'The Degree of Status Incongruence and its Effects', in R. Bendix and S. M. Lipset (eds.), *Class, Status and Power* (2nd edn., London, 1967).

[27] On incremental and decremental relative deprivation, see T. R. Gurr, 'A Comparative Study of Civil Strife', and I. K. Feierabend *et al.*, 'Social Change and Political Violence: Cross National Patterns', in H. D. Graham and T. R. Gurr (eds.), *The History of Violence in America* (New York, 1969). W. Korpi has made an important contribution by sketching out a 'power balance' model of conflict which incorporates the central elements of the competing 'relative deprivation' and 'political process' models of conflict ('Conflict, Power and Relative Depriva-

Durkheim, persons enjoying a sudden increase in resources are quick to raise their aspirations, whereas those who are suddenly thrust into adversity are slow to adjust their customary level of wants to their new conditions. When faced simultaneously with a relative decline in its power and the claim by Beta-plus that it should be its status equal, Alpha is likely to react by 'hardening' its status boundary. In other words, it will raise the power-status exchange rate by becoming more exclusive than before; for example, by reverting to purely ascriptive criteria of member-ship.[28] This reaction on the part of Alpha is a necessary condition of the escalation of conflict to the level of beliefs and values which legitimate the hierarchy of status in contrast to the norms which regulate mobility within the hierarchy. If this happens, Beta-plus can only resolve the incongruity between its increased power and subordinate status by challenging the basis of the existing status system and formulating new principles of social classification which undermine the superior status of Alpha. This action on the part of Beta-plus is no longer status usurpation but status renovation.

4. One further conflict-maximizing reaction of Alpha in this situation is worth noting because it leads to two further forms of status incongruity which are frequently associated with the process of declassification. A common feature of pre-revolutionary situations is that the blockage of the status aspirations of a newly powerful class by the traditional ruling class coincides with the latter's abandonment of its customary obligations towards, or actual invasion of the rights of, subordinate status groups.[29] Here

---

tion', *American Political Science Review*, 68 (1974)). None of these discussions, however, takes full account of the distinctive feature of declassification; that is, the interdependency, or the chain reaction, of relative deprivations.

[28] 'When a class feels threatened it tends to close its ranks', says March Bloch, *Feudal Society* (London, 1961), 322. In a similar vein, B. Moore writes that 'reactionary social theories are liable to flourish in a landed upper class that manages to hang onto political power successfully although it is losing out economically or perhaps is threatened by a new and strange source of economic power' (*The Social Origins of Dictatorship and Democracy* (Boston, 1966), 490).

[29] See, e.g., E. R. Wolf, *Peasant Wars of the Twentieth Century* (London, 1971), 282–6; R. Hilton, *Bond Men Made Free* (London, 1973), 114–19; N. Hampson, *A Social History of the French Revolution* (London, 1966), 11–13; Levenson, *Confucian China and its Modern Fate*, pp. 79–86; Stone, *The Causes of the English Revolution*, p. 84.

the incongruity consists in the discrepancy between the way in which the dominant class exercises its power and the norms that define and legitimate the status relationship between itself and subordinate groups. Whereas the incongruous position of Beta-plus arises from its power mobility and is expressed in its demand for status recognition by Alpha, the legitimation of the relationship between Alpha and Beta-minus is undermined by actions on the part of Alpha which may be described as 'status dereliction' and 'status abrogation'. Status dereliction means the neglect by a higher status group of its traditional obligations towards a lower one (for example, the duty to provide protection). Status abrogation is, by contrast, an act of commission rather than omission. It is the revocation of the customary status rights of Beta-minus. Both kinds of action relate to the exercise of power in a way that violates established status expectations. They undermine the authority of the higher status group and increase the sense of relative deprivation on the part of the lower one. Since status dereliction and abrogation are means of increasing the exploitation of lower status groups, they are measures which are likely to be resorted to by a group such as Alpha when it is faced with the need to maintain its traditional status against the demand for status elevation by Beta-plus at the very same time that its command over economic power has diminished relative to Beta-plus.

5. The initial change in the power position of Beta-plus can thus be seen to lead indirectly to a sense of relative deprivation among the members of Beta-minus. But this effect is also likely to be produced directly through the example of Beta-plus's power mobility and its claim for status enhancement. First of all, if those in Beta-minus feel that they can legitimately compare their present position with that of those in Beta-plus because of the pre-existing equality between the two groups, then they will feel deprived relative to Beta-plus. But in respect of what will they feel deprived? This will depend in large part on the conflict between Alpha and Beta-plus, which will be maximized if Alpha reacts to Beta-plus's claim for incorporation by increasing its exclusivity as a status group.[30] In this case, the unresolved incongruity between

---

[30] A less extreme reaction by Alpha is still likely to lead to an increase in the status aspirations of Beta-minus. For example, if Alpha admitted as status equals

the power and status of Beta-plus is a condition under which the values underlying the status hierarchy could be brought into question. This, in turn, would unsettle the subordination of the whole of group Beta to Alpha. The effect of Beta-plus's failure to resolve its own status incongruity would be to arouse new status aspirations on the part of Beta-minus. In this scenario the demonstration effect of Beta-plus on Beta-minus is therefore twofold: first the direct effect of the former's mobility upon the expectations of the latter; and secondly the indirect effect on the status aspirations of Beta-minus of Beta-plus's questioning of the principles underlying the status hierarchy. Finally, disorder would be maximized if Beta-plus endeavoured to mobilize the support of Beta-minus in its own struggle against Alpha; and this, according to Marx, among others, is a general tendency of revolutionary classes.

Like its predecessors, the last assumption merely serves to indicate one possible consequence of an initial condition of status incongruity—an outcome which, in this imaginary society, combines with others to maximize the potential for conflict. Their several effects are depicted in Fig. 5.1, which shows not only how Durkheim's inchoate notion of declassification can be given conceptual substance through the idea of status incongruity, but also how the latter might acquire a systematic relevance.

The main conclusion so far, then, is that social declassification may best be understood as a state of disorder characterized by structurally interrelated incongruities of power and status. The social conflicts centring on such incongruities may be said to be anomic in that they are likely to lead to a questioning of the values legitimating the existing status hierarchy. In these terms also it is possible to conceive how anomic conflict could take on a schismatic form. At least, it is reasonable to think of proliferating status incongruities as the structural precondition of moral polari-

---

only a part of the membership of Beta-plus according to some non-ascriptive criterion (such as the amount of economic power), then this would lead to an elevation of the status aspirations of Beta-minus for the same reason that the excluded membership of Beta-plus would feel that their exclusion was unjust or weakly justified: namely, because of the introduction of a quantitative in the place of a qualitative criterion of status. A concrete example is the weak legitimating principle of a property franchise in the place of an hereditary one.

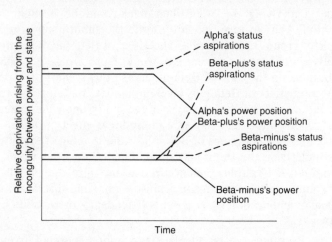

FIG 5.1. The incongruity of power and status: a model of maximum relative deprivation

Notes:

1. The upturn in Alpha's status aspirations represents its growing exclusivity as a status group.
2. The upturn in Beta-minus's status aspirations represents the effect of the example of Beta-plus.
3. The downturn in the power position of Beta-minus represents the effect of Alpha's status abrogation.

zation. This is not a hypothesis Durkheim entertained, but it is certainly consistent with his portrayal of the causes and consequences of declassification.

However, this conclusion is not the end of the matter. Status incongruity may be a necessary condition of delegitimation and of the growing polarization of social conflict; but it is not a sufficient one. To assume otherwise would imply that changes in values and beliefs are to be understood simply as the result of the intensification of social forces. This, of course, is what has already been shown to be the premiss of Durkheim's theory of moral innovation: namely, the idea of hyper-ritual. But that concept arises from his analysis of a socially undifferentiated society, or at any rate one that knows nothing of power and status relations. Now that these terms have been used to explicate the theory of anomic declassification, it would seem appropriate to return to the prob-

lem of moral innovation, this time asking whether what Durkheim's successors have had to say on the subject accommodates
the kind of criticisms that can be levelled against his own treatment
of it.

6.

MORAL INNOVATION

I

The most important of the assumptions entering into the foregoing argument is that, if a class such as Beta-plus cannot resolve its status incongruity through its incorporation into Alpha, then it will attempt to delegitimate the existing status hierarchy by promoting a counter value system. This assumption is vital to the explanation of declassification as moral polarization. In the literature on social stratification it seems to be fairly well accepted that chronic relative deprivation resulting from unresolved status incongruity is a structural precondition of the mobilization of disaffected groups around a new set of values and beliefs that undermines the legitimacy of the status order. For example, Gurr makes the point that ideological conversion is a function of relative deprivation. 'The greater the intensity of relative deprivation the more prone people are to seek out and be receptive to norms and beliefs that justify new expectations and that promise means of attaining them.'[1] This general consideration underlies the more specific formulation of Malewski that,

if an individual of incongruent status cannot raise the lower factors of his status, he will tend to reject the system of evaluation which justified his humiliations and to join those who are opposed to that system. If these others represent a tendency towards changing the existing order, the above individual mentioned will be particularly inclined to accept their total programme.[2]

While the propensity to ideological conversion may be understood, in general terms at least, as the result of the incongruity between power and status, there remains the problem of explaining the values and beliefs to which the status disaffected are attracted. This problem is in effect twofold. First, there is the

---

[1] Gurr, *Why Men Rebel*, p. 101.
[2] Malewski, 'The Degree of Status Incongruence', p. 306.

question of the sheer availability of counter values. Secondly, there is the question of the effects which these values and beliefs are likely to have on the process of declassification.

The first question is the less intractable from the viewpoint of Durkheimian theory, since it is basically that of whether ideological innovation occurs randomly or is socially structured. On general grounds, as was shown in Chapter 2, it would be quite inconsistent with the basic assumptions of Durkheim's sociology to imagine that changes in belief are unrelated to other kinds of social change. This is also in line with what is generally known: that periods in which new values and beliefs are most frequently generated are also periods of rapid and profound economic and social change. To suppose that the innovation of belief systems is concomitant with the emergence of the kinds of structural incongruity that have been discussed so far is also consistent with the thesis already established that declassification is associated with hyper-ritualism. It can be assumed then that the conditions which lead to declassification and the relative deprivation of status incongruity will also provide an environment especially conducive to the production of new values and beliefs. If these beliefs have the capacity of delegitimating the existing status order, adhesion to them by groups who are disaffected because of the discrepancy between their command over resources and their position in the social hierarchy will move conflict towards the pole of moral disunion.

It is, however, an indulgent reading of Durkheim to find this possibility in his argument. Although he indicates that anomie is somehow associated with moral innovation, this line of argument is never made explicit. At several stages of the preceding discussion it has been noted that Durkheim's theory of society is singularly ill equipped to deal with the effects upon social order and disorder of the variability in the structure of values and beliefs. The same point is of even greater significance in the case of moral innovation. It is quite remarkable that a theory which identifies social solidarity with a system of common values and beliefs should seek to explain disorder by a sudden discontinuity in the distribution of power and wealth. What is even more striking is that Durkheim does not consider the declassifying effects of changes in expectations that result from ideological innovation. The case he refers to is one in which relative deprivation is created either by expectations rising in consequence of a sudden increase in resources (incremental deprivation) or by resources suddenly decreasing while the level of expectation remains the same (decremental deprivation). But there is a third possibility, what has been called 'aspirational' deprivation. This occurs when people's expectations suddenly increase while the level of their resources does not alter, and when the source of their rising expectations is their exposure to new values and beliefs. It is ironic that one of the most precise statements of this kind of normatively engendered disorder is to be found, not in the work of Durkheim, but in a classic treatise on class and power.

It may happen in the history of a nation [writes Mosca] that commerce with foreign peoples, forced immigrations, discoveries, wars, create new poverty and new wealth, disseminate knowledge of things that were previously unknown or cause infiltrations of new moral, intellectual and religious currents. Or again—as a result of such infiltrations or through a slow process of inner growth, or from both causes—it may happen that a new learning arises, or that certain elements of an old, long forgotten learning return to favour so that new ideas and new beliefs come to the fore and upset the intellectual habits on which the obedience of the masses has been founded.[3]

That the 'infiltration' of alien beliefs into a religiously homogeneous society is often productive of social division is an observation that Durkheim's theory is well able to cope with. But what of Mosca's view that social order can be impaired by the impact of new ideas and beliefs that have their origin in a religion's 'slow process of inner growth'? Whether the inner growth is slow or fast, it raises once again the problem of the sect. Originally, the inability of Durkheim's theory of religion to explain the disunion of church and sect was taken to represent in its most acute form its inability to explain variations in the strength of attachment to a common value system. This particular difficulty no longer arises if declassification is understood as conflict determined by a structural incongruity between power and status. But the explanation

---

[3] Mosca, *The Ruling Class*, p. 67. It is worth noting that, in this short passage, Mosca introduces all four sources of change which one modern student of revolutions makes central to his account of 'the disequilibrated social system' namely, changes in the environment and in the values of a society, each of which, in turn, may be exogenous or endogenous in origin, see Johnson, *Revolutionary Change*, ch 4.

of differences in adhesion to new beliefs does not account for the emergence of these beliefs. On this matter, Durkheim's sociology is silent. And it must be, because, in so far as the inner growth of religion is amenable to sociological enquiry, its explanation depends on concepts referring to precisely those aspects of religion that Durkheim excluded from his purview on the grounds that they introduced unnecessary 'complications'. The two principal aspects he chose to ignore were variations in the structure of religious beliefs themselves, and differences in the division and organization of religious labour.[4] In spite of his claim to reveal what is fundamental about religion, Durkheim's theory has absolutely nothing to say about such matters. Since his investigation of elementary religion concentrates on the socially integrative function of common values and rituals *tout court*, it is unsurprising that his theory of disorder cannot begin to explain why some religious institutions are more likely than others to be doctrinally fissiparous. The same is true of his theory that moral effervescence and innovation is likely to increase in a period of declassification. But it would be naïve to assume that the incidence of the creation of new beliefs is unrelated to the particular religious beliefs and to the particular form of the religious division of labour through which the work of preserving and transforming beliefs primarily takes place. To ignore these features of the religious life is

---

[4] As in the sphere of economic production, the 'separation of the worker from the means of production' is a prominent feature of the religious division of labour. Quite generally, this phenomenon has a twofold aspect. The appropriation of the means of salvation by a church separates the laity of believers from a class of owners of 'spiritual technology'. Within the latter class, the dogmatization of belief and the routinization of charisma could easily lead to a further class division between those who own and those who are expropriated from the means of ideological production. Given such an ecclesiastical stratification, a most interesting question is whether ideological innovation is more likely to emanate from the centre or from the periphery of the church. Centrality and peripherality may be defined in terms of *de jure* control over doctrinal and liturgical matters, full-time intellectual specialization, and exposure to profane, secular environments. At one extreme might be found full-time experts on matters of doctrine who are authorized to control the forces of ideological production and are insulated from worldly contamination; at the other extreme would be those functionaries who administer to the laity and who are, as regards doctrinal innovation, a dispossessed ecclesiastical proletariat. For a stimulating discussion of this sort of problem, see P. L. Berger, 'Charisma, Religious Innovation and the Israelite Prophecy', *American Sociological Review*, 28 (1963).

tantamount to assuming that they are unrelated to ideological innovation.

These considerations have even greater force when it comes to explaining not the rate of production of new beliefs but the way in which they differ in their capacity to focus and intensify the sense of deprivation among those groups in the society who are attracted to them. For it is central to the idea of aspirational deprivation that exposure to new beliefs can have an effect that is independent of incremental (or decremental) deprivation arising from a change in the distribution of resources. Aspirational deprivation is a function of the capacity of new beliefs to raise expectations to a higher level than they would have reached if the beliefs had not existed. A more meaningful way of putting this is to say that what is especially crucial about new beliefs is their capacity not only to raise expectations but to create expectations that cannot be realized within the existing social hierarchy. This is, after all, the prime characteristic of utopian beliefs, which may be regarded as the example *par excellence* of aspirational deprivation. But, since the utopian potentiality of ideologies is highly variable, it cannot be taken for granted that all new beliefs provide equally powerful means of raising aspirations, increasing relative deprivation, and delegitimating the existing status hierarchy.

The significance of this whole problem of the variability of belief systems, which is so strikingly absent in Durkheim's analysis of declassification, is brought out by Merton's theory of anomie. This is premised on the assumption that a high degree of aspirational deprivation is engendered by the distinctive features of the American value system. Merton's argument is that the latter has the effect of creating strivings for 'success', particularly in the form of upward occupational mobility, for all sections of the society. But, given the norms defining the legitimate means of pursuing this goal, and the fact that classes vary in their command over the resources that enable them to succeed in realizing the goal, there is, as a result, a strong sense of relative deprivation among those in the lower reaches of the class structure which, in turn, leads to various forms of mainly individual deviance.[5] There

---

[5] This is only the briefest summary of Merton's influential essay, 'Social Structure and Anomie', which is to be found in his *Social Theory and Social Structure*.

are three aspects of Merton's thesis which are noteworthy in the present context. The first is that his idea of class differentiation, or what he calls the 'opportunity structure', is very similar to Durkheim's concept of 'resources' in that it refers to the distributional, rather than the relational, nature of class structure; that is, it refers to the distribution of resources, for example, wealth, rather than to the relations between persons that are determined by their differential possession of these resources. Secondly, unlike Durkheim's theory of declassification, Merton's analysis deals with a relatively mild form of anomie, which is, so to speak, a normal feature of a stable social classification. Moreover, a principal component of this classification is a system of institutionalized mobility which operates generally to make the unsuccessful individual blame himself rather than the structure of the society for his lack of achievement.[6] Thirdly, and most importantly, Merton's analysis of anomie introduces the idea of the significance of a particular system of beliefs. If his argument is correct, the American value system not only creates relative deprivation by the universalization of the success goal, but it also provides the ideological means of preventing the radical collectivization of this discontent by the way in which the norm of 'equality of opportunity' individualizes the causes of success and failure.[7] To say that the value system does these things is, of course, elliptical. The

[6] On the conditions under which this mechanism is effective, see especially R. A. Cloward and L. E. Ohlin, *Delinquency and Opportunity* (London, 1961).

[7] The question of whether all sections of the American population do in fact share the same levels of aspiration has been challenged. One of the earliest critics of Merton's theory was H. H. Hyman, 'The Value Systems of Different Classes', in Bendix and Lipset (eds.), *Class, Status and Power*. Although this and other studies show that levels of aspiration and the 'success' goals aspired to among the lower classes are adjusted to the realistic conditions of their situation, Merton's main point that the aspirations of the American lower class are high relative to their chances of fulfilling them and to those of lower classes in other comparable societies would seem to be a valid one. The argument that the widespread acceptance of the norm of 'equality of opportunity' helps to prevent the collectivization of discontent is equivalent to saying that in this respect the value system is unexploitable; this would also partly explain why, as Merton shows, discontent leads mainly to individual forms of deviance. Against this, the ideal of equality has been highly exploitable, and the collective movements aimed at its more substantial implementation have no place in Merton's analysis, even though they come closer to being examples of the more chronic form of anomic declassification. For a general historical account, see J. R. Pole, *The Pursuit of Equality in American History* (Berkeley, Calif., 1978).

social and economic conditions under which the beliefs Merton is referring to can be deeply and extensively inculcated in the population lie outside the scope of his analysis. Nevertheless, what is relevant here is that, in identifying these two salient aspects of the American value system, Merton opens up the general question of the relationship between aspirational deprivation and the variability in beliefs.

Durkheim's lack of interest in the problem of whether values and beliefs vary in their contribution to social disorder parallels in a curious manner his *ad hoc* conceptualization of the factors that play the principal role in his theory of declassification: namely, power, wealth, and resources. The relationship is curious because of the disproportionate attention he pays to the sacred, by comparison with the profane, sphere of society. Yet his theory of the social functions of religious beliefs and ritual is formulated in very general terms. Moreover, his account of change, whether in the sacred or the profane region of society, reflects a fundamental tendency of his sociology as a whole, one that has been referred to before on several occasions. This is his propensity to think of social forces in quantitative terms. It is only from this viewpoint that it is possible to understand why his theory of declassification excludes all consideration of the part played by values and beliefs in the disordering of society. His quantitative concept of social transformation is the reason why the causes and effects of variability in the structure of both the profane and sacred spheres of social life constitute empty boxes in his theory of disorder. What causes declassification is not any particular structure associated with the distribution of wealth, power, or resources but rather the suddenness and extensiveness of their redistribution. And if, as has been argued, declassification is accompanied by moral innovation, the latter is not to be understood by reference to the structure of values and beliefs but simply in terms of the intensification of the moral life, which, in turn, is reducible to the intensification of social interactions. There is then, in both cases, the assumption of a threshold effect, whereby changes in degree result in changes in kind. If the change in the distribution of 'men and things' is sufficiently profound and extensive, then the social classification begins to break down. Correspondingly, if the moral effervescence due to increased social interaction reaches a certain pitch, then new ideals and values are created.

Durkheim's theory of declassification is very rudimentary. The assumptions underlying it can only be discovered by placing it in the context of his most general assumptions about society. In attempting to make something positive of the theory, the foregoing discussion has quite possibly given an interpretation of it that is highly contentious. Nevertheless, the two major criticisms on the basis of which the argument has proceeded so far may be thought to have some force. The first is that the analytical priority which Durkheim gives to the normative structuring of action necessitates the introduction of concepts that are residual to his theory. The second is that, despite the central place which values and beliefs occupy in his theory of society, the latter is distinguished by its lack of concepts by which the relevance to social order and disorder of variations in values and beliefs can be systematically analysed. Because these criticisms are of such importance to the overall argument, it would seem desirable to subject them to further test. This can be done fairly decisively by examining the key assumptions of Smelser's theory of 'collective behaviour', which is the most detailed and sophisticated analysis of social disorder within the normative functionalist tradition.

II

Although Smelser's conceptual scheme is much more elaborate than Durkheim's, and is expressly designed to explain the emergence of sectarian and other collective movements, his theory is founded on basically Durkheimian assumptions. These are that a common value system is indispensable to social stability and the primary source of the integration and structuring of social action. These assumptions are built into the most fundamental concept of his theory: namely, the 'hierarchy of the components of action'.[8] This hierarchy is made up of the following levels. Values, which occupy the topmost place, are 'the most general statement of legitimate ends which guide social action'. Next in order are norms which are 'the rules governing the pursuit of these goals', and which derive their legitimacy from the values. Below norms is

---

[8] Smelser, *Theory of Collective Behaviour*, ch. 2. See also Parsons, *Societies: Evolutionary and Comparative Perspectives*, ch. 2, esp. pp. 11–14. Page references are given only for those quotations not taken from Smelser, ch. 2.

what Smelser calls 'the mobilization of motivation into organized
action'—this means the way in which the actions of specific agents
'will be structured into concrete roles and organizations, and how
they will be rewarded for responsible participation in these roles
and organizations'.[9] Finally, at the lowest level of the hierarchy,
are 'situational facilities' which are 'the means and obstacles which
facilitate or hinder the attainment of concrete goals in the role or
organizational context'.[10]

The main feature of the hierarchy is that, 'as we move from top
to bottom, we approach components which are progressively less
central to the integration of the social order'. Thus values are of
greatest significance in this respect and most resistant to change.
If they do change, this necessarily results in changes in all the
components below them: norms, mobilization, and facilities.
Conversely, situational facilities are least central to social integration and their change does not necessarily result in changes at the
higher levels of the hierarchy. A further characteristic of the
schema is that it is put forward as a general analytical device
which is meant to be applicable to any institutional sphere of
society, although Smelser does suggest that 'some institutional
clusterings of concrete action' have an 'especially close connection
with one or more components of action': for example, that
between religious institutions and the component of values.

In general, however, the fact that values are placed highest in
the hierarchy clearly signifies that Smelser's concept of society as
a system is one that gives analytical priority to the normative
structuring of action. The normative element is also crucially
involved in the mobilization of motivation, which is basically a
matter of socialization.

The most general level involves the formation of an individual's basic
character. The most general set of predispositions to motivational commitment is generated at a very early age in the family setting. In this first

[9] The level of mobilization is roughly equivalent to 'most of what sociologists
call "Social organization" or "Social structure"—families, churches, hospitals,
government agencies, business firms, associations, political parties'.

[10] For each of the four levels of the hierarchy, Smelser differentiates between
more general and more specific elements. For example, the most general element
in the component of situational facilities is 'preconceptions concerning causality',
and the most specific, 'allocation of facilities within organization to attain concrete
goals'. This refinement of the schema is not relevant to the present discussion.

stage of socialization the individual learns to curb his most blatant anti-social impulses and to acquire the basic capacity to enter roles of various sorts.

But socialization, the generation of motivational commitment, must be socialization into, and commitment to, something, even at the most elementary level. What this something is, is indicated by the correspondingly most general aspect of the level of norms. 'At the first level, the definition of normative regulation involves general conformity to norms, no matter what the content.' It is on this basis of a socialization into general conformity to norms that more specific forms of mobilization are built.

The normative structuring of action, then, reaches very far down the hierarchy. But what about the level of situational facilities? Here there is a lack of clarity, and some inconsistency, in Smelser's exposition. At one point facilities are said to 'include knowledge of the environment, predictability of consequences of action, and tools and skills'. Another definition appears to limit them exclusively to 'the actor's knowledge of the opportunities and limitations of the environment and, in some cases, his knowledge of his own ability to influence the environment'— although, in an example that directly follows this formal definition, facilities denote 'how much capital is available for investment; and how well is the businessman able to finance his projected enterprise'. In yet other contexts, Smelser refers to 'wealth, power and prestige' as facilities.[11] Still more confusing, wealth, power, and prestige reappear at the level of mobilization, this time in the form of rewards: 'Around this component we find the operative play of rewards, such as wealth, power, and prestige, which accrue as a result of effective performance in roles and organizations.'[12]

The fact that wealth, power, and prestige have no definite place in Smelser's analytical scheme and enter into it in an entirely *ad hoc* manner is in one way surprising, and in another not. It is surprising because, although, like Durkheim, Smelser attributes to values a central significance in social integration, he has no concept of status as a macro-social structure. Yet, whether prestige is treated as a facility or a reward, its effectiveness in either

---

[11] Smelser, *Theory of Collective Behaviour*, pp. 31, 325.
[12] Ibid. 28; see also p. 233.

respect presupposes a status system which is maintained through acts of social acceptance, deference, and derogation. The analytically residual place occupied by wealth and power in Smelser's theory is not surprising given its Durkheimian provenance. They are mentioned only briefly, as examples of facilities and rewards. In other words, as in Durkheim's theory, wealth and power are conceived of as distributions of discrete resources rather than as constituting social relations. The idea of class structure is completely lacking in Smelser's formal depiction of the social system. The index of his book confirms this, since it contains no reference to class, status, or social stratification. Yet these concepts do crop up, quite adventitiously, when his discussion turns from the components of social action in general to the explanation of particular cases of 'value-oriented' collective movements.

The hierarchy just described serves two main purposes. First, it is used to identify the various forms of 'strains' that underlie collective movements. Secondly, it serves to classify the different types of collective movements, which are, in order of their increasing threat to social integration, the panic, the craze, the hostile outburst, the norm-oriented movement, and the value-oriented movement. Each type of collective behaviour is characterized by the component of action which it seeks to reconstitute in the 'name of a generalized belief'. It is Smelser's analysis of value-oriented movements which bears most directly on the problem of moral innovation, and for this reason the following remarks are restricted to his account of the 'collective attempt to restore, protect, modify or create values in the name of a generalized belief'.[13] Some kind of generalized belief is an essential feature of all collective behaviour. Leaving on one side for the moment the question of how these beliefs are created, here is how Smelser defines those that distinguish value-oriented movements:

Such beliefs concentrate on a source of evil which overshadows all of life. As such, this evil is a threat to the very foundation of the social order (Values) and by implication to the normative arrangements, and to the organized social life in general. In the same belief a positive set of values is put forth. A new social order is envisioned; institutional chaos will give way to harmony and stability; the evil will be eradicated, and human happiness will result.[14]

---

[13] Smelser, *Theory of Collective Behaviour*, p. 313.   [14] Ibid. 348.

This type of belief, Smelser argues, is common to a wide variety of movements. 'Our definition encompasses the phenomena designated by the labels "nativistic movement", "millenarian movement", "utopian movement", "sect formation", "religious revolution", "nationalist movement", "charismatic movement", and many others.'[15] Furthermore, all such movements can be explained by a set of general conditions, of which the most fundamental are 'structural conduciveness', 'strain', and 'the crystallization of generalized beliefs'.[16] These categories are used to explain all forms of collective behaviour, but value-oriented movements differ from lower level ones in respect of the nature of their structural preconditions, the strains they express, and the beliefs that mobilize them.

Among the structural conditions that are conducive to the emergence of value-oriented movements, the most important is the lack of differentiation between norms and values. In this case, as Smelser rightly argues, breaking a norm involves defiance of a general value: 'Specific dissatisfactions with any social arrangements eventually become religious protests, or, more generally, protests against values.'[17] This is not a novel observation. Engels makes exactly the same point when he writes that the 'supremacy of theology in the entire realm of intellectual activity' had the consequence that 'all the generally voiced attacks against feudal-

[15] Ibid. 313. Political revolutions are also included as 'secular' value-oriented movements (p. 316).

[16] Ibid. 12–21. The remaining factors—precipitating events, mobilization of participants for action, and the operation of social control—are not of central interest to the present discussion, and what Smelser has to say about them is fairly commonplace. It may be noted, however, that the explanation of each type of collective behaviour involves reference to all six factors mentioned here and in the text above. Structural conduciveness, strain, generalized beliefs, precipitating factors, mobilization for action, and the response of agencies of social control constitute a series of progressively more determinate conditions, which (depending on the nature of each factor in the series) are the necessary and sufficient conditions of the various types of collective behaviour. This is 'the logic of explanation' that Smelser calls 'the value-added process'.

[17] Ibid. 320. Smelser lists four conditions of structural conduciveness: lack of differentiation between values and norms; the perceived unavailability of alternative means for reconstituting the social situation; inability to control the movement by its isolation or insulation; and the possibility of communication, of disseminating a generalized belief. The last proposition is true but trivial, and the third, as Smelser realizes, is more relevant to the problem of 'social control' than to the question of why value-oriented movements arise in the first place. The first and second conditions are discussed in the text above.

ism, above all the attacks against the church, and all revolutionary social and political doctrines, had mostly and simultaneously to be theological heresies. The existing social conditions had to be stripped of their halo of sanctity before they could be attacked.'[18] Moreover, Smelser's key proposition that moral innovation is more likely to occur the more completely specific norms are integrated with ultimate values and beliefs remains a highly formal one. What is lacking is a consideration of the problem of whether, quite independently of the degree of differentiation of values and norms, some kinds of values and beliefs are more conducive than others to the development of value-oriented movements. It is from Engels again that instruction can be sought. The peasant and plebian heretics of medieval Europe, he writes,

demanded the restoration of early Christian equality among members of the community and the recognition of this equality as a prescript for the burgher world as well. From the 'equality of the children of God' it inferred civil equality, and even partly equality of property. Equality of nobleman and peasant, of patrician, privileged burgher and plebian, abolition of the corvée, groundrents, taxes, privileges, and at least the most crying differences in property. These were demands advanced with more or less determination as natural implications of the early Christian doctrine.

These implications could be drawn because

Luther had put a powerful weapon in the hands of the plebian movement by translating the Bible. Through the Bible he contrasted the feudalized Christianity of his day with the unassuming Christianity of the first century and the decaying feudal society with a picture of a society that knew nothing of the complex and artificial feudal hierarchy. The peasants had made extensive use of this instrument against the princes, the nobility and the clergy.[19]

These internal contradictions of Christian religion, to say nothing of its inextinguishable chiliasm, were certainly 'conducive' to the outbreak of value-oriented movements; but with a specific force that cannot be explained simply by the lack of differentiation

---

[18] F. Engels, *The Peasant War in Germany* (Moscow, 1956), 55.
[19] Ibid. 58, 67.

between values and norms.[20] This meagre formula cannot take account of the way in which differences in the structure of particular value and belief systems affect the propensity to social conflict. In this respect, Smelser's theory of value-oriented movements has much in common with Durkheim's theory of religion. The distinction between values and norms corresponds very closely to Durkheim's distinction between beliefs and rituals. To say that, when values and norms are undifferentiated, breaking a norm is repudiating a value is more or less the same as saying that, when ritual conformity is the salient feature of the religious life, failure to comply with rituals is tantamount to heresy.[21]

The second major element of structural conduciveness is the unavailability to aggrieved groups of alternative means of remedying the situation that causes their distress, and in particular their inability to change the norms defining that situation. According to the logic of Smelser's schema, the means that are unavailable are of three kinds, corresponding to the three levels of the hierarchy of action below that of values: namely, facilities, mobilization, and normative components.

In terms of our scheme of analysis [he writes] this unavailability has three main aspects: (a) The aggrieved group in question does not possess the facilities whereby they may reconstitute the social situation; such a group ranks low on wealth, power, prestige, or access to means of communication. (b) The aggrieved group is prevented from expressing hostility that will punish some person or group considered responsible for the disturbing state of affairs. (c) The aggrieved group cannot modify the normative structure, or cannot influence those who have the power to do so.[22]

Since (c) is the condition that is decisive for the transformation of a norm-oriented into a value-oriented movement, it deserves some, but only brief, comment. The first and most obvious point is that it would seem to add little to what has already been said about the lack of differentiation of values and norms being a condition of the development of value-oriented movements. For,

---

[20] Which is, in fact, Smelser's explanation of these self-same movements: 'Political and religious authority were little differentiated during medieval times,' he writes, and 'Under such circumstances protests of all sorts tended to be expressed in religious terms and treated as heresies against the values of medieval Christianity' (*Theory of Collective Behaviour*, pp. 321–2).

[21] See above, ch. 3, s. III.

[22] Smelser, *Theory of Collective Behaviour*, p. 325.

if the attempt to modify norms implies an attack on values, it must by definition be true that an 'aggrieved group' is unable to 'modify the normative structure' without at the same time seeking to change values. Rather than being a separate condition of the emergence of value-oriented movements, the inability to modify the normative structure is simply the counterpart of the major condition of structural conduciveness, since the lack of differentiation of values and norms excludes the possibility of changing the normative structure as a means of 'reconstituting the social situation'. Secondly, the argument seems to suppose that the inability to alter the normative structure results in the generalized beliefs of the collective movement in question jumping, so to speak, to the value-oriented level. It is only possible, at a later stage, after having summarized Smelser's account of the creation of generalized beliefs, to appreciate how closely this escalation from norm-oriented to value-oriented beliefs corresponds to Durkheim's theory of moral innovation.[23]

So far, the exposition of Smelser's theory has dealt with those aspects of structural conduciveness that are particularly relevant to the explanation of the emergence of value-oriented movements. But such movements, indeed all forms of collective behaviour, arise in response to what is called 'strain'. Strain can originate at any level of the hierarchy of action, but its bearing on types of collective movements is said to be highly indeterminate. 'No direct causal link exists, however, between a *particular* kind of strain and a *particular* kind of collective episode.'[24] In fact, Smelser concludes his discussion of this topic with two 'cautions', which are '(a) Structural strain is a necessary, but not sufficient, condition for an episode of collective behaviour; (b) Any type of

---

[23] A third possible criticism of Smelser's argument about the unavailability of alternative means is that it is difficult to see how a group's 'inability to modify the normative structure' or to 'influence those who have the power to do so' is analytically or empirically distinguishable from the first of the three conditions he cites: namely, a lack of 'facilities to reconstitute the social situation'. Given that these facilities include 'wealth, power, prestige, or access to means of communication', it is not at all clear by what other means a group might be able to modify the normative structure or to influence those who have the power to do so. This distinction, it may be thought, is enforced by the logic of Smelser's 'hierarchy of the components of action', which creates conceptual boxes that must be filled by something.

[24] Smelser, *Theory of Collective Behaviour*, p. 48.

structural strain may give rise to any type of collective behaviour.'
He then goes on to say, 'We wish, therefore, to explain collective
behaviour not in extremely refined statements of the direct
relations between specific strains and specific collective episodes,
but in an investigation of how these inherently indeterminate
strains combine with other factors.'[25] The concept of strain,
therefore, plays a vital but highly ambiguous role in the theory of
collective behaviour. The different kinds of strains which Smelser
defines by reference to the levels of the hierarchy of action are
multifarious and defy any brief summary.[26]

What is of much more interest are his examples of the kinds of
strains underlying particular value-oriented movements. Here it
becomes clear that the elaborate analysis of the concept of strain,
which is supposed to be applicable to all forms of collective
behaviour, is in fact largely irrelevant. One chief case, which also
happens to be Durkheim's foremost example of 'great creative
rituals', is the French Revolution. In referring to the 'multiplicity
of strains' that 'lay behind the French Revolution', Smelser no
longer speaks of the levels of the hierarchy of the components of
action, but rather of much more familiar actors and interests. The
'nobility' was 'left without traditional local responsibilities' and it
was 'threatened' by the 'increasing wealth of the bourgeoisie and
by the growing tendency of the King to sell titles of nobility'. At
the same time, the aristocracy's 'continuing privileges and
demands rankled with several other classes in France at that time'.
The 'middle classes' in particular, found themselves 'improving
with regard to wealth and education' but were 'excluded from
certain occupations, privileges, and entrance to high society'. The
position of 'peasants' was also 'generally improving from the
standpoint of land ownership' but they were burdened 'with
demands, duties, and taxes from the feudal masters who had,
from the standpoint of the exercise of responsible authority,
deserted them'. Smelser goes on in a similar vein to write of the
interests of the clergy, the military, and the independent
craftsmen.[27]

---

[25] Ibid. 66. These other factors are 'precipitating factors', 'mobilization of
participants', and 'social controls'. See n. 16 above, on the 'value-added process'.
[26] Ibid., ch. 3, 'Structural Strain Underlying Collective Behaviour'.
[27] Ibid. 343–4; see also p. 349.

In effect, what he provides is a thumbnail sketch of the conflicting interests of various classes in a particular society at a particular time. What is to be concluded from this exercise? First of all, while it is conceivable that he could subsume these specific strains under the categories of his own conceptual scheme, it seems extremely doubtful that in doing this he could improve upon accounts of causes of the French Revolution advanced by historians bereft of his theory of collective behaviour.[28] Secondly, and more importantly to the course of the present discussion, is the fact that, when Smelser analyses a critical case of declassification and moral innovation, he, like Durkheim, appears to have to invoke concepts relating to the class and status structure of a society that have no place in his theory.

After structural conduciveness and strain, the third most general determinant of collective behaviour is the creation of 'generalized beliefs'. Some indication of the nature of these beliefs has already been given. For a value-oriented movement to occur, there must be available a value-oriented belief, and the 'crystallization of value-oriented beliefs' is a function of the first two basic determinants. There must be the right conditions of structural conduciveness, particularly the lack of differentiation of values and norms; and strain must be such that it affects the highest level of the hierarchy of the components of action, namely values. But Smelser's argument about the conditions promoting the emergence of value-oriented beliefs cannot be understood in isolation from the way in which he conceives of the creation of all generalized beliefs.

Strain may occur at any level of the hierarchy of action, and, when it does, a generalized belief will emerge. These beliefs serve to reduce ambiguity and provide a meaningful interpretation of the source of strain and thus indicate the way in which the social situation can be reconstituted to remove the strain. Smelser identifies four broad classes of generalized beliefs which corres-

---

[28] For example, by N. Hampson, *A Social History of the French Revolution* (London, 1966), 1–33. The question of whether Smelser's theory could provide a better explanation of any of the value-oriented movements he refers to does not, however, really arise, since his references to detailed empirical studies of these movements have the limited purpose of providing materials to illustrate his own concepts, which, given their very general nature, allow of a considerable degree of freedom in this respect.

pond to the four levels of the hierarchy of action. 'Thus hysteria and wish-fulfilment [characterizing panics and crazes] restructure the Facilities Series; hostility restructures the Mobilization Series; the norm-oriented belief restructures the Normative Series, and the value-oriented belief restructures the Value-Series.' But Smelser is quick to point out that

this formal connection between strain and types of beliefs is not a causal connection. Many different kinds of strain may give rise to one type of belief, and one kind of strain may give rise to many different types of belief. Which type of generalized belief, if any, arises is a function of both the character of strain and the character of other determinants (e.g., conduciveness and the response of agencies of social control).[29]

Whilst enjoying this considerable indeterminacy, Smelser's basic argument rests on three broad assumptions which are of especial interest to the present discussion.

The first is what might be called escalation. It will be remembered that Smelser distinguishes between more general and specific levels for each of the four components of the hierarchy of action, namely values, norms, mobilization, and facilities. Strain arises only at the lower levels of each component, because these are what he calls the 'operative' levels, those which 'define social action in progressively more detailed ways'. But, as the strains accumulate at these lower levels and as dissatisfaction spreads, 'attention turns to a search for the source of operative failures', and the 'higher levels of the components are activated'.[30] Without going into further detail, it may simply be noted that, whichever component of action is subject to strain, if the strain persists, there is a spontaneous tendency for the search for solutions to be directed to the highest level of that particular component.[31] These solutions take the form of generalized beliefs.

[29] Smelser, *Theory of Collective Behaviour*, p. 30 .
[30] Ibid. 49–50.
[31] For example, as regards situational facilities, the operative levels that may come under strain are, in ascending order of specificity: ambiguity in allocating facilities to sectors of society (level 5); ambiguity in allocating facilities to organizations (level 6); and ambiguity in allocating facilities to attain operative goals (level 7). If strain occurs at these levels, the search for solutions to it escalates to the highest level of the component (1) which is 'preconceptions concerning causality'. The generalized belief that is created at this level is termed, by Smelser, 'hysterical': that is 'a belief empowering an ambiguous element in the environment with a generalized power to threaten or destroy'.

The second aspect of Smelser's argument about the nature of generalized beliefs is what he calls 'short-circuiting'.

> Generalized beliefs restructure an ambiguous situation in a short-circuited way. In fact, this process of short-circuiting constitutes the central defining characteristic of a generalized belief as opposed to other kinds of beliefs. Short-circuiting involves the jump from extremely high levels of generality to specific, concrete situations.[32]

In other words, just as the accumulation of strains and dissatisfaction centring on the operative level of one component of action leads to the escalation of the search for solutions to the highest level of that component and to the creation of a generalized belief, once this belief has been created it immediately provides the rationale for reconstituting the operative levels of that component of action and thereby removing the source of strain.

The third point relates to the creation of value-oriented beliefs in particular. The most striking feature of Smelser's very brief discussion of this type of generalized belief is his exclusion of all consideration of the content or structure of the beliefs. 'We shall not inquire into the intellectual origins of the beliefs,' he writes. 'We shall even ignore the issue of whether a value-oriented belief is a revival of past cultural patterns, the invention of new ones, or the importation of foreign ones,' and, quite emphatically, 'we shall not be interested in the particular content of value-oriented beliefs'.[33] Apart from a restatement of what all such beliefs have in common, which in fact seems to be over-dependent on the characterization of millenarian beliefs,[34] Smelser's main concern is to identify, by reference to the components of the hierarchy of action, the various stages of the creation of a value-oriented belief. Since values stand highest in the hierarchy, and since any generalized belief 'includes all the components of the beliefs

---

[32] Smelser, *Theory of Collective Behaviour*, p. 82.

[33] It is only fair to point out that these remarks are prefaced by the qualification 'for the moment' (ibid. 121). But it is also necessary to point out that nowhere, later on in the book, does Smelser attempt to go further into these questions that he has set on one side. The chapter devoted to value-oriented movements contains only scanty illustrative materials on four particular beliefs: the Father Divine cult; the ideology of the French eighteenth-century enlightenment; nationalistic ideologies in underdeveloped areas; and Marxism (ibid. 348–50).

[34] See ibid. 122, where Smelser, following Shils's definition of millenarianism, appears to take this type of belief as the model of value-oriented beliefs in general.

below it in the hierarchy, plus one new ingredient which gives this belief its distinctive character',[35] the creation of a value-oriented belief means that generalized beliefs of a lower order are incapable of removing the source of strain by specifying which aspects of the social situation need to be reconstituted. But this is a purely logical implication of Smelser's scheme. It does not mean that in fact a value-oriented belief will only be created after attempts to handle the source of strain by recourse to lower order beliefs (those which specify changes in facilities, roles, and organizations, or norms) have failed.[36] This is because there is no causal connection postulated between any particular strain and any particular type of belief.

The foregoing account of Smelser's explanation of value-oriented movements has attempted to do no more than identify the key features of a very complicated conceptual scheme. But, it can nevertheless serve as the basis for several broad conclusions. It has already been seen that Smelser's social theory bears a close resemblance to Durkheim's in two major respects. First, there is the central importance attributed to values and norms in the structuring of action and in the constitution of social systems. Secondly, the analytical status of the concepts of wealth, power, and prestige remains uncertain and obscure. Although these terms are never defined, they are frequently introduced as examples of 'facilities' and 'rewards'. But nothing is said about their interrelationship, and consequently there is no conception of structured social inequality. Yet incongruities of power, wealth, and status are clearly the major sources of strain underlying the only value-oriented movement Smelser discusses at any length. These incongruities surely imply the existence of class and status systems.

Another important feature of his explanation of value-oriented movements is that he explicitly discounts the significance of

[35] Ibid. 130.

[36] Smelser's depiction of the 'stages' of the creation of value-oriented beliefs (ibid. 124) might be taken to suggest that, in the search for a solution to strain, there occurs first an escalation up to the highest level of the facilities component and an abortive 'short-circuiting' down it, then so to speak a jump to the next higher component (mobilization) and a similar escalation and short-circuiting, and so on, until the highest level of the values component is activated to produce a value-oriented belief. But this is not the case. All that is implied is that value-oriented beliefs must include components of the lower level beliefs (i.e. norm-oriented, hostile, wish-fulfilment, and hysterical beliefs).

different types of beliefs. This is reminiscent of Durkheim's wish to avoid consideration of the 'complicating' aspects of religion which obscure its elementary forms. The implication is that differences in the nature of beliefs are irrelevant to understanding both the emergence and the socially disordering effects of value-oriented movements. This leads to another closely related problem. New beliefs arise principally as a result of what is called strain. But there is no determinate relationship between particular kinds of strains and particular kinds of beliefs; 'many different kinds of strain may give rise to one type of belief, and one kind of strain may give rise to many different types of belief'. However, it is possible to say something in general terms about the way in which strain results in the creation of new beliefs. The key hypothesis is that accumulation of strain at the lower, operative, levels of a component of action leads quickly to the search for a solution at the very highest level, where a generalized belief is created. This bears some similarity to Durkheim's theory of hyper-ritual, to his view that changes in values and beliefs result from the growing intensity and frequency of social interaction. Although Smelser's analysis of the sources of strain is very detailed, it excludes the possibility that strain itself might be heightened or reduced by particular types of beliefs. Consequently, the creation of new beliefs is very much a function of the accumulation of strain *per se*. Basically this is not very different from Durkheim's view that the underlying cause of those 'great creative rituals' which give birth to new ideals is an increase in social and moral density. The same point can be given added emphasis by reference to the other major precondition of the emergence of value-oriented movements: namely, structural conduciveness. If values and norms are undifferentiated, it is impossible to remove the source of strain by changing norms without at the same time challenging the value system as a whole. It has already been noted that the distinction between values and norms is akin to that between beliefs and ritual. From Smelser's theory it should follow that, when religions become highly ritualistic, strains are more likely to give rise to value-oriented movements. Yet religions sharing this trait have also differed markedly in their theodicies and soteriologies; and there is much evidence to show that these differences have been of crucial significance in determining both the incidence and the goals of social movements. The fact that Smelser fails to take account of the structure of belief systems is the most fundamental shortcoming of his theory of collective behaviour, and the most basic respect in which it resembles Durkheim's account of moral innovation.

7.

THE PROBLEM OF DISORDER

This chapter will not attempt to summarize arguments that have been presented so far in the book. It is hoped that the conclusions of each particular line of argument have been stated clearly enough to make this task unnecessary. What might be useful, however, is a brief review of the basic thesis of the Durkheimian 'problem of disorder'. This problem, which is also traceable in the work of the neo-Durkheimian school of normative functionalism, has two main sources. The first is to be found in the analytically residual nature of those aspects of society which Durkheim often refers to under the general rubric of the 'utilitarian'. The second is to be found in the way in which Durkheim's theory of society represents an extreme reaction to, and rejection of, what Parsons has called the 'utilitarian theory of action'. They are really different aspects of the same conceptual problem, but for purposes of exposition it is convenient to treat them separately.

The relatively undifferentiated or residual position of the 'utilitarian' element in Durkheim's theory accounts for both the ambiguity in his conceptualization of disorder and his *ad hoc* explanation of declassification. The analytical priority accorded to normative elements in the structuring of social action serves well enough to provide a limiting notion of order as solidarity. But it proves inadequate for the understanding of disorder. The notion of anomie is the root cause of the difficulty, as may be seen from Fig. 7.1, in which the implications of the concept of solidarity are shown by solid arrows and the implications of the theory of anomie by broken ones.

Anomie differs from solidarity in two main respects. The first is a matter of definition. Given the central importance of normative elements in Durkheim's theory of order, anomie comes to be defined negatively, as a state of affairs in which a common value system is lacking. The second difference is that whereas solidarity is merely a concept that defines a limiting case of order, and by implication disorder, anomie is a theory of disorder. It is more-

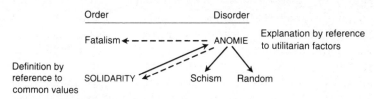

FIG 7.1. Major implications of Durkheim's key concepts

over a theory that attributes the causes of disorder to utilitarian factors.

Taken simply as a concept of disorder, anomie is ambiguous. This is because the antithesis of solidarity can find its limit either in random and interminable conflict or, via moral polarization, in schism. The interpretation of anomie as random conflict must be rejected because it is incompatible with Durkheim's idea of reclassification, which is integral to his theory of disorder. But the interpretation of anomie as schism raises an equally acute problem since, within Durkheim's schema, there are no conceptual means of explaining the causes of moral polarization. While schism is just as much a 'religious' phenomenon as solidarity, the structural basis of moral polarization cannot be accounted for by Durkheim's rag-bag concept of the utilitarian life (that it cannot be accounted for either by his analysis of the religious life, which offers no grounds for thinking that values and beliefs differ in their conduciveness to order and disorder, indicates a gap in his theory of an altogether different kind). This difficulty can only be overcome if the forces that originate in the utilitarian sphere of activity and disrupt the common value system are conceived of as systematic rather than random. That is to say, the structure of social relationships that is implied by Durkheim's vague ideas about the distribution of 'men and things', and of 'wealth', 'power', and 'resources' must be promoted to the same analytical status as that enjoyed by the privileged concept of normative structure. Irrespective of whether schism is taken as the limiting case of disorder, the duality of structure is a notion indispensable to the theory of anomic declassification. For, unless the latter is founded on the concept of the incongruity between normative and non-normative relationships, there is no alternative but to regard disorder as random conflict.

From a slightly different point of view, what is basically at issue here is the question of the determination of wants. While Durkheim lays greatest stress upon the influence of moral factors in this respect, it is fairly clear that he recognizes that wants are also determined by command over resources. But since wants are thus co-determined, the only way of dispensing with the notion of non-normative structure would be to assume one of two things. The first is that the resources possessed by individuals do not entail social relationships. The second is that these relationships are not distinct from, and do not vary independently of, the normatively defined relationships. Neither of these assumptions is empirically valid. Some notion of non-normative structure, therefore, is latent in both Durkheim's theory of disorder and his view of the determination of wants.[1]

These considerations introduce important qualifications into his explanation of order. First of all, since declassification is caused by a sudden and widespread change in the distribution of wealth and power, it must follow that a relatively stable distribution of these resources is a necessary condition of solidarity.[2] In Fig. 7.1 this implication is shown by the dotted arrow going from anomie to solidarity. The second consequence is that, although the concept of solidarity might still serve as the limiting case of order, something approximating fatalism is an alternative and perhaps the more usual state of affairs. The latter is understood here as 'conditional fatalism', that is, as an attitude of resignation in the face of extremely adverse and stable social conditions. This is the type of fatalism that is strictly entailed by Durkheim's theory of anomie. The idea of 'ethical fatalism' cannot be derived from anomie or from solidarity, since neither of them presupposes that variations in the contents of values and beliefs are of any significance in the explanation of order or disorder.

---

[1] The unavoidable conclusion that wants are determined by both norm and resources also disposes of the notion of 'egoism', which Durkheim always equates with 'utilitarian' interest. It is in any case never clear from his writings whether it is the lack of moral regulation which releases egoism or the eruption of egoism which weakens regulation and integration.

[2] But if it is accepted that a stable distribution of power and wealth is a precondition of solidarity, it may be wondered how in this respect solidarity differs from conditional fatalism. Given Durkheim's predisposition to think of social forces in quantitative terms, the only consistent answer would have to be that fatalism differs from solidarity only in the degree of the stability, oppressiveness, and perceived unalterability of the 'distribution of men and things'.

The residual nature of Durkheim's conception of the socially disruptive forces that stem from the utilitarian sphere of society is revealed most clearly in his theory of anomic declassification. But the same kind of *ad hoc*-ery is no less notable in the work of other theorists within the Durkheimian tradition. This has already been demonstrated at some length in the discussion of Smelser's theory of collective behaviour, and the following statement by Parsons may serve as a further exemplification of this claim.

Perhaps the most important and necessary functional focus of positive institutionalization of stratification is the tendency of societal differentiation to lead to bases of polarization of conflicting interests. The two most obvious bases of polarization are political power and wealth, ie., command of more or less generalized facilities. Here the focus of institutionalized stratification is legitimizing differential power and wealth, and, more generally, access to valued objects and statuses . . . the major function of the institutionalization of class status is to minimize class conflict; but often it is not very successful.[3]

The terms entering into this highly compressed hypothesis about the functions of status stratification are of exemplary significance. First of all, although Parsons employs the idea of polarization, this concept can hardly be said to play a central role in any version of his theory of society. Moreover, the cause of polarization has nothing to do with values and beliefs. It is due rather to the conflict of interests that results from inequalities of power and wealth. Secondly, the latter appear to be conceived of in distributional rather than relational terms, even though the reference to class conflict implies a structure of class relations. This leads to the third point, which is that, although Parsons invokes the idea of class conflict to explain the need for the institutionalization of 'class status', the former concept is entirely marginal to his theory of society and the latter refers fairly predictably not to class but to status.[4]

---

[3] Parsons, 'Introduction' to Parsons *et al.*, *Theories of Society*, p. 59.
[4] See also *The Social System*, p. 172, where, after referring to the 'sorting out of kinship units relative to prestige status within the social system', Parsons says, 'This is what we call social class, a class being an aggregate of kinship units of approximately equal status in the system of stratification.' This usage is wholly consistent with his definitions of 'class', 'class status', 'social class', and 'social stratification' in his other writings. But these definitions are so full of such a consistent confusion of the meaning of class and status that this, taken in the context of his professed intellectual indebtedness to Weber, must be regarded as perverse.

But the crux of the matter is not the specific manner in which 'utilitarian' elements enter into the explanations of disorder advanced by any particular adherent of normative functionalism, nor indeed the degree to which they receive some formal recognition. The basic issue concerns the general tendency to demote these determinants of social action by comparison with the emphasis on normative factors. This is closely connected with the other characteristic feature of the Durkheimian solution of the problem of disorder: namely, the extent to which his theory of society and those of his successors owe their distinctiveness to their rejection of, and over-reaction to, the utilitarian schema of action. As far as Durkheim's work is concerned, this is clearly the case. His implacable opposition to utilitarian explanations of order, represented above by Spencer's idea of industrial solidarity as a spontaneous equilibration of self-interest through contractual exchange, led to the overriding importance placed on the normative integration of ends in his own conception of social solidarity. But, as the preceding discussion has endeavoured to show, the price to be paid for such a thoroughgoing anti-utilitarianism is that the only way of explaining disorder is resort to precisely the concept of action the rejected theory takes as axiomatic: a purely rational 'egoism' oriented to material ends such as power and wealth. A no less striking feature of a theory aiming to establish the importance of common values and beliefs in the integration of social systems is the almost total neglect of the significance of their variability for explanations of both order and conflict.[5]

Finally, and in anticipation of the discussion yet to come, it may be noted how much of a surface resemblance Durkheim's description of declassification bears to Marx's depiction of the socially disordering effects of capitalist industrialization:

[5] The inexorability of this idealistic tendency in Durkheim's social theory has been demonstrated by Parsons. Ironically, others have been able to document a similar shift in his own writings: from a voluntaristic theory of action in his early work to his later exposition of a cybernetic theory of social change, where he declares himself to be a 'cultural determinist' because he believes that 'normative elements are more important for social change than material interests' (*Societies: Evolutionary and Comparative Perspectives*, p. 113). This is also the only work in which the significance of historically specific values and beliefs is dealt with in a general and systematic way; and then, rather schematically, and in relation to long-run social change rather than the explanation of order and disorder. An important early contribution to the subject is J. F. Scott, 'Changing Foundations of the Parsonian Action Scheme', *American Sociological Review*, 28 (1963).

Constant revolutionizing of production, uninterrupted disturbance of all social conditions, everlasting uncertainty and agitation distinguish the bourgeois epoch from all earlier ones. All fixed, fast-frozen relations, with their train of ancient and venerable prejudices and opinions, are swept away, all new-formed ones become antiquated before they can ossify. All that is solid melts into air, all that is holy is profaned.[6]

But the similarity is no more than superficial. The disturbances Marx describes are merely the epiphenomena of a social system whose inner mechanism is held to be comprehensible only in terms of a particular version of the utilitarian theory of action. But, just as the Durkheimian rejection of this type of theory leads inevitably to the *ad hoc* introduction of utilitarian elements, the basic dependence of Marxism on a form of utilitarian theorizing leads equally inevitably to the increasingly problematic nature of normative determinants of social action. In a sense, the Marxist problem of disorder is the mirror image of the Durkheimian problem of disorder. In exactly what sense this is the case requires no small proof.

---

[6] K. Marx and F. Engels, *Selected Works* (2 vols.; Moscow, 1950, 1949), i. 36. Essentially the same, but rather more informative, observation is provided by Weber when he writes that 'if merely economic acquisition and naked economic power still bearing the stigma of its extra-status origin could bestow upon anyone who has won it the same honour as those who are interested in status by virtue of style of life claim for themselves, the status order would be threatened at its very root . . . When the bases of the acquisition and distribution of goods are relatively stable, stratification by status is favoured. Every technological repercussion and economic transformation threatens stratification by status and pushes the class situation into the foreground.' (*From Max Weber: Essays in Sociology*, ed. H. H. Gerth and C. W. Mills (London, 1948), 193–4.)

PART THREE
SCHISM

8.

REVOLUTIONARY POLARIZATION

I

That polarization of the moral community of the church which for Durkheim had to be the utter negation of a society has always been of central importance for Marxist theory and practice, and there is a clear sense in which the ideological class division of society into 'two great hostile camps' represents the antithesis of solidarity as consensus on ultimate values and beliefs. In a state of revolutionary class conflict, inter-class antagonism is inversely related to intra-class solidarity, and both attain their extreme limits when they partake of 'religious' phenomena in Durkheimian terms; that is, when classes are coextensive with churches and when their mutual relationship is one of schism. Parsons makes the point nicely when he writes that 'Marx saw only two antagonistic systems of mechanical solidarity, one for each of the two principal classes in his capitalistic system'.[1]

It might be said then that the idea of revolutionary class conflict has the merit of providing a 'correct' Durkheimian definition of disorder, in that moral polarization represents the extreme state of social declassification entailed by his key idea of social solidarity. Moreover, through the concept of economic structure as a system of production or economic power relations, Marxism also offers an explanation of the basis of moral polarization which is analytically far superior to Durkheim's invocation of the vague notion of the 'distribution of men and things'. To make this point it is unnecessary to go into the question of whether the concepts of forces and relations of production are applicable only to the economic sphere or whether they have a more general relevance suggested by Marx when he notes that military and ideological

---

[1] Parsons, *Sociological Theory and Modern Society*, p. 133.

institutions have to be understood as having their own specific modes of production. Finally, there can be no doubt that the general categories of Marxist sociology help to elucidate problems arising from Durkheim's preoccupation with the 'religious life' but which find no satisfactory solution within the terms of his own theory—most importantly the nature of the relationship between economic change and ideological innovation.

These considerations merely serve to indicate that the concepts of social action entering into Marxist explanations of order and disorder are likely to be more complicated and difficult to identify than those characterizing Durkheim's work or, more generally, that of normative functionalism. Yet in one way the task is easier, since the most important types of explanation have a much sharper focus in the paramount problem of why no advanced capitalist society has experienced the kind of proletarian revolution Marx envisaged. This is also the most obvious sense in which there exists a Marxist 'problem of disorder', even though its solution has increasingly taken the form of theories of ideological domination which, except for their terminology of class and class conflict, are strikingly similar to normative functionalist explanations of the problem of order. The chief characteristic of Marxist theory, however, is its claim, and apparent ability, to account for both order and disorder, for both the absence and yet unextinguished potentiality of revolutionary consciousness. Yet it is just this theoretical versatility that indicates a more deeply seated problem which is very much the same as that pervading Durkheimian sociology because it concerns the nature of the underlying action schema. Durkheim's difficulty in accommodating the residual concept of 'utilitarian' factors to his basically normative conception of the structuring of social action arises most acutely in his theory of anomic declassification. In Marxism, the problem is just the opposite: that of accommodating to a basically utilitarian action schema normative elements whose lack of differentiation and thereby uncertain analytical status introduces a chronic instability into the range of possible explanations of class action. This is most evident in the oscillation between 'positivistic' and 'idealistic' theories of revolutionary consciousness (or the lack of it)— the one extreme being represented by the supposedly revolutionizing effects of some form of economic conditions, and the other by the apparently unconditional nature of some form of global ideological domination. One reason for this latitude is that, by contrast with the economic theory of capitalist system contradiction, the political sociology of class conflict is analytically underdeveloped; as a result the relation between them is open to highly generalized interpretations.[2] But this particular theoretical imbalance is only one aspect of a wider range of problems having to do with the incoherence of the underlying action schema.

These are the principal themes of the following discussion. First of all, however, it is necessary to clarify two preliminary issues. The first concerns the limiting case of revolutionary disorder. How is this to be understood, and in what sense can it be said to be the outstanding problem of Marxist class theory? Secondly, the hypothesis that the concept of production relations provides the prototypical concept of structure which Durkheim's theory of disorder both requires and lacks is one that has to be examined in the light of criticisms that these relations involve irreducibly normative elements. Following the discussion of these matters, which relate respectively to the ultimate end and the principal structural conditions of proletarian revolution, the argument then turns to consider a variety of theories seeking to explain the emergence or absence of revolutionary consciousness.

II

As to the exact nature of revolutionary class polarization, Marx is nowhere explicit. Nevertheless, it might be supposed to have two general features. On the one hand there is a structural simplification of class relations due mainly to the growing concentration and centralization of capital and the concomitant socialization of labour; on the other a polarization of class consciousness and ideological confrontation. The idea of class revolutionary conflict, then, refers to both a structural and a moral division of society, terms that correspond closely to Durkheim's distinction between group attachments and moral regulation as the twin sources of

---

[2] As Poggi puts it, 'The attempt to locate the specific conditions that effect the subversion of power relations characteristic of modern society is an integral part of Marx's theory of that society. Again, it is a complex attempt; and it does not easily lend itself to sociological interpretation and assessment, since Marx conducted it largely in economic rather than sociological terms.' (*Images of Society*, p. 155).

social order. These two dimensions are conflated in the otherwise valuable definition provided by Kuper, who writes:

Polarization implies a division into two camps—the oppressors and the oppressed—with few relationships that transcend group barriers and restrain conflict by the ties of cross-cutting loyalties. Interests are in dialectical opposition and values antithetical: the subject peoples deny legitimacy to the social order and the rulers respond with increasing repression. Social cleavages are superimposed so that domination in political structures coincides with domination in other institutional structures. The dichotomy of values is pervasive, unresolved conflicts cumulate, and minor, seemingly isolated, issues quickly escalate to the level of the total society. There is no neutral ground of detachment from the struggle, which drives all strata into opposing camps; there is no appreciable intermediate area of living which might serve as the foundation for a more inclusive system of relationship.[3]

There are two points that need to be made about this definition. The first is that it might be taken to imply that moral polarization is simply a by-product of social division. The second is that it is a concept that has been developed in the context of the study of plural societies whose populations are divided principally according to ascriptive criteria, such as race, ethnicity, religion, and language. As regards the first point, experience shows that structural cleavage is neither a sufficient nor even a necessary condition of moral polarization. For, while it is true that cross-cutting group attachments generally have the effect of weakening any tendency to polarization, it is equally the case that social order, if not social solidarity, is perfectly compatible with a high degree of superimposition of political, economic, and social inequality, provided that the status classification of society enjoys an undisturbed dominance, such as that which may rest simply on a fatalistic belief in the unalterability of the status quo. Furthermore, moral or ideological polarization can have the effect of over-riding, and thus 'simplifying', what might otherwise appear to be complex lines of structural differentiation by resolving cross-pressures to which individuals are subjected; that is, by forcing a commitment to one pole of conflict or the other. This would in turn be expected

---

[3] L. Kuper, 'Conflict and the Plural Society', in L. Kuper and M. G. Smith (eds.), *Pluralism in Africa* (Berkeley, Calif., 1971), 160–1.

to have quite radicalizing consequences, because of the catharsis involved in the dissolution of ambivalent group attachments.

It is in this connection that the second aspect of the definition of polarization just given becomes most relevant. Lenin predicted that social revolution would never take the form of two classes lining up like opposing armies, the bourgeoisie declaring itself for capitalism and the proletariat for socialism.[4] But something closely approximating this degree of extreme polarization is all too common in the case of communal conflicts in plural societies where groups are divided on the basis of race, ethnicity, language, or religion. Generally speaking, communal conflicts appear to over-ride cross-cutting class cleavages much more easily than class conflicts over-ride cross-cutting communal cleavages. Whether class conflicts in what Schumpeter calls 'ethnically homogeneous societies'[5] are every likely to reach the pitch of communal conflicts in plural societies is, therefore, a question of the utmost importance for Marxist class theory and for the sociology of stratification in general.[6] But, compared with primordial attachments of race, ethnicity, and, in some cases, religion, it would seem that class divisions are much less powerful forces for social disorder, and class ideologies much less effective means of mobilizing intermediate strata. Even in ethnically homogeneous societies the development of class antagonism, not to mention the once hoped for spread of proletarian internationalism, has undoubtedly been greatly impeded by the ethnic solidarity of nationalism.

Quite apart from these considerations, Marxist theories of revolutionary class consciousness have encountered the fact that the class structure of advanced capitalist societies has not become progressively simplified in accordance with Marx's expectations. As a result, the major task of contemporary Marxist analysis has become that of locating the class position of those 'intermediate'

---

[4] In fact, in Sweden, where the national organizations of 'capitalists' and 'workers' represent an extremely high proportion of their respective potential memberships, classes—or their agents—do 'line up' against each other regularly, but not in the revolutionary relationship Lenin had in mind.

[5] J. A. Schumpeter, 'Social Classes in Ethnically Homogeneous Environment', in his *Imperialism and Social Classes* (Oxford, 1951).

[6] On this, see L. Kuper, *Race, Class and Power* (London, 1974), esp. chs. 7, 8, and F. Parkin, *Marxism and Class Theory: A Bourgeois Critique* (London, 1979), ch. 3.

Schism

groups of white-collar and service employees whose growing representation in the labour force is one of the most striking features of the most recent phase of capitalist development. Yet, despite the difficulties of establishing a hard and fast line between them, the capitalist and working classes are still regarded as the only centres of social gravity towards which intermediate groups with less clearly defined class positions will be attracted in situations of critical class conflict. The expectation is that the ideological polarization of the two main classes will overcome the lack of structural polarization, and that those groups who do not belong to the working class proper, but who are subject to an increasing 'proletarianization', will be brought into alliance with the working class as a result of a correct socialist strategy.[7]

Nothing, therefore, has been more disconcerting to Marxist theory than the massively awkward fact that no advanced capitalist society has produced anything resembling a revolutionary proletariat since the upsurges in working-class protest after the First World War which reached their peaks with the 'revolt' in the Ruhr and the factory occupations in Turin. Even then, the extent to which the mass of workers were imbued with a revolutionary consciousness appears to have been limited.[8]

The most obvious sense in which one can speak of a Marxist

---

[7] See N. Poulantzas, *Classes in Contemporary Capitalism* (London, 1978), which is one of the very few general treatises to have appeared in the last decade which is concerned with other than purely structural analysis.

[8] As regards the more significant of these two cases, B. Moore, relying extensively on Lucas's account of the March 1920 revolt in the Ruhr, refers to this struggle as 'the most significant uprising by industrial workers that has so far taken place in any modern industrial society' (*Injustice: The Social Bases of Obedience and Revolt* (London, 1978) p. 328). But, at most points, he qualifies this by showing that the evidence reveals a lack of widespread revolutionary consciousness among the working class. J. Tampke, in his *Ruhr and Revolution* (London, 1979), describes the general strike of 1919 as the 'first revolution in a fully industrialized country' (p. xiv). But his account of the limits and variability of working-class consciousness during this critical period is amply supported by several other authorities, such as E. Lucas, *Zwei Formen von Radikalismus in der deutschen Arbeiterbewegung* (Frankfurt, 1976) and M. Nolan, *Social Democracy and Society: Working Class Radicalism in Düsseldorf, 1890–1920* (Bonn, 1974). The general difficulties of inferring workers' consciousness from the data available from this time are carefully presented by D. Geary, 'Identifying Militancy: The Assessment of Working Class Attitudes towards State and Society', in R. J. Evans (ed.), *The German Working Class, 1888–1933* (London, 1982). On the 'Red Two Years' in Italy, see M. Clark, *The Revolution that Failed* (New Haven, Conn., 1977), and G. A. Williams, *Proletarian Order* (London, 1975).

'problem of disorder', therefore, is the absence in modern capitalist societies of anything approximating the degree of class polarization envisaged by Marx, and by many of his successors right up to the present day. The other side of this is the amount of recent Marxist theory that has been devoted to explaining the failure of capitalist societies to dig their own graves. As a part of this exercise, it has become increasingly fashionable to argue that Marx's work provides no grounds for thinking that revolution would necessarily occur only in the most advanced capitalist countries. Thus, for example, Hobsbawm: 'No interpretation of Marx is more grotesque than the one which suggests that he expected a revolution exclusively from the advanced industrial countries of the West.'[9] Whilst this may be a valid comment on Marx's fluctuating hopes of revolution, it surely has to be taken in conjunction with the equally relevant observation that, 'concerning the conditions necessary to produce a successful revolution, Marx was more or less sanguine according to the historical situation in which he found himself',[10] and that 'any attempt to systematize Marx's various predictions may be quite confusing, if not outright senseless'.[11] Moreover, Marx's view of the possibility of revolution in less developed societies was not only highly tentative but stipulated that the success of such a revolution, in Russia for example, would depend on its being 'the signal for a proletarian revolution in the West'.[12] In any case, to argue that Marx did not expect revolution 'exclusively' in the most advanced societies can hardly be taken to imply that he thought that proletarian revolution would pass them by. Unless the relations between his theory of system contradiction and class conflict is held to be a purely contingent one[13] (in which case much of what

[9] E. J. Hobsbawm, 'Introduction' to his edition of K. Marx, *Precapitalist Economic Formation* (London, 1964), 49.

[10] D. McLellan, *The Thought of Karl Marx: An Introduction* (London, 1971), 199.

[11] S. Avineri, *The Social and Political Thought of Karl Marx* (Cambridge, 1970), 256.

[12] McLellan, *The Thought of Karl Marx*, p. 101.

[13] In the writing of Althusser, this is a distinct possibility. Judging from his *post hoc* 'explanations' of the Bolshevik, Chinese revolutions, it is difficult to avoid the conclusion that his concept of 'overdetermination' is little more than an analytical blank cheque which guarantees that revolutions will occur whenever and wherever the sufficient conditions of their occurrence (superimposed 'conflicts' and 'contradictions' of an indiscriminate kind) happen to exist.

is distinctive about a Marxist interpretation disappears), then the whole logic of his major work points to one and only one conclusion: namely, that the conditions of proletarian revolution will be found in the most advanced, and the most capitalist, of capitalist societies. What he has to say on this score in the famous Preface to *A Contribution to the Critique of Political Economy* finds almost identical expression in the *Grundrisse*: 'If we did not find concealed in society as it is the material conditions of production and the corresponding relations of exchange pre-requisite for a classless society, then all attempts to explode it would be quixotic.'[14] *Capital* is replete with similar statements. For example: 'in theory, it is assumed that the laws of capitalist production operate in their pure form. In reality there exists only approximation; but this approximation is the greater, the more developed the capitalist mode of production and the less it is adulterated and amalgamated with survivals of former economic conditions'.[15] From this standpoint,[16] the United States of America has always been the chief embarrassment. To the naming of the factors making for US 'exceptionalism' there is hardly any end.[17] But, in that case, at what point does one admit that the sociological law of motion of capitalist society has ground to a halt in the

[14] K. Marx, *Grundrisse*, trans., with a foreword by M. Nicolaus (Harmondsworth, 1973), 159.

[15] K. Marx, *Capital*, iii (London, 1972), 175.

[16] It may be said that the above quotations refer only to the capitalist mode of production considered abstractly, and that this has no direct relevance to the understanding of class conflict, which must be analysed by reference to specific social formations. This is not the case. First, in so far as Marx's writings yield a systematic account of the conditions making for proletarian revolutionary consciousness, these conditions progress *pari passu* with the development of the capitalist mode of production itself. (This is as clear in the Preface to the *Critique of Political Economy* as it is in the chapter on 'The Historical Tendencies of Capitalist Accumulation' in *Capital*.) Secondly, while no one would wish to deny that a full understanding of class movements involves a study of specific historical situations, the main function of the term 'social formation' is to disguise the fact that Marxism lacks any well-formulated sociology of class formation. On this, see below, ch. 16.

[17] These are discussed thoroughly in J. H. M. Laslett and S. M. Lipset (eds.), *Failure of a Dream? Essays in the History of American Socialism* (Garden City, NY, 1974). See also the editorial Introduction by C. T. Husbands to W. Sombart, *Why is there no socialism in the United States?* (London, 1976): H. Klehr, 'Marxist Theory in Search of America', *Journal of Politics*, 35 (1973); M. Davis, 'Why the U.S. Working Class is Different', *New Left Review*, 123 (1980); E. Foner, 'Why is there no socialism in the United States', *History Workshop*, 17 (1984).

sands of historical particularity—or in what some prefer to call the 'concrete of social formation'?

In general, these sorts of problems have led not to the abandonment of the idea that the most advanced capitalist societies are the most likely sites of socialist revolution but rather to a much greater emphasis upon the structural changes that have caused its postponement. The belief that, in the long run at any rate, the contradictions of capitalist societies will lead to increasing class polarization and to the revolutionary, though not necessarily violent, transformation of capitalism into socialism has remained intact. The example of countries that embarked on a course of socialist transformation in the name of Marx has also given new meaning to his admonition that the essential precondition of an authentic socialist revolution is the emergence of a revolutionary consciousness among the mass of the working class. The problem of revolutionary class polarization is therefore still very much on the agenda of Marxist theory. As Miliband puts it, 'Marxists have always believed that the working class would eventually want to go beyond partial reforms inside the system—that it would, in other words, come to acquire the "class consciousness" needed to want a thoroughgoing, revolutionary transformation of capitalist society into an entirely differently based and differently motivated system.'[18]

The ways in which class theorists have attempted to take account of major structural developments in advanced capitalist societies will be discussed at some length at a later stage. For the time being, however, the more basic problem has to do less with changes in production relationships than with the question of the assumptions entering into theories seeking to relate structural conditions to class action. The matter at issue then is not whether capitalist societies have changed in ways that Marx did not expect but whether, even under the conditions he and his successors have thought most conducive to revolutionary consciousness (or for that matter to the lack of it), the assumptions underlying theories relating class situation to class conflict are coherent and well founded. From this viewpoint, for example, whether or not capitalism has produced a proletariat which has become increasingly impoverished in either an absolute or a relative sense is less

[18] R. Miliband, *Marxism and Politics* (Oxford, 1977), 41.

significant than the question of how impoverishment (or affluence) is understood to affect class consciousness. Answers to questions of this kind must take the form of generalizations 'confirmed by observation to the effect that under certain conditions an expected course of action will occur, which is understandable in terms of the typical motives and typical subjective intentions of the actors'.[19] The major issue then is whether, informing all the various hypotheses put forward to explain variations in class consciousness, there can be said to be a something approximating a unitary theory of action.

What chiefly distinguishes one type of action scheme from another are assumptions about the standards according to which actors select their ends and use the means available to them for the achievement of these ends under given conditions. To anticipate an argument that has yet to be substantiated, it may be said that in general, and usually implicitly, Marxist theorizing has approximated the utilitarian action schema in postulating 'rationality' as the standard governing the actor's adaptation of means to ends. This, as will be seen, is incompatible with a systematic analysis of normative standards, which in the last analysis have to be regarded positively as nonrational rather than as irrational deviations from a purely rational course of action. The most important categories in this connection are shared values and beliefs, and the modes of action related to them—paradigmatically 'religion' and 'ritual' in the Durkheimian sense. Given the predominantly utilitarian assumptions of Marxist theorizing, there are only two ways in which the problem of nonrational norms can be dealt with, and, for reasons still to be gone into, both prove less than satisfactory. One solution is to reduce these normative elements to conditions of action: that is, to treat them as being somehow determined by conditions of production; the other is to treat them as means: that is, as ideological resources by which one class dominates another. These typical ways of explaining deviations from rational action are of course integrally bound up with two other familiar assumptions that distinguish Marxism from purely individualistic versions of the utilitarian action scheme. The first is that the ultimate as well as the proximate ends of

[19] M. Weber, *Economy and Society*, ed. G. Roth and C. Wittich (Berkeley, Calif., 1978), 18.

actors (classes) are 'given', in the sense that they are determined by their location in relations of production. The second is that these production relations somehow determine a wide variety of 'superstructural' factors, including the type of normative elements just referred to.

Production relations are taken to be by far the most important set of conditions 'structuring' social action. Class position is the principal determinant of the ends of actors and of the means available to them for the realization of these ends (including their chances of collective action). The system of production also structures action indirectly, through the unintended consequences of actors pursuing ends in such a way as to bring about a contradiction between the forces and relations of production. But production relations are only a necessary, not a sufficient, condition of class action, the explanation of which also involves assumptions about the nature of the actors themselves.[20] Nevertheless, the concept of production relations is of such crucial importance in the action schema as to warrant separate treatment.

At first sight the Marxist and Durkheim concepts of structure seem poles apart. Yet, to make sense of Durkheim's theory of declassification, terms such as 'power and wealth' and 'the distribution of men and things' have to be taken to refer to power relationships which possess a structure which is sufficiently distinct for it to be said that it becomes incongruent with the normative order or system of social classification. It may be thought that much the same kind of incongruity is involved in the Marxian notion of a contradiction between the increasingly socialized nature of production and the institution of private property. However, this apparent point of convergence must remain rather superficial, unless it is possible to show in what precise sense non-normative relationships represent more than a deviation from institutional norms and come to take on the form of an incipient anti-system[21] such as that Marx refers to when he writes of the

---

[20] As one authority puts it: 'If, however, the proletariat is still unaware of its historical position, if it does not possess an adequate world view, then the objective conditions by themselves will not create a revolution until and unless the proletariat grasps that by shaping its own view of the world it also changes it' (Avineri, *The Social and Political Thought of Karl Marx*, p.144).

[21] This term is taken from S. N. Eisenstadt, 'Institutionalization and Change', *American Sociological Review*, 29 (1964), 247.

progressive 'abolition of capitalist relations of production within the capitalist system of production'. In approaching this problem, the first and basic question is whether production relations can be defined except by reference to the laws and customs regulating these relations. An alternative formulation is to ask whether class relations can be distinguished from status relations. This may be the more useful starting-point, since it also offers the opportunity to review and revise the notion of social classification.

9.

CONTRADICTION AND ANTI-SYSTEM

I

For Durkheim and normative functionalism generally, the status system is of strategic importance, since it is the social mechanism by which the ends or interests of individuals and groups are hierarchically integrated by reference to ultimate values and beliefs. For Durkheim at least the social classification includes not only moral standards defining the differential worth of social functions but also legal norms such as those of property and contract which regulate and legitimate the 'distribution of men and things'. Status is therefore directly implicated in the power structure of a society and is not simply a purely normative, ideational representation of it. Only in a superficial sense can status be equated with a hierarchy of honour or prestige based on values about which there is more or less consensus. The fundamental aspect of status has to do with rights and duties defining the powers and resources appropriate to particular groups. 'For all practical purposes', Weber notes, 'stratification by status goes hand in hand with a monopolization of ideal and material goods and opportunities. Besides the specific status honour, which always rests on distance and exclusiveness, we find all sorts of material monopolies.'[1] In most societies, the prerogatives of status groups, sanctioned by custom, law, and ritual, have been shaped by and have imposed their legitimation on all major forms of power, including the economic (the right to own certain kinds of property, consume certain kinds of goods, pursue certain types of vocations). It is principally to these rights that Weber refers when introducing the idea of 'status situation' as a determinant of life chances, and also when stating that status groups, just as much as

---

[1] *From Max Weber*, p. 191.

classes, are 'phenomena of the distribution of power within a community'. In one way Durkheim's term 'social classification' captures this meaning of status rather well, since it conveys the fact that class or production relations are always encompassed and partially determined by status relations.

Whichever term is preferred, the importance of this view of status cannot be sufficiently emphasized, because there is a tendency among a great many students of social stratification to treat status merely as prestige ranking or as, at the most, purely conventional status relationships, maintained by informal means of social inclusion and exclusion, which are manifested in, for example, patterns of intermarriage and interdining.[2] Fairly typical is the following statement:

Weber uses the concept of 'status situation' to point to the normative determination of life chances. Weber argues that an agent's status situation is that aspect of his or her life chances which is determined by the agent's social standing in terms of some normative order. The central mechanism here is social honour, the estimation of which derives from the normative order and the cultural values which underpin it.[3]

Although it is true that any stable form of status involves 'estimations of social honour' by reference to values, it also consists, and

[2] And, very typically, by Marxist writers. Here are some examples: 'status groups are to be distinguished according to such essentially subjective criteria as prestige, social honour, and so on, which are expressed in a particular "style of life"' (R. Crompton and J. Gubbay, *Economy and Class Structure* (London, 1977), 7); 'the sensitivity of people to gradations of prestige; the rituals and etiquette of interpersonal relationships within and across lines that divide the population in some sort of hierarchy of esteem. The concern is with what sociologists usually call social "status"' (J. Westergaard and H. Resler, *Class in a Capitalist Society* (London, 1975), 1-2); 'I propose to define the peasantry as a class, as determined by its place in the production of a society's material needs; not as a status group determined by attributed esteem, dignity, or honour' (R. Hilton, *The English Peasantry in the Later Middle Ages* (Oxford, 1975), 12). It is however, precisely a Weberian notion of status groups that Hilton requires when he seeks an explanation of peasant revolts. The outbreak of these revolts, he argues, needs to be explained by something more than the fact that 'peasants and landlords had incompatible interests in the division of the social product' or 'the natural antagonism between an exploiting and an exploited class'. This something more was action 'which altered the customary relationships or disappointed normal expectations', and it was just such 'innovation by the lords which (in peasant eyes) seemed to justify their own renunciation of their humble role in the social hierarchy'. See Hilton, *Bond Men Made Free*, pp. 113-19.

[3] J. Scott, *The Upper Classes* (London, 1982), 2.

much more substantively, of rights and obligations, privileges and disabilities, which are guaranteed by legal sanctions—that is, ultimately, by the application of physical force, whether by the state or some other corporate group. In no society, then, are status groups constituted merely, or even mainly, by anything so fragile as social honour or 'public opinion'. Status rights and duties are always an expression of the distribution of political, military and economic power. For example, immunity from the corvée and from punishment by the bamboo were not privileges of the Chinese mandarin which derived from a status situation guaranteed simply by estimations of social honour. This cultural dominance was merely one aspect of the formidable resources (economic and ideological as well as political) concentrated in the hands of the Chinese bureaucratic élite. And in principle the status of the citizen of the modern democratic state is no different. His or her right to cast the ballot is no less an expression of the distribution of power and is in the last resort guaranteed by the coercive power of the state. As a status order, citizenship merely substitutes equality for hierarchy.

Only in the case of conventional status groups can it be said that status is a normative order resting on purely social sanctions; even then, conventional status inhabits the interstices of legal status. In modern democracies any advantages conferred by conventional status are so stringently limited by the various legal status rights enjoyed by all citizens so as to make the former feeble by comparison with earlier societies. From this perspective the styles of life which now differentiate conventional status groups are, with very few trivial exceptions, neither legally inaccessible nor of any major significance in the determination of life chances, however important they may be as standards of emulation or social worth. That citizenship is the core status order of these societies is only difficult to understand as long as the legal rights and duties defining status are thought to entail hierarchy rather than equality. Indeed, the removal of this misconception is prerequisite to a proper understanding of the nature of class relations, to which status is usually thought to be in some vague sense epiphenomenal. And since citizenship confers the same right on all adults to acquire property and to enter into contracts, the egalitarian status order of capitalist societies has profound consequences for the constitution of production relations as well as for the nature and extent of any consciousness of class division these relations are likely to give rise to.

As a general rule, class conflict appears to vary inversely with the degree to which production relations are embodied within a stable system of hierarchical status. Conversely, as the foregoing discussion has sought to establish, where there occurs a marked incongruity between status and economic (not to mention other forms of) power, status declassification may be seen to be both a consequence of unanticipated changes in production relations and a direct cause of class conflict. In other words, classes, born of production relations, only become active social forces, or 'classes for themselves', when economic power is momentarily disengaged from the status order in which it was previously incorporated and legitimated. In this, Weber's generalization has still to be faulted. Class formation is inhibited when opportunities for the disposition of goods and labour are institutionalized as the prerogatives of status groups; conversely, it is promoted when rapid economic and technological change undermines the status order, and life chances become largely a function of market economic power exercised through the market. In the same vein, Lukács writes that 'status consciousness—a real historical factor—masks class consciousness; in fact it prevents it from emerging at all'. Like Weber, he sees this factor as characteristic of pre-capitalist societies, in which 'the structuring of society into castes and estates means that economic elements are inextricably joined to political and religious factors' and in which 'legal institutions intervene substantively in the interplay of economic forces'. Only in capitalist societies 'does economic class interest emerge in all its starkness as the motor of history'.[4]

---

[4] G. Lukács, *History and Class Consciousness* (London, 1971), pp. 56–8. The subsumption of class relations under status relations is also implied in the passage where Marx writes that 'in all forms in which the direct producer remains "the possessor" of the means of production and labour conditions necessary for the production of his own means of subsistence the property relationship must simultaneously appear as a direct relationship of lordship and servitude, so that the direct producer is not free'. Under such conditions, surplus labour can only be extorted by 'other than economic pressure', and, although the relationship between rulers and ruled 'grows directly out of production', the former reacts upon the latter as 'a determining element' and the connection between relations of production and relations of domination 'can be ascertained only by analysis of the empirically given circumstances'. *Capital*, iii. 790–2. From this, it has been concluded that 'pre-capitalist modes of production cannot be defined except via

However, this way of characterizing societies by their predominant forms of social inequality is a hindrance to understanding the
dynamic between class and status that occurs in all of them. For
example, Weber can write that 'depending on the prevailing mode
of stratification, we shall speak of a "status society" or a "class
society"'.[5] But a society ordered by status is not devoid of
production relations, and, however closely the distribution of
economic power may correspond to status rights and obligations,
the two structures can never be identical. However strongly
buttressed by legal and ritual sanctions, no status order is immune
from the effects of changes in class situation, even when the latter
do not eventuate in class formation. Studies of the Indian caste
system, for example, show how the ritually sanctioned status
hierarchy has constantly had to accommodate itself to redistributions of economic and other forms of power.[6]

The opposite case is provided by societies ordered (or perhaps
more correctly disordered) by the predominance of class relations.
But even when capitalist, market-mediated, economic power had
greatest scope, the status determination of life chances was never
absent, although it guaranteed little more than a relation of formal
legal equality between employers and wage-earners.[7] Neverthe-

---

their political, legal and ideological superstructures, since these are what determines the type of extra-economic coercion that specifies them' (P. Anderson,
Lineages of the Absolutist State (London, 1974), 404). This has the effect of making
'pre-capitalist' society a vast residual category, within which distinctions can be
made only by reference to 'superstructural' factors. See the sharp critique of this
position by A. Cutler *et al.*, *Marx's Capital and Capitalism Today* (London, 1977),
i. 244–7.

[5] Weber, *Economy and Society*, p. 306. This sentence is omitted from the
corresponding section of *The Theory of Social and Economic Organization*, ed. T.
Parsons (London, 1947). It is also quite perverse that in the latter work *Klassenlage*
is translated as 'class status'. In Weber's 'Class, Status Groups and Party' it is
possible to identify a continuum of class and status-group formation of the
following kind: (1) 'societalized class actions', (2) 'communal class actions', (3)
'mass reactions of a class kind', (4) 'mass reactions of a status kind' (not mentioned
by Weber but implicit in his schema; for example, the case of individuals of a
lower status adopting the life-style of a higher status group), (5) 'conventional'
status groups, (6) 'legalized' status groups, and (7) 'ritualized' status groups. The
elucidation of these distinctions could yield an index of social integration.

[6] See the literature cited above, ch. 3 n. 31.

[7] Even then, 'conventional' status shaped the very core of class relations, that
is, the 'labour process'; see P. Joyce, *Work, Society and Politics: The Culture of
the Factory in Later Victorian England* (Brighton, 1980).

less, this acute incongruity between formal rights and factual powers meant that it was a status structure which exacerbated the sense of class division.[8]

It was also a configuration of status rights that was short-lived. As Avineri points out, 'for Marx, the heyday of unfettered capitalism, when economic activity, at least in England, was not encumbered by any limitation at all, pre- or post-capitalist, was short: from the Repeal of the Corn Laws to the introduction of the Ten Hours Bill'.[9]

For Marx, the reduction of the working day presaged the transformation of capitalism into socialism, and was the latter's most essential precondition.[10] With hindsight, however, the Ten Hours Bill appears as the first of a series of legislations through which market powers have been progressively circumscribed by civic rights to an extent Marx could never have foreseen.

The relation between class and status is therefore highly complex. At this stage, it is sufficient to conclude that a status-ordered society can no more immobilize economic forces than, at the other extreme, class interests and class conflicts can wholly escape the constraints of the status system in which production relations are always embedded. The distinction between class and status situation is not between economic power and social honour or prestige, but rather between a situation in which life chances are minimally conditioned by legal status defining entitlements and one in which the latter play the preponderant role.

II

Although the fact that status and class situations are always interdependent means that there can be no purely 'status' or 'class' structured societies, it by no means rules out the possibility of class relations becoming incongruent with status relations. Yet it is just this contingency which seems to go unrecognized in the argument that, since production relations cannot be understood except by reference to the legal norms by which they are defined,

---

[8] See T. H. Marshall, *Citizenship and Social Class*, and R. Bendix, 'The Lower Classes and the "Democratic Revolution"', *Industrial Relations*, 1 (1961).

[9] Avineri, *The Social and Political Thought of Karl Marx*, p. 161.

[10] Marx, *Capital*, iii. 820.

it is impossible to distinguish between the 'economic structure of society', or 'real foundation', and its 'legal and political superstructure'. This is, for example, the core of the criticism advanced by Parsons, who regards law as 'the primary structural focus of society', and legal norms as 'first line mechanisms regulating the pursuit of the type of interests which predominate in Marxist theory'. From these assumptions he concludes that 'a primary focus of ambiguity in Marxian thought lies in the problem of the relation of legal order to the famous concept of *Produktionsverhältnisse*'.[11] This ambiguity arises because,

by grounding the conception of capitalistic interest in the concrete structure of the family firm, certain property institutions, and market structures regulated by the institutions of contract, Marxians have generally tended to *include* basic legal institutions within the famous material factors, the relations of production. At other times, however, they have treated law as a component of the 'superstructure' and thus as 'determined by' rather than as a *part of*, the relations of production.[12]

Plamenatz makes basically the same criticism when he writes that:

it is quite impossible to define these relations except in terms which men make upon one another and recognize—except in terms of admitted rights and obligations. There are such rights and obligations, there are accepted rules of conduct, rules which require and forbid and are supported by sanctions; there are, in the broad sense of the word, laws.[13]

In another sense, however, this formulation also assumes what it sets out to prove, since to assert that norms are 'recognized', 'admitted', and 'accepted' is in effect to postulate the limiting case of order, solidarity, in which the parties to a social relationship do in fact act in conformity with rules because they are rules that embody shared values. As a consequence, it does not allow for the possibility that actual social relationships may assume a markedly different structure from that defined in law or custom.[14]

---

[11] Parsons, *Sociological Theory and Modern Society*, pp. 9, 183.

[12] Ibid. 183.

[13] Plamenatz, *Man and Society*, ii. 291. See also G. Leff, *The Tyranny of Concepts* (London, 1969).

[14] For example, Plamenatz's definition would imply that, if oligarchy is the actual form of government of ostensibly democratic organizations, this would on closer inspection nevertheless turn out to be a sub-legal order constituted by customary norms that are recognized, admitted, and accepted by all concerned. This construal would be difficult to reconcile with R. Michels's explanation of 'the

On this subject, the scattered remarks of Marx and Engels, if not unequivocal, lead to the fairly clear conclusion that actual production relations must not be confused with the legal concepts which arise from and sanction these relations, and which, due to the separate division of legal labour, come to acquire an independent and consequently artificial existence.[15] The terms in which this process is portrayed are hardly distinguishable from those that Durkheim uses to describe the spontaneous emergence of the moral rules expressing relations of organic solidarity arising from the division of labour. For example, after noting that the legal sanctioning of the existing order is in the interest of the ruling section of society, Marx goes on to say that,

Apart from all else, this, by the way, comes about of itself as soon as the constant reproduction of the basis of the existing order and its fundamental relations assumes a regulated and orderly form in the course of time. And such regulation and order are themselves indispensable elements in any mode of production, if it is to assume social stability and independence from mere chance and arbitrariness.[16]

This distinction between actual relations of production and the legal norms that enshrine them is maintained so consistently

---

development in such parties of the very tendencies against which they have declared war' (*Political Parties* (Glencoe, Ill., 1949), 11). Michels's argument would be that any customary norms oligarchy gives rise to are the unintended and unwelcome product of technical and organizational imperatives.

[15] For example, 'The existing relations of production between individuals must necessarily express themselves also as political and legal relations. Within the division of labour these relations are bound to assume an independent existence *vis-à-vis* individuals. In language, such relations can only be expressed as concepts. The fact that these universals and concepts are accepted as mysterious powers is a necessary consequence of the independent existence assumed by real relations whose expression they are. Besides this acceptance in everyday consciousness, these universals are also given a special validity and further development by political scientists and jurists who, as a result of the division of labour, are assigned to the cult of these concepts, and who see in them, rather than in the relations of production, the true basis of property relations.' (*Karl Marx: Selected Writings in Sociology and Social Philosophy*. ed. T. B. Bottomore and M. Rubel (London, 1956), 78.) See also Engels, in Marx and Engels, *Selected Works*, i. 565.

[16] Marx, *Capital*, iii. 793. Similarly, Engels: 'At a certain, very primitive stage of the development of society, the need arises to bring under a common rule the daily recurring acts of production, distribution and exchange of products, to see to it that the individual subordinates himself to the common conditions of production and exchange. This rule, which is at first custom, soon becomes law.' (Marx and Engels, *Selected Works* , p. 564.)

throughout Marx's writings and is also so obviously indispensable to his theory of system contradiction, that it is difficult to understand the argument that his idea of social structure is fundamentally flawed by his inability to appreciate the need, in his own words, to study 'property relations as a whole, not in their *legal* expression as *relations of volition* but in their real form, that is, as *relations of production*'.[17]

The basic issue then is not whether legal and customary institutions are in Parsons's term 'part of' the relations of production, or whether, as Plamanatz puts it, the definition of these relations necessarily involves reference to such norms. For, although both statements are obviously true, they do not dispose of the more important problem of whether it is possible and useful to distinguish between the legal and customary norms defining the legitimate rights and duties of economic agents and the actual form production relations assume within this institutional framework. This question in turn raises the broader and much more complicated one of how far it is possible to explain changes in production relations without reference to the normative structure in which they develop; and, even more generally, the whole question of the role of normative factors within the Marxist action schema. The latter is a subject discussed at length below,[18] and for present purposes the former can be set on one side, for the answer to the question of whether it is possible to distinguish production relations from their legal or customary matrix does not presuppose judgements about the relative importance of legal and economic factors in explaining changes in these relations.

To argue that production relations are distinct from the legal norms that define and regulate and thus partly constitute them it is not enough to show that the former may deviate from the latter, since such a discrepancy could be seen as a characteristic feature of the grounding of all rules or norms, which, however specific they may be, are never devoid of ambiguity and exploitability when applied to concrete social situations. It is necessary to show rather that it is possible for production relations to be so incon-

---

[17] In particular, see the critique of Dahrendorf in A. Giddens, *The Class Structure of the Advanced Societies* (London, 1973), 70 ff. The quotation is from Marx and Engels, *Selected Works*, p. 355. The same distinction is maintained by Engels and in almost exactly the same terms (ibid. 564–5).

[18] See ch. 10.

gruent with legal and customary norms that they may be said to be structurally distinct in the sense that the incongruity is systematic and requires distinctive, non-legal terms to describe and account for it. A classic example of this is given by Renner, who contrasts the functions of private law in the two limiting cases of simple commodity and pure capitalist production. The former case exemplifies his thesis that there is 'always a moment in the history of human institutions when the legal system is the adequate expression of the economic relations, when superstructure and substructure are in conformity'.[19] This is the starting-point of his account of how capitalist development led to a divergence between norm and substratum, due to the fact that, whilst the norms of private property and contract remained essentially the same, changes in the ownership of the means of production led to the capitalist exercising a *de facto* power over his employees which became increasingly incongruent with the legal norms governing their relationship. In this case, as no doubt generally, the incongruity is inexplicable without reference to the content of the specific norms in question. As Kahn-Freund puts it, 'the contract itself is, like all legal institutions, a blank without intrinsic social significance, and adaptable to an infinite number of social objectives', so that, 'the employer, by exercising his power of command, fills in the blank, and that power vests in him by virtue of his dominium, his ownership of the means of production'.[20] But the essential point he and Renner both wish to emphasize is that, at this stage, the capitalist's untrammelled power of command over his workforce not only has no directly corresponding right but is in effect a public power of command which is totally foreign to the institution of private law which enables its exercise. 'The employment relationship', writes Renner, 'is an indirect power relationship, a public obligation to service, like serfdom of feudal times. It differs from serfdom only in this respect, that it is based on contract, not upon inheritance.' In particular, the direction and co-ordination of labour resulting from the capitalist's power to control the labour process is tantamount to a 'compulsory association'.[21]

---

[19] K. Renner, *The Institutions of Private Law and their Social Functions*, ed. with an introduction by O. Kahn-Freund (London, 1949), 83.

[20] Ibid. 28.

[21] Ibid. 115. See also the comment by Kahn-Freund, p. 163 n. 128. Renner

That this example refers to a particular and, in its pure form, short-lived, period of capitalist development does not detract from the importance of the general order of facts it signifies. The capitalist's powers of compulsion over his workforce under the legal fiction of free contract arose in the same manner in which, at a later stage, most owners of capital lost the right of control over the disposition not only of labour but of capital itself, as a result of the concentration of capital and the divorce of legal and real economic ownership. Many other examples could easily be adduced. For instance, the fact that in the twelfth century the position of villeins was improving at the same time as the institution of villeinage became more rigid and oppressive has to be explained in very much the same terms: namely, by the landlords' inability to enforce their authority and collect labour dues from manorial estates too remote to allow of direct control.[22] What these examples demonstrate is the need for a clear distinction between formal legal rights and the powers that render them effective or ineffective; and this is the most general ground for rejecting the argument that the concept of production relations is ambiguous and untenable.[23]

It is a distinction that is also crucial to understanding the sense in which Marx's theory of system contradiction posits the growing socialization of production relations within the capitalist mode of production as the major structural condition of the occurrence and success of proletarian revolution. This idea of the immanent socialization of capitalist production relations taking on the form of an 'anti-system' also stands in starkest contrast to the purely negative notion of 'deviation' from institutional norms which is

---

elaborates by saying that 'the subordination of the workers which at the same time effects their mutual co-ordination is a corresponding phenomenon. Is this co-ordination also based on contract? The workers are not asked whether their neighbour appeals to them, yet they are forced into close proximity and in this way become united into an association of workers.' He concludes that 'there is no doubt that these workers who contribute partial operations form a compulsory association according to all rules of legal doctrine' and that this association is 'essentially determined by compulsion yet based on free contract' (ibid. 107). Once again, see the commentary by Kahn-Freund.

[22] M. M. Postan, *The Medieval Economy and Society* (Harmondsworth, 1975), 105, 167.

[23] G. A. Cohen, 'On Some Criticisms of Historical Materialism', *Proceedings of the Aristotelian Society*, Supplement (1970).

the main way of conceptualizing social change within Durkheimian and normative functionalist sociology. From the latter perspective, deviation is seen either as a form of individual pathology or as a 'subcultural' adaptation to the dominant institutional order.

Completely alien to this viewpoint is Marx's general thesis that 'new higher relations of production never appear before the material conditions of their existence have matured in the womb of the old society'.[24] These conditions, he believed, were already highly developed in the most advanced capitalist societies of his day, in which there existed a glaring contradiction between 'the general social power into which capital develops on the one hand, and the private power of the individual capitalists over these social conditions of production on the other'.[25] This is why he could argue that 'the transformation of scattered private property, arising from individual labour, into capitalist private property is, naturally, a process, incomparably more protracted, violent, and difficult, than the transformation of capitalistic private property, already practically resting on socialised production, into socialised property'.[26] The agency of this transformation is the proletariat, 'a class always increasing in numbers and disciplined, united, organised by the very mechanism of the process of capitalist production itself'.[27] But these and other equally familiar statements provide no more than a very general understanding of how the contradiction between socialized production and private ownership creates conditions conducive to proletarian revolutionary action.

[24] Marx and Engels, *Selected Works*, i. 329.

[25] Marx, *Capital*, iii. 264.

[26] Ibid. i. 789. This transformation, the expropriation of the capitalist class, is facilitated by the cannibalistic propensity of capitalists themselves: by the action of the immanent laws of capitalist production itself, by the centralization of capital. 'One capitalist kills many' (ibid. 788). Nevertheless, Marx has little to say about the crucial question of communist relations of production, except that 'Surplus labour in general, as labour performed over and above given requirements, must always remain' because it will be required as 'an insurance against accidents, and by the necessary and progressive expansion of the process of reproduction in keeping with the development and needs and growth of population' (ibid. iii. 819). But the institutional means by which this surplus is consensually set on one side remain as obscure as those which would ensure the free association of producers rationally regulating their 'interchange with nature'. These are naturally just the sort of problems Durkheim seizes upon in *Socialism*, ed. A. Gouldner (London, 1962).

[27] Marx, *Capital*, i. 789.

In approaching this problem it is useful to distinguish between those conditions resulting from system contradictions which take the form of periodic crises and those conditions which take the form of structural changes in production relations themselves. For Marx, economic crises reflected the way in which the growing concentration and centralization of capital within private ownership relations simultaneously promoted and restricted the development of productive forces. In this sense, the 'real barrier' to the socialization of productive forces was 'capital itself'; and the diversity of system contradictions or crisis mechanisms identified by Marx's successors in economic theory have been variations on this central theme. But, like Marx himself, these writers have had remarkably little to say about the relationship between changes in macro-economic conditions and the development of class consciousness and class formation.[28] Either economic factors (such as levels of wages and unemployment) are assumed to have fairly direct consequences for class action or else their mediation is treated as highly complex and marginal to, if not outside the scope of, the economic theorization of the crisis mechanism *per se*. It is therefore convenient to postpone the discussion of the effects of changes in these kinds of economic conditions to a later stage, when more has been said about the nature of the Marxist action schema. There remains, however, the question of how the contradiction between the growing socialization of production and the private ownership of the means of production is to be understood at the level of social integration; that is, as a form of structural change which is seen as being directly conducive to the development of class struggle over the control of the production process itself.

III

The socialization of production refers to the progressive transformation of the two kinds of production relations which Marx identifies as the twin characteristics of the labour process: first,

---

[28] See, e.g. P. A. Baran and P. M. Sweezy, *Monopoly Capital* (New York, 1966), J. O'Connor, *The Fiscal Crisis of the State* (London, 1973), A. Glyn and B. Sutcliffe, *British Capitalism, Workers and the Profits Squeeze* (Harmondsworth, 1972). The chief exception to this is E. Mandel, *Late Capitalism* (London, 1978).

the control of the capitalist over the work of the labourer; and, secondly, the capitalist's appropriation of the product of this work.[29] Later reformulations of the distinction have taken account of the growing separation of economic powers and legal ownership. For example, Ohlin Wright uses the term the term 'possession' to refer to 'control over the production process, or control over *how* things are produced'; and 'economic ownership' to refer to 'control over the flow of investments into production, or, more concretely, over *what* is produced'.[30] Both are powers that may be and often are exercised by others than the formal legal owners of the capital. Marx regarded the divorce of ownership and control as one of the most important aspects of the socialization process, since it signified the increasingly redundant, purely rentier, nature of ownership *per se* and the transference of powers of possession and real ownership to salaried managers, part of whose function— the co-ordination of the labour process—already placed them with other productive workers in the category of the 'collective labourer'. The way in which capitalists, in pursuing their immediate ends, create conditions that progressively augment the powers attaching to the collective labourer is at the heart of Marx's idea of socialization of production relations and of the sense in which the forces of production come into contradiction with the relations of private property.

'Forces of production' is a term that has given rise to much controversy, largely because it is unclear whether it should be taken to refer simply to the means of production and labour power or should also include *de facto* production relations expressing powers of possession and real economic ownership. But unless the latter is the preferred interpretation, it is difficult to see what

[29] Marx, *Capital*, i. 165.

[30] E. O. Wright, *Class, Crisis and the State* (London, 1978), 68–74. In a similar way, E. Balibar distinguishes between 'real appropriation' ('the technical division of labour' with the 'function of the capitalist as organizer of production'), and 'relations of expropriation' ('the function of the capitalist as exploiter of labour power'). ('The Basic Concepts of Historical Materialism', in L. Althusser and E. Balibar, *Reading Capital* (London, 1972), 214, 235, 246.) Cohen's distinction between 'work' and 'ownership' relations is comparable: the former refer to those 'between persons and persons or between persons and productive forces which obtain when persons employ productive forces to make products', whereas the latter 'stipulate ownership by persons of productive forces or of persons *or* relations which entail such ownership relations' ('On Some Criticisms of Historical Materialism', p. 127).

meaning can be attached to the idea that the contradiction between forces and relations of production manifests itself socially as that between the growing socialization of the labour process and the private ownership of the means of production.

On this subject, Marx's views are far from unequivocal. In a frequently cited source, the Preface to *The Critique of Political Economy*, he identifies the 'economic structure' with 'relations of production' in contrast to the 'material forces of production'; and elsewhere likewise equates the 'forces of production' with the 'material forces of production'.[31] This narrow view of productive forces is further emphasized by his observation that 'Machinery is only a productive force. The modern workshop, which is based on the use of machinery, is a social relation of production, or economic category.'[32] According to these definitions, the actual organization of production would appear to be placed in the category of the relations rather than the forces of production. Yet Marx also writes that 'a certain mode of production, or industrial stage, is always combined with a certain mode of co-operation, or social stage, and this mode of co-operation is itself a "productive force".[33] He also speaks of 'the productive forces resulting from co-operation and division of labour' as 'natural forces of social labour'.[34]

It is presumably this ambiguity which has licensed widely divergent definitions of forces of production which range all the way from the narrowly technological to those that include a

---

[31] Marx, *Selected Writings in Sociology and Social Philosophy*, ed. T. B. Bottomore and M. Rubel, p. 147.

[32] Ibid. 93.

[33] K. Marx and F. Engels, *The German Ideology* (London, 1940), 18.

[34] Marx, *Capital*, i. 382. It is implausible that this identification of co-operation and division of labour as 'productive forces' can be dismissed by the argument that Marx's lack of consistency in equating forces of production with the means of production and labour power is due to the fact that *Produktivkraft* can mean either productive force or simply productivity. This is the view taken by W. H. Shaw, *Marx's Theory of History* (London, 1978), in seeking to maintain a strictly 'technological-determinist' interpretation. Following Cohen, 'On Some Criticisms of Historical Materialism', he assigns work relations to the category of relations of production. In a later work, however, Cohen has modified his position by placing what he calls 'material work relations' 'alongside the productive forces as a substratum of the economic structure', while maintaining that they are not in themselves productive forces. See G. A. Cohen, *Karl Marx's Theory of History: A Defence* (Oxford, 1978), 113.

variety of cultural and even political elements.[35] In the face of this
definitional choice it is necessary to bear in mind that, in whatever
form it is manifested at the level of system integration (e.g.
economic crises), the contradiction between forces and relations
of production at the level of social integration has to do with class
struggle whose primary locus is powers of possession and real
economic ownership. It is a conflict between existing and emerging
powers; between the legally defined but increasingly ineffective
powers of owners of the means of production and the potential
and increasingly effective powers of the emergent 'collective
labourer'. In an early and incisive contribution, Martynow argued
that 'the contradiction between the forces and relations of production takes the form of a contradiction between two kinds of
production relations, that is, an internal contradiction in a society's production relations'. On the one hand there are 'socio-
economic production relations (capitalistic private ownership of
the means of production)' and on the other 'the work relationships
associated with the technical organization of production (the social
nature of labour)'. At a certain stage, the two types of relations
correspond. But this unity is transformed into its opposite when
property or ownership relations cease to facilitate the development of the technical relations of production and come to act as
their fetters. 'Technology advances, and, closely related to, and
parallel with this, the organisation of labour is transformed, so
that increasingly socialised production relations come into ever
greater contradiction with socio-economic, capitalist, production
relations, until finally the capitalist integument is burst asunder.'[36]

[35] An example of the former is that the concept of productive forces 'denotes,
roughly, the physical "hardware" of production and communication (plant,
machinery, computers, railways, etc.) and also the system of knowledge on which
their development and application depends', whereas the 'social relations of
production' refers to 'the property institutions, work organization, class structure,
and the various other institutions whereby a given productive system is located
within a specific political economy' (R. Hyman and I. Brough, *Social Values and
Industrial Relations* (London, 1975), 248). A wider interpretation of productive
forces is that they 'ultimately include not only technical instruments, but also the
application of scientific knowledge to the perfection of those instruments and
ultimately science itself; not only a population of working strengths but also the
technical and cultural customs of this population . . . not only techniques, but also
a certain organization of labour, or even a social and political organization
("planning" is an obvious example), etc.' (Balibar, 'The Basic Concepts of
Historical Materialism', p. 234.)

[36] A. Martynow, 'Die Theorie des beweglichen Gleichgewichts der Gesellschaft

Work relations, immediate production relations, the technical division of labour: some such term is obviously crucial for referring to the social relations associated with the forces of production. A most useful one, which also serves to bring out their potentially oppositional nature, is Burawoy's concept of relations *in* production, in contradistinction to relations *of* production.[37]

From this viewpoint, the importance Marx attached to the socialization of production relations might be understood as follows. This process not only created conditions conducive to collective action on the part of the proletariat, but also one of the major conditions under which the proletariat as 'collective labourer' would become increasingly aware of the way in which its *de facto* powers of control over the production process came into irreconcilable opposition to the more and more purely formal rights of control vested in the private owners of the means of production. At one pole stood the collective labourer, objectively and potentially in control of production; at the other the pure rentier. For Marx, both were the outcome of the concentration and centralization of capital.

In an elaboration of this thesis, Engels speaks of the 'socialization of great masses of means of production which we may meet with in the different kinds of joint stock companies', a development that reaches its culmination in the formation of 'trusts', through which 'the whole of the particular industry is turned into one gigantic joint stock company' and 'production without any definite plan in capitalistic society capitulates to the production upon a definite plan of invading socialistic society'.[38] This growing

---

und die Wechselbeziehungen zwischen Gesellschaft und Milieu', *Unter dem Banner des Marxismus*, 4 (1930), 109–10. Martynow cites many different contexts in which Marx refers to the forces of production as including the division of labour or organization of work. Martynow's chief target is Bukharin, whom he criticizes for failing to grasp that Marx conceives of productive forces from two different standpoints: the 'materialistic' and that of 'political economy', which correspond to the 'natural' and 'social' aspects of the phenomenon. A section of the original article is reprinted, under the title 'Kritik an Bucharins Identifikation der Produktivkraefte mit der Produktionstechnik', in *Der Marxismus*, i, ed. I. Fetscher (Munich, 1963), 215–21.

[37] M. Burawoy, *Manufacturing Consent* (Chicago, 1979), 15; also 'The Politics of Production and the Production of Politics', in M. Zeitlin (ed.), *Political Power and Social Theory* (Greenwich, Conn., 1980), i. 264–5.

[38] Marx and Engels, *Selected Works*, ii. 135. Engels is careful to note, however, that 'this is so far still to the benefit of the capitalists', and that, even though the

interdependence of centralized capitals, which increasingly reveals the social character of production and inherent instability of the capitalist economy, is a development which Lenin describes as follows:

The socialization of labour by capitalist production does not consist in the fact that people work under one roof (that is only a small part of the process), but in the fact that the concentration of capital is accompanied by the specialization of social labour, by a reduction in the number of capitalists in any given branch of industry and an increase in the number of special branches of industry—in the fact that many scattered processes of production are merged into one social process of production.

The result is that,

when work comes to a standstill in a larger enterprise, which is engaged in a highly specialized branch of industry and is therefore working almost for the whole of society and which, in turn, is dependent on the whole of society (for the sake of simplicity I take a case where socialization has attained a culminating point), work is bound to come to a standstill in all the other enterprises of society . . . the whole of production thus becomes fused into a single social process of production; yet each enterprise is conducted by a single capitalist, is dependent on his will and pleasure and turns over the social products to him as his private property. Is it not clear that the form of production comes into irreconcilable contradiction with the form of appropriation?

In this account of the objective nature of socialization, Lenin concludes: 'I have described only the material process, only the change in the relations of production, without touching on the social aspect of the process, the fact that the workers become united, welded together and organized, since it is a derivative and subsidiary phenomenon.'[39]

But like Marx's writings on the subject, this leaves rather obscure the exact manner in which the development of relations in production creates conditions under which it would be possible for the proletariat to entertain and make demands that went beyond what would now be called 'aggressive economism and

---

state will 'ultimately have to undertake the direction of production', this would not 'do away with the capitalistic nature of the productive forces' (ibid. 135–6). This is now a common theme in some Marxist writings on the limits of the socialization of production.

[39] V. I. Lenin, *Selected Works* (2 vols.; Moscow, 1950, 1947), i. 148–9.

defensive control'. Indeed, Marx's observations on the labour process suggest quite a different outcome. A very important instance is his conclusion that there is an 'absolute contradiction between the technical necessities of Modern Industry and the social character inherent in its capitalist form'.[40] This arises because the manufacturing division of 'detail' labour, which was a precondition of the introduction of machinery, has now become incompatible with technological requirements of modern industry, with 'associated labour' and the 'co-operative character of the labour process'. This technical necessity

compels society, under penalty of death, to replace the detail-worker of today, crippled by life-long repetition of one and the same trivial operation, and thus reduced to a mere fragment of a man, by the fully developed individual, fit for a variety of labours, ready to face any change of production, and to whom the different social functions he performs are but so many modes of giving free scope to his natural and acquired powers.[41]

Marx was no doubt encouraged in this belief by the syndicalist movement of his day. Nevertheless, everything in his analysis of the organization of the labour process under capitalism led to just the opposite conclusion: namely, that, far from promoting the kind of polytechnical workers who would be able to take over production in the factory and society at large, manufacturing industry was creating a proletarianized mass of unskilled workers for whom the assumption of such a task was objectively more and more remote. It is this theme, rather than his hopeful observations on the technical necessities of 'Modern Industry', which prefigures and authenticates the now prevalent view that it is the nature of relations of production which is decisive for the development of forces of production and correspondingly for the reproduction of relations in production.[42] After the First World War the factory councils' movement briefly gave some credence to the idea of the power of 'associated labour', to its capacity to 'set to work' the system of production. But the growing concentration and central- ization of capital, the increasing complexity of the social division

[40] Marx, *Capital*, i. 493.
[41] Ibid. 494.
[42] See, e.g., O'Connor, *The Fiscal Crisis of the State*, pp. 111, 121; Burawoy, 'The Politics of Production and the Production of Politics'.

of labour, and the ever closer control over the labour process by capital that itself became more and more depersonalized and objectified—all of which Marx had correctly anticipated—created conditions under which the prospect of the emergence of an anti-system of the associated producers can now be well described as 'the myth of collective appropriation'.[43] In one sense, Marx was correct in thinking that capitalism produces a collective worker (not to mention a 'global' capital whose agents and beneficiaries are less and less meaningfully distinct as a class fit for prospective expropriation). But capitalist relations of production have also led to relations in production which prevent workers in particular from identifying themselves with such as abstract, objective entity. For this reason, it is understandable that the idea of the collective worker, so central to Marx's understanding of revolutionary transformation, seldom finds mention in contemporary theories of capitalist society.

IV

In the theory of the collective worker, the assumptions about social action that relate objective conditions to collective behaviour are rudimentary. The same is true of more recent theories seeking to account for the lack of revolutionary working-class consciousness in contemporary capitalist societies. In general, they take two forms. One is that capitalism has not yet produced conditions conducive to revolutionary consciousness because the nature of system contradiction has undergone substantial change since Marx identified its basic form. The other is that Marx's theory was in any case only a statement of abstract tendencies and that the consequences of system contradiction for working-class consciousness depend on specific historical circumstances. In other words, there is a distinction between the theorization of the dynamics of the mode of production and the exigencies of the 'concrete social formation', or the particular form of social integration. But what is significant about both types of argument is that they are not very explicit about the action schema linking system

---

[43] The term is that of A. Gorz, in his book *Farewell to the Working Class* (London, 1982), which stands out for its full and uncompromising treatment of this vital, but neglected, theme of the 'collective worker'.

contradiction and class polarization, or conversely system integration and social cohesion.

In the case of theories of system contradiction or integration, attention is concentrated on factors exacerbating or ameliorating some kind of crisis mechanism which in turn is seen as resulting in changes in broadly defined economic conditions or class situations. But such theories seldom go far towards explaining how these conditions give rise to class action or inaction, and usually rest on some simple utilitarian assumptions which posit a fairly direct connection between economic circumstances and social behaviour. The search for ever newer types of structurally determined crisis tendencies and counteracting mechanisms has certainly been the orthodox way of attempting to deal with the basic Marxian problem of disorder. But whether the latter can be resolved satisfactorily simply by reference to conditions of the situation of action is much more debatable. First of all, the argument that capitalism has not yet produced conditions conducive to proletarian revolution might be said to imply not only a serious deficiency in Marx's own estimation of the connection between growing system contradiction and imminent class polarization, but also the shortcomings of any general theory that postulates a quick and ready connection between economic conditions and resultant class action. Ollman puts the general point very well when he writes that

both critics and defenders of Marx alike have sought to explain the failure of the working class to assume its historic role by tampering with his account of capitalist conditions. Thus, his critics assert that the lot of workers has improved, that the middle class has not disappeared, etc., and, at the extreme, that these conditions were never really as bad as Marx claimed. His defenders have tried to show that it was relative pauperization he predicted, that big businesses are getting larger, etc., and, after Lenin, that imperialist expansion permitted capitalists to buy off workers. Such rejoinders, however, whether in criticism or defence, miss the essential point that for the whole of Marx's lifetime the situation in the capitalist world was adequate, by his own standards, for the revolution he expected to take place.[44]

---

[44] B. Ollman, 'Towards Class Consciousness Next Time: Marx and the Working Class', *Politics and Society*, 3 (1972).

The evidence certainly supports the view that Marx held fairly consistently to the belief that, under the conditions present in his own day, 'the proletariat would develop revolutionary consciousness with relative ease'.[45] Against this, of course, it is not difficult to extract from his writings passing observations presenting quite different scenarios, including one that places revolution well into the future, when capitalism will, so it is held, face its ultimately insoluble contradiction with the advent of fully automated production.

Whether or not this proves to be the case, the fact is that present-day theories of capitalist contradictions rest on motivational assumptions which are far less explicit than those that can be found in Marx's writings. Such issues appear to have been swept aside in the wake created by the search for ever newer endemic sources of disorder underlying the remarkable endurability and social equilibrium of advanced capitalist societies.[46] The same can be said of recent developments in Marxist political theory, the chief feature of which has been a variety of functionalist interpretations in which the state is seen as a structure that works objectively to secure the conditions necessary to capitalist accumulation, and in which actors are the bearers of 'structural determinisms'. Since they are premissed on it, these theories cannot abandon the idea of fundamental system contradiction. But they go a long way in providing a hedge against the likelihood of its proving a source of social and political disequilibirum.[47]

This embarrassment of theoretical riches is only the latest expression of a century-long attempt to accommodate the Marxian canon to the refractoriness of capitalism. But, although modern Marxism in its multifold identity enjoys such a wide range of

[45] This is the conclusion of a careful survey of the Marxian corpus by Carol Johnson, 'Reformism and Commodity Fetishism', *New Left Review*, 119 (1980), 93.

[46] One result is the ingenuity required to reconcile the radically divergent assumptions of competing schools and to find in them some common Marxian provenance. A familiar conclusion is that the different forms of system contradiction should be conceived of as marking progressive stages in capitalist development; see Wright, *Class, Crisis and the State*, ch. 3.

[47] For an exposition and critique of these theories, see C. Crouch, 'The State, Capital and Liberal Democracy', in C. Crouch (ed.), *State and Economy in Contemporary Capitalism* (London, 1979); also the short but incisive section on 'Class Conflict and the State', in A. Przeworski, *Capitalism and Social Democracy* (Cambridge, 1986).

options that it can hardly be faulted, any one of its prognoses is just as likely to be overtaken by events as is any of those of 'bourgeois' political, economic, or social theory. For the latter, however, this is less serious, in the sense that the felt need for an integrated theory of society is, for better or worse, less exigent. But, from the present viewpoint, the most striking feature of these exercises in Marxist revisionism is that the analysis of what is seen in the particular case as the basic system contradiction is not matched by a correspondingly thorough analysis of its consequences for class action. This deficiency in political economy is complemented by the increasingly structuralist nature of recent theories of class on the other. As will be seen in due course, the latter have been preoccupied with the definition and location of class boundaries, a debate in which the traditional problem of class formation has been either neglected or explicitly rejected. In one way or another, then, attempts to provide systemic or structuralist explanations of the lack of revolutionary consciousness have not led to any comprehensive review of the assumptions entering into what might be identified as a Marxist action schema.[48]

These assumptions are even less likely to be made explicit in historical studies of class formation. It is sometimes claimed that there is a necessary distinction between the analysis of modes of production and the analysis of 'concrete social formations'; and that the work of the historian complements the abstract theory of system integration and contradiction by showing how the latter has to be modified to take account of specific conditions in each particular case. This co-operation is most evident in Marxist economics and economic history, mainly because it is here that the theory of system dynamics is most explicit. Marx's formulation of the law of the tendency of the rate of profit to fall is exact enough to take account of a limited number of exacerbating and

---

[48] It is only relatively recently that this problem has been raised from a quite different perspective with the advent of 'rational choice' Marxism. In the latter, the utilitarian action schema basic to, but hitherto implicit in, most Marxian and Marxist explanations of class action has found a novel and powerful application. At the same time, this type of theorizing has indicated its distinct and familiar limitations. These are most generally to be found in the need to reintroduce the notion of nonrational, or normatively oriented, action. On this, see especially, J. Elster, *The Cement of Society: A Study of Social Order* (Cambridge, 1989).

counteracting factors which in turn can be drawn upon and adapted to explain a variety of historically unique contradictions, such as a 'fiscal crisis' in the United States or that brought on by a 'profits squeeze' in Britain.[49] But the analytical precision and versatility of these theories is due to their being theories of a very special kind, and this incurs a certain cost. They are primarily economic theories, having small, if any, relevance to the explanation of social integration and conflict. This is mainly because they are theories based on a utilitarian action schema, which, like that of 'bourgeois' economics, predicates rational actors oriented to narrowly 'material' ends.

When it comes to explanations of class polarization or social equilibrium, theorists and historians can be epistemological poles apart.[50] Quite generally the historical sociology of concrete social formations is characterized less by the strict application or testing of well-defined theories of class than by the identification of unique conditions accounting for the presence (or more usually the absence) of proletarian revolutionary consciousness. The action schema linking conditions to consciousness remains implicit in such accounts, being embedded in the interpretation of a particular course of events. Consider, for example, the following summary of the fate of the English working class, which attributes the deflection of its revolutionary impulse to the peculiar consciousness of the bourgeoisie:

To become a new hegemonic force, capable of dominating society in its turn, the English working class absolutely required a consciousness containing the elements ignored by, or excised from, the consciousness of the English bourgeoisie. This was the task that was completely, tragically, beyond the powers of the English working class. Nothing else was beyond its powers. In numbers, in essential solidarity and homogeneity, in capacity for organization, in tenacity, in moral and civil courage, the English working class was, and still is, one of the very greatest of social forces. And it has always existed in one of the least militarized of bourgeois states. No external fetters could ever have withstood this

---

[49] See, respectively, O'Connor, *The Fiscal Crisis of the State*, and Glyn and Sutcliffe, *British Capitalism, Workers and the Profits Squeeze*.

[50] The principal example being the excoriation of Althusserian Marxism by E. P. Thompson, *The Poverty of Theory* (London, 1978).

colossus. It was held by intangible threads of consciousness, by the mentality produced by distinctive conditions and experience.[51]

It is not the merit, but the form, of this argument that is significant, since it is fairly typical of appeals to equally distinctive conditions and experience in most other explanations of the lack of a revolutionary working-class consciousness in mature capitalist societies.[52] In this respect, Marxist historical sociology is no different from any other.[53] As a result, what is distinctively Marxist about it is unclear. If a diversity of conditions, the most important of which are accidentally related to the capitalist mode of production as such,[54] prove to be so decisively important in shaping class consciousness, then it is disingenuous to argue that the historical analysis of concrete social formations is in any strict sense complementary to the abstract theory of the capitalist mode of production in general. It is as if a scientific law was invariably overridden by initial conditions it could not even anticipate. This does not imply that it is impossible to arrive at generalizations about the determinants of class consciousness; only that on present evidence there is nothing specifically Marxist about them.

Within Marxist theory, then, it is necessary to distinguish between well-articulated economic theories of various forms of system contradiction on the one hand, and on the other the much less theoretically precise historical or sociological accounts of how

---

[51] T. Nairn, 'The English Working Class', in R. Blackburn (ed.), *Ideology and Social Science* (London, 1975), p. 201. It is notable that Nairn carries this 'historical accident' thesis to its full limits by arguing that 'the formation of the English working class was a major tragedy. It was also one—and perhaps the greatest single—phase of the tragedy of modern times, the failure of the European working class to overthrow capital and fashion the new society that material conditions long ago made possible . . . If the working class of only one major industrial nation had succeeded, the course of history would have been radically changed.' (p. 199)

[52] For an equally particularistic interpretation, see Davis, 'Why the U.S. Working Class is Different'.

[53] For example, in the case of the French working class, D. Gallie singles out the effects of the First World War as being crucial for its subsequent development; see his *Social Inequality and Class Radicalism in France and Britain* (Cambridge, 1983). On the significance of 'archaic' pre-capitalist institutions during the formative stages of capitalist industrialization as well as other historically contingent determinants of working-class movements, see M. H. Mann, *Consciousness and Action among the Western Working Class* (London, 1973).

[54] Mann's conclusion that 'I have located major determinants of class consciousness outside the necessary structure of capitalism itself' (ibid. 43) is one that finds strong support in the subsequent literature.

conditions resulting from these contradictions are related to class consciousness and class conflict. Whilst the former are based on a more or less explicit utilitarian action schema, they have little bearing on class formation. The latter, by contrast, usually provide such dense interpretations of particular phases or instances of class formation that it is difficult to extract from them any common body of assumptions that might constitute what might be identified as a distinctively Marxist theory of the structuring of social action.[55]

Before pursuing this theme, a most important qualification is called for. The foregoing account of the ways in which Marxist theory has found an accommodation to its major problem of disorder might be thought to be seriously incomplete in failing to mention attempts to explain the lack of revolutionary consciousness as the outcome of some form of systematic ideological domination or indoctrination. This type of theory is indeed the chief conceptual means which has been used to accommodate the political sociology of class formation to the implications of the political economy of system contradiction. But, because theories of ideological domination have now come to play such a prominent role in Marxist class analysis, they deserve special discussion. This will come later, after establishing the need for their promotion, which is to be found in the properties of original Marxian action schema.

[55] The following discussion therefore does not take account of the kind of Marxist functionalism in which workers, like any other 'agents', are demoted to the status of 'bearers' of structural (especially ideological) determinations. Such theories 'solve' the problem of disorder by banishing the 'problematic of the subject' but only at the cost of having it reappear and run riot in the contingency of the 'concrete' or 'conjectural' class struggle. On this, see ch. 16 below.

10.

THE THEORY OF ACTION

I

On the face of it, it seems improbable that there is any such thing as *the* Marxist theory of action. Marxists have always laid claim to a uniquely privileged understanding of society through their possession of a body of theory which by its singular unity transcends the artificial specialism of the 'bourgeois' social sciences. But this claim is surely invalid and lacking in force. It is not simply that Marxism is now in such a state of epistemological disarray that some of its illuminati have denied the very possibility of one of the two subjects in which Marxist scholarship has excelled: namely, history.[1] It is also that, in practice, Marxism exhibits very much the selfsame division of intellectual labour as that of 'bourgeois' social science. Economic theorists go their several ways without paying much attention to problems of class formation and class consciousness.[2] On the other hand, students of the political sociology of class do not as a matter of course relate their work to Marxist economic theory in any systematic way, if at all.[3] Finally, there is a quite distinctive school of philosophical anthropology which centres its attention on the concept of alienation.[4]

---

[1] B. Hindess and P. Q. Hirst, *Pre-capitalist Modes of Production* (London, 1975). The other subject is the much more untouchable discipline of Marxist economic theory.

[2] Note, e.g., the exiguous treatment of the problem of class formation in expositions of Marxist economic theory. This is just as evident in more recent writings as it was in the earlier classical statements such as P. M. Sweezy, *The Theory of Capitalist Development* (London, 1949); Baran and Sweezy, *Monopoly Capital*, and Mandel, *Late Capitalism*.

[3] This applies to R. Miliband, *The State in Capitalist Society* (London, 1969), and N. Poulantzas, *Political Power and Social Classes* (London, 1973), the two works that have dominated the discussion of the subject in the last decade.

[4] Representative of this genre are A. Heller, *The Theory of Need in Marx* (London, 1976), B. Ollman, *Alienation: Marx's Concept of Man in Capitalist Society* (Cambridge, 1971), and I. Meszaros, *Marx's Theory of Alienation* (London, 1970).

Writings on this subject have only the most tenuous connection
with the substance of Marxist economic theory, and the majority
of leading Marxist political sociologists find the whole notion of
alienation of small relevance, if not downright heretical.

Given that contemporary Marxism exhibits such a heterogene-
ity of persuasion, is it reasonable to suppose that underlying this
diversity there is a coherent theory of class action? This is not
a question that can be answered within the confines of the
present work without drastic simplification. But it may be that
there is some advantage to be gained from pursuing this matter
without too much subtlety, and even with a certain bluntness,
since no small part of the discussion that complicates the subject
appears, in however sophisticated a manner, to fudge the basic
issues.

From a sociological viewpoint, the most crucial aspect of the
problem is the link between system and social integration; and in
Marxism the economic theory of system contradiction is the only
chain of reasoning that is at all well forged. What is at stake, then,
is whether, underlying the diverse strands of Marxist interpretation, there exists a unitary action schema which is both internally
coherent and capable of relating the economic theory of capitalist
accumulation to the political sociology or the philosophical anthropology of proletarian revolution. The elucidation of this connection has always been, and still is, the most problematic feature of
Marxist social thought. The thesis that will be pursued from now
on is that the link between system and social integration has been
established mainly by means of a basically utilitarian concept of
action which leads to unstable and contradictory explanations of
conflict and order.

In concentrating on the extent to which the Marxist theory of
class action represents a modified version of the utilitarian action
schema, there is no intention of trying to demote the significance
of the Hegelian influence on Marx's general view of the nature of
historical development and the ultimate goal of unalienated
human existence. That would be preposterous. Nevertheless, it is
quite clear that, in working out his 'law of motion' on the capitalist
mode of production, and thereby giving concrete meaning to the
idea of 'economic determinism', Marx was, as he readily admitted,
very heavily influenced by the thinking of those political economists who represented a certain stage in the development of the

utilitarian theory of action.[5] It is arguable that this theory of action, which plays such a central role in Marx's account of the internal contradictions of the capitalist economic system is also the linchpin of his much less clearly articulated analysis of the dynamics of class revolution. At any rate, this is the hypothesis that will be explored in the following discussion.

II

The two chief distinguishing characteristics of the classical utilitarian position are, first, that the ultimate ends of actors are 'random', and, second, that, in adapting their means to their given ends, actors are governed by the standard of 'rationality'. The randomness of ends implies that ultimate ends are idiosyncratic and that they are 'given' in the sense that the problem of the social determination and moral integration of the ends of actors lies outside the scope of the theory of action. The rationality of action is measured against the norm of a scientific knowledge of the conditions of action and of the most efficient use of means to attain given ends. By the time of Malthus and Ricardo, however, the Hobbesian concept of the actor as a rational individual egoist had been replaced by the notion of equally rational class egoists whose proximate ends are systematically determined by their position within specific production relations. By this time also the post-Hobbesian solutions of the problem of order, which took the form of a political or economic theory of the 'natural identity of interests' (thereby solving at least the problem of the integration of the proximate ends of actors), had been replaced by a theory of the 'natural divergence of interests'.[6] The assumption that the ends of actors are random because they are purely idiosyncratic and not subject to social determination had, therefore, been abandoned. But the idea that ends, even proximate ends, are random in the sense that they lack integration through a 'common value system' is one that may be said to have persisted, at least implicitly. The problem of moral integration was peripheral to the

[5] See Parsons, *The Structure of Social Action*, pp. 107–10, 488–95, and A. D. Lindsay, *Karl Marx's Capital: An Introductory Essay* (London, 1925), ch. 3, 'Economic Determinism'.

[6] See E. Halevy, *The Growth of Philosophic Radicalism* (Boston, 1955), 319, and, on the class nature of this divergence of interests, pp. 329–33.

type of theory that centred increasingly on the antagonisms of interest between capitalists, labourers, and landlords. Moreover, the key assumption that class actors pursued their given interests according to the standard of rationality precluded systematic consideration of the normative determination of action.[7]

Marx modified this reconstituted utilitarian action schema in two main ways, both of which are related to his claim that his predecessors in political economy had treated the behaviour and motives of individuals in capitalist society as universally valid instead of historically specific. First of all, he postulates an asymmetry between the ends of capitalists and proletarians by ascribing to the latter class the extra-systemic end of its self-transformation while the former is confined to acting out its self-destructive role as pure *homo economicus*. This introduces the problem of what may be called the end-shift of the proletariat. But, despite this Hegelian gloss,[8] Marx's operative theory of action remains confined within the same limits of the utilitarian problematic he sought to supercede, because it is still characterized by the fact that the ends of the two main actors are 'random' and 'given'. Ends are random in the sense that, although they are structured by production relations (that is in the last analysis by command over resources), they are also for the same reason fundamentally irreconcilable and thus beyond the scope of any moral integration through a system of common values. The extra-systemic end of the proletariat is also 'given', in the sense that it is an objectively necessary end. It is not simply a moral goal which the proletariat has to be socialized into accepting, but rather one that is determined by the social logic of capitalist society itself. Although the proletariat must play an active role in becoming

---

[7] In the sense, for example, that Adam Smith's *Theory of Moral Sentiments* contains assumptions about constraints on self-interest which complement, but are not explicitly related to, the economic analysis of *The Wealth of Nations*.

[8] But not only a Hegelian way of thinking of class interests. M. Seliger, *The Marxist Conception of Ideology* (Cambridge, 1977), 232–3, is certainly correct in arguing that the 'attribution of interests, systems of values and ideologies to social classes in a certain stage of historical development is a corollary of the historicist attribution of unique characteristics to a given era'. However, the tendency to attribute interests to classes was by no means foreign to the tradition of British political economy within which Marx's theory took shape. The fact that neither body of theory facilitates an understanding of concrete class action receives belated recognition by Cutler, *Marx's Capital and Capitalism Today*, pp. 232–3.

conscious of its true aim, this ultimate end is not in itself dependent on individual volition. Hence the famous aphorism:

It is not a matter of knowing what this or that proletarian, or even the proletariat as a whole, *conceives* as its aims at any particular moment. It is a question of knowing *what* the proletariat *is*, and what it must historically accomplish in accordance with its *nature*. Its aim and its historical activity are ordained for it, in a tangible and irrevocable way, by its own situation as well as by the whole organisation of present-day civil society.[9]

The proletariat's goal of transforming capitalism into communism is an end that is as analytically unproblematic as the capitalist's restricted, but equally given motive of profit maximization.

Secondly, this 'end-shift' of the proletariat is integrally bound up with Marx's revision of the rationality assumption of the utilitarian action schema. Corresponding to the asymmetry of the ends of capitalists and proletarians is the assumption of differential class rationality. The distinction between rationality in the sense of a technologically or economically rational adaptation of means to given ends, and 'reason' in the sense of a capacity to understand that rational action can be self-defeating, and hence, 'unreasonable', is a notion already present in the work of Locke,[10] who attributed this higher order rationality or reason to the propertied classes.[11] By contrast, Marx endows the proletariat with this same kind of reason, and it is indeed through its exercise, under conditions created by capitalist accumulation, that the end-shift of the proletariat occurs.

These rather compressed introductory remarks on the asymmetry of the ends of class actors and on the distinction between

---

[9] Marx, *Selected Writings*, pp. 232–3.

[10] See Parsons, *The Structure of Social Action*, p. 96. Referring to Locke's concept of the state of nature, Parsons notes that 'instead of being a *bellum omnium contra omnes*', it is, for Locke, 'a beneficent state of affairs, governed by Reason, the law of nature', and that what this implies is that 'men "being reasonable" ought to, and in general will in pursuit of their ends subordinate their actions, whatever these may be, to certain rules. The essential content of these rules is to respect the natural rights of others, to refrain from injuring them. This means that the choice of means in pursuit of ends is not guided solely by considerations of immediate efficiency, but that 'reason' in this sense is limited by "reason" in the other.'

[11] C. B. MacPherson, *The Political Theory of Possessive Individualism* (Oxford, 1977), 221–38.

rationality and reason will now be developed in such a way as to indicate the basic source of instability in explanations of the relationship between system contradiction and proletarian revolution.

III

Marx's view of the capitalist class is epitomized by his description of the 'rational miser' whose 'subjective aim' and 'sole motive' is the 'restless, never-ending process of profit making alone'. The rational pursuit of capital accumulation is determined by two conditions. The first draws on the distinction between production aimed at use value and production based on exchange value. In the former case, 'surplus-labour will be limited to a given set of wants which may be greater or less' and 'no boundless thirst for surplus-labour arises from the nature of production itself'. Production is 'kept within bounds by the very object it aims at, namely, consumption or the satisfaction of definite wants, an aim that lies altogether outside the sphere of circulation'. In a capitalist system, however, 'the circulation of money as capital is, on the contrary, an end in itself. The circulation of capital has therefore no limits.' The second condition is the competition between capitalists.

That which in the miser is a mere idiosyncracy, is, in the capitalist, the effect of the social mechanism of which he is but one of the wheels. Moreover, the development of capitalist production makes it constantly necessary to keep increasing the amount of capital laid out in a given undertaking, and competition makes the immanent laws of capitalist production to be felt by each individual capitalist, as external coercive laws.[12]

Marx's rational miser is thus the product not of fixed human nature but of specific social conditions. Nevertheless, the question of whether Marx was correct in accusing his forerunners in political economy of conflating this distinction is unimportant, because his concept of the capitalist as a rational accumulator is, in effect, just as utilitarian in character as his theory that individual capitalists, in rationally pursuing their given ends, unintendedly produce conditions that are irrational from the viewpoint of the

---

[12] Marx, *Capital*, i. 130–1, 219, 128, 129, 603, respectively.

capitalist class as a whole. He presents the capitalist only as the 'personification of an economic category', but his construct of the rational miser does not differ in its essentials from the concept of the actor which is to be found in theories of the natural identity or divergence of interests put forward by previous writers within the utilitarian tradition. Without this postulate of the capitalist as a rational class egoist, Marx's system cannot work. Each capitalist finds himself in a situation whose logic dictates that capital accumulation becomes his ultimate end, and, as a result of his rationally pursuing it, scientific knowledge in the form of technology becomes progressively incorporated into the means of production as the chief method of obtaining relative surplus value. This rising organic composition of capital not only provides the key to Marx's theory of system contradiction but serves to explain how capitalism creates all the major conditions conducive to proletarian revolt.

In turning to the concept of proletarian action the picture becomes more complicated. Like capitalists, workers are assumed to act rationally in pursuit of an end that is immediately given by the existing system of production. This is the wage that is necessary for maintaining and reproducing labour at a level of existence which is either purely physical or one that involves some 'traditional' standard of life. And, like the class situation of capitalists, that of the proletariat is characterized, initially at least, by competition among workers. But, unlike the capitalist class, the proletariat possesses a higher-order rationality, or faculty of reason, which enables it to acquire an understanding that the rational pursuit of its immediate ends is self-defeating, and that it has an ultimate end which can only be realized through the abolition of the capitalist system.[13] The nature of this postulated

---

[13] It is not altogether clear why capitalists should lack reason and be unable to grasp that the pursuit of their immediate individual ends is detrimental to their fundamental interests as a class. As Elster points out, Marx explains the introduction of factory legislation 'as being partly the result of the political activity of the workers and partly as the defence of the capitalist class against its own members, the idea being that the over-exploitation of the workers might threaten their physical reproduction and thus capitalism itself. The latter explanation either requires the collective interests of capitalists to overcome their individual interests or their long-term interest to overcome their short-term interest. Both ideas, however, are hard to square with what Marx says elsewhere about the possibility of solidarity between capitalists.' (J. Elster, *Logic and Society* (Chichester, 1978),

end-shift is identified by the distinction between a struggle over
the level of wages and a struggle over the 'wages system' itself.
The first goal is determined simply by a zero-sum conflict between
capitalist and proletarian, by 'a continuous struggle between
capital and labour, the capitalist constantly tending to reduce
wages to their physical minimum, and to extend the working day
to its physical maximum, while the working man constantly presses
in the opposite direction'.[14] From the viewpoint of Marx's theory
of 'human nature', this goal represents the alienated need engendered by capitalist relations of production: 'The need for money
is, therefore, the real need created by the modern economic
system, and the only need which it creates.'[15] By contrast, the
extra-systemic end of the proletariat is the unalienated condition
of 'socialised man, the associated producers, rationally regulating
their interchange with Nature, bringing it under their common
control, instead of being ruled by it as by the blind forces of
Nature; and achieving this with the least expenditure of energy
and under the conditions most favourable to, and worthy of, their
human nature'.[16] According to Marx, this end is not simply an
ideal standard but a state of affairs that is already prefigured in
the existing society. 'The working class ought not to forget that
they are fighting with effects but not with the causes of these
effects . . . they ought to understand that, with all the miseries it
imposes on them, the present system simultaneously engenders
the *material conditions* and the social forms necessary for an

---

139.) What Marx says elsewhere is 'that the individual bourgeois is always ready
to sacrifice the overall interests of his class to this or that private matter, and that
at each moment the bourgeoisie is prepared to sacrifice its general interest to the
most narrow-minded and squalid of interests ' (quoted by Seliger, *The Marxist
Conception of Ideology*, p. 68. Seliger also demonstrates fully the inconsistency of
Marx's assumption of the irrationality of bourgeois actors (pp. 50–7). The
conventional Marxist solution of this problem is to be found in the role of the
state. As Sweezy puts it, 'it is not inconsistent to say that State action may run
counter to the immediate interests of some or even all of the capitalists provided
only that the overriding aim of preserving the system intact is promoted' (Sweezy,
The Theory of Capitalist Development, p. 248). And, of course, the greater the
emphasis on the 'relative autonomy' of the state's economically and socially
stabilizing functions, the more the state can take on the role of the 'cunning of
reason' as far as the capitalist class is concerned.

[14] Marx and Engels, *Selected Works*, i. 402.
[15] Marx, *Early Writings*, p. 168.
[16] Marx, *Capital*, iii. 820.

economic reconstruction of society.'[17] This goal is not to be confused with any immediate interests of the working class or with any beliefs that might momentarily inform them. It is an 'ultimate end' that is determined by the operation of the capitalist system. Engels actually uses this term in his assessment of the situation of the US working class in 1887.

The causes that brought into existence the abyss between the working class and the capitalist class are the same in America as in Europe; the means of filling up that abyss are equally the same everywhere. Consequently, the platform of the American proletariat will, in the long run, coincide as the ultimate end to be attained with the one which, after sixty years of dissensions and discussions, has become the adopted platform of the great mass of the European militant proletariat. It will proclaim as the ultimate end the conquest of political supremacy by the working class, in order to effect the direct appropriation of all means of production by society at large, to be worked in common by all and for the account and benefit of all.[18]

The conditions that make this ultimate or extra-systemic end of the proletariat realizable are produced by capitalists rationally pursuing their own intra-systemic end. The increasing concentration and centralization of capital, the progressive socialization of the labour process, and the growing material and moral misery of the working class are all consequences of the general tendency of capitalist accumulation. But the mediating factor between these conditions and revolutionary action is the proletariat's faculty of reason, its capacity to grasp the connection between its immediate and its fundamental interest.[19]

  This is brought out very clearly by Wright when he says that

---

[17] Marx and Engels, *Selected Works*, i. 404.
[18] K. Marx and F. Engels, *Basic Writings in Politics and Philosophy*, ed. L. Feuer (New York, 1959), 491–2.
[19] The rationality assumption underlying Marx's conception of proletarian action is stressed at many points in Ollman, *Alienation*, pp. 114–15, 122–3, and esp. 238–9. See also C. W. Mills, *White Collar* (Oxford, 1951), 326, where he writes that 'underlying the general Marxian model there is always, in Louis Clair's words, the political psychology of "becoming conscious of inherent possibilities". This idea is just as rationalist as liberalism in its psychological assumptions. For the struggle that occurs proceeds on the rational recognition by competing classes of incompatible material interests; reflection links material fact and interested consciousness by a calculus of advantage. As Veblen correctly pointed out, the idea is utilitarian, and more closely related to Bentham than Hegel.' The inconsistencies between this rationality assumption of Marx and the 'public goods' assumption of

Class interests, therefore, are in a sense hypotheses about the objective of struggles which would occur if the actors in the struggle had a scientifically correct understanding of their situations. To make the claim that socialism is in the 'interests' of the working class is not simply to make a historical, moralistic claim that workers ought to be in favour of socialism nor to make a normative claim that they would be 'better off' in a socialist society, but rather to claim that if workers had a scientific understanding of the contradictions of capitalism, they would in fact engage in struggles for socialism.[20]

Marx did expect that workers would be able to come close to such an understanding, and mainly as a result of their own experience and powers of ratiocination. Indeed, this revolutionary consciousness of the proletariat would be a necessary condition of the success of genuine socialist revolution. His assumption that the proletariat could achieve its historically ascribed end-shift through the exercise of its faculty of reason is a view of action in which the utilitarian source of Marxian thinking merges into the Hegelian. Unlike previous revolutionary classes, the proletariat cannot simply pursue its immediate interests and entrust the consequences of its action to the 'cunning of reason'. As Lukács puts it, 'the dialectical relationship between immediate interests and objective impact on the whole of society is located *in the consciousness of the proletariat* itself'.[21] The fusion of immediate and fundamental interests comes about, so it is argued, through the process of revolutionary practice in which the proletariat's unfolding power of reason plays a crucial role. As it stands, however, the famous formula that the changing of men goes hand in hand with the changing of their circumstances possesses no more cogency than an incantation. To grasp its concrete meaning

---

his theory of collective proletarian action are brought out well by Olson, *The Logic of Collective Action*, pp. 105–10, and further elaborated by A. Buchanan, 'Revolutionary Motivation and Rationality', *Philosophy and Public Affairs*, (1980). The rationality assumption is also indispensable to the thesis of the primacy of productive forces, on which see Cohen, *Karl Marx's Theory of History*, pp. 151–3.

[20] Wright, *White Collar*, p. 89. It should be noted, however, that the 'scientific understanding' in question is not clarified. Moreover, careful examination of the problem of whether, in rationally pursuing even their material interests, workers would be led to opt for socialism does not necessarily yield a positive answer. See A. Przeworski, 'Material Interests, Class Compromise and the Transition to Socialism', *Politics and Society*, 10 (1980).

[21] Lukács, *History and Class Consciousness*, p. 71.

requires a specification of the nature of the men and circumstances in question. But, before turning to consider what these are, it is necessary to deal with one final issue that arises from the assumption that action is governed by the standard of scientific rationality. This is the explanation of 'irrational' action.

IV

Marx's belief that history would vindicate his theory is inseparable from his belief that his theory would prove to be a real historical force in just the same way as the reason of the proletariat with which it had an assignation. But this does not alter the fact that his theory *qua* theory only works by attributing rationality and reason to the actors it creates and must, therefore, also be able to account for irrational action. Moreover, it can hardly be said that history has been backward in providing cause for treating this problem very seriously. In general, social theory has found only two main ways of explaining deviations from rational action. The first, an integral part of utilitarian thinking, relies heavily on the concepts of 'ignorance' and 'error'. In other words, irrational action is seen to be due either to the actor's inadequate knowledge of the facts of the situation or to his imperfect understanding of the most efficient, that is, scientifically rational, means of attaining his ends. This type of explanation has always been central to Marxist theory, and it has figured more prominently as the problem of accounting for the aberration of the proletariat has become more exigent. What is referred to here is the analytical promotion of the concept of capitalist ideological domination, and, by implication, that of the false consciousness of the proletariat.[22] This concept has taken different forms, but, as will be seen in due course, the general use to which it has been put has had the effect of creating a high degree of instability in the theory of proletarian action.

The second way of explaining deviation from rational action does not play a systematic role in either utilitarian or Marxist thought. It rests on the distinction between irrational and nonra-

---

[22] Although Marx did not use the term 'false consciousness', he used terms that carried the same meaning, see Seliger, *The Marxist Conception of Ideology*, pp. 30–1.

tional action.[23] Whereas the former is defined negatively by the actor's 'failure' to conform to the standard of scientific rationality in adapting his means to his ends, the latter is defined positively by the actor's conformity to rules or norms that he regards as obligatory because they embody some ultimate end or value. This type of action, which finds its limiting case in Durkheim's notion of religious ritual, is, therefore, nonrational only in the sense that it is finally inexplicable in terms of ignorance or error. Although some norms may be partly justified as the most appropriate means of attaining proximate ends, and thus capable of being judged according to criteria of scientific rationality, progression up the means–ends chain sooner or later reaches a point where the rationale of the rule is grounded in an end that is ultimate in that it is scientifically irrefutable. It is true that ultimate values are still open to rational scrutiny; but, at the same time, it is unlikely that a society made up entirely of moral philosophers would be at all durable. Nevertheless, the fact that most people do not acquire, hold to, and sometimes change their ultimate ends purely as a result of logical reflection does not imply that they are simply socialized into an unquestioning conformity to the rules that these values underpin. The view of action now being considered merely serves to bring into focus questions that the utilitarian schema leaves obscure. The most basic of these is the extent to which the ultimate ends of actors are integrated with one another through a system of common values. This then concentrates attention on the factors that determine the extent to which the values and norms defining the ends and means appropriate to different classes of actors come to constitute conditions of their action in the form of internal, rather than external, constraints. From this perspective, the central problem is no longer that of accounting for deviation from scientifically rational action but rather that of explaining variations in the institutionalization of values.

The position of values and norms within the Marxist theory of class action is very uncertain. Recognition of their significance grows as the evident weaknesses of explanations of ideologically induced ignorance and error call for a much more explicit treatment of the 'cultural', as opposed to the 'cognitive', obstacles to revolutionary consciousness. In general, however, these cultural

---

[23] See Parsons, *The Structure of Social Action*, pp. 712–13.

factors have been incorporated into the category of ideology. The main reason for this is the lack of a clear distinction between irrational and nonrational action, which rules out the possibility of the rigorous analysis and empirical study of the conditions determining the institutionalization of values. In default of this, explanations that depart from the basic utilitarian action schema have the tendency to resort to an 'over-socialized' concept of man, which accentuates the instability of the Marxist theory of class action by encouraging 'idealistic' forms of explanation closely resembling those of normative functionalism.[24]

Before examining the ways in which explanations of the absence of revolutionary class consciousness have led to an increasing emphasis on the ideological and cultural barriers to proletarian reason, it may be worthwhile to consider in some detail how the problem of dealing with normative elements arises directly from Marx's account of the conditions making for proletarian revolution. For purposes of exposition it is convenient to separate out three main strands of Marx's argument. First, there is an 'economic' theory which centres on the absolute or relative material impoverishment of the working class. Secondly, there is the 'philosophical anthropology' of alienation, which locates the revolutionary impulse of the proletariat in the degradation of its species-being or its moral impoverishment. Thirdly, there is what

[24] See Parsons, *The Structure of Social Action*, ch. 2, for the distinction between the 'utilitarian ' and 'idealistic' action schemas, the former being one version of a more general, 'positivistic', model. Parson's shortest and most incisive statement is as follows: 'Just as positivism eliminates the creative, voluntaristic character of action by dispensing with the analytical significance of values, so idealism has the same effect for the opposite reason—idealism eliminates the reality of the obstacles to the realization of values' (ibid. 466). It is in this sense that it can be said that Marxist theory has a tendency to oscillate between the utilitarian and idealistic poles. This has occurred because, in the face of the actual development of capitalist societies, the assumption of proletarian reason, which underlies the theory of revolution, has had to give way to a growing emphasis on ideological obstacles to revolution. The undefined relationship between these two highly general, and radically divergent, hypotheses is the root cause of the instability of modern Marxism. This said, it needs to be added that this impasse has its counterpart in 'bourgeois' social theory. Despite Parsons's ecumenical advocacy of a voluntaristic theory of action, explanations based on competing notions of 'rational' versus 'socialized' man persist, and have so far proved to be irreconcilable. In Marxism, this problem is merely magnified because its claim to provide a unified theory of system and social integration brings out any inadequacy of the underlying action schema in a much more dramatic fashion than is the case in theories of less ambitious scope.

might be called a 'sociological' theory which sees revolution as the outcome of a process of proletarian self-education or revolutionary practice. Since capitalist crises may be thought to have an educative function in this sense, their effects on proletarian class consciousness will be discussed under the third heading. This way of distinguishing the various strands of Marxian theory is rough and ready, and many might object to the terms used to describe them. But there is good reason for treating the three kinds of explanation separately. For, although it is possible to claim that they are parts of an indivisible whole, it is not the case that all Marxist writers give equal emphasis to what have been called the economic, philosophical, and sociological interpretations of class action. Indeed, it is just the opposite tendency for modern Marxism to be divided according to which of these kinds of explanation is preferred that makes it so hard to identify anything that resembles a unitary action schema. Moreover, by treating these themes one by one it is much easier to identify the main weaknesses of the latter.

II.

MATERIAL AND MORAL
IMPOVERISHMENT

I

To begin with the 'economic' theory, the most basic question about the material impoverishment of the working class concerns the concept of action that links this condition with working-class revolt. As De Man puts it, 'Of what use is it to prove that economic crises have assumed other forms than those foreseen by Marx? What matters to us is whether there really is, as Marx believed, a necessary connection between economic crises and the social revolution.'[1] Impoverishment is, of course, only one aspect of this connection. The other is the way in which recurrent crises that plunge the proletariat into poverty also provide the conditions of the self-education of the class. It may be thought, therefore, that it is factitious to isolate the discussion of these two aspects of the problem. But this procedure is not entirely unwarranted, because it is still a common, albeit implicit, assumption of Marxist writers that impoverishment, or affluence, *per se* does have a direct and immediate effect on working-class consciousness. And Marx and Engels often talk in these terms. Moreover, as will be shown in due course, this assumption is made less rather than more plausible by the introduction of the notion of self-education, since the latter does not usually take into account the importance of the distinction between human and organizational life spans, and thus confuses the learning embodied in the tradition of a corporate group with the learning of its individual members. Furthermore, the self-education of the working class is not a problem that can be considered in isolation from the wider system of status classification within which working-class struggle unfolds

[1] H. De Man, *The Psychology of Socialism* (London, 1928), 23.

and which plays an important part in defining the objectives of this struggle.

The question of whether Marx predicted an absolute or a relative impoverishment of the proletariat in an objective, strictly economic sense, is not a matter of great importance in the present context, however controversial it might be from other points of view.[2] The starting-point must surely be that the hypothesis that impoverishment leads to radicalism, or conversely that affluence leads to conservatism, is neither empirically supportable nor logically sound. It is not the case that the most impoverished and economically insecure workers are invariably, or even usually, the most radical, or that periods of falling real wages and high unemployment are invariably those of working-class radicalism, still less of revolution. What seems to be more significant is the manner in which impoverishment occurs. If the theory refers to the reduction of living standards due to long-run employment, such as that experienced on a large scale by workers during the inter-war depression, then it must be regarded as defective. The usual response of the working class thus afflicted was far more likely to be fatalistic than revolutionary.[3] Moreover, in such periods of protracted economic stagnation, labour organizations are weakened not strengthened. If, on the other hand, the theory of immiserization refers to crises which bring about a sharp reduction in living standards after a period of economic advance, Marx is on surer ground. As Runciman puts it, 'It is only poverty which seems irremediable that is likely to keep relative deprivation low. Marx and Engels were not foolish to hope for economic crises as the catalysts of revolution, for when a stable expectation is suddenly disappointed this is just as likely to promote a relative deprivation as when an expectation is suddenly heightened.'[4] Moreover, Marx himself provides the reasons for doubting that there should be a simple and direct relation between the economic condition and the class consciousness of the proletariat. First of

[2] M. M. Bober, *Karl Marx's Interpretation of History* (New York, 1948), 213–21, is probably still the best short account.
[3] See, e.g., J. Stevenson and C. Cook, *The Slump* (London, 1979), ch. 14, 'The Revolution That Never Was'; and S. Verba and K. Lehman, 'Unemployment, Class Consciousness and Radical Politics: What Didn't Happen in the Thirties', *Journal of Politics*, 39 (1977).
[4] Runciman, *Relative Deprivation and Social Justice*, p. 25.

all, like Ricardo before him, Marx recognized that the needs of labourers, and hence the value of labour, were variable, determined not only by the necessities of sheer physical existence but also by 'a traditional standard of life', by 'a historical and moral element'.[5] This means that there is introduced into the very notion of impoverishment a concept of the relativity of deprivation and that the effects of economic circumstances on class consciousness are mediated by the structure and variability of 'moral' factors. Most significantly, in the last analysis, the concept of a traditional standard of life involves reference to the phenomenon of status-group stratification. Thus, quite apart from the possibility noted by Durkheim that poverty can just as easily lead to fatalism as to revolt because 'actual possessions are partly the criterion of those aspired to',[6] the notion of tradition or the moral element introduces into the Marxian concept of action a normative factor of fundamental importance, but one that remains analytically residual.[7]

[5] In *Wages, Price and Profit*, the value of labour power is defined by two elements: 'the one merely physical, the other historical or social. Its *ultimate limit* is determined by the *physical* element, that is to say, to maintain and reproduce itself, to perpetuate its physical existence, the working class must receive the necessaries absolutely indispensable for living and multiplying.' But 'besides this mere physical element, the value of labour is in every country determined by a *traditional standard of life*. It is not merely physical life, but it is the satisfaction of certain wants springing from the social conditions in which people are placed and reared up' (Marx and Engels, *Selected Works*, i. 400–1.) The same point is made in *Capital*, i. 140–50, where Marx refers to the 'historical and moral element' entering into the determination of labour power. For an extended discussion of this subject, see E. Browder, *Marx and America: A Study of the Doctrine of Impoverishment* (London, 1959).

[6] Durkheim, *Professional Ethics*, p. 254. It has been argued that the fatalistic response to impoverishment should have entered more centrally into Marx's thinking from his reading of factory inspector's reports. See Ollman, 'Towards Class Consciousness Next Time'.

[7] The notion of 'tradition' has always been introduced *ad hoc*, and has remained a principal means of referring to a whole range of undifferentiated normative elements whose place in the scheme of action is obscure and whose significance in the analysis of concrete social situations is therefore imponderable. Bober, *Karl Marx's Interpretation of History*, provides ample documentation of the first point. It is interesting that one recent treatment of tradition should concentrate on its 'invention', an approach that is completely consistent with the assumption of actors' rational, instrumental orientations to normative elements in general. See E. J. Hobsbawm, 'Inventing Traditions', introduction to E. J. Hobsbawm and T. Ranger (eds.), *The Invention of Tradition* (Cambridge, 1983). Tradition has usually been treated as a 'given' condition of action, and principally as an obstacle to the development of class consciousness. As a result, the double-edged nature of tradition has been ignored, and most particularly the radicalizing effects of

The systematic nature of this moral element becomes more evident if it is accepted that Marx predicted not the absolute, but only the relative, impoverishment of the working class.[8] Whatever the merits of this interpretation,[9] it has far-reaching sociological implications. For, unless it is held that it means no more than an objective divergence of wages and profits, both of which increase in absolute terms, then the explanation of the feeling of unjust deprivation associated with relative impoverishment must involve reference to the normative interrelationship of the ends of capitalists and proletarians. In other words, the sense of deprivation on the part of the proletariat results not from a comparison of their means relative to their traditionally defined standard of living, but rather from a comparison of their standard of living with that of the capitalist class. If the idea of relative impoverishment does not refer to this kind of comparison, then it is a purely statistical notion with no implications for the action of the proletariat. But, if it does have this connotation, then it entails the concept of a status order. If the standard of living of a class contains a moral element, then the relationship between the standard of living of one class and that of another must imply a moral relationship; that is, a status hierarchy defining the ends, or standards of living,

---

incongruities of class and status, such as those referred to in ch. 5 by the terms 'status abrogation' and 'status dereliction'. As C. J. Calhoun has shown, radicalism has not only been sustained by the cohesive nature of traditional communities but has frequently arisen from 'the defence of traditional practices and the demand for the practical implementation of traditional goals long unrealized' ('The Radicalism of Tradition', *American Journal of Sociology*, 88 (1983), 900).

[8] This interpretation is based mainly on the passage in *Wage Labour and Capital* in which Marx argues that even 'in the most favourable situation for the working class', when wages are going up, 'the material position of the worker has improved', but at the cost of his social position. The social gulf that divides him from the capitalist has widened.' This is because, 'although the enjoyments of the worker have risen, the social satisfaction that they give has fallen in comparison with the increased enjoyments of the capitalist, which are inaccessible to the workers, in comparison with the state of development of society in general. Our desires and pleasures spring from society; we measure them, therefore, by society and not by the objects which serve for their satisfactions. Because they are of a social nature, they are of a relative nature.' (Marx and Engels, *Selected Works*, i. 87, 91.)

[9] 'The most favourable case for the working class', which Marx takes for his introduction of the idea of relative impoverishment, is clearly distinct from the 'general tendency of production' in which the 'progress of accumulation' takes the form of a '*progressive* change in the *composition* of capital'. The result of this is 'to sink the average standard of wages, or to push the *value of labour* more or less to its *minimum limit*' (ibid. 404).

to which different classes may legitimately aspire. Although Marx and Engels were not oblivious of the fact that class solidarity could be impaired by status differentiation, the concept of status entered into their explanations of class action in an entirely *ad hoc* manner; and this has remained characteristic of subsequent Marxist theory. If what Marx calls the 'social satisfaction' of the worker is a function of the comparison he makes between his lot and that of other classes, then the extent to which the worker experiences his relative impoverishment as relative deprivation will depend on his choice of reference groups, and this, in turn, will be determined by both his pre-existing status aspirations and changes in his material position. In this respect, there is a basic point of convergence between Marxian and Durkheimian sociology. Whereas Durkheim concentrated on the socially stabilizing effects of the status classification to the neglect of the problem of how structural changes in the 'distribution of men and things' impinge upon the aspirations of status groups, in Marxism the opposite tendency is all too apparent. But, since the concept of a status system has no place in Marxist theory, there can be no means of analysing the principal way in which the effects on class interest of changes in material circumstances are mediated by the aspirations of class actors.[10]

This defect is not specific to the hypothesis that impoverishment leads to revolt. It will shortly be shown that very similar assumptions support those explanations of proletarian action which are based on the concepts of alienation and self-education. Most generally, the failure to differentiate the institutionalization of status from the all-purpose category of the ideological is a main reason why Marxism exhibits a marked tendency to oscillate between two equally untenable action schemas: at the one extreme, the positivistic, of which the impoverishment thesis is

---

[10] Influenced by 'bourgeois' sociology, some Marxist writers have at least broached this problem, though in fairly general terms. See, e.g., H. Wolpe, 'Some Problems Concerning Revolutionary Consciousness', *Socialist Register* (1970), and L. Clements, 'Reference Groups and Trade Union Consciousness', in T. Clarke and L. Clements (eds.), *Trade Unions under Capitalism* (London, 1977). The frequency with which Marxist writers refer to the pioneering study by Runciman, *Relative Deprivation and Social Justice*, emphasizes the need for a more general treatment of the whole problem, such as that essayed by J. Urry, *Reference Groups and the Theory of Revolution* (London, 1973).

archetypal; and, at the other, what can only be called, though in a necessarily qualified sense, the idealistic.

At this stage, however, it simply needs to be emphasized that the foregoing criticisms of the impoverishment thesis apply with equal force to the opposite kind of argument, which seeks to explain working-class acquiescence or conservatism in terms of relative affluence. Lenin's theory of the 'labour aristocracy' is the *locus classicus* of this type of explanation. His (or rather Hobson's) idea that proletarian revolution was averted by leading sections of the working class being 'bribed' or 'bought off' by their sharing in imperialist 'super profits' is based on the familiar positivistic assumption that reduces the determination of ends to changes in material conditions. Subsequent research has demonstrated the inadequacy of this theory, and recent Marxist investigations into the subject have focused on the social rather than the simply economic factors determining the position of this stratum of the working class, whose boundaries have thereby become analytically less and less certain.[11] Most interestingly, detailed case studies of the labour aristocracy have documented the importance in its formation of status innovation. They have shown that, far from its being bribed into acquiescence or being 'bourgeoisified' through its indoctrination with ruling-class ideology, the labour aristocracy constituted itself as a separate status group, and hence as a reference group for other sections of the working class, by creating distinctive values and beliefs which stood at some distance from, and were in certain crucial respects antagonistic to, those of the bourgeoisie.[12]

[11] For a critical summary of the literature, see H. F. Moorhouse, 'The Marxist Theory of the Labour Aristocracy', *Social History*, 3 (1978). The crude bribery argument is, however, not extinct. See, e.g., W. M. Gallacher and J. R. Campbell, 'Direct Action', in Clarke and Clements (eds.), *Trade Unions under Capitalism*, pp. 127–8. Their argument that technicians in particular are bought off by employers is not exactly compatible with the more fashionable Marxist theory, to be discussed below, which holds that it is just this 'new working class' that possesses revolutionary potential.

[12] See, especially, G. Crossick, 'The Labour Aristocracy and its Values', *Victorian Studies*, 19 (1976), and R. Q. Gray, 'Styles of Life, the "Labour Aristocracy" and Class Relations in Later Nineteenth Century Edinburgh', *International Review of Social History*, 18 (1973). Work of this kind, reflecting the influence of the sophisticated theory of hegemonic domination yet to be discussed, introduces into the cruder versions of Marxist theory a mode of analysis that has long been characteristic of sociological studies of the working class. See, e.g., the classic study by Chinoy, *Automobile Workers and the American Dream*.

II

The significance that Marxist writers attach to the economic impoverishment of the working class is highly variable,[13] and the logic of the relation between impoverishment and class consciousness remains decidedly undeveloped. These considerations also apply to the second main strand of the Marxian argument: namely, the theory of moral impoverishment or alienation. It is important to begin by noting that, although this idea is used chiefly to account for working-class passivity, it is also capable of yielding an explanation of working-class revolt. The fact that contradictory conclusions can be drawn from the theory may of course be regarded as a demonstration of the merit of 'dialectical thinking'; but the fact that very few of these conclusions are specific enough to be demonstrable hardly commends it as a rigorous explanation of class action.[14]

The root of the difficulty is to be found in the ambiguity of the two basic terms that enter into its formulation: on the one hand, the concept of 'human nature', and, on the other, that of the conditions making for alienation. As regards the former, it is well known that Marx refers to 'human nature in general' as well as to 'human nature as modified in each historical epoch'. At the same time, the relative importance of these two aspects of human nature for explaining the action of the proletariat remains highly indeterminate. Fromm expresses the general source of this problem very well when he writes:

---

[13] Compare, e.g., A. Gorz, *Strategy for Labor* (Boston, 1964), Introduction and pp. 20–4, with H. Braverman, *Labor and Monopoly Capital* (New York, 1974), 398–401.

[14] Meszaros, *Marx's Theory of Alienation*, p. 13, argues that Marx's concepts 'must sound extremely odd, if not altogether meaningless or self-contradictory, to all those who are used to the misleading 'common-sense simplicity' of positivistic empiricism'. The sense in which the 'complexities of a dialectical framework of discourse' are inaccessible to the practitioners of 'commonplace-mongering neo-empiricism' is, however, debatable. It is at least arguable that the 'positivistic empiricist', who, it might be expected, would possess some knowledge of multivariate analysis, would not have too much difficulty in grasping the possibly only exact meaning of the idea that an element of a system is a 'determined determinant' (ibid. 155). The real difficulty lies not so much in the difficulty of dialectical reasoning as in the paucity of its specific conclusions. Ollman, *Alienation*, p. 232, is nearer to the point when he says that Marx's conception of human nature and his theory of alienation 'are for the most part not amenable to the evidence of experience, whether actual or potential'.

Marx argues against two points of view here: the ahistorical, which postulates the nature of man as a substance existing since the beginning of history, as well as the relativistic, which endows the nature of man with none of its own properties but considers it the reflection of social conditions. However, he never formulated conclusively his own theory of the nature of man to transcend both the ahistorical and the relativistic points of view. For this reason the interpretations of his theory are so variant and contradictory.[15]

Although it is generally held that Marx did not have a conception of a fixed human nature, he did nevertheless have a notion of what man had it in him essentially to become, and his theory of alienation only makes sense in the context of his idea of the powers and needs which distinguish man as 'species being', a potentiality that would only be actualized with the abolition of the division of labour. The difference between this idea and that of a fixed or basic human nature is very fine.[16] What is fixed and basic is a capacity and therefore in some sense also a need to engage in many-sided activity, mental as well as manual work. For Marx, men's powers and needs develop in a reciprocal way through the labour (in the widest sense) by which they transform their natural and social environment. In this process needs are satisfied, essential powers achieve new expression, and further needs emerge. Any particular stage of this process is to be measured against the unalienated activity which is the end state of social development,[17] and in which, subject to the realm of necessity which even the full development of productive forces under communism does not entirely eliminate, man is able to realize his inherent abilities in 'free, conscious activity' which is the 'species-character of human beings'. By contrast, in capitalism, alienation reaches

---

[15] E. Fromm, *Beyond the Chains of Illusion* (New York, 1962), 31.

[16] According to Meszaros, Marx 'denies that man is an essentially *egoistic* being, for he does not accept such a thing as a *fixed* human nature', yet 'what emerges as the "essence of human nature" is not *egoism*, but *sociality*'. Furthermore, 'sociality' 'is actually inherent in every single individual' (*Marx's Theory of Alienation*, pp. 149, 175). As noted above (ch. 1 n. 5), Marx's concrete depiction of this 'sociality' has a distinctively Durkheimian ring to it.

[17] Though note Meszaros's claims that the 'Marxian system remains open because in this account the very "goal" of history is defined in inherently historical terms, and not as a fixed target' and that there cannot be 'a point in history at which we could say: "human substance has been fully realized". For such a fixing would deprive the human being of his essential attribute: his power of "self-mediation" and "self-development"' (*Marx's Theory of Alienation*, pp. 118–19).

its climax. The way in which Marx conceived of the worker as being alienated from the act of production, from his product, from his fellow-men, and from his species-being has been analysed at great length in general terms, and is in no need of repetition here. The main point is that, under the capitalist mode of production, essential human powers are stunted and human needs are correspondingly distorted—egoism, the very opposite of sociality, being their predominant expression. But in degrading man capitalism at the same time creates the objective conditions requisite for the abolition of this degradation. Whether these conditions are also experienced as degrading is, however, a different matter. And it is in this respect that the ambiguity of Marx's conception of 'human nature' yields the most contradictory conclusions.

What is essentially at stake is the extent to which the socially determined and false needs of the proletariat inhibit the emergence of its essential need to engage in that kind of activity that fully expresses its species-being. Depending on which of the two aspects of the formation of needs is emphasized, the reaction of the proletariat to alienating conditions can be either passive or active. Marx provides authority for both views. 'The class of the proletariat', he writes, 'is abased and indignant at that debasement, an indignation to which it is necessarily driven by the contradiction between its human nature and its condition of life, which is the outright, decisive and comprehensive negation of that nature.'[18] And again, 'From the start, the worker is superior to the capitalist in that the capitalist is rooted in his process of alienation and is completely content therein, whereas the worker who is its victim finds himself from the beginning in a state of rebellion against it and experiences the process as one of enslavement.'[19] Yet, at the same time, there is ample evidence in Marx's writings to support the opposite interpretation, which has become more prominent in subsequent Marxist literature and which lays much greater stress on the passive response to alienating conditions, and thereby on the power of these conditions to induce false wants.

Corresponding to the ambiguity in the conception of human

[18] McLellan, *The Thought of Karl Marx*, p. 113.
[19] Ibid. 119.

nature and further compounding the difficulty of arriving at a clear
view of the dynamic of alienation in capitalist society is the
problem of whether the conditions making for alienation are to be
understood as variable or invariable. If, as is usually the case, the
source of alienation is located in capitalist relations of production
per se, then alienation is global. Since it is held to be inherent in
capitalism as a system of generalized commodity production, most
Marxists have been content to do little more than merely repeat
Marx's own fairly general analysis of the basic sources of alienation in capitalist society. Unfortunately, it is a theory whose
decisive test presupposes a state of affairs in which alienation no
longer exists. The latter, according to Mandel, would imply 'the
withering away of commodity production, the disappearance of
private ownership of the means of production and the elimination
of the difference between manual and intellectual labour, between
producers and administrators'.[20] A society possessing these characteristics would provide the only true measure of the extent to
which the pervasive alienation that is said to be the product of
capitalist social relations is both peculiar and avoidable. But such
a society has yet to come into being.[21]

Nevertheless, Marx appears to give grounds for thinking that,
although all workers are alienated by the basic conditions of
capitalist production relations, some workers might be more
alienated than others. This is quite clearly the conclusion to be
drawn from his account of the need for capitalists to increase the
social productiveness of labour. The imperative of profit maximization results in some of the most crucial features of alienated
labour becoming intensified. Thus the state of alienation is not
only a constant feature of capitalist production as such but one
that is associated with the rising organic composition of capital
and with the technical and organizational concomitants of this
means of increasing the productivity of labour. In the passage of
Capital in which Marx concludes that 'in proportion as capital
accumulates, the lot of the labourer, be his payment high or low,
must grow worse', he refers quite explicitly to the alienating effect

[20] E. Mandel, *The Marxist Theory of Alienation* (New York, 1973), 30.
[21] For an interesting attempt to compare alienation in capitalist and state
socialist societies, see D. Lane and F. O'Dell, *The Soviet Industrial Worker*
(Oxford, 1978), ch. 3.

of 'all methods for raising the social productiveness of labour' which are 'brought about at the cost of the individual labourer'. These advances in the means of production 'mutilate the labourer into a fragment of a man, degrade him to the level of an appendage of a machine, destroy every remnant of charm in his work and turn it into a hated toil; they estrange him from the intellectual potentialities of the labour process in the same proportion as science is incorporated in it as an independent power'. Marx finishes by saying that 'all methods for the production of surplus value are at the same time methods of accumulation; and every extension of accumulation becomes again a means for the development of these methods.'[22] Since these technological and organizational methods of increasing productivity differ in the extent to which they diminish, or in some cases enlarge, the autonomy of the worker, their development introduces an important element of variability into the conditions of proletarian alienation. It is one that is bound up not so much with capitalist production relations as such but rather with the way in which the further socialization of the forces of production occurs within these relations. In comparison with the notion of global alienation, the idea that the advance of technology alters the conditions of alienation is one that has led to some unusually specific Marxist theories of class action.

These ambiguities in the Marxian concepts of human nature and of the conditions making for alienation allow a considerable degree of freedom in the interpretation of class action. There are two extreme possibilities and they yield contradictory conclusions. The first may be simply stated without too much comment here, since it is a strand in the safety-net thesis of the ideological repression of proletarian reason which will be considered at length in Part Two. It is an argument designed to account for the lack of a working-class revolution in advanced capitalist societies and the unlikelihood of such an event in the foreseeable future. In this explanation what is emphasized is the plasticity of the wants of the proletariat and the global character of the conditions making for its alienation. In some versions of the argument the extinction of the capacity of the working class to exercise its reason and comprehend its essential human needs is apparently complete. In

[22] Marx, *Capital*, i. 661.

others, this capacity is regarded as inextinguishable but too enfeebled to assert itself save by the intervention of an external agency. However, in marked contrast to this pessimistic view of alienated proletarian passivity, there is another line of argument which stresses workers' revolt against their degradation, and which in some versions seeks to link this revolt with the growing socialization of production.

It rests partly on the assumption that capitalism 'produces not only alienation but the consciousness of alienation, in other words, radical needs'.[23] This clearly invokes Marx's conception of the proletariat being forced to revolt 'by the contradiction between its *humanity* and its situation, which is an open, clear and absolute negation of its humanity', of 'the proletariat as proletariat, poverty conscious of its moral and physical poverty, degradation conscious of its degradation, and for this reason trying to abolish itself'.[24] The humanity referred to consists of the powers and needs that seek actualization in free conscious activity; and, for the worker to become conscious of his alienation and to develop 'radical' needs, implies, as Ollman argues, that the worker's capacity for rational purposive activity, his ability 'to grasp the nature of what it is he wants to transform and to direct his energies accordingly', is inextinguishable.

For Marx, rather than inhibiting understanding, the very extremity of the worker's situation, the very extent of his suffering, makes the task of calculating advantages relatively an easy one. All the facts stand out in stark relief, and the conclusion to be drawn from them cannot be missed. His needs, too, urge recognition of the general means for their satisfaction, both those available within the system and those requiring the system's transformation.[25]

---

[23] Heller, *The Theory of Need in Marx*, pp. 93–4. See also Meszaros, *Marx's Theory of Alienation*, p. 181: 'Alienation is an inherently dynamic concept: a concept that necessarily implies change. Alienation activity not only produces "alienated consciousness", but also the "consciousness of being alienated".'

[24] Marx, *The Holy Family*, in *Selected Writings*, pp. 231–2.

[25] Ollman, *Alienation*, pp. 239, 114. Ollman goes on to argue: 'Proletarian class consciousness, when it occurs, is the result of workers using such reasoning powers on themselves and their life conditions. It flows necessarily from what they are, both as rational human beings and as workers caught up in an inhuman situation. Thus, even when Marx recognizes that the weight of evidence is against him, he is handicapped in accounting for the absence of proletarian class consciousness by his operating assumption, encased in his conceptual framework, that it already exists, actually or potentially.'

This is a far cry from the worker as a 'one dimensional man', from a passively suffering proletariat whose dehumanization is complete. Nevertheless, even if this interpretation of Marx is correct,[26] and it is accepted that 'the essence of man develops within alienation itself, and thereby creates the possibility for the realization of man',[27] in exactly what do the radical needs of the proletariat consist? Generalities apart, what the argument boils down to is that Marx attributed to the proletariat two kinds of needs that capitalism would be unable to meet fully. One is the 'need for free time'. It is seen as a potentially revolutionary need because Marx is convinced 'that from a certain point onwards capitalism is incapable of shortening labour time any further: the need for free time then becomes in principle a radical need, which can only be satisfied with the transcendence of capitalism'.[28] This argument is certainly consistent with the importance he attaches to the shortening of the working day as a focus of class struggle, with his conception of the hiatus between work and leisure created by capitalist production relations, and also with his view that the reduction of necessary labour time would be the major prerequisite of the self-realizing activity of 'socialist man'.[29] It is also consistent with the argument that capitalism cannot bring about the full automation of productive forces since this would mean the end of the valorization process. But it is not a thesis that is sufficiently precise to identify the point at which the denial of this postulated need breeds revolutionary claims and becomes the site of class struggle which would threaten the existence of the capitalist mode of production.

Similar objections can be levelled against the other postulated human capacity that capitalism denies, namely, that of 'universality', or the need for the 'all round development of individuals'.[30] The source of this idea is the passage in *Capital* where Marx predicted that 'Modern Industry compels society, under penalty of death, to replace the detail-worker of today' by the 'fully

---

[26] Seliger, *The Marxist Conception of Ideology*, p. 65, is among those who dispute its validity.

[27] Heller, *The Theory of Need in Marx*, p. 46.

[28] Ibid. 91.

[29] Marx, *Capital*, iii. 820.

[30] Heller, *The Theory of Need in Marx*, pp. 91–3. See also A. Swingewood, *Marx and Modern Social Theory* (London, 1975), 105–9.

developed individual, fit for a variety of labours'. What the argument in question only faintly recognizes, however, is that Marx believed that this 'imperative' was already negated by the development of 'Modern Industry' of his own day. Therefore, once again, the crucial question is at what point capitalism's denial of the worker's need for polyvalent labour will lead to proletarian revolt against these alienating production relations. On this, as on the question of the radical nature of the need for free time, the philosophical anthropology of alienation as revolt is silent.[31]

The findings of industrial sociology certainly lend credence to the view that the most alienating conditions of production lead to high levels of job dissatisfaction and industrial unrest. The reduction of worker autonomy through the intensification of detail labour, which is carried to its extreme in mass-production industries, has usually been associated with low morale, high rates of turnover, and absenteeism; and it is also true that these industries have been marked by relatively high levels of strike action and other kinds of collective protest. But it is also found that, the longer workers are exposed to such conditions, the more pathologically inured to them they become, and work becomes less and less a central life interest.[32] On the whole, then, there is little in this research to support the idea that the denial of the worker's 'radical need' for autonomy will lead to revolutionary consciousness. The predominant mode of response might be described rather as routine recalcitrance or passive alienation, punctuated by periodic industrial disputes over issues that reflect a highly instrumental, 'economistic' orientation to work.[33]

A more ingenious and precise formulation of the idea that alienation leads to radicalism is Mallet's theory of 'the new

[31] Heller, *The Theory of Need in Marx*, p. 95, at least admits that, 'As yet, history has not yet answered the question as to whether capitalist society *in fact* produces this "consciousness exceeding its bounds", which in Marx's day did not exist, and whose existence Marx had to *project*.' (Italics in original.)

[32] The classic summary statements and basis of much subsequent work are C. Argyris, *Personality and Organization* (New York, 1957), and R. Blauner, *Alienation and Freedom: The Factory Worker and his Industry* (Chicago, 1964).

[33] It can of course be argued that the alienation of the worker cannot be understood simply by reference to his work situation. This usually means, however, that theories of the radicalizing effects of alienation give way to interpretations of proletarian passivity which stress the global nature of alienation in capitalist society, no matter under which specific working conditions wage labour is performed. This line of argument is considered in Part Four, esp. ch. 14.

working class', which is based on his study of technicians in some of the most technologically advanced industries in France at the time.[34] The ingenuity of his argument consists in inverting the usual thesis that the proletariat will become revolutionary as their conditions of work become more dehumanized. In a dialectical *tour de force*, he holds that the most radical workers are those who work under the least objectively alienating conditions. However, since these conditions are also associated with the most advanced forces of production, there is at least one straw of orthodoxy to clutch at. This is Marx's belief—though one that is hard to square with his assessment of the tendency of technological development in capitalist society of his own day—that human powers and needs will unfold with people's increasing command over nature through progressively socialized production relations.[35] Underlying the 'new-working-class' thesis then is a concept of human nature which postulates some in-built hierarchy of needs, which appears to be very similar to that proposed by Maslow.[36]

According to Mallet then, it is because workers in advanced technological industries are relatively well paid and secure in their jobs that they are capable of developing needs of a qualitatively

[34] S. Mallet, *The New Working Class* (Nottingham, 1975).
[35] Attempts to establish that Marx foresaw the development of modern automated technology are well known. See, e.g., D. McLellan, *Marx's Grundrisse* (St Albans, 1973), foreword to extracts 22, 23, and 24, M. Nicolaus in his Introduction to *Grundrisse*, pp. 51–2, and his 'The Unknown Marx', in C. Oglesby (ed.), *New Left Reader* (New York, 1969), 106. But these interpretations are based on one isolated passage in his work, and it is fanciful to suppose that he imagined that proletarian revolution would be postponed until the advent of automated production. His lengthy discussions of the distinction between manufacture and Modern Industry in *Capital* suggest that what he is chiefly talking about in the *Grundrisse* (and indeed by reference to the same sources that are used in the former work) are simply the tendencies of Modern Industry. His major theme is the deskilling of work. The highly skilled, polytechnical workers who make up but a small minority of the labour force of most modern automated industries, and in whom some Marxists perceive the prototype of socialist man, bear no resemblance to the worker serving the 'automaton' who is portrayed at length in those sections of the *Grundrisse* which read more than anything else like the script for the factory scenes in Fritz Lang's *Metropolis*. Whether Marx did or did not foresee automated production is of course irrelevant to the question of whether its modern form will be the site of a revolutionary potential. For such an argument, see Mandel, *Late Capitalism* pp. 582–3, where he nicely makes the most of the 'free time' and 'polyvalent labour' theses referred to above.
[36] A. H. Maslow, *Motivation and Personality* (New York, 1954).

different kind from those of other workers; in particular demands for worker control and self-management as opposed to merely economistic ones. These interests, which are held to pose the most fundamental threat to capitalist production relations, are also prompted by the workers' integration into the enterprise. Unlike the passively alienated workers employed in mass-production industries, the new working class is in a situation where individual labour loses all meaning, and where workers' knowledge, skills, and collective involvement in production not only give them a high disruptive capacity but also make them increasingly aware of the contradiction between the socialized character of the labour process as a whole and the private character of its control. In pursuing their goals, the trade unions of the new working class are able to use new strike methods and are self-educated into making demands that encroach increasingly on the prerogatives of management, even in areas of financial decision-making. In short, the new working class is the incarnation of Marx's idea of the collective labourer.

Compared with most Marxist interpretations of alienation the merit of this argument is that it is refutable: and it has been, fairly definitively.[37] The basic respect in which it is faulty concerns the now familiar problem of workers' aspirations; and, in particular, the sources of their aspirations for control. Mallet's thesis is wrong because it assumes a technological determination of class action which is unable to account for marked national differences in the attitudes and behaviour of workers employed in technologically identical plants. The radicalism of the French new working class appears to be due more to the radical stance of the French labour movement than to the fact that they work in 'advanced' industries. In consequence, the explanation of the attitudes and behaviour of this section of the working class has to be sought in the wider system of industrial and political relations. The deficiency of the

[37] By D. Gallie, *In Search of the New Working Class: Automation and Social Integration within the Capitalist Enterprise* (Cambridge, 1978). His work also shows that the postulated need for 'free-time' is far from being met by automated production, of which shift working is an integral part; and that only a minority of workers possess what might be regarded as 'polytechnical' skills. Two other recent studies which support Gallie's general argument are J. R. Low-Beer, *Protest and Participation: The New Working Class in Italy* (Cambridge, 1978), and R. Scase, *Social Democracy in Capitalist Society: Working Class Politics in Britain and Sweden* (London, 1977).

theory of the new working class thus brings to the fore once again the significance for class action of the status system in which class relations are embedded. And since the basic constituent of status in capitalist societies is citizenship, it is perhaps not surprising that there is a close relationship between the way in which this status has been institutionalized and the nature of working-class consciousness. Generally speaking, the earlier and more easily the working-class has acquired effective rights of citizenship, the less radical it has been. The failure to take account of this process of civic incorporation, or, in Durkheimian terms, status reclassification, is not simply the chief defect of Mallet's theory of the new working class; it is also, as will now be shown, a major weakness of the theory of 'self-emancipation' or revolutionary praxis.

12.

REVOLUTIONARY PRACTICE

I

The idea of revolutionary practice is considered here solely from the point of view of its relevance to the explanation of class action, and in particular to the understanding of the process of proletarian self-education.

An initial difficulty of this approach is that the concept of praxis has yielded much more in the way of a political philosophy of the class struggle than anything resembling a sociology of working-class action and consciousness. The former has aimed at a conception of the unity of theory and practice modelled on Marx's dictum that, 'just as philosophy finds its *material* weapons in the proletariat, so the proletariat finds its *intellectual* weapons in philosophy'. In the most influential statements of this view,[1] the unity of theory and practice is absolutely guaranteed, because, just as the proletariat is the only class capable of becoming conscious of its real, historically determined interest, so Marxism possesses a uniquely privileged insight into the nature of this historical process. As the authentic expression of proletarian consciousness, not only can Marxism enter into history by articulating the nascent interest of the proletariat; in performing this function it thereby demonstrates its own truth and scientific validity. If the proletariat is slow to reach out to clasp the philosophical helping hand, that merely signifies its immaturity.[2]

In the present context, the reasons for the emergence of the concept of praxis,[3] its epistemological status, and its function in

---

[1] The best short account is T. B. Bottomore, *Marxist Sociology* (London, 1975), ch. 4.

[2] 'The proletariat cannot abdicate its mission. The only question at issue is how much it has to suffer before it achieves ideological maturity, before it acquires a true understanding of its class situation and a true class consciousness' (Lukács, *History and Class Consciousness*, p. 76).

[3] Whilst undoubtedly in part the result of the failure of history to bear out Marx's wavering, but on the whole optimistic, belief in the proletariat's capacity

political rhetoric are matters of less direct concern than the question of what the idea of revolutionary practice has to contribute to a sociology of class action. Protagonists of the philosophy of praxis would no doubt consider this a misguided and futile aim. The contempt in which Lukács and Gramsci held attempts to 'sociologize' Marxist doctrine is well known; and this attitude has persisted.[4] Against this, however, it might be argued that the Lukácsian interpretation of praxis, in which 'imputed rational consciousness' is opposed to actual 'psychological' consciousness, has simply provided a ground for avoiding any analysis of concrete class formation that aims to discover some pattern in its 'contingency' and 'particularity'. It has also demoted the significance of the idea of proletarian self-emancipation, Marx's own chief example of the 'coincidence of the changing of circumstances and of human activity or self-changing'. It is on this concept of revolutionizing practice, and its implications for class action, that the following discussion will concentrate. Practice in this sense could be taken to mean, unexceptionably, that actors, in pursuing their immediate ends under given social conditions, intentionally or, more often than not, unintentionally, bring about changes in these conditions which in turn afford them with the possibility of pursuing new ends which present themselves during the selfsame process of social action. It is very much in these terms that Marx sought to explain the growing class consciousness of the English workers of his day. In the event, his expectation of the revolutionary potential of the working class was misplaced. But this is not a sufficient reason for replacing his arguments about, say, the politicizing effects of the struggle for the Ten Hour Bill with a theory of praxis in which the proletariat reverts to being a subject whose objective consciousness exists independently of its manifestation at any one time or under any particular set of conditions. If Marx was wrong about the nature of revolutionary practice, it is more than likely that he was wrong for reasons that have to do

---

for self-emancipation, the philosophy of praxis was also a reaction against the deterministic Marxism of the Second International, in which, mainly due to the influence of Engels, the theory of the unintended consequences of action became predominant.

[4] See, e.g., I. Meszaros, 'Contingent and Necessary Class Consciousness', in I. Meszaros (ed.), *Aspects of History and Class Consciousness* (London, 1971), 94 ff.

with his assumptions about the structuring of class action, or actual 'psychological' class consciousness. At any rate, this will be the major theme of the following discussion. But, as a preliminary step, it may be useful to examine the idea of revolutionary practice from the more general perspective of what it contributes to an understanding of the Marxist action schema.

II

Prima facie, the idea of the coincidence of the changing of conditions and of 'self-changing' involves a concept of action that is very similar to what Parsons calls the 'voluntaristic'.[5] The principal respect in which this is so is that action is conceived of not as passive adaptation to conditions but rather as a creative activity in which the actor strives to realize ends that represent an ideal prefiguration of a state of affairs that does not yet exist. This is brought out clearly by Marx's description of what is distinctive about human action:

A spider conducts operations that resemble those of a weaver, and the bee puts to shame many an architect in the construction of her cells. But what distinguished the worst architect from the best of bees is this, that the architect raises his structure in imagination, before he erects it in reality.[6]

At the same time, action does not consist in the effortless actualization of the ideal end prefigured in consciousness. The reality that individuals seek to transform in accordance with their ends is obdurate. In pursuing their ends, by adapting their means to bring about the ideal result, they do sometimes alter the natural and the social conditions of their action. But for the most part both their means and conditions set limits on the realization of their ends. In practical activity, actual outcomes seldom represent perfect states of affairs in comparison with the originally conceived project. Moreover, the ends themselves are constantly modified in the face of realistic exigencies as well as in the light of the actor's values and beliefs.

In portraying action as the interplay between subjective and

---

[5] This is not to be confused with voluntarism in the Marxist sense of a strategy opposed to economism, though it has some affinities with it.

[6] Marx, *Capital*, i. 157.

objective factors, the idea of practice emerged as a reaction against both idealistic and materialistic determinism in much the same way as Parsons's concept of voluntarism was arrived at negatively through a rejection of what he calls the positivistic and idealistic action schemas.[7] There is, however, one important respect in which the two approaches would seem to differ. This concerns the standards that are seen to govern the actor's selection of his ends and his use of means to achieve these ends. The main distinction, already referred to several times in the course of this discussion, is that between theories that emphasize the rationality of actors and those that emphasize the orientation of actors to ultimate values. Rational man and socialized man are not congenial companions. Indeed, they are apparently so incompatible that social theories usually give pride of place to the one or the other and differ only in the manner in which this is done. On the centre stage of economic theory and rational choice theory more generally, socialized man either has no role at all or awaits his call in the wings. In sociology, the preference is less clear-cut. It tends to be revealed in the form of categories, which, while not declared residual at the outset, can be seen to possess this analytical status when the theory in question seeks to provide solutions of the problems it sets itself. This applies to both Parsons's concept of voluntarism and the Marxist idea of practice.

The former was mainly a product of Parsons's critique of what he took to be the sociologically unqualified assumptions about the rationality of actors which he detected in utilitarian social theory and showed to be incapable of yielding a satisfactory solution of the problem of order. Nevertheless, in principle, the notion of voluntaristic action does not seek to dispense with the idea that, in pursuing their ends and even in selecting and modifying them, people act rationally. Its purpose is rather to focus attention on the institutional context of rational action, that is to say, on the values and norms which define the kinds of goals that it is 'rational' for actors to strive after and the sorts of means that it is 'rational' for them to employ. This system of normative constraint is itself

---

[7] Compare, e.g., A. S. Vazquez, *The Philosophy of Praxis* (London, 1977), ch. 4, with Parsons, *The Structure of Social Action*, ch. 2, and his 'The Place of Ultimate Values in Sociological Theory', *International Journal of Ethics*, 45 (1935). See also A. Gouldner, *The Coming Crisis of Western Sociology*, pp. 185–95.

wholly explicable neither as the product of a rational accommodation of interests in the sense of an original 'social contract' nor as the unintended system effect of the interactions of individuals, each one rationally pursuing his immediate ends. From this viewpoint, then, what becomes of primary concern is the extent to which the ends of actors are integrated with one another through a system of common values and beliefs. But this does not imply that individuals are socialized into an unquestioning acceptance of values and an undeviating compliance with norms. Socialization is highly imperfect, values are always more or less exploitable, norms situationally ambiguous in some degree, and the means legitimately available to different classes of actors are never commensurate to the realization of their respectively prescribed ends. For these reasons, the insistence upon the importance of treating action as normatively regulated does not exclude the possibility of rational choice in the selection of means and ends. It merely assumes that the actor's orientation to norms is typically never a purely instrumental one.[8] For the same reasons, there is no force in the argument that there is a contradiction between holding to a voluntaristic concept of action and attributing a socially integrative function to common values.[9] This contradiction would only exist if the common-values assumption implied that people were socialized into a perfect consensus on values (in which case ends would be reduced to conditions of action) and if voluntarism implied that actors were perfectly autonomous in their choice of ends (in which case their ends would stand in a random relationship to one another). But neither position is entailed by anything Parsons has written about social action and system integration. The 'over-socialized' actors who inhabit the social system in his later works are not logical products of his taking the institutionalization of values as the focal problem of the structuring of social action. They are rather creatures of his conviction that the essential preliminary task of sociology is to

---

[8] Also that social stability is incompatible with the majority of actors adopting a purely instrumental attitude towards major social institutions.

[9] Such as that advanced by A. Dawe, 'Theories of Action', in T. Bottomore and R. Nisbet (eds.), *A History of Sociological Analysis* (London, 1979), 401 ff. The best short account of the growing emphasis on the role of common values in Parsonian sociology is still J. F. Scott, 'The Changing Foundations of the Parsonian Action Scheme', *American Sociological Review*, 28 (1963).

provide an account of the stability of social systems in distinctively non-utilitarian terms.

Since the theory of revolutionary, or revolutionizing, practice has a diametrically opposite explanatory purpose, it is perhaps not surprising that it should rest on a conception of action which is much closer to that of rational man. The assumption that capitalists and proletarians act rationally in pursuit of their immediate ends within the constraints of the 'wages system' is one that has already been shown to be indispensable to Marx's theory of the growing internal contradictions of capitalism. And it is difficult to avoid the conclusion that the idea of proletarian self-emancipation implies a course of action that is rational to an even higher degree. There are two senses in which this is so. First, it must be assumed that, by pursuing its immediate ends, the proletariat not only brings about changes in conditions but also acquires, and acts on, the understanding that these new conditions are simply means of achieving its now more ambitious ends. It is only through its progression up this means–ends chain of action that the proletariat arrives at a consciousness of its ultimate interest in abolishing the 'wages system' and at the same time helps to create the conditions under which this interest can be realized. Secondly, since conditions are social as well as natural, it must be assumed that the proletariat has, or develops, a highly instrumental orientation towards institutions other than those it creates for itself, and for its own historically inscribed end. This claim may seem hard to reconcile with the fact that Marx and Engels were obviously not unaware of the specific institutional obstacles in the path of the working-class movements of their day. They usually refer to them by such general terms as 'tradition', 'custom', and 'prejudice'; and Marxist social historians have not been slack at filling in the particulars. Nevertheless, there is nothing in this to suggest that such concepts have more than a residual status in the theory of revolutionary practice.[10] Unless the latter signifies nothing more

---

[10] To show that concepts are not residual, it is not enough to assert their importance in general terms or to demonstrate their significance in explaining specific events; they have to be incorporated into a theory systematically. That is to say, the general terms have to be identified with sufficient precision for their component elements to enter into the theory as variables of the same analytical status as those that are central to it. The accumulation of instances that exemplify the importance of taking account of residual factors may well testify to the need for theoretical reconstruction but will not in itself bring it about.

than the historical complexity and contingency of class struggle, it must imply that in the course of this struggle the proletariat is led step by step to a realization that all customary and traditional arrangements standing in the way of its ultimate goal are irrational.[11] At best they are means capable of being used to further its interests; at worst they are purely external conditions to which for the time being it has to adapt.

Since Marx nowhere refers to proletarian action as rational,[12] the foregoing interpretation of revolutionary practice is hypothetical. Yet how else is it possible to understand his depiction of the unfolding of working-class consciousness? 'The proletarian movement,' he writes, 'is the self-conscious, independent movement of the immense majority in the interests of the immense majority.' The proletariat is a class 'from which emanates the consciousness of the necessity of a fundamental revolution' and it is only 'in a practical movement, a *revolution*', that 'the production on a mass scale of this communist consciousness' and 'the alteration of men on a mass scale' can occur. And nothing could be more explicit than the statement that 'the emancipation of the working classes must be conquered by the working classes themselves. We cannot, therefore, co-operate with people who openly state that the workers are too uneducated to emancipate themselves.'[13] From these and similar passages, it is hard to conceive that revolutionary practice can readily be assimilated to the more general Marxian idea of the unanticipated consequences of social action and thereby understood as a kind of 'unintentional praxis'.[14]

---

[11] 'Law, morality, religion are to him [the proletarian] so many bourgeois prejudices, behind which lurk in ambush just as many bourgeois interests' (Marx and Engels, *Selected Works*, i. 42).

[12] This term is reserved to describe the activity of 'socialized man' in communist society; see *Capital*, iii. 820. There is an interesting parallel here between the revolutionary proletarian who has a rational, instrumental orientation to the institutions of bourgeois society and his successor, 'socialized man', who rationally regulates his activity in an institutional vacuum. Marx's unwillingness to go into too much detail about the institutional framework of socialist and communist society is partly to be explained by his aversion to 'utopian socialism'. A major aspect of Durkheim's critique of socialist doctrine is, of course, precisely concerned with this issue: the problem of the moral regulation of socialist economic life; see *Socialism*, ch. 10.

[13] The quotations are from McLellan, *The Thought of Karl Marx*, pp. 206, 20, 178 respectively.

[14] See Vazquez, *The Philosophy of Praxis*, pp. 265–7.

The classical formulation of this idea is Engels' account of historical events as the outcome of 'an infinite series of parallelograms of forces', a process in which

What each individual wills is obstructed by everyone else, and what emerges is something that no one willed. Thus past history proceeds in the manner of a natural process and is essentially subject to the same laws of motion. But from the fact that individual wills—of which each desires what he is impelled to by his physical constitution and external, in the last resort economic, circumstances (either his own personal circumstances or those of society in general)—do not attain what they want, but are merged into a collective mean, a common resultant, it must not be concluded that their value is equal to zero. On the contrary, each contributes to the resultant and is to this degree involved in it.[15]

In this conception of practice, human purpose does not disappear but it definitely takes second place to force of circumstances. In effect, the rationality of the actor is limited to the pursuit of his immediate ends, and his capacity to calculate that these ends are the means of achieving higher ends is replaced by some idea of objective or structural rationality[16] which operates behind his back to secure the same outcome. This is indispensable, because, if human action generally produces unintended consequences, how can it be guaranteed that proletarian action will result in the overthrow of capitalism? System effects of this sort are naturally central to Marx's general social theory. Both the condition of alienation which obstructs the development of proletarian class consciousness, and the inner contradictions of capitalism, which he believed would promote that consciousness, are explained in this way. The connection between intention and outcome is thus guaranteed by unanticipated consequences of social action, which, presenting themselves as conditions, constrain the proletariat to move towards its ultimate goal.

How is this view of social action to be reconciled with that which appears to be implicit in the idea of revolutionary practice? Or, rather, how can it be resolved in terms other than vague assertions about the need for a dialectical understanding of the complex relation between 'objective' and 'subjective' elements? One serious student of the problem arrives at the conclusion that

---

[15] Marx and Engels, *Selected Works*, ii. 444.
[16] Vazquez, *The Philosophy of Praxis*, pp. 283 ff.

there is no consistent solution of it, and that there is an inherent ambiguity in Marx's

alternation between the possibility and even necessity of consciously rational action, and a determinism which, while it precludes such action and accounts for men's necessarily false consciousness, simultaneously guarantees the ineffectiveness of false consciousness in the long run, and in this way ensures the rational outcome of irrational action-orientation.[17]

But how, however long the run may be, could a rational outcome result from unintentional practice? For Marx it would be inconceivable that the proletariat, in rationally pursuing its immediate ends, could inadvertently help to bring about revolutionary conditions without acquiring a revolutionary consciousness: that would be a contradiction in terms. A rather more plausible interpretation might be that the proletariat inadvertently acts in such a way as to produce such conditions and acquires a revolutionary consciousness only very suddenly, at the last moment, so to speak. This conception is by no means excluded by the idea of revolutionary practice, and has been called the 'explosion of consciousness' thesis.[18] It is a line of argument that will be considered in due course; but it is not one that is easy to square with Marx's own scattered comments on the subject, which seem to favour the alternative 'self-emancipation' thesis. The latter is constantly advanced. Even the famous and much-quoted passage in which he announces that the goal of the proletariat is historically ordained for it is preceded and followed by the equally emphatic, but much less frequently noted, statements that 'the proletariat can and must emancipate itself', that 'it is not in vain that it passes through the rough and stimulating school of labour', and that 'a large part of the English and French proletariat has already become *aware* of its historic mission, and works incessantly to clarify this awareness'. It is to a closer examination of the idea of self-emancipation that the discussion now turns.

III

Marx gives all too few indications of how precisely he expected the end-shift of the proletariat would occur, and of what revolu-

---

[17] Seliger, *The Marxist Conception of Ideology*, p. 73.
[18] For a pithy critique of the contemporary relevance of the idea, see Mann, *Consciousness and Action among the Western Working Class*, ch. 6.

tionary consciousness consists of. The view that Marxism itself is necessarily the theoretical expression of working-class consciousness has no real authority.[19] His own analysis concentrates attention on two main stages in the development of class struggle. The first is when workers in particular trades and industries become aware that they have economic interests in common which are opposed to those of their respective employers. This rudimentary class consciousness emerges in the face of the competition between workers, which capitalist production relations engender and which trade unions have constantly to combat. The second stage is the elevation of consciousness which Marx thought would be brought about when workers sought to enforce their general class interests through political, that is, legislative demands. This broad distinction between the particularity of the economic struggle and the revolutionizing effects of political class confrontation has been decisive for all subsequent debate on the nature of working-class consciousness; and attempts to arrive at more exact definitions have gone little beyond Marx's formulation. For example, in one scheme, levels of class consciousness are arranged in a hierarchy made up, in ascending order, of class identity, class opposition, an awareness of the operation of the class system as a totality, and, finally, the consciousness of an alternative, socialist, society.[20] Class identity and class opposition, which anyway may be thought to be opposite sides of the same coin, would seem to correspond more or less to Marx's first level of working-class consciousness. And the awareness of class inequality as a systematic product of the operation of capitalist society as a whole is very similar to the type of consciousness he expected to emerge from the politicization of the class struggle. The final level, the conception of an alternative social order, is not, however, something that Marx identifies as part of revolutionary consciousness, chiefly because he eschewed attempts to provide blueprints for

---

[19] See Miliband, *Marxism and Politics*, pp. 34–5, and T. Bottomore, editorial introduction to *Karl Marx* (Oxford, 1973), 31.

[20] The first three criteria are proposed by A. Touraine, *La Conscience ouvrière* (Paris, 1966), 17, 311 ff. The fourth is added by Mann in his modification of Touraine's scheme in *Consciousness and Action among the Western Working Class*, p. 13. See also J. H. Goldthorpe, 'L'Image des classes chez les travailleurs manuels aises', *Revue française de sociologie*, 11 (1970).

the socialist society of the future. 'Utopian socialism' did not sit easily with his idea of revolutionary practice.

Nevertheless, the concepts of identity, opposition, totality, and alternative are useful bench-marks for the analysis of working-class consciousness, since they differentiate the range of social comparisons entering into the notion of relative deprivation. Workers who possess a sense of class identity and class opposition are not thereby necessarily led to compare their lot with that of higher status groups. Indeed, the term 'trade union consciousness' was coined to accommodate Marxist theory to the fact that most workers normally compared themselves with other, and usually adjacent, sections of the working class. In other words, workers' interests are usually informed by some kind of status distinction within their own ranks. In contrast, a consciousness of the operation of the class system as a whole, and presumably of the need for, and the possibility of, its abolition, must also involve a repudiation of the society's status hierarchy. It might be expected, then, that this form of class consciousness would be heralded by the working class progressively widening the range of its social comparisons. Finally, if revolutionary consciousness is taken to include the conception of an alternative social order, then this plainly refers to what were earlier termed inter-societal comparisons.

What is gained by translating concepts of class consciousness into concepts that have to do with social comparison and relative deprivation? There are two main justifications. The first is that the language of reference groups and relative deprivation is the most convenient means of establishing a common ground between the conception of revolutionary practice and Durkheim's theory of anomic declassification. If this were the sole purpose, it should be considered factitious. But it is not the only consideration. As the discussion of material and moral impoverishment has shown, Marxist theories of revolutionary change cannot avoid raising crucial issues concerning the moral expectations of actors and the institutional sources of the variability of these expectations. The same, it may be supposed, applies to the idea of practice. In this respect, concepts such as identity, opposition, and totality have little to offer, because they merely redescribe what has to be explained: that is, the upward slope of consciousness which a self-emancipating proletariat has to traverse. In so far as these concepts contain a theory of action that could account for such a change in consciousness, it is one that is indistinguishable from the idea of revolutionary practice as a process in which the proletariat is endowed with instrumental rationality, by means of which, under the constraint of purely external conditions, it is able to attain an even wider and deeper understanding of the nature of class oppression. But elevated class consciousness is not, as Marx most often seems to suggest, simply a matter of improved understanding or clearer cognition; it has also to do with a sense of injustice, and hence with the structure of legitimate expectations which enters into definition of class interest at every level. Since Marx's general underestimation of the significance of these 'moral elements' also appears to be a major flaw in his theory of proletarian self-education, there is every reason to take them seriously. And there is no other way of doing this save through the idea of a status order, which is the principal source of social comparisons that have the most direct bearing on the problem of class formation.

In attempting to justify this line of argument, the best starting-point is provided by Marx's most specific observations on working-class self-emancipation, commentary on which has added little of real sociological significance.[21] Although his writings on the subject are difficult to piece together and open to different emphases,[22] the central thrust of his argument is fairly clear. While his belief in their effectiveness vacillated, there can be little doubt that he thought that trade unions were the major vehicles of revolutionizing practice. At one point, he could declare that

---

[21] For example, in one of the most highly thought of interpretations of Marxian social theory, the meaning of the 'social context of praxis' has no more specification than the following: 'Revolutionary *praxis* has thus a dialectical aspect. Objectively, it is the organization of the conditions leading towards ultimate human emancipation. Subjectively, it is the self-change the proletariat achieves by its self-discovery through organization. Through its organization the proletariat prepares the conditions for its self-emancipation. Organization and association, even considered apart from their immediate aims, constitute a crucial phase in the liberation of the workers. They change the worker, his way of life, his consciousness of himself and his society.' (Avineri, *The Social and Political Thought of Karl Marx*, pp. 136–7). Perhaps even more surprising, Marxist sociologists who consider praxis to be a concept of crucial importance do not seem to find it easy to say what in particular they think it is useful in illuminating. See, e.g., H. Lefebvre, *The Sociology of Marx* (London, 1968), and Swingewood, *Marx and Modern Social Theory*.

[22] Lozovsky, *Marx and the Trade Unions* (London, 1935), brings together practically all of the relevant material.

trade unions are the schools of socialism. It is in trade unions that workers educate themselves and become socialists because under their very eyes and every day the struggle with capital is taking place. Any political party, whatever its nature and without exception, can only hold the enthusiasm of the masses for a short time, momentarily; unions, on the other hand, lay hold of the masses in a more enduring way; they alone are capable of representing a true working-class party and opposing a bulwark to the power of capital.[23]

Yet only four years before he can be found castigating trade unions for 'limiting themselves to a guerilla war against the effects of the existing system, instead of simultaneously trying to change it'.[24] On balance, though, it would be hard to fault the conclusion that Marx 'places the main emphasis upon a spontaneous development of working class consciousness'.[25]

Of particular significance in his view of the advance of proletarian consciousness are the supposedly revolutionizing effects of the transformation of the economic into the political class struggle. This is held to be a qualitative change of the first importance, because it is only by engaging in a political confrontation with the capitalist class that the working class becomes a 'class for itself'. Through merely economic action particular sections of the proletariat may achieve specific interests within the overall constraints of the law. But in acting directly to change the law, the general interest of the class is asserted and thereby class conflict is raised to a higher level.

For instance, [Marx writes], the attempt in a particular factory or even in a particular trade to force a shorter working day out of individual capitalists by strikes, etc., is a purely economic movement. On the other hand the movement to force through an eight-hour day, etc., *law*, is a *political* movement. And in this way, out of the separate economic movements of the workers there grows up everywhere a political movement, that is to say, a movement of the class, with the object of enforcing

---

[23] McLellan, *The Thought of Karl Marx*, p. 175.

[24] Marx and Engels, *Selected Works*, i. 405.

[25] Bottomore, *Karl Marx*, p. 30. See also Miliband, *Marxism and Politics*, pp. 119, 131–2, and R. Hyman, *Marxism and the Sociology of Trade Unionism* (London, 1971), 11, where he concludes that, 'at the level of general theory, their early revolutionary interpretations of trade unionism remained unquestioned by Marx and Engels'.

its interests in a general form, in a form possessing general, socially coercive force.[26]

This escalation of the class struggle from the particularity of interest involved in economic conflict to the generality of interest revealed through political struggle would, Marx believed, lead to increasing class polarization. There is no doubt that this belief stemmed mainly from his study of the 'struggle for the normal working day'. Twice within a few adjacent pages of *Capital* he refers to this struggle as 'a civil war of half a century', and as 'a civil war, more or less dissembled, between the capitalist class and the working class'.[27] Whether or not it deserves the epithet of 'civil war', the campaign for the Ten Hours Bill was, together with Chartism, Marx's chief example of how the working class of the most advanced capitalist country of his day was, in the words of the *Communist Manifesto*, 'dragged into the political arena', and of how, embroiled in the conflict between capitalists and land-lords, it was furnished with 'its own elements of political and general education'. In fact, it is virtually the only concrete example of proletarian revolutionary practice that he provides; nowhere else in his writing does he give a more precise indication of the conditions that would bring about an alteration of working-class consciousness on a mass scale. But in his lengthy account of the campaign, he does not expand on this crucial theme. What principally concerns him is the ingenuity displayed by factory owners in exploiting the loopholes of legislation. On the effects of the politicization of the economic struggle on working-class consciousness he is practically silent.[28] Nevertheless, these have been amply documented by others, and there is no doubt that this phase of the English labour movement can be interpreted quite plausibly as a process of proletarian self-education.[29]

[26] McLellan, *The Thought of Karl Marx*, p. 17.

[27] Marx, *Capital*, i. 282, 285.

[28] Engels's brief sketch of changing class alliances is, from this point of view, the more useful. See his 'The English Ten Hours Bill', in K. Marx and F. Engels, *Articles on Britain* (Moscow, 1971), 96–108.

[29] And most explicitly by M. Vester, *Die Entstehung des Proletariats als Lernprozess: Die Entstehung antikapitalistischer Theorie und Praxis in England, 1792–1848* (Frankfurt, 1970). Vester seeks to identify six distinct 'learning cycles', each one culminating in the use of more effective means or the adoption of more realistic goals, so that the period as a whole represents in the main a 'progressive' learning process, with Chartism its high point. There are, however, also 'regressive'

In retrospect, however, the importance Marx attached to this episode seems extravagant, even allowing for the absolutely central place the reduction of the working day occupies in his view of historical progress and in his conception of communism in particular. The struggle over the working day, or even over factory legislation in general, has hardly proved to be the epicentre of class conflict in capitalist societies since his day. Of much greater consequence, it is now possible to appreciate how seriously he misjudged the effects of the entry of the working class into the political arena. In the most advanced capitalist countries, working-class organizations have generally had as their foremost, most enduring, and practical political goal not the overthrow of the existing order but rather the establishment of a secure status within it. The most acute class conflicts have characteristically centred on such issues as the legal status of trade unions, institutions of collective bargaining, and the right to the vote. Naturally, there are exceptions to this rule, but the struggle to gain rights that redefine the industrial and political status of the worker has been the most important long-run objective of the most powerful trade union movements. In this development, which has been aptly termed 'civic incorporation' (and is surely an instance of what Durkheim meant by 'social reclassification'), it has been status consolidating, rather than class revolutionary, interests which have predominated.

All of this is very difficult, if not impossible, to square with the idea of practice as a process of self-education in which the proletariat rationally acquires a progressively deeper understanding of the system of class exploitation and thereby an interest in its revolutionary transformation. It is equally indisputable that the drastic revision of this version of the theory of practice at the hands of Kautsky and Lenin was a necessary accommodation to these inconvenient facts of labour history. But the revised theory of practice does not obviate the need to explain how the proletariat will attain something close to revolutionary consciousness; otherwise, the 'elective affinity' between mass and 'vanguard' would be inconceivable. It is here that the 'explosion of conscious-

---

aspects of the process and these come to predominate after 1848 with 'the depoliticization and bureaucratization of trades unions and the labour movement abandoning its political autonomy'.

ness', rather than the 'self-emancipation', thesis acquires its significance. And, although it may be an alternative or auxiliary hypothesis to Marx's principal one, there is no great difficulty in authenticating it: the ambiguity of his sparse observations on the working class sees to that.

Despite his claim that communists had the 'theoretical' advantage over the great mass of workers in possessing a clear understanding of 'the line of march, the conditions, and the ultimate general results of the proletarian movement',[30] this knowledge of the conditions of class formation was nowhere handed down in systematic form. For this reason also it was also impossible for him to say anything about how long revolutionary consciousness would take to emerge, or even much in particular about the circumstances that would promote or forestall its emergence. Would revolution, as he sometimes thought, be triggered off by the next economic crisis; or would it, as he thought on yet other occasions, involve a protracted political struggle over several generations? At what stage in the socialization of production relations would the working class achieve that level of consciousness which transformed it into a critical revolutionary mass, in the absence of which 'it is absolutely indifferent for practical developments, as the history of communism proves, whether the idea of that revolution has already been formulated a hundred times?' The fact that Marx did not go deeply into such matters was not of course incompatible with, and was probably due to, the certainty of his belief that proletarian revolt was imminent; and not having a well-worked-out theory of revolution imposed few restrictions upon his expectations of when and where that event would occur.[31] The precipitating conditions remain obscure, but presumably pre-eminent among them would be the economic crises 'whose periodical return put on trial, each time more threateningly, the existence of the entire bourgeois society'.[32]

---

[30] McLellan, *The Thought of Karl Marx*, p. 172.

[31] 'Every crisis that seems to shock the stability of the established order he projects into a portent and prelude to revolution. His philosophical system is quite unable to help him to greater discrimination about the precise location of the next revolutionary outburst. All that philosophical system, with all its richness, insight, complexity and intellectual brilliance could offer him was the evangelical truth that the millenium was around the corner.' (Avineri, *The Social and Political Thought of Karl Marx*, p. 256).

[32] Marx and Engels, *Selected Works*, i. 38.

The legacy of Marx's vacillating hopes of proletarian revolt has been a conception of practice whose chief feature is the volatility of working-class consciousness. This idea of the possibility of an 'explosion' of consciousness stands in fairly marked contrast to that of self-education, understood as a process in which the working class, through its experience of the class struggle, gradually learns that its interests can only be realized through the revolutionary transformation of the capitalist system. This hard-won education goes hand in hand with the growing strength of trade-union organization and a progressive widening and intensification of political class conflict. By contrast, the key assumption of the alternative, explosion thesis is that working-class consciousness is capable of undergoing a sudden, fundamental, and largely unpredictable alteration.[33] This possibility of a 'jump' or 'leap' in consciousness makes revolution an ever-present eventuality whenever class conflict is heightened by economic crisis and industrial strife. And naturally, since there is always a 'next time', it is an assumption that makes this theory of practice inherently irrefutable. Nevertheless, the idea of such a radical discontinuity in class consciousness is to be found not only in Marx's work, but also in that of his successors, where it plays a more specific and important role. It is integral to both Lenin's reformulation of the Marxian theory of revolution and to Luxemburg's strategy of the 'mass strike'. Despite his demotion of the idea of proletarian self-emancipation and his view that the spontaneous tendency of the working class was in favour of trade-union consciousness and reformism, Lenin held to the assumption that the proletariat of the advanced capitalist societies possessed a revolutionary potential that could be quickly actualized; and this assumption is a fundamental part of his theory of practice. 'Revolution', he writes, 'enlightens all classes with a rapidity and thoroughness unknown in normal, peaceful times,' and 'during a revolution millions and

---

[33] For example, one of the most acute writers on the sociology of class conflict concludes his survey by saying that the 'limits of trade union consciousness can vary markedly between historical contexts and can shift radically with only a brief passage of time', and hence 'no *general* theory is available to relate the struggle for material reforms to the development of consciousness', so that 'the theoretical issue, in other words, can be resolved only through the *praxis* of the struggle itself' (Hyman, *Marxism and the Sociology of Trade Unionism*, pp. 52–3).

tens of millions of people learn in a week more than they do in a year of ordinary, somnolent life'.[34]

In so far as the explosion-of-consciousness thesis can ever be challenged, its credibility is much diminished by the selfsame facts of labour history that cast doubt on the alternative idea of proletarian self-education. Just as Marx misjudged the outcome of the initial politicization of the class struggle, Lenin was not alone in overestimating the revolutionary potential of the working class at a later stage of capitalist development. If the waves of industrial unrest that swept through Western Europe after the First World War make it easy to understand how Lenin could have entertained hopes of a revolutionary outbreak, the events of the subsequent sixty years provide no instance of an explosion of consciousness that is at all comparable. That neither theory of revolutionizing practice possesses much explanatory power is, moreover, all too evident from the fact that, in so much of contemporary Marxism, the discussion of them resembles nothing more than a recriminatory post-mortem. Even attempts at resurrection through exegesis have produced little more than the familiar remains. For this reason, it is proposed to examine these problems from an entirely different viewpoint, since so many of the facts that are an embarrassment to both conceptions of practice fall conveniently into place when seen from the perspective of Durkheim's theory of anomic declassification and reclassification, which, as was shown above, supercedes in every significant respect his rudimentary idea of moral innovation through hyper-ritual. But, at this stage, the latter is the more relevant starting-point.

IV

What is first of all most striking about the explosion-of-consciousness thesis is its similarity to Durkheim's attempt to explain changes in the collective conscience as the result of hyper-ritual. In both cases, there is the assumption of a threshold effect: beyond a certain point the intensification of social forces results in

---

[34] Quoted by Parkin, *Marxism and Class Theory*, pp. 158–9, who also notes the similarity between Lenin's views and 'Durkheim's notion of the creative powers of "effervescence" generated by collective social action'.

an alteration of class consciousness or the creation of new beliefs. There is a clear parallel between the view that new moral standards emerge spontaneously when collective interactions become extraordinarily 'dense' and 'effervescent', and the view that revolutionary consciousness is generated by exceptionally acute class conflict. The 'general' or 'mass' strike, large-scale factory occupations, and political demonstrations of class solidarity are the prime examples of those critical breaks in social routine when, if only momentarily and partially, authority and status are peremptorily challenged, the limited social horizons of the ordinary worker are suddenly and dramatically widened, and hitherto dormant aspirations are aroused and seek a new dispensation. On these occasions, which take on the quality of political hyper-rituals, it is assumed, in a typical Durkheimian fashion, that the sheer increase in the frequency of social interactions or moral density has as its almost direct and unmediated effect a profound alteration in consciousness.

Before reconsidering this crucial assumption of the explosion-of-consciousness thesis, it is important to note that the necessity of its introduction is in large part due to the failure of Marxist theory systematically to take into account the category of ritual action in general; that is to say, the actor's non-rational commitment to ultimate ends. The most important example of this, which has already been referred to several times before, is civic incorporation, a process which can best be understood as status reclassification. But there are also at least three other ways in which ritual elements enter into the determination of working-class action.

First, the ceremonial occasions, ranging all the way from craft initiation ceremonies to national galas, on which workers in particular trades and industries gather together, locally, regionally, or nationally, to express and reaffirm their sense of identity, are identical with the rituals through which Durkheim understood that every social group was periodically in need of strengthening its unity through the celebration of collective values and beliefs.[35] Protracted industrial disputes sometimes have the same function

---

[35] This point is very well made by S. Lukes, 'Political Ritual and Social Integration', *Sociology*, 9 (1975), and by E. J. Hobsbawm, *Social Bandits and Primitive Rebels* (London, 1959), ch. 9.

of evoking similar sentiments and of reinforcing a sense of occupational cohesion. But, while these ritual gatherings and secular conflicts may serve to bring out a consciousness of a wider class solidarity, very often their chief effect is to strengthen traditional status demarcations by investing the primarily utilitarian nature of intra-class divisions with a moral significance. Secondly, the familiar tendency towards oligarchy, from which trade unions are not exempt, can result in goal displacement or the transformation of organizational means into ends in themselves. This process, commonly associated with the interests of leaders in acquiring and securing status within and outside the organization, is a typical case of ritual action.[36] Thirdly, adherence to such organizations involves a ritual element in so far as there is a disparity between the life span of the organization and that of its membership. In this disparity lies a major flaw in the idea of practice conceived of as the progressive self-education of the proletarian subject. For the learning from experience of the individual worker must be distinguished from that of an organization whose capacity to learn is in large part a function of the tradition it embodies, which is in turn a crystallization of the experiences and learning of past generations of its membership. Through the tradition of an organization, a ritual element inevitably enters into the determination of what is a rational course of action for the individuals who comprise its present membership. Working-class organizations are not in any way privileged to remain immune from Marx's dictum that 'the tradition of all the dead generations weighs like a nightmare on the brain of the living'.[37]

It could, of course, be argued that these kinds of factors are subsumed under the accepted Marxist formula of 'trade-union consciousness'. But this is not a position that can easily be maintained. The theory of trade union consciousness is far too sweeping and undiscriminating to provide a satisfactory explanation of variations in working-class consciousness both within and between capitalist countries. A major reason for this is that it is a theory in which concepts such as tradition, status, and ritual have no real standing, since all action oriented to ultimate ends other than that of socialism is treated as irrational, the product of

---

[36] See Merton, *Social Theory and Social Structure*, pp. 149–53.
[37] Marx and Engels, *Selected Works*, i. 225.

ignorance and error, whether on the part of leaders or led. In acknowledging the extent of this 'irrationality', the concept of trade-union consciousness is then more a symptom of the inadequacy of the theory of proletarian self-education than any improvement upon it, since the underlying action schema remains the same. It is also a concept that finds its complement in the explosion-of-consciousness thesis, since the latter offers an explanation of how workers' irrational, or at least limited, aspirations can be more or less instantaneously transformed into revolutionary goals.[38]

The closest approximations to explosions of consciousness are, as was noted above, the mass strikes that swept through several European countries after the First World War, and, most notably in Germany and Italy, the establishment of workers' councils, and the occupation of factories. Although the background of these movements naturally included many particular historical circumstances, it is nevertheless safe to say that they were all shaped by certain social and economic changes which were greatly accelerated by the war and were the kinds of discontinuities that Durkheim would have considered to be 'anomic'. In more or less marked degree, these were the rapid mobilization of the workforce, its industrial and urban concentrations, the threat to traditional skills due to the influx of semi-skilled labour, and a harsher factory discipline, all of which resulted in the accumulation of grievances and discontents which, by the end of the war, had become fused with expectations of major social and economic reform and further heightened by conditions of political uncertainty if not downright governmental instability.[39] There can also be little doubt about the spontaneity of working-class protest which then broke out, or the fact that its more radical expression received only lukewarm support from, if it was not seen as a direct challenge to trade union and socialist party establishments. Yet, at the same time, it is highly debatable whether, even among the

---

[38] The only other solution of the problem of trade-union consciousness is, of course, the Leninist strategy of 'arraignment'. It seems appropriate to postpone consideration of this until the discussion turns to the subject of ideological domination. See ch. 13, s. II.

[39] See the excellent summary in D. Geary, *European Labour Protest, 1848–1939* (London, 1981), ch. 4; and C. L. Bertrand (ed.), *Revolutionary Situations in Europe, 1917–1922* (Quebec, 1977).

workers drawn into these movements, revolutionary goals pre-dominated; as indeed is the efficacy of such action as a means of generating, not to say sustaining, a revolutionary consciousness.[40] Finally, comparable currents of socialist enthusiasm have been virtually absent in advanced capitalist countries: their modern exemplar is surely *Solidarność*. So the explosion-of-consciousness thesis draws its support mainly from one historical conjuncture, which was the product of a concatenation of very special and unusual conditions.

This crucial episode in the history of the labour movement draws attention once again to the chief weakness of this version of the theory of practice. For, while it is impossible to disprove the hypothesis that the proletariat possesses a latent revolutionary potential which will sooner or later be released in a situation of acute class conflict, the failure to specify the conditions under which it is likely to occur means that all the explanatory emphasis is placed on the intensity of the conflict. Because of this, the explosion-of-consciousness thesis rests on the same, highly ques-tionable, assumptions as Durkheim's theory of hyper-ritual: namely, that changes in the collective conscience are the direct, structurally unmediated, effect of the 'effervescence' caused by extraordinarily 'dense' social interactions. It is true that in Marxist theory this social ferment is seen as the product of fundamental class relations. But the link between them is hard to perceive and the postulated effect comes about in a similar manner and differs from the Durkheimian model only in that it results in class polarization rather than moral innovation, which from a certain viewpoint might be considered as equivalent. Beyond this, it has to be said that it would be to take a very impoverished view of what a society consists of to suppose that the only structurally significant determinants of class consciousness are reducible to the basic capitalist–proletarian relationship.

V

It is in this connection that Durkheim's theory of anomic disorder as a process of status declassification becomes of more direct

[40] On the latter point, see P. Anderson, 'The Limits and Possibilities of Trade Union Action', and E. Mandel, 'The Leninist Theory of Organization', both in Clarke and Clements (eds.), *Trade Unions under Capitalism*.

relevance than that of hyper-ritual, of which it is a logical extension. It will be remembered that the latter is the chief way in which he seeks to account for moral innovation within the terms of his analysis of the normally socially integrative function of ritual in a society exemplifying the features of an 'elementary religious life' and possessing only the most rudimentary division of labour. In this case, ordinary rituals serve to reinforce collective beliefs which are periodically weakened by the physical dispersal of individuals and their absorption in utilitarian activities. Hyper-ritual is said to occur when the moral effervescence associated with ordinary rituals becomes exceptionally intense due to some kind of extraordinarily heightened social interaction. Why this should happen is not immediately obvious. But it would appear that the most general cause of this kind of creative ferment has to be found in the collapse of what Durkheim calls a social hierarchy, or social classification, which defines the legitimate aspirations of different social classes and thereby limits the range of invidious comparisons with respect to the distribution of power and wealth. Although this scenario only unfolds in his explanation of anomie, it is nevertheless the necessary complement to his theory of elementary religion, because social classification and declassification are the sole conceptual means of providing a structural explanation of the moral innovation associated with hyper-ritual. It may be that these terms can also help to throw some light on the cognate problem of revolutionary consciousness.

Under normal conditions, incongruities in power, wealth, and status are usually confined to particular regions and levels of a society, affecting only marginally the pre-existing aspirations of contiguous social groups. These dislocations are usually easily reparable through incorporation, or by some other, perhaps more informal, means of reclassifying 'men and things'. By contrast with such local disturbances, anomic declassification proper involves a far more widespread social upheaval, which results in such gross disparities of class and status that the entire social hierarchy may be brought into question. This eventuality depends on whether the existing status order can accommodate itself to the sudden redistribution of 'men and things'; on whether new wealth and power enjoy appropriate status elevation through incorporation or suffer persistent status exclusion; on whether status demotion is accepted by those groups whose power and wealth has diminished; and on whether these types of status rivalry set in train a chain reaction of relative status deprivation which affects the least, as well as the most, privileged social classes.[41] In the situation of extreme anomic declassification, social reference points widen, moving progressively from intra-status-group to inter-status-group comparisons, which, especially if these also invoke inter-societal comparisons, compromise ultimate values and beliefs and threaten the integrity of the status hierarchy in its entirety. But this complete delegitimation of the status system is very much a limiting case of disorder; the important point is that throughout the process of declassification, class interests are first and foremost informed by considerations of status, and that it is through the existing status order that these interests are in turn negotiated and contained.

Whatever its deficiencies in other respects, Durkheim's idea of anomic declassification does at least serve to clarify the shortcomings of any theory of practice whose central assumption is that, under conditions of acute economic crisis, working-class consciousness can rapidly achieve a revolutionary pitch. Translated into Durkheimian terms, the assumption is that working-class interests can easily escape the constraint of intra-class comparisons (which is one way of defining 'trade-union consciousness') and become informed by inter-class, and even inter-societal, reference points. Using different terms, which have been introduced above, the postulated 'jump' in consciousness is from a level at which sentiments of cohesion and opposition predominate to one at which the proletariat's awareness of deprivation is heightened by its acquiring an understanding of the systematic nature of class oppression and of the possibility of the abolition of this oppression through revolutionary action. But what this perspective lacks, and what Durkheim's notion of declassification provides, is an appreciation of the extent to which the status order of a society can undergo quite considerable destabilization and readjustment without class conflict eventuating in ideological polarization. Another way of putting this is to say that the idea of a rapid escalation of class consciousness to the revolutionary level does not sufficiently take into account the tendency of socially deregulated, or status incongruent, classes to seek first and foremost the reclassification

---

[41] For the detailed argument supporting this interpretation, see ch. 5, ss. II, III.

of their position within the existing social hierarchy, and to limit their interests to seeking marginal adjustments of traditional status boundaries.

All of this is of direct relevance to Marx's idea of the self-education of the proletariat, a process characterized above all by the movement of the class struggle from the economic to the political level. His chief reason for thinking of this transition as crucial is that political confrontation reveals the general nature of class relations, which remain opaque as long as conflict remains confined to the competition between particular groups of workers and capitalists. It is assumed that the politicization of industrial conflict leads fairly directly to the working class acquiring a clear and comprehensive understanding of its collective interest. One way of describing this effect is to say that the range of social comparisons not only widens but undergoes a qualitative change: instead of the worker remaining oriented to the conventional status hierarchy defining position within the working class by reference to such attributes as skill, respectability, and remuneration, his awareness becomes focused on the rights and duties governing the relationship between the proletariat and the bourgeoisie as two distinct and antagonistic classes. Instead of each particular group of workers pursuing their specific interests through the use of economic sanctions within the existing legal framework, political action may be considered proto-revolutionary because it brings into question rights of private property and free contract, and thereby the legitimacy of the entire structure of class relations and class powers. Marx simply argues that the political struggle makes particular groups of workers conscious of the wider class interest they share in common. But if such a consciousness were not also associated with a belief in the iniquity of capitalist institutions, how could it be revolutionary? The answer must be that Marx took it for granted that the proletariat was already sufficiently well acquainted with the injustice of class relations, and that what it needed above all was an understanding of the possibility of changing them, fundamentally. What was needed, then, was not moral education or indignation, but enlightenment, an antidote to fatalism.

Durkheim's theory of reclassification carries almost the opposite implications: namely, that the corporate actions of disaffected social groups are more likely to be oriented initially to the protection, acquisition, or augmentation of status rights within the existing social order. In this case, and to the extent that such demands are acceded to, if only partially, there is no inherent reason why the politicization of class conflict should lead to a wholescale repudiation of dominant institutions and to revolutionary consciousness. With hindsight, the Durkheimian perspective would seem to be the more informative in that the political objectives of organized labour have generally centred on such issues as the extension of the franchise, the establishment of collective bargaining, and the enlargement of social welfare entitlements. The struggle over, the gradual achievement of these political, industrial, and social rights making up the modern structure of citizenship represents a profound change in the status, and thereby also the class, position of the working class—a process much more akin to Durkheim's idea of social reclassification than to Marx's notion of revolutionary practice.

Indeed, according to the basic presuppositions of Marxist theory, action in pursuit of these interests is ultimately irrational, because an attachment to 'mere' trade unionism, or to what used to be called the 'sham' of bourgeois democracy, is nothing more than a form of ideologically induced false consciousness which prevents the proletariat from becoming aware of its interest in socialism. Nevertheless, this hypothesis is not very useful in explaining why such 'irrational' interests should have been so enduringly important at so many different critical stages in the development of the labour movements of so many different countries. As will be seen later on, the thesis of ideological domination is far too general to provide a satisfactory explanation of the historical diversity and particularity of working-class consciousness. Nor does it provide an adequate basis for understanding how working-class interests are likely to unfold in contemporary capitalist societies. At the same time, these problems are unlikely to be elucidated by adopting the opposite assumption: namely, that courses of action that Marxism considers to be irrational can best be explained as being informed by, and the outcome of, wholly rational choice, based on a scientific understanding of the situation and an irrefragable logic. For this also would leave no place for action that is neither rational nor irrational, but rather nonrational, in the positive sense that it is oriented to standards of ultimate value which lie beyond scientific calculation. It is through their embodiment in the status order of a society that these standards most concretely and systematically exert their social force, which includes the shaping of class interest. Whether status interests are anchored in the metropolitan or some local region of society, whether they are informed by expectations of legal entitlement or customary recognition, these interests—including the need to win respect and to avoid derogation—are at least as powerful in shaping conduct as the seemingly more 'material' interests which derive from antagonistic class relationships.[42] Indeed, there is a sense in which, under normal conditions, class position is, to use Dumont's term, 'encompassed' by status position.[43] That is to say, class interests are generated within the matrix of a status order, which does quite literally order these interests by providing them with direction, significance, and legitimation.

The major weakness of the theory of revolutionary practice, then, is one that it can be seen to share with other theories of proletarian action. It inheres in the impossibility of incorporating into a basically utilitarian action schema concepts that would give due recognition to the structuring of nonrational orientations, particularly status interests, while at the same time preserving the identity of Marxism as a distinctive social theory. This defect, already noted in several contexts, is hardly surprising, since the exclusion of status interests is central to Marx's definition of the proletariat as a 'universal' class: 'a sphere of society which claims no *traditional* status but only a human status'.[44] Such a class has never existed and never will; and, if exchanging aphorisms is at all useful, then Dawley's observation that, for the US working class, 'the ballot box was the coffin of class consciousness'[45] is a generalizable dictum of much greater acuity.

---

[42] This is true of revolutionary action also. For example, salient among the demands of the Kiel sailors whose mutiny triggered off the revolution of 1918 was that for 'less overbearing treatment by their officers and the right to use less deference in addressing them', see A. J. Ryder, *The German Revolution of 1918* (Cambridge, 1967), 141.

[43] Dumont, *Homo Hierarchicus*, p. 165.

[44] Marx, in the 'Critique of Hegel's "Philosophy of Right"', in *Early Writings*, p. 58 (italic in original).

[45] A. Dawley, *Class and Community: The Industrial Revolution in Lynn* (Cambridge, Mass., 1976), 70.

VI

If the Marxist theory of class conflict needs, but cannot provide, a way of dealing with the relationship between class and status, because it has no concept of a status system to set against that of class, Durkheim's theory of anomie is vitiated for the exactly opposite reason. While social theory awaits a thoroughgoing analysis of the interrelationship between class and status, a model for it and one that is highly germane to the present discussion is provided by T. H. Marshall in his study of citizenship and social class.[46] Dealing partly with the same period of British history from which Marx drew many of his generalizations about class action, Marshall seeks to show how the dissolution and reconstitution of the status order was decisive for understanding the development of class conflict. Moreover, the sequence of stable classification, declassification, and reclassification postulated by Durkheim in his theory of anomie has flesh put on its bones by Marshall's account of the twofold transition from a society organized in estates to an almost purely market-dominated class society, and then to one in which a new framework of citizenship becomes established.

The first change is that from a society in which the three basic strands of civil, political, and social privilege were 'wound in a single thread', and in which there was 'no principle of equality of citizens to set against the principle of inequality of classes', to a system where inequalities of political power and welfare came to be determined by the outcome of a market competition between classes who were at once highly unequal in their possession of economic resources and yet formally equal in their possession of civil rights. Such a situation is highly conducive to class antagonism, and this is not so simply because, as Weber argued, life chances are determined and seen to be determined largely by market power, but also because of the other reasons that Marshall points to. The coexistence of vast disparities in economic advantage with a basic equality of rights to acquire property and enter into contracts encourages precisely the kind of inter-class comparison and sense of relative deprivation that the previous order discouraged, despite, or rather because of, its more thoroughgoing inequality. Simultaneously, dissent is engendered because the

[46] Marshall, *Citizenship and Social Class*.

allocation of political status and welfare is no longer tied to a 'natural' principle of all-encompassing status ascription but rather to a weak legitimating principle of market success and failure, the arbitrary nature of which is most evident in the property franchise. Under these circumstances, it is natural that a 'class in civil society which is not a class of civil society', which is how Marx describes the proletariat, should have as one of its main immediate interests the acquisition of political rights. Finally, because economic, political, and welfare inequalities tend to be aligned with and superimposed upon one another, there is a strong propensity to class polarization that is once again conditioned by the presence of a standard of equality in the form of civil rights which are indispensable to the workings of the market economy.

Marshall's analysis of how, from this juncture, the further development of citizenship status contributed to the abatement and institutionalization of class conflicts has been absorbed into the orthodoxy of sociological theories of working-class consciousness.[47] The extension of the franchise, the creation of social rights, and the establishment of a 'secondary system of industrial citizenship parallel with and supplementary to the system of political citizenship' have been seen as having had important effects upon the structure of class relations: namely, the diminution of the scope of market-based power and the increase in the status determination of life chances; the separation of industrial and political arenas of conflict; and the creation of cross pressures between the divisive solidarities of class and the status common to citizens of the wider society.

While Marshall confines his attention to Britain, his concepts of the civil, political, social, and industrial rights of citizenship are indispensable to the understanding of variations in the radicalism of working-class movements in other countries. In general, the earlier the working class has acquired effective industrial and political rights the less radical the labour movement has been. Plainly it cannot be claimed that the form of the institutionalization

---

[47] See, esp., R. Bendix, *Nation Building and Citizenship* (New York, 1964), ch. 3; S. M. Lipset, *Political Man* (London, 1960), ch. 3; A. M. Ross and P. T. Hartman, *Changing Patterns of Industrial Conflict* (New York, 1960); E. Shorter and C. Tilly, *Strikes in France, 1830–1968* (Cambridge, 1974), esp. ch. 12. By far the best general survey of the subject is J. M. Barbalet, *Citizenship: Rights, Struggle and Class Inequality* (Milton Keynes, 1988).

of citizenship provides a complete explanation of national differences in class formation.[48] Yet the values and institutions of citizenship must be a major part of any such explanation. All capitalist societies have been faced with the problem of the incorporation of the working class, and the various modes of its resolution go some considerable way in accounting for national differences in the saliency of class consciousness at the present time. This is to imply neither a legal nor a moral determinism or that citizenship is purely integrative in its consequences. The several strands of citizenship do not emerge as the unfolding of some immanent principle of order, with classes, status groups, and parties acting merely as the vehicles of its expression. The extension of citizenship is a history of class struggle and the term 'civic incorporation', which modern Marxism has found congenial and has adopted, is obviously grossly misleading if it is used to suggest that the working class has been successfully domesticated by skilful ruling-class manipulation. This would not only ignore the extent to which citizenship rights have been the outcome of class struggle and its accommodation; it would also exaggerate the unity and prescience of the capitalist class, and its capacity to constitute social relations for its advantage. Nevertheless, citizenship does possess an inner dynamic, and the conflicts of interest which shape its institutional form at any one particular stage are themselves changed in the process and have their social force redirected as a consequence of both the practical working out of new forms of citizenship and of the principles still dormant in them—principles that are as yet unrealized in social action and have the potential for exacerbating as well as diminishing class and other kinds of conflicts.[49]

For these reasons alone, it would be erroneous to suppose that the social cohesion of present-day capitalist societies is guaranteed

[48] A factor of crucial importance—though not one that can be readily fitted into the Marxist schema—is the superimposition of unresolved religious cleavages on emergent lines of class division. The development of a radical working-class movement in France and Italy is due at least as much to its being bound up with a radical–secular/Catholic–traditionalist opposition as to any purely economic factors. It is this factor which, as much as anything else, has contributed to the relative weakness of civic incorporation. See esp. S. M. Lipset and S. Rokkan (eds.), *Party Systems and Voter Alignments* (New York, 1967).

[49] For an elaboration of these points, see D. Lockwood, 'Schichtung in der Staatsbuergergesellschaft', in B. Giesen and H. Haferkamp (eds.), *Soziologie der sozialen Ungleichheit* (Opladen, 1987).

by their movement in the direction of what Parsons has called 'full citizenship'.[50] Yet this is what was announced by erstwhile proponents of the idea of the 'institutionalization of class conflict' and its cultural outrider, the 'end of ideology'. But it is unlikely that capitalism is peculiarly privileged in having the kind of homoeostasis celebrated by such ideas. In all societies, the legitimation of the unequal distribution of wealth and power is of necessity always imperfect. This is partly because the accumulation and dissolution of power has a momentum of its own which is often inconsiderate of established status expectations of who should get what, when, and how. But moral regulation is also imperfect because the logic of status reaches beyond the world of inequality as it finds it and to which it must accommodate. Its horizons are ideal, and the tension between ideology and reality is an additional reason why adherence to a status order is never unconditional, even on the part of those who are most indulged by its dispensation. Indeed, the tendency of status orders to call forth their own negation in the ideal of equality is very widespread. In many cases, the influence of this ideal has been only very feeble, peripheral, and intermittent; but in others some notion of equality is at the very core of the common morality. Citizenship is an institution embodies values which are more exploitable than most because of its diffuse egalitarian promise, the limits of which are highly uncertain. Thus 'full citizenship' is a chimera, its acclamation merely the ground for claiming a 'fuller' citizenship. But if fuller citizenship were to involve a substantial enlargement of social as opposed to civil and political rights, the lack of consensus on principles of distributive justice would quickly be apparent. The elaboration of this point is worthwhile not only for its own sake, but also because it will provide a further example of how inattention to status interests both characterizes and vitiates the theory of revolutionary practice.

In contemporary capitalist societies, the legitimation of inequality rests to a very considerable extent upon the effectiveness of the economic system to 'deliver the goods', that is its ability to meet aspirations for a certain standard of living or style of life, which vary according to occupation or profession, and which are

---

[50] T. Parsons, 'Full Citizenship for the Negro American?' in his *Sociological Theory and Modern Society*.

determined both by customary or traditional expectations of the relative rewards due to different occupational groups and by changes in bargaining power. The degree to which the determination of inequalities is displaced from the political to the economic sphere, and thereby legitimated by 'market efficiency' rather than by specific status entitlements, is a measure of the extent to which citizenship is still limited to what may be called formal as opposed to substantive rights. Formal citizenship in this context is taken to mean those civil, political, and social rights which segregate industrial from political conflict, redress the balance of industrial bargaining power of capital over labour, and provide some modicum of security for persons who are unable to compete in the market at all or to equip themselves to do so on anything like equal terms. These are the status rights that limit, regulate, and legitimate capitalist market exchanges—what Durkheim called the 'non-contractual elements of contract'. More specifically, the institutionalization of formal citizenship might be understood as a movement in the direction of bringing about that 'equality in the external conditions of conflict' which Durkheim considered essential for organic solidarity. At the present time, rights of social and industrial citizenship vary very considerably from country to country, and have correspondingly more or less marked effects on the overall pattern of economic and social inequalities. But in most cases they remain marginal to, because primarily enabling rather than invasive of, market-exchange relationships. This type of citizenship is very different from one that would take the form of social rights and was aimed at bringing about a distribution of income and welfare embodying an ideal of social justice and standards of economic efficiency. Some appreciable movement towards this kind of 'institutional' as opposed to 'marginal' citizenship is already discernible in the Scandinavian social democracies, especially in Sweden, where the 'solidaristic' wages policy pursued through centralized collective bargaining has complemented a high level of social welfare provision.[51] As an ideal type, this form of citizenship entails not only a more robust notion of equality of

---

[51] See R. Erikson and R. Åberg, *Welfare in Transition: A Survey of Living Conditions in Sweden, 1968–1981* (Oxford, 1987), and W. Korpi, *The Democratic Class Struggle* (London, 1983). The distinction between marginal and institutional social policy is made by R. Titmus, *Social Policy* (London, 1974), 30–1.

opportunity but a clarification of what Durkheim referred to as the 'dim perception, in the moral consciousness of societies, of the respective value of different social services, the relative reward due to each, and the consequent degree of comfort appropriate on the average to workers in each occupation'.[52] Substantive citizenship is therefore qualitatively different from formal citizenship, since it is built on values that run counter to the market and point beyond this mode of income determination. Whereas formal citizenship has served to ameliorate market outcomes and thereby legitimate market relations (including collective bargaining), substantive citizenship rests on principles that point to a very different institutional order in which status rights would more and more encroach on contractual relations, and status entitlements on market-determined rewards. As such, substantive citizenship is a natural, if unintended, extension of the ethos and practice of citizenship.

But what is natural in logic is seldom so in social practice, and a principal reason for the arrestment of citizenship at its formal level is the lack of a 'moral calculus' by means of which a planned income distribution could command lasting support on grounds of both rightness and efficiency. A glimpse of this problem is afforded by the experience of attempts to implement 'incomes policies' as a means of achieving that elusive combination of economic growth, full employment, and low rates of inflation.[53]

[52] The Swedish model is again instructive. When, in a 1984 national survey, respondents were asked to choose between different principles of wage distribution, it was the norm of 'responsibility' which found the most widespread popular support. See A. S. Olsson, *The Swedish Wage Negotiation System* (Uppsala, 1989), ch. 6. 'Responsibility' can, of course, be interpreted in several different ways. But a certain degree of ambiguity is a necessary feature of any norm that could serve the purpose of social reclassification.

[53] Here the discussion is based principally on the British experience, in which the politicization of industrial conflict has been most evident and relevatory of industrial anomie. Countries have differed greatly in the extent to which governments have been constrained to introduce incomes policies, which themselves have differed considerably in their form, efficiency, and the resistance they have met with. In general, some kind of income policy has come closest to being institutionalized in countries where there are highly centralized and internally well-disciplined organizations of capital and labour, and where social democratic governments have been in power, or have participated in coalition governments, for long periods of time. The literature on this subject is vast, but a useful conspectus is provided by H. Clegg, *Trade Unionism under Collective Bargaining* (London, 1976). See also S. Barkin (ed.), *Worker Militancy and its Consequences, 1965–75* (New York, 1975), and C. Crouch and A. Pizzorno (eds.), *The Resurgence of Class Conflict in Western Europe since 1968* (London, 1978).

The most interesting cases are those which have led to the politicization of industrial conflict, since they show how easily the segregation of industrial and political disputes, the precondition of a system of institutionalized class conflict, can give way to something like incipient anomie. Once market forces or bargaining power are in abeyance, there are no widely agreed upon norms of distributive justice to fill the vacuum. The major consequence of incomes policy, therefore, is to displace the explosive issue of the justice of differential rewards from the industrial to the political arena.

Under these conditions, disorder arises most immediately from the breakdown of the institutional segregation of conflict, which politicizes industrial disputes by bringing any trade-union action that seriously challenges incomes policy into direct confrontation with state coercive power. Disorder is heightened further since the suspension of the machinery of collective bargaining means also the jettisoning of the complex system of 'custom and practice' indispensable to the settlement of disputes, particularly those originating in inter-union rivalries. But the most fundamentally disordering effect of incomes policies of any comprehensiveness and duration is that they throw responsibility for the determination of relativities on government.[54] This means nothing short of the political determination of what Durkheim called 'the coefficient of well-being to be assigned to each function' or 'the maximum degree of ease of living to which each class may legitimately aspire'. A concrete idea of what this entails was provided by Lord Brown in 1977. Summarizing the decisions on income distribution which any government bent on a serious attempt at incomes policy would be faced with, he wrote:

There are about six different levels of differential as follows: (a) those between individual employees; (b) between groups of employees working at the same level in the hierarchy; (c) between different levels in the hierarchy; (d) between different hierarchies in the same industry; (e)

---

[54] For a brief, in parts truly Durkheimian, formulation of these issues see *Relativities* (Advisory Report No. 35 of the Pay Board; HMSO, London 1974). Indispensable to this discussion is B. Wootton, *The Social Foundations of a Wage Policy* (London, 1955). An incisive review of the practice of incomes policies is to be found in C. Crouch, 'The Drive for Equality: Experience of Incomes Policy in Britain', in L. L. Lindberg (ed.), *Stress and Contradiction in Modern Capitalism* (Lexington, Mass., 1975).

between different 'industries', e.g., engineering, civil service, mining, teaching, etc.; (f) between citizens in different categories, e.g., those employed, unemployed, pensioners, disabled, etc.[55]

It is redundant to add that the requisite equations were unavailable. But the identification of the need for them simply underlined the fact that, in the absence of a society-wide consensus on relativities, incomes policies would impose a rough-and-ready justice, one that was highly disruptive of the customary wages differentials arrived at through a long practice of collective bargaining in particular industries and occupations.

The fact that incomes policies focus attention on relativities is what weakens the argument that the politicization of industrial conflict resulting from such policies may be seen as conducive to heightened class consciousness and even proto-revolutionary situations. For example, at more or less the same time as Lord Brown was warning the government that its policies were likely to result in industrial anomie, a representative Marxist theorist saw the same type of situation in very different terms:

The most critical field of State intervention in the advanced capitalist economy is that of incomes policies. The attempt to regulate the overall level of profits and wages is potentially the most explosive development of all those which constitute the new form of capitalism . . . The introduction of attempts to co-ordinate incomes unintentionally makes possible a return to something like the pre-capitalist visibility of exploitation but in a more universal context . . . whatever the state of the political development of a given working-class movement, it is likely that the application of incomes policies will render more palpable the fundamental class antagonisms between workers and capitalists, creating favourable conditions for intervention by revolutionary workers' organizations.[56]

The chief difficulty with this kind of argument is that the social conflict created by attempts to implement an incomes policy or a 'wage freeze' is less likely to expose 'fundamental class antagonism' than to lay bare the absence of consensus on intra-class relativities. Indeed a principal feature of the substitution of even the shortest lived dirigisme for a collective-bargained income distribution is the extent to which it heightens awareness of

---

[55] Letter to *The Times*, 13 Apr. 1977.
[56] R. Blackburn, 'The New Capitalism', in R. Blackburn (ed.), *Ideology and Social Science* (London, 1975), 183, 185, 196.

internal class differentials. In such situations, there does not occur any dramatic widening of social comparisons, still less a questioning of the status hierarchy as a whole. Rank-and-file workers do not usually start comparing their incomes with those of professionals, managers, or entrepreneurs. On the contrary, it is position within the customary manual-wage hierarchy that proves to be their major point of reference and the major ground of any disaffection. It is these sorts of conflicts rather than revolutionary demands that have been generated by, and have led to the abandonment of incomes policies. Moreover, where the latter have been at all comprehensive and of appreciable duration, they have usually involved some form of overt or tacit 'social contract' between government and trade unions: an incipient form of industrial and political representation prototypical of Durkheim's ideal of corporativism.[57]

That this has been the central tendency casts further doubt on the relevance of the theory of revolutionary practice to the elucidation of the working-class action in contemporary capitalist society. It is certainly true that any attempt to impose a planned distribution of income is likely to lead to the politicization of industrial conflict. But experience does not favour the hypothesis that under these conditions the working class is likely to extend its range of comparative reference groups to the point at which the legitimacy of the whole social order is brought into question. To make this assumption would seem to be another instance of the tendency to invoke the idea of a proletariat as a unitary collective actor; as an undifferentiated subject that can quickly acquire a clear and compelling understanding of the class system as a totality, completely unclouded by the kind of parochial comparisons that have for so long played such an important role in shaping contingent rather than necessary class consciousness.

One way of concluding this brief excursis into the morality of industrial relations might be to argue that the preface to the second edition of Durkheim's *Division of Labour* has proved to be strikingly prescient of the institutional changes by means of

---

[57] The facility with which some Marxist scholars have first of all been able to theorize corporativism as a new and inevitable stage of capitalist development and then, only several years later, to reject this thesis in favour of some version of Thatcherite, populist, hegemonic, domination, is disconcerting.

which advanced capitalist societies have so far been able to manage their problems of social integration. His prognoses certainly have the edge on the scenario of class polarization presented in Marx's concluding passages in 'The Historical Tendency of Capitalist Accumulation'. Yet within capitalist societies there still remains a considerable zone of 'industrial anomie'. This is partly due to the socialization of production relations which Marx anticipated. But it is also due to the lack of consensus on relative rewards, which is not only the most important cause of distributional conflicts, corporatist measures, and incomes policies, but also the most important obstacle to their implementation.[58] It is, however, noteworthy that such measures have been most successful in societies where the socialization of labour and social citizenship are relatively most advanced.[59]

This last observation leads to the further point that industrial anomie is not a problem peculiar to contemporary capitalist societies—at least in the sense that it could be expected to disappear with a change in ownership relations. In a socialist society that was also democratic, it is inconceivable that consensus on principles of distributive justice would not be an even more pressing issue. The reasons for this were elaborated by Durkheim almost a century ago in his critique of Saint-Simon.[60] Yet the nature of social classification in a future socialist society remains as vague as it was then, mainly because the anti-utopianism of Marxist theory eschews speculation about social ethics and leaves the question of who will get what, when, and how to the grace of revolutionary practice. But if this is the guide, then it is perhaps once again in the expansion of substantive citizenship status that the evolution within capitalism of some kind of post-capitalist and pre-socialist order has to be discussed.

Marx saw the future taking shape in such institutions as joint stock companies and co-operative societies. But today it is through pension and insurance funds that capital has acquired an even

[58] See J. H. Goldthorpe, 'The Current Inflation: Towards a Sociological Account', in F. Hirsch and J. H. Goldthorpe (eds.), *The Political Economy of Inflation* (London, 1978).

[59] See G. Esping-Andersen and W. Korpi, 'Social Policy as Class Politics in Post-war Capitalism: Scandinavia, Austria and Germany', in J. H. Goldthorpe (ed.), *Order and Conflict in Contemporary Capitalism* (Oxford, 1984).

[60] Durkheim, *Socialism*, ch. 10.

more impersonal and yet inherently social form. Since Marx saw
social insurance as one of the main purposes to which the surplus
of a socialist society would be put, it is by no means fanciful to
suppose that he would have regarded these institutions as a
further, and perhaps the most important, instance of the immanent socialization of capitalist economic relations. While the
prospect of these forms of collective capital being brought under
democratic control seems remote, their existence is nevertheless
likely to continue to arouse this aspiration.[61] A different route to
the same goal—wage-earner's investment funds—is now being
sought in the country whose welfare policies already represent the
most advanced form of the limitation of market forces by rights of
substantive citizenship: namely, Sweden. If, as many believe, this
is where democratic socialism is now starting to shrug off the
institutional carapace of capitalism (and where else is there
another candidate?), the implications for the theory of revolutionary practice are once again fairly clear. A striking feature of the
Swedish form of corporation has always been the degree to which
it expresses and promotes class interest *en bloc*. Contra Lenin, the
working class and the capitalist class—or at least their corporate
representatives—do regularly line up in two camps against each
other. But their relationship is not one of revolutionary class
polarization. It is part of the wider democratic class struggle over
the expansion of citizenship rights.[62]　.

VII

The argument so far suggests that, as an explanation of revolutionary action, the idea of praxis has singularly little to offer in the
way of specific hypotheses; and it is in the nature of the idea that
it cannot be conclusively disproved. Nevertheless, the course of
working-class action since the time Marx wrote does nothing to
increase confidence in the view that the proletariat gains a

[61] See T. Schuller, *Democracy at Work* (Oxford, 1985), ch. 5.

[62] The strategy behind employee investment funds has been described as the
introduction of 'a new set of citizen rights to collective capital ("economic
citizenship") as a means of resolving the existing contradictions between social
citizenship with full employment and economic growth' (Esping-Anderson and
Korpi, 'Social Policy as Class Politics', p. 190). See also Korpi, *The Democratic
Class Struggle*.

revolutionary understanding of its situation through either a gradual or a precipitate learning process. Marx's theory of the self-emancipation of the working class has not been borne out. This is uncontroversial. When Kautsky coined the phrase *Nur Gewerkschaftlerei* he wrote the epitaph to proletarian reason, and Lenin drove home the point that from then on philosophy would have to work much harder to find its material weapon in the proletariat. Yet Leninist theory turned out to be just as inadequate an explanation of working-class praxis in advanced capitalist societies.[63] And, most damaging for Marxist theory, it is paradoxically in the most purely capitalist of the advanced countries that the working class has evidenced least of the makings of the revolutionary consciousness which the theory of praxis requires.

There are only two ways of dealing with these sorts of facts. The first, which modern Marxism has eschewed, is to abandon the basic utilitarian action schema of the theory of practice. The other is to seek reasons for the absence of working-class revolution in conditions of action brought about by the development of modern capitalism. These conditions can only be twofold: the historically specific; and the structural or systemic. There is obviously an unacceptable cost in giving too much weight to the former, since the admission that their significance is such that proletarian revolution could suffer an indefinite delay would be tantamount to the dissolution of Marxism as a distinctive social theory. This conclusion is all the more unavoidable because, compared with the counteracting forces that can readily be seen to offset the general tendency of the rate of profit to fall, the factors affecting working-class consciousness are far more numerous and heterogeneous, and any theory of class formation that sought to encompass them would be correspondingly far less well defined. It is, therefore, quite understandable that the main way of seeking to repair the concept of revolutionary practice should have taken the form of a generalized explanation of proletarian passivity in terms immediately derivable from the utilitarian action schema.

To account for the short-circuiting of proletarian revolution, for faltering trade-union consciousness, and reformism, there has been an increasing reliance on explanations emphasizing the role of ideological obfuscation resulting either from purposive ruling-

---

[63] See the trenchant critique by Miliband, *Marxism and Politics*, ch. 6.

class indoctrination of the proletariat or from the false consciousness that is generated by capitalist production relations as such
and affects both capitalists and proletarians alike. These kinds of
explanations have tended to replace the once much favoured
theory that revolutionary tendencies were averted by the working
class being misled by its 'bourgeoisified' leadership. The evident
weakness of this argument is not only that it leaves unexplained
how workers could be so easily and consistently misled; it also
rests on the highly questionable assumption of a potentially
revolutionary proletarian mass.[64] Both these problems disappear
in the newer versions of global ideological domination. What is of
greatest interest about the latter is that they seek to save the
theory of practice by resorting to some form of explanation which
ultimately rests on the notions of ignorance and error which in the
utilitarian action schema are the key concepts for explaining
deviations from rational action. The ways in which this resort to
explanations of class action in terms of global ideological constraint introduce a chronic instability into Marxist theory is a
matter that will be taken up in Part Four. At this point, however,
it is instructive to consider that aspect of the thesis of ideological
domination which bears most directly upon, and indeed superficially appears to resemble, the foregoing account of the institutionalization of citizenship. This will bring into focus the way in
which utilitarian assumptions about social action continue to
characterize much Marxist theory and also serve as an introduction
to the discussion of ideology proper.

'In the developed countries,' writes Therborn, 'all major sections of the revolutionary labour movement have now openly
acknowledged that bourgeois democracy cannot be dismissed as a
mere sham.'[65] In similar vein, Miliband argues that any explanation of the failure of proletarian revolt must include a factor 'of

[64] Such as, e.g., what Miliband (ibid. 172), calls Lenin's 'absurd' pronouncement
that 'in all civilized and advanced countries . . . civil war between the proletariat
and the bourgeoisie is maturing and is imminent'. In what is probably the closest
approximation to a revolutionary situation in an advanced capitalist society,
namely Germany after the First World War, the evidence does not support the
view that the working class was a revolutionary mass 'betrayed' by a leadership
unwilling to lead it. For a detailed review of the literature, see Moore, *Injustice:
The Social Bases of Obedience and Revolt*, pt. 2, esp. chs. 8 and 9.

[65] G. Therborn, 'The Rule of Capital and the Rise of Democracy', *New Left
Review*, 103 (1977), 5.

the greatest importance: this is the extremely strong attraction which legality, constitutionalism, electoralism and representative institutions of the parlimentary type have had for the overwhelming majority of people in the working class movements of capitalist societies'.[66] Similar authoritative statements suggest that a great many, probably the majority of, Western Maxist theorists now acknowledge that working-class adherence to bourgeois social democratic institutions is not wholly irrational, and also place enough value on present forms of democracy to regard them as the basis of the higher form of socialist democracy yet to come. This reassessment has no doubt been heavily influenced by the experience of actual state socialist societies as well as by the fact that even the ostensibly radical sections of the Western working class appear to favour the pursuit of egalitarian goals by democratic means.[67]

Nevertheless, from any authentic Marxist viewpoint, this working-class commitment must be considered irrational, induced by an ideological cloaking of real class relations, and thus an obstacle to a necessary and feasible socialist reconstruction of society. Indeed, it is difficult to see how Marxism can preserve its theoretical distinctiveness if its proponents do not conclude that the political and civil relations of capitalist society continue to serve to the function of preventing the emergence of a revolutionary proletariat by atomizing society into a mass of legally isolated citizens and thereby obscuring the reality of class relations and class exploitations. This is certainly the view of one leading authority on the subject, who has no doubt that 'the fundamental form of the Western parliamentary State—the juridical sum of its citizenry—is itself the hub of the ideological apparatuses of

[66] Miliband, *Marxism and Politics*, pp. 189–90.

[67] A review of evidence relating to the attitudes of the French working class concludes that 'it is far from clear that this relatively high level of mobilization behind Marxist parties of the French Left signifies the prevalence of "revolutionary" consciousness in the working class in the sense of the desire for a wholesale and sudden transformation of the existing social order. The evidence is substantial that French workers are deeply committed to parliamentary institutions, and, perhaps as a consequence of this, the majority of French workers would appear to prefer the scenario of change through gradual reform. Indeed, it is far from clear that a major part of the French working class has ever been in favour of revolution in the conventional sense.' (D. Gallie, 'Social Radicalism in the French and British Working Classes: Some Points of Comparison', *British Journal of Sociology*, 30 (1979), 509.)

capitalism'.[68] And complementing this individualization of political relations, the civil institutions of private property and free contract (including collective bargaining) continue to have the effect of obscuring the reality of class relations at their very core. In stressing the socially integrative, or at least socially stabilizing, functions of the institutions of citizenship, this kind of continuing emphasis on the malformation of proletarian consciousness is brought into a fairly close approximation to 'bourgeois' theories of the institutionalization of class conflict. But it is distinguishable from the latter in several ways, most significantly by its implicit derogation of the intelligence of the working class. However objectionable this may be—if only from the viewpoint of Marx's original project—it is nevertheless a fairly direct result of the action schema underlying this particular version of utilitarian theorizing. For, given that the ultimate end of the proletariat is an interest in socialism, it must necessarily follow that any lasting commitment of the working class to the institutions of citizenship, parliamentary democracy, and collective bargaining is finally, with however many qualifications, irrational. This then is the source of the ambivalence displayed by modern Marxism towards capitalist social democracy. On the one hand there is a recognition that the adherence of the working class to social democratic institutions reflects a realistic appraisal of its circumstances and of the real if limited merits of this essentially bourgeois dispensation. On the other, there endures the conception of a proletariat for whom the acquisition of status rights within the existing social order is completely rational only if they are used to bring about its radical transformation.

Little such ambivalence is present in Marx's work. Indeed, his conception of the proletariat, self-educated into an increasing awareness of its interest in the abolition of the wages system, allowed him to envisage the imminent possibility of an enfranchised working class voting itself into socialism. 'If in England or the United States, for example, the working class were able to gain a majority in Parliament or in Congress, then it could by legal means set aside the laws and structures that stood in its way,' he wrote; and again, 'we do not deny that there are countries like

---

[68] P. Anderson, 'The Antinomies of Antonio Gramsci', *New Left Review*, 100 (1976), 29.

England and America and, if I am familiar with your institutions, Holland, where labour may attain its goals by peaceful means'.[69] Leaving on one side the fact that Marx could hardly have chosen more unfortunate prospective sites of revolutionary socialist transformation, what these comments serve most of all to indicate is the unquestioned assumption that the proletariat's acquisition of citizenship rights has to be regarded only as a prelude to their being used as a means of enforcing its ultimate class interest. Here there is no appreciation of the possibility that both the struggle to attain political and industrial rights and the use subsequently made of them could reflect at least as much status as opposed to class interest; that is an interest in rights through which the material and moral position of the working class within the existing system might be enhanced, rather than rights regarded in a purely instrumental manner as the means of revolutionizing that status system. It may be objected that Marx's and Engel's several observations on a matter such as the 'bourgeois prejudices' of the working class give the lie to this interpretation. But this is not so. The putative instrumentalism of the proletariat is but the mirror image of the orthodox version of the dominant ideology thesis, which holds that the capitalist class can be counted upon to act in an equally rational manner by using all the means at its disposal to safeguard its class interest. These include the piecemeal granting of a whole range of citizenship rights whereby the proletariat is deflected from its revolutionary path towards an interest in civic incorporation. Thus proletarian and bourgeois instrumentalism are part and parcel of the same utilitarian action schema. In this conspectus, the proletariat entertains 'bourgeois prejudices' only because it is momentarily unable to see through them, and not because they represent its real interest, which it will eventually be able to grasp through a progressively acquired understanding of the limited, class-based nature of capitalist civic integration. The view that the working class can have no enduring commitment to bourgeois values and institutions, and will sooner or later exploit them to bring about revolutionary and not just reformist change,

[69] The first quotation is from McLellan, *The Thought of Karl Marx*, p. 201. The second from Avineri, *The Social and Political Thought of Karl Marx*, p. 216. For a general survey o f Marx's and Engels's views on democratic institutions, see W. R. Schonfeld, 'The Classical Marxist Conception of Democracy', *Review of Politics*, 33 (1971).

is one that has been and remains central to Marxist political sociology. Only fairly recently has it become fashionable to acknowledge that citizenship is both much more commanding of working-class allegiance and less of a 'sham'.

It is understandable that in response to the conception of working-class reformism as irrational, some critics of Marxism should seek to argue the contrary: namely, that the commitment to social democracy on the part of workers in the most advanced capitalist societies must be in large part explained by their sensible appraisal of the realistic alternatives open to them. One forceful exponent of this case presents it as follows:

Given what we know about Marxist societies-without-blueprints built elsewhere, it should come as no great surprise if western workers were to show some scepticism about the reliability of this architectural procedure. It is not, after all, as if the unflattering image of existing socialist states is a malicious fabrication of the bourgeois mind. Western Marxists of many breeds and dispositions have been just as disparaging of state socialism as any mere liberal . . . the working class could easily be forgiven for thinking that something must be very badly wrong with state socialism after all . . . only if it were patently and unambiguously the case that the forcible overthrow of bourgeois regimes elsewhere had resulted in the reclamation of the proletariat would a social democratic commitment on the part of western workers seem especially odd.

And, in addition to this external demonstration effect, it is held that 'the fact that the majority of the west European working class continue to give their political allegiance to social democracy is no doubt a judgement of sorts upon its overall performance'.[70]

This kind of argument has a certain sociological, as well as polemical, appeal. Nevertheless the assumption that the working class has a democratic commitment based on a well-informed appraisal of the balance of economic and political advantages and disadvantages of its present position as compared with those that it would be likely to experience in any socialist alternative is just as sweeping and unfounded as the opposite claim that, due to its indoctrination into bourgeois ideology, the working class is incap-

---

[70] Parkin, *Marxism and Class Theory*, pp. 199, 202. For a similar argument that, if workers sought rationally to maximize their material welfare, they would not have an interest in socialism, see Przeworski, 'Material Interests, Class Compromise and the Transition to Socialism'.

able of understanding its real class situation and thus discovering its ultimate interest in socialism. That such a high degree of rational calculation underlies what is taken to be a widespread working-class allegiance to social democracy is itself an assumption that seems somewhat implausible in the view of survey data which indicate that the range of working-class social comparisons is very narrow, and that the electorates of Western democracies are distinguished by their extremely low levels of political conceptualization and by their low rating of the political realm as a determinant of the quality of life.[71] These data, such as they are, would rather tend to support the view that the worker's sociopolitical attitudes lack any overall consistency and that his orientation to dominant institutions is essentially one of 'pragmatic' or fatalistic acceptance.[72] But the fact of the matter is that there is insufficient evidence to discriminate between the competing claims of these three, equally overgeneralized, depictions of working-class consciousness. Indeed, their common *explanandum* is far from having been firmly established. Survey research has hardly begun to provide any definite answers to the questions of what it is about democratic instititions that the 'Western working class', or for that matter the population at large, regards as possessing or lacking legitimacy. However, such evidence as there is does suggest that ordinary people's commitment to democracy rests less on their estimation of governments and politicians (which is largely negative) than on their evaluation of the regime as such (which is largely positive).[73] But almost nothing is known about

[71] The pioneering work on ideological conceptualization is P. E. Converse, 'The Nature of Belief Systems in Mass Publics', in D. Apter (ed.), *Ideology and Discontent* (New York, 1964). See also S. H. Barnes, M. Kaase, *et al.* (eds.), *Political Action: Mass Participation in Five Western Democracies* (Beverley Hills, Calif., 1979).

[72] The most influential statement of this view is Mann, 'The Social Cohesion of Liberal Democracy'. However, the evidence he presents is not only inadequate to provide the basis of generalizations about liberal democracies as a whole; it also falls far short of demonstrating that the generally negative or ambivalent attitudes of workers towards social and economic inequalities are matched by a repudiation of democratic political institutions. Moreover, the argument is methodologically very suspect, since to a large extent it infers individual attributes from ecological data.

[73] See D. Kavanagh, 'Political Culture in Great Britain: The Decline of Civic Culture', in G. A. Almond and S. Verba (eds.), *The Civic Culture Revisited*, (Boston, 1980), 152–3, and, esp., A. I. Abramowitz, 'The United States: Political Culture Under Stress', in ibid. 195–6. The relevance of the distinction between

the question of which of the several institutions making up social democratic regimes enjoys most widespread support among the working class. For example, it is possible that, in their conception of democracy, free trade unions and collective bargaining figure at least as prominently as political institutions proper. But the extent to which such ideas of extra-parliamentary democracy are central or marginal to workers' allegiance is not a problem that has preoccupied students of civic culture. Nor does the historical record provide unequivocal answers to such questions, mainly for the reason that there is little evidential constraint on imputing motives to working-class action or inaction. It is arguable, for example, that the acid test of working-class commitment to the complex set of arrangements making up social democracy is how this class reacts when these institutions have been put under greatest strain, particularly at times of chronic economic depression and massive unemployment. In this respect, it is evident that in countries where citizenship rights have been most fully and effectively institutionalized working-class adversity has not been accompanied by anything like the extent of radical social protest that could be expected on the grounds of Marxist theory. Even so, the fact that economic crisis has failed to generate revolutionary consciousness cannot be taken as proof that the stability of democratic institutions is to be explained by the extent of their popular support. An equally plausible hypothesis, for which, unlike the preceding one, there is considerable supporting evidence, is that the long-run unemployed become socially isolated and apathetic and in general make up an inert, demoralized mass.[74] Under these conditions, what appears to be decisive for the stability of democratic institutions is the extent to which they continue to enjoy the support of élites, including not least the leadership of trade unions and labour parties.

---

government and regime is brought out strongly by D. Halle, *America's Working Man* (Chicago, 1984). His respondents—manual workers employed in a New Jersey chemical plant—despised politicians but displayed a strong commitment to the freedoms enjoyed by citizens of a democracy, especially when compared with their perceptions of the communist system.

[74] The pioneering work is M. Jahoda, P. Lazarsfeld, and H. Zeisel, *Marienthal* (London, 1972; originally published in 1933). See also E. Ginzberg, *The Unemployed* (New York, 1943), E. W. Bakke, *Citizens without Work* (New Haven, Conn., 1940), and J. A. Garraty, *Unemployment in History* (New York, 1978).

PART FOUR
IDEOLOGY

13.

INDOCTRINATION

I

The foregoing survey of the three kinds of explanations entering into the theory of proletarian revolution shows that, while they comprise a very versatile set of arguments not easily capable of empirical disproof, all have the same basic flaw. This is to be found in the assumption that, through their powers of reason, workers will be quick to learn from their experience of capitalist production relations that their ends can only be realized by the abolition of these relations. Moreover, the fact that material and moral impoverishment, and self-education through collective action and class struggle, have not led to proletarian revolution in the most advanced capitalist societies has long since suggested, and not least to many Marxist theoreticians, that the assumption of proletarian reason is faulty. By according the standard of rationality such a central role in explaining the means–ends relationship, Marxism shares the same weakness as utilitarian theory in that it excludes systematic consideration of nonrational action. In contrast with irrational action, which can always be explained in terms of ignorance and error, nonrational action can only be understood by reference to the normative integration of ends. At the outset, it was stated that in the utilitarian scheme the ends of actors are treated either explicitly or implicitly as 'random', in the sense that the problem of their interrelationship lies outside the scope of the theory. It was also claimed that the same tendency is characteristic of the Marxist action schema. This is now in need of qualification.

At first sight, the concept of ideology would seem to offer an explanation of why ends are not random and thus demolish the argument that Marxism is a version of a basically utilitarian theory of action. But, in order to understand exactly the extent to which this is the case, it is necessary to examine in some detail the main variants of the Marxist theory of ideology. However, it cannot here be the aim to present anything like a full account of the subject. All that can be done is to isolate and appraise the chief assumptions underlying the explanation of ideologically induced social order. The principal line of argument will be that the tendency to explain the lack of proletarian revolution in terms of ideological constraints has the effect of introducing into the Marxist action schema a fundamental instability, which takes the form of an oscillation between, at one extreme, the utilitarian position, and at the other what may in a qualified sense be termed the idealistic.

In approaching this highly complicated subject-matter, it is useful to identify three major versions of the theory of ideology. First of all, there is what may be called the indoctrination thesis, which originates in certain well-known passages in the *German Ideology*, and acquires a more highly developed formulation in Lenin's *What Is To Be Done?* It will be shown that this theory of how the capitalist class inculcates in the proletariat a false consciousness of its interests rests on a fairly explicit utilitarian action schema. The latter can also be shown to underpin the second theory, that of 'commodity fetishism', in which false consciousness is seen to be the result of ideological effects that are produced by the capitalist system of production itself. In both these theories great emphasis is placed on the cognitive obstacles to proletarian revolutionary action. However, because of the failure to specify the conditions under which ideological domination of the one kind or the other is likely to vary, there is in both cases a strong tendency to attribute to it a quite pervasive and global influence. The result of this is that the underlying utilitarian action schema veers towards the opposite, idealistic pole. This tendency is less pronounced in the third theory—that of 'hegemony'. This is mainly because Gramsci's concept of 'contradictory consciousness' opens up the whole question of how ideologies are grounded in action; a process that is necessarily always imperfect. But it is also because, in contrast with the idea of ideological indoctrination, hegemony refers to a much more diffuse intellectual and cultural dominance, in which a variety of values and beliefs coexist more or less coherently and have greater or lesser appeal to different classes and social strata. In this way, Gramsci also brings Marxist theory much closer to the other main body of social theory discussed above: namely, normative functionalism. This convergence, however, is much more evident in the work of some of his interpreters who have used the concept of hegemony to advance highly generalized explanations of proletarian passivity which tend in the direction of a cultural determinism. The most egregious example of this is the concept of 'ideological state apparatuses', which serves to denote ideological effects of a quite pervasive and apparently unconditional kind.

II

The orthodox version of ideological domination, or indoctrination, originates in certain passages of *The German Ideology* and finds its clearest and most forceful statement in Lenin's *What Is To Be Done?* It has the following, characteristically utilitarian, elements. Control over the production of ideas, and thereby the ability to inculcate into the proletariat a false consciousness of its position, is one of the means by which the ruling class rationally pursues its intra-systemic end. This is possible because the ruling class possesses overwhelmingly superior resources for the creation and dissemination of its ideas. As far as the subjugated class is concerned, dominant ideas presumably constitute an internalized condition of its situation of action, so that it remains ignorant of the means–ends chain that would lead it to recognize its extra-systemic, or ultimate end.

It will no doubt be said that this is a caricature of Marx's view of ideology. But the fact of the matter is that Marx and Engels did not have a well-worked-out theory of ideology at all,[1] and ideological factors do not figure prominently, much less systematically, in their explanations of class action, particularly proletarian action. Indeed, a strong case can be made out for thinking that the Marxian solution of the problem of order is one in which the familiar utilitarian notions of force and fraud play a major role.[2] Nevertheless, the makings of a theory of ideological indoctrination are certainly evident in the work of Marx and Engels. With Lenin, it acquired a novel form, and greater political significance, and thereby became a long lasting orthodoxy which has only fairly

---

[1] As is shown by Seliger, *The Marxist Conception of Ideology*, ch. 2.
[2] See Poggi, *Images of Society*, ch. 5; also N. Birnbaum, 'Conflicting Interpretations of the Rise of Capitalism: Marx and Weber', *British Journal of Sociology*, 4 (1953), 130, and J. Femia, 'Hegemony and Consciousness in the Thought of Antonio Gramsci', *Political Studies*, 23 (1975), 31.

recently been modified by more sophisticated interpretations.[3] Its main source is the passage in which Marx and Engels write that, 'The class which has the means of material production at its disposal has control at the same time over the means of mental production, so that in consequence the ideas of those who lack the means of mental production are, in general, subject to it.' They go on to say that, 'The individuals composing the ruling class . . . regulate the production and distribution of the ideas of their age.'[4]

This formula is the way in which, as Birnbaum points out, Marx attempted to

account for consensual phenomena of an interclass sort. To meet this difficulty, Marx advanced the proposition that the class which controlled the means of production could and did impose its ideology on the rest of society. The failure of the members, leaders or ideologists of a class to comprehend their real interests leads them to accept the ideology of another, opposed stratum and so underlies this imposition.[5]

Since Marx, this view of ideological domination, or solution of the problem of integration of the ends of class actors, has in one form or another become the most widely favoured explanation of the lack of proletarian revolution. The question of whether its underlying assumptions can easily be reconciled with other scattered comments through which Marx and Engels convey their general views on the nature of ideological production is a matter that for the time being can be postponed. At this stage, it is more important to indicate how the utilitarian scheme of action implied by this concept of ideological indoctrination appears much more explicitly in the interpretation of working-class consciousness put forward by Lenin in *What Is To Be Done?*

This seminal work[6] represents a fairly radical break with the

---

[3] See, e.g., J. Mepham, 'The Theory of Ideology in Capital', in J. Mepham and D. H. Ruben (eds.), *Issues in Marxist Philosophy*, iii (Brighton, 1979), 141–3.

[4] Marx and Engels, *The German Ideology*, p. 39.

[5] Birnbaum, 'Conflicting Interpretations of the Rise of Capitalism', p. 313.

[6] Despite the fact that it was addressed to problems arising at a specific historical stage, there would seem to be widespread agreement that until fairly recently the general theory put forward in this work has exerted the greatest influence on Marxist interpretations of the possibility of proletarian revolt in advanced capitalist societies. For an account of Lenin's changing views on the working-class movement, see T. T. Hammond, *Lenin on Trade Unions and Revolution, 1893–1917* (New York, 1957).

concept of proletarian self-emancipation which is central to the Marxian theory of praxis. At the same time, Lenin's explanation of the limits of the spontaneous movement of the working class is essentially a restatement and elaboration of the thesis of ideological indoctrination outlined by Marx and Engels. In particular, Lenin's account of ideology rests on the same basic utilitarian action schema that informs the latter; and it is chiefly for this reason that it is best understood as an embellishment of the indoctrination thesis rather than as a precursor of the hegemony thesis. As will be seen in due course, the difficulties of working with a simple indoctrination model, which arise principally from its utilitarian presuppositions, have lead many Marxist exponents of it towards a position that is much closer to the hegemonic thesis. There is, however, little in Lenin's theory that suggests the need for any major revision of the view of ideology that is sketched out in *The German Ideology*.

With Lenin, ideological conflict and polarization come to play a much more central role in the class struggle than they were ever accorded by Marx.[7] The development of revolutionary consciousness is most generally conceived of by Marx as a relatively spontaneous change in which the working class acquires the knowledge of its system-transcending interests in the course of class struggle that becomes more widespread and acute with the growing contradiction between the forces and relations of production and its own growing self-awareness and organization as a class for itself. In this process, the role of ideology is summed up by his statement that 'the existence of revolutionary ideas in a particular period presupposes the existence of a revolutionary class'. But the exact significance of 'revolutionary ideas' for the self-transformation of the proletariat from a class in itself to a class for itself remains obscure. Although he repudiates utopian socialist ideas, it is not clear which kinds of ideas he thought would serve the interests of a revolutionary proletariat. There are certainly many Marxist scholars who would definitely reject the view that Marx thought that his own ideas would necessarily serve as the ideology of the proletariat in this sense. Moreover, at several points, he and Engels appear to demote the importance of

---

[7] The concept of ideology itself also undergoes a significant change; see Seliger, *The Marxist Conception of Ideology*.

the particular form of revolutionary ideas. Unless the material conditions of revolution exist, 'then, as far as practical development is concerned, it is absolutely immaterial whether the "idea" of this revolution has been expressed a hundred times already; as the history of communism proves'.[8] Revolutionary ideas are seen as variations on the same external theme, merely different expressions of the same basic class antagonism.[9] Moreover, quite apart from the problem of the appropriate form of revolutionary ideas, it is by no means obvious from Marx's work how he conceived of such ideas entering into and aiding proletarian revolution. Would these ideas become a 'material force' only when the proletariat had, by its own efforts so to speak, passed the threshold of inter-class comparisons, or are they a necessary precondition of the 'production on a mass scale of this communist consciousness'?

It might be argued that Marx's view of the dialectical nature of change in consciousness and change in conditions renders such questions otiose, if not meaningless. But, if that were the case, then the whole purpose of Lenin's theory would also lack significance. It may be assumed that it does not, since it is clear that, in taking as his premiss 'There can be no revolutionary movement without a revolutionary theory',[10] he throws into relief the basic question that for Marx simply did not arise. Marx never thought it necessary to ask what would happen to the proletarian movement if revolutionary conditions were unaccompanied by a revolutionary ideology.[11] Lenin faced a situation in which he judged that this was a real possibility, and this was the occasion for his attack on 'spontaneity'. His target was not Marx himself, but those who ostensibly saddled him with this deviation. His warrant

---

[8] Marx and Engels, *The German Ideology*, pp. 29–30.

[9] *The Communist Manifesto*, in Marx and Engels, *Selected Works*, i. 50. There are, however, as will be noted below (ch. 13, s. IV), instances where Engels clearly suggests that the form of ideologies and particularly the manner in which they are exploitable is important for the development of revolutionary movements.

[10] V. I. Lenin, *What Is To Be Done?*, trans. and ed. S. V. and P. Utechin (London, 1970), 75.

[11] By no means merely a counterfactual supposition of small importance. For example, Stone, *The Causes of the English Revolution*, p. 103: 'It is as safe as any broad generalization of history can be to say that without the ideas, the organization and the leadership supplied by Puritanism there would have been no revolution at all.'

for absolving Marx of such a theoretical error was Kautsky; and Kautsky's warrant was his own. Be this as it may, the assumption that 'the existence of revolutionary ideas in a particular period presupposes the existence of a revolutionary class' was the Marxian premiss whose terms Lenin decisively reversed.

His thesis is familiar, but bears repetition because of the need to establish the conception of social action it entails. He begins with the observation that it is a mistake to believe that 'the purely worker movement by itself can and will work out an independent ideology for itself' for 'the history of all countries shows that the working class, solely by its own forces, is able to work out merely trade union consciousness'.[12] Even the goal of '"lending the economic struggle *itself* a political character", which sounds "frightfully" profound and revolutionary, is in fact hiding the traditional striving to *demote* Social-Democratic politics to tradeunionist politics'. Thus the way in which Marx seems to have conceived of the escalation of the economic to the political level of conflict does not necessarily lead to revolutionary interest.[13] Class conflicts remain within the bounds of the capitalist system, and the 'ideological enslavement of the workers by the bourgeoisie' continues. What then is the nature of this ideological constraint, and why is it so powerful? An answer to the first question can be found in Lenin's assertion that there are only two, classbased, ideologies, which are totally opposed to one another.

Since there can be no question of an independent ideology being worked out by the working masses in the very process of their movement, then the *only* question is *this*: the bourgeois ideology or the Socialist ideology. There is nothing in between (for humanity has not worked out any 'third' ideology and, in general, in a society torn by class contradictions, there can never be an ideology that is outside or above classes). Hence *any* belittling of the Socialist ideology, *any* withdrawing from it, means by the same token the strengthening of the bourgeois ideology.[14]

[12] Lenin, *What Is To Be Done?*, pp. 89, 80.
[13] Ibid. 108. It is precisely the political goals to which Marx attributed such importance in developing proletarian class consciousness that Lenin dismisses as ineffective for this purpose, that is: 'struggling for freedom of strikes, for the removal of all and sundry legal obstacles to the co-operative and trade union movement, for laws protecting women and children, for the improvement of conditions of work by means of health and factory legislation, etc.'
[14] Ibid. 89–90.

This rules out the possibility of any lasting consensus on ultimate beliefs and leads to a notion of class struggle as ideological polarization.[15] In developing this theme, Lenin provides the answer to the second question.

But why, the reader will ask, does the spontaneous movement, the movement along the line of least resistance, lead precisely to the domination of the bourgeois ideology? For the simple reason that the bourgeois ideology is far older in origin than the Socialist ideology, because it is more completely developed, and because it possesses *immeasurably* greater means for being spread.[16]

Here, as in the passages of *The German Ideology* cited above, the argument rests on what is basically a utilitarian action schema. Ideological indoctrination is possible because the ruling class has far greater means of disseminating its ideas than has the proletariat. The claim that the power of bourgeois ideology is due to its being far older in origin than the socialist ideology is an extension of this type of assumption, since it can only be taken to imply that prolonged exposure to these ideas results in their becoming even more strongly a condition of proletarian action. What is meant by the third reason for the superior efficacy of bourgeois ideology is not clear. That it is 'more completely developed' could mean that it is a more logically consistent and closed system of ideas than socialism: not a view that could easily be maintained. Alternatively, it could mean that bourgeois ideology is more developed, in the sense that it is socially more widespread; this argument would then again become simply an extension of the first. So far then it cannot be said that Lenin's elaboration of this aspect of the indoctrination thesis goes much beyond its formulation by Marx and Engels.

But, given that bourgeois ideological domination leads the

---

[15] This does not mean, however, that there is a complete hiatus between bourgeois and socialist ideology, since 'the teaching of Socialism has grown out of the philosophical, historical and economic theories that were worked out by the educated representatives of the propertied classes—the intelligentsia' (ibid. 80). Lenin did not draw from this observation the conclusion that has become the central theme of post-Gramscian Marxism: namely, that the most difficult task of a socialist party aiming at 'hegemony' is that of detaching class neutral values and beliefs from their bourgeois nexus and rearticulating them within a 'popular democratic' socialist discourse. See E. Laclau, *Politics and Ideology in Marxist Theory* (London, 1979), esp. ch. 3.

[16] *What Is To Be Done?*, pp. 90–1.

working class towards trade-union consciousness, the vital question is how this spontaneous tendency can be counteracted. Lenin's answer is both clear and novel. Since the ideological enslavement of the workers by the bourgeoisie is so profound that it is proof even against conditions favouring revolution,[17] the creation of revolutionary consciousness becomes a task of ideological conversion. This in turn requires a very special body, an organization of highly disciplined and professional revolutionaries. It is through the party that the struggle to weaken the hold of bourgeois ideology over the working class is largely to be carried out: a struggle that involves 'lifting the movement to the level of "its own programme"'.[18] Of greatest interest about this process of ideological conversion are the means by which it is to be carried out: namely, propaganda and agitation. The task of 'political education' is to articulate the worker's experience of oppression, his consciousness of which is 'embryonic',[19] by making him aware of the connections between particular injustices and the oppressiveness of the class system as a whole.

It is not sufficient to *explain* the political oppression of the workers (as it was not sufficient to *explain* to them the antagonism between their interests and the interests of the employers). It is necessary to agitate in connexion with every concrete manifestation of such oppression. And since *this* oppression falls on the most diverse classes of society, since it manifests itself in the most diverse spheres of life and activity—professional, civic, personal, family, religious, scientific, etc., etc.,—is it then not obvious that *we shall not fulfil our task* of developing the political consciousness of the workers if we do not *take upon ourselves* the organisation of an *all-embracing political arraignment* of the autocracy?

The consciousness of the working class cannot be a truly political consciousness if the workers have not been trained to respond to *all* and

[17] Ibid. 99, where other socialist factions are castigated for not keeping theoretical pace with the 'spontaneous upsurge of the masses in Russia'. See also Parkin, *Marxism and Class Theory*, pp. 155 ff.

[18] Lenin, *What Is To Be Done?*, p. 98. Also p. 129, where he speaks of the need 'to *raise* the trade-unionist politics of the working class to Social-Democratic politics'.

[19] 'Propaganda and agitation are not enough. For this the masses must have their own political experience' (Lenin, *Selected Works*, ii. 626). But 'The "spontaneous element" in effect represents nothing but consciousness in an *embryonic form*' (*What Is To Be Done?*, p. 80). This term is also used by Gramsci to describe the 'concrete' element of 'contradictory consciousness', on which see below, ch. 15, s. II.

sundry cases of arbitrariness and oppression, violence and misdeeds, *whatever classes* may be affected by these cases—to respond, moreover, precisely from a Social-Democratic and not from any other point of view. The consciousness of the working masses cannot be truly class-conscious-ness if the workers do not learn on the basis of concrete and, what is essential, topical political facts and events to observe *every* other social class in *all* the manifestations of the intellectual, moral and political life of these classes.[20]

The aim of propaganda and agitation conveyed in these passages obviously reflects conditions peculiar to Russian autocracy, whose internal disintegration, a process accelerated by war, was decisive for the Bolshevik seizure of power. Nevertheless, Lenin's strategy of political education is regarded as having a general relevance, and what is most striking about it is the underlying assumption that the ends of actors can be changed through the impartation of 'scientific' knowledge.

In its essentials, his theory of the ideological conversion of the working class to socialist beliefs is the mirror image of the theory of the ideological indoctrination of the working class by the bourgeoisie. Both rest on the assumption that what is crucial for the formation of class consciousness is which class, or its represen-tatives, has the superior means of defining the worker's conception of his situation. These means are above all cognitive. That is to say the worker's evaluation of his situation is considered to be problematic only in the sense that, under conditions of bourgeois indoctrination, his understanding of the relationship between his own position and that of other groups and classes is obscured only by a lack of knowledge. It is to correct this state of 'ignorance' that socialist propaganda and agitation are directed. Again and again, Lenin returns to this fundamental theme.

He who draws the attention, the power of observation and the conscious-ness of the working class exclusively or predominantly on to itself is not a Social Democrat, for the self-understanding of the working class is inseparably bound up with a complete clarity of ideas on the inter-relationship of *all* classes of contemporary society.[21]

'A clear idea' of the class system, 'A complete clarity of ideas'— these are phrases that he never tires of using. And they mean the

---

[20]   *What Is To Be Done?*, pp. 105 and 115 respectively.
[21]   Ibid. 115.

impartation of knowledge. The working class 'needs before and above all else all-sided, live political knowledge'; 'the most pressing need of the working class' is 'for political knowledge and political education'; the aim of Social Democracy is 'to provide the workers with real, all-round, and live political knowledge'; and so on.[22] In this respect, then, Lenin's major contribution is to have complemented Marx's utilitarian theory of ideological indoctrination with a consistently utilitarian theory of ideological conversion.

III

Before turning to examine the problems presented by this interpretation, it is worth noting the ways in which Lenin's conception of ideological polarization brings Marxism into an approximation to Durkheimian sociology. First of all, the distinction between socialist and trade-union consciousness corresponds closely to that between sacred and profane activity, the main difference being that, whereas the latter refers to separate spheres of activity within society, the former refers to different levels of activity by a class. Classes take shape within antagonistic economic relationships, which for Durkheim were the epitome of the profane or 'utilitarian' life and the primordial sources of friction and conflict. For Durkheim, these divisive conflicts undermine social solidarity and their effects can only be counteracted through ritual and the reaffirmation of shared beliefs. For Lenin, trade-union consciousness is equally divisive of class solidarity, and to counteract proletarian egoism, to 'lift' the working-class movement to 'the level of its own programme', requires 'agitation' and 'arraignment', a heightening of the awareness of collective life through the promulgation of a socialist creed which fixes attention and affect on the injustice of society as a whole. It might not be too much to say that this programme aims at the 'sacralization' of profane interest, not least because the decisive moment of socialist intervention is when class conflict heightens class solidarity and when class consciousness is most open to revolutionary transformation. This is surely very similar to Durkheim's understanding that new beliefs are created out of the 'moral effervescence' that

[22] Ibid. 132, 122, 130.

results when social interactions become exceptionally frequent and intense.

In a way, then, Lenin was a good Durkheimian. But, as a Marxist, he was able to identify one of the most general causes of heightened social interaction in structural conditions which Durkheim's sociology merely hinted at, necessitated, but could find no conceptual room for. And Lenin went beyond Marx by identifying and creating the agency required to transform values and beliefs—the kind of organization Durkheim deliberately excluded from his purview in order to grasp religion's basic form, devoid of the 'complicating' features of sects and heretical creeds. This observation leads immediately to the second point, not particularly new, which is that Lenin's conception of the role of the party, struggling not only against bourgeois ideology, but also against heretical tendencies within its own ranks, and thus demanding the utmost conviction and loyalty from its adherents, is very close to that of a sect seeking the authority and ascendancy of a new church. It hardly needs to be added that the chief means of securing party solidarity—ideological correctness and strict discipline—are exactly the features Weber singled out as the predominant characteristic of protestant sects. What may be less obvious is that the revolutionary party represents in an extreme form the combination of what for Durkheim were the two basic constituents of social cohesion: namely, the strength of an individual's attachment to social groups and the strength of the moral discipline to which he is thereby subjected. By the same token, the dissociation of such a social group from the wider society approximates corporate egoism; just as its revolutionary goal, and its activity in revolutionizing or deregulating the aspirations of the masses, are distinctly anomic.

Nevertheless, Lenin's theory of the preconditions of ideological polarization has no counterpart in Durkheim's conception of disorder and differs substantially from that of Marx. In not too dissimilar ways, both Durkheim and Marx tended to think that systemic forces, either in the form of sudden redistributions of 'men and things' or in the form of capitalist crises, would precipitate fundamental social conflicts in the course of which the existing social classification or the relations of production would undergo radical change. Lenin departs from this view to the extent that, while he accepts that such system contradictions might exacerbate class conflict, he does not assume that they will produce a sense of unjust deprivation of revolutionary proportions, because the working class will tend to confine its demands to objectives that are defined as legitimate by the dominant ideology. Qualitatively different ends do not arise simply from the intensification of the class struggle, but only through ideological conversion. In Durkheimian terms, the chain reactions of relative deprivation that are triggered off by sudden discontinuities in the distribution of men and things are not in themselves sufficient to delegitimate the existing system of status and authority. It is rather the ideological intensification of class struggle which supposedly achieves this end. The primary function of the revolutionary party is to manufacture relative deprivation among the proletariat; as Lenin puts it, 'to *arouse* in the mass dissatisfaction and indignation'.[23] By placing every concrete aspect of the class struggle in the context of a socialist critique which demonstrates not only the systematic nature of social injustice, but also the inevitability of its breakdown and supersession by a new social order, the sense of deprivation of the working class is deepened as its point of reference widens from intra-class, to inter-class, to inter-societal comparisons.[24]

A fitting conclusion, then, might be to say that this theory of a revolutionary party or sect aiming at the ideological polarization of class conflict carries to its logical extreme the only coherent concept of anomic declassification implied by Durkheim's idea of social solidarity: namely, schism. Conflict brought about by the generation and dissemination of new beliefs, deriving from but antithetical to the pre-existing collective conscience, would certainly be more in keeping with Durkheim's general views on the nature of social solidarity than the concept of anomic disorder resulting from inexplicable discontinuities in the distribution of power and wealth. For these reasons, then, Lenin's theory of revolutionary class consciousness may be said to provide a Marxist

[23] *What Is To Be Done?*, p. 113.

[24] For Lenin, as for Marx, all attempts to mobilize the working class by appeals to 'utopian' socialist ideas are rejected. Scientific socialism 'restricts itself to the most general allusions to the future and traces only those already existing elements from which the future system is growing' (Lenin, *Selected Works*, i. 158–9). This, however, does not take account of the fact that there are always important respects in which the critique of an existing totality necessarily posits an alternative totality.

solution of the Durkheimian problem of disorder, just as his elaboration of the Marxian theory of ideological indoctrination prefigures the quasi-Durkheimian solution of the Marxist problem of order which culminates in Gramsci's notion of hegemony.

IV

From this excursion to view points of convergence between Leninist and Durkheimian perspectives on disorder, it is appropriate to return to the fundamental point of divergence, which is that the theory of ideological indoctrination rests on just the kind of utilitarian action schema which Durkheim believed to be incapable of yielding an adequte explanation of social order. This was because, in the last analysis, it was shared moral beliefs that held a society together. In the indoctrination thesis, moral beliefs are analytically indistinguishable from other kinds of 'irrational' orientations; and the chief consequence of their assimilation to the general category of the ideological is that, like any other misconceptions, they are treated as scientifically corrigible. Conversely, there is no conceptual space for nonrational commitment to moral beliefs, especially to bourgeois values. At any rate, these would appear to be the implications of this type of theory, whose chief assumptions may now be recapitulated.

The first is that the ruling class has a purely instrumental orientation towards the production and dissemination of ideas, so that from its standpoint ideas are reduced to the status of means by which it can most effectively realize its ends. That is to say, in the last instance, the 'productivity' of ideas, their 'value', is measured against the norm of scientific knowledge: ideas are judged as more or less efficacious in producing the result intended (i.e. indoctrination) according to a rational, scientific knowledge of the situation of action. This assumption, without which it would be meaningless to talk of control over, or regulation of, the means of mental production, may be called 'manipulation'. The second assumption is that the ruling class does in fact have at its disposal overwhelmingly superior means for implanting its ideas into the consciousness of the proletariat. This may be called the 'monopoly' assumption, and it is the one that most Marxist writers have tended to concentrate on, perhaps because it is thought that this is the issue on which evidence is most plentiful and least equivocal.

Thirdly, there is the question of the receptivity of the subjugated class to ruling-class ideas. The assumption here is that, lacking the means of producing and disseminating its own ideas, the proletariat is in fact manipulable by the bourgeoisie and will internalize dominant beliefs as the key definitions of its own situation. This may be called the 'ignorance' assumption, since its principal implication is that as a result of its ideological indoctrination the proletariat is unable to grasp its real and ultimate end.[25] The reverse of 'ignorance' is Lenin's idea of 'arraignment', that is, the possibility of the correction of this condition of ignorance and of the conversion of the proletariat to a socialist consciousness by providing workers with a correct knowledge and understanding of their situation.

Manipulation, monopoly, and ignorance are the core concepts of the ideological indoctrination thesis which has been derived from Marx, Engels, and Lenin. In general, the exponents of this thesis have not enquired too closely into its analytical coherence or empirical validity. The idea that the bourgeoisie does in some way or another impose a false consciousness of its situation on the proletariat tends to be regarded as almost self-evidently true. While it might be going too far to suggest that the lack of proletarian revolution in advanced capitalist societies often seems to be taken as a sufficient proof of the theory that was developed precisely to explain this non-event, it is nevertheless the case that the theory has been subject to little detailed scrutiny. Before examining its core assumptions in turn, one further general feature of the idea of indoctrination is worth commenting on.

This is the way in which it reverses the asymmetry between

---

[25] This theory is less than consistent with the opposing Marxism doctrine that each class generates its own distinctive consciousness. See N. Abercrombie and B S. Turner, 'The Dominant Ideology Thesis', *British Journal of Sociology*, 29 (1978), 151, where they claim that 'The two theories are in conflict with one another. The first suggests that each class forms its own system of belief in accordance with its own particular interests which will be basically at variance with those of other classes. The second suggests that all classes share in the system of belief imposed by the dominant class.' This 'conflict', however, is easily resolved by the monopoly assumption referred to above. And, since the indoctrination thesis emphasizes the means available to actors, it can much more easily account for the possibility of a proletarian revolutionary consciousness emerging than can those alternative theories which conceive of ideological domination as an unintended system effect, as an impersonally imposed condition of class actors in general.

bourgeois 'rationality' and proletarian 'reason' noted above.[26] The latter, it will be remembered, involved the distinction between a type of rationality whose operation was confined to the pursuit of intra-systemic ends and a superior capacity for reason which would lead to the understanding that the pursuit of these immediate ends entailed the ultimate end of the abolition of the system that produced them. In the indoctrination thesis, the assumptions of bourgeois manipulation and proletarian ignorance reverse, at least momentarily, this fundamental disparity in cognitive competence. While the asymmetry of the ends of the two main class actors has not changed, the capacity of manipulation attributed to the bourgeoisie now places it at an advantage *vis-à-vis* the proletariat. This advantage consists in its having an instrumental orientation towards ideas justifying its position of dominance, and, further, not only the material means of spreading these ideas, but also, in the limiting case, a full scientific knowledge of the means of most effectively using ideas to deceive the proletariat. This must imply that its understanding of the class system as a totality is superior to that of the proletariat. Correspondingly the ignorance assumption somehow denies the proletariat this faculty. Not only is it incapable of comprehending the reality of its situation; its miscomprehension is in large part a function of its inability to resist indoctrination by the ruling class. Unlike the latter, far from being able to treat ideas instrumentally, the proletariat is constrained to internalize them, to make them conditions of its action. In this way then, the notion of differential class rationality, which plays such a crucial role in the theory of proletarian revolution, reappears, but in a directly opposite form.

But is the manipulation assumption authentically Marxian and integral to the indoctrination thesis? As far as Marx is concerned, it is possible to argue that he never thought of ideological domination in such simple terms. According to Bottomore, for instance,

Marx's view seems to be that a rising class (for example, the bourgeoisie in feudal society) is able to develop, through its representative intellec-

---

[26] Ch. 10 above. In doing so, moreover, the indoctrination thesis plainly reveals the fact that it rests on the same type of utilitarian action schema, and, specifically, upon the assumption that a rational scientific knowledge of the situation of action is the chief 'norm' by which the actor's adaptation of his means to his ends can be understood.

tuals, a realistic science of society, whereas the social thought of a class that is established in power becomes more ideological as the need emerges to conceal the special interests and privileges of the rulers and to prevent social changes which would diminish their power.

In a footnote, he adds: 'This is not a matter of *conscious* deception. Marx always emphasized that the production of ideology is a social and cultural process that occurs without individual thinkers being aware of it.'[27] Yet in the same author's collection of Marx's writings, the passage that deals precisely with the ideological activity of the 'established' ruling class does strongly suggest that it is engaged in just such 'conscious deception'; or, as Marx puts it, 'mere idealising phrases, conscious illusions and deliberate deceits'.[28] Nor is this an isolated example: similar charges of bourgeois hypocrisy are not difficult to find elsewhere in his and Engels's work.[29] It is nevertheless also true that their passing comments on the nature of ideological production do suggest that a closer view of this activity would invest it with considerable autonomy; indeed, that it deserves investigation as a mode of production in its own right. Marx speaks of the need to study 'the reciprocal action' between the mode of material production and the specific form of 'intellectual production which corresponds to it',[30] a form of production which it may be thought has its own forces and relations of production, even its own distinctive internal contradictions. In adumbrating their thesis of ideological indoctrination Marx and Engels also distinguish between 'the active conceptualising ideologists' of the ruling class 'who make it their chief source of livelihood to develop and perfect the illusions of the class about itself', and those who 'have a more passive and receptive attitude to these ideas and illusions, because they are in reality the active members of this class and have less time to make

[27] T. B. Bottomore, editorial introduction to *Karl Marx*, p. 32.

[28] Marx, *Selected Writings*, p. 81.

[29] Seliger, *The Marxist Conception of Ideology*, p. 69, concludes his survey of the subject by saying that 'The bourgeois who offends as a matter of course against property and family knows that he must insist on the sanctity of these institutions because they are the foundation of the dominance of the bourgeoisie. The admission that the bourgeois ruling class practises its deceptions not only consciously but also more or less consciously is, therefore, only the opening of a flagrant contradiction of the assertion that the will to perpetuate domination conceals the perception of reality.'

[30] Marx, *Selected Writings*, p. 82. See also above, ch. 6 n. 4.

up ideas and illusions about themselves'. Furthermore, in consequence of this 'division of mental and material labour' within the
ruling class, there can even develop 'a certain opposition and
hostility between the two parts'.[31] With Engels especially, there is
the beginnings of a view of ideological production that Marxism
has yet to incorporate within its general theory, one that very
substantially reduces the force of the manipulation assumption.
For example, ideological production has an inner logic because of
the 'given concept-material' on which it works.[32] In almost Weberian terms, Engels also argues that 'religions are founded by people
who feel a need for religion themselves and have a feeling for the
religious needs of the masses';[33] that what was decisive for the
spread of Christianity was, in the social and religious context of
the time, its specifically universalistic belief system and lack of
exclusive ritual practices;[34] and that it was socially marginal, or
declassified, strata who were most receptive to the most radical
chialistic currents of the Reformation.[35] At several points, what
he is concerned to stress is not the indoctrinating power of
dominant beliefs but rather their 'exploitability' by the masses.[36]
In these and other respects, Engels advances a view of ideology
that is difficult to reconcile with any simple indoctrination thesis.
He could thus perfectly well argue that,

> where Luther failed, Calvin won the day. Calvin's creed was one fit for
> the boldest of the bourgeoisie of his day. His predestination doctrine was
> the religious expression of the fact that in the commercial world of
> competition success or failure does not depend upon a man's activity or
> cleverness, but upon circumstances uncontrollable by him.[37]

---

[31] Marx, *Selected Writings*, p. 79.

[32] *Marx and Engels on Religion*, ed. with an introduction by R. Niebuhr (New
York, 1964), 263: 'Every ideology, however, once it has arisen, develops in
connection with the given concept-material, and develops this material further;
otherwise it would not be an ideology, occupation with thoughts as with independent entities, developing independently and subject only to their own laws. That
the material life conditions of the persons inside whose heads this thought process
goes on in the last resort determine the course of this process remains of necessity
unknown to these persons, for otherwise there would be an end to all ideology.'

[33] Ibid. 197.

[34] Ibid. 194–204; a view incidentally in which A. D. Nock, *Conversion* (Oxford,
1933), basically concurs.

[35] *Marx and Engels on Religion*, p. 102.

[36] For example, ibid. 101, 108, 271.

[37] Ibid. 300–1. Similar observations about the homology between belief systems

But it would be hard to saddle Engels with the manipulation assumption that Calvin was just the public relations man of Geneva capitalism.

In the light of these necessary qualifications of the argument that finds the makings of the indoctrination thesis in the work of Marx and Engels, is it possible to maintain that the manipulation assumption is a necessary part of that thesis? There is certainly an unresolved conflict between statements such as those just referred to and the well-known dicta of *The German Ideology*. As regards the explanation of capitalist ideological domination, however, it is the latter view that has prevailed; and it is difficult to see what is left of the argument that the ruling class does 'control' and 'regulate' ideological production unless it is assumed that this class has a manipulative orientation to ideas. Moreover, as is often pointed out by the adherents of this view, in capitalist societies the means of such potential domination are much more highly concentrated and technologically vastly more developed than in those societies to which the foregoing qualifications principally refer.

At any rate, the manipulation assumption is not hard to discover in writings on this theme. It is necessary only to turn to the work of a leading Marxist political sociologist to find a most explicit statement of it. After referring to the axiom that 'the ideas of the ruling class are in every epoch the ruling ideas', Miliband goes on to say that this 'is not simply something which happens, as a mere superstructural derivative of economic and social predominance. It is, in very large part, the result of a permanent and pervasive *effort*, conducted through a multitude of agencies, and deliberately intended to create what Talcott Parsons calls a "national supra party consensus" based on "higher order solidarity".' This theme is repeated at many points in Miliband's subsequent discussion. It is argued that 'much of the process is intended, in these regimes, to foster acceptance of a *capitalist* social order and of its values, an adaptation to its requirements, a rejection of alternatives to it; in short, that what is involved here is very largely a process of massive *indoctrination*'. Again the various forms of political persuasion 'must be seen as engaged, together with the state, in a

and social structure are to be found in the writings of Durkheim and Weber. Probably the most thorough attempt to demonstrate such connections is G. Swanson, *Religion and Regime* (Ann Arbor, Mich., 1967).

combined and formidable enterprise of conservative indoctrination'. This enterprise is 'made immeasurably more formidable' by the role of the mass media, which are described as 'weapons in the arsenal of class domination'. Finally, 'the failure of the working classes to rise in revolt' against capitalism must be explained in large measure by the 'cultural hegemony of the dominant classes over the subordinate ones—in the manufacture, as it were, of a false consciousness by the former for the latter'.[38]

There could be obtained no clearer evidence in support of the argument that the manipulation assumption still plays a major role in the ideological indoctrination thesis. Moreover, the basic idiom (effort, deliberate intent, combined enterprise, weapons, manufacture) is in keeping with the hypothesis that the assumption belongs to the utilitarian action framework. It is the definite claim that the ruling class regards the ideas legitimating its position as a means by which it can pacify the working class; and indeed that in this 'enterprise' it is largely successful. Leaving on one side for the moment the latter part of the argument, the principal problem arising from this interpretation becomes evident when it is asked what these ideas consist of. Their

essential content, in the conditions of advanced capitalism, is much the same everywhere, with the defence of the free enterprise system as its very kernel. Surrounding that kernel, and often serving to conceal it, there stand guard many different ideological sentinels, called freedom, democracy, constitutional government, patriotism, religion, tradition, the national interest, the sanctity of property, financial stability, social reform, law and order, and whatever else may be the pot-pourri of conservative ideology at any given time and place.[39]

---

[38] Miliband, *The State in Capitalist Society*, pp. 181, 182, 218, 236, and 262, respectively (italics in original).

[39] Ibid. 189–90. But see also pp. 266–7, where it is recognized that some of the most central of these values and beliefs, which serve to buttress the rule of the economically dominant class, also possess *intrinsic* value: 'Yet, when all this and more has been said about the limits and contingent character of civic and political liberties under "bourgeois democracy", and when the fact has been duly noted that some of these liberties are a mere cloak for class domination, it remains the case that many others have constituted an important and valuable element of life in advanced capitalist societies; and that they have materially altered the encounter between the state and the citizen, and between the dominant classes and the subordinate ones. It is a dangerous confusion to believe and claim that, because "bourgeois freedoms" are inadequate and consistently threatened by erosion, they are therefore of no consequence.'

Now what appears to be the basic premiss of the thoroughgoing manipulation hypothesis is that this highly differentiated and internally unstable set of values and beliefs can somehow be regarded as a unitary ideological means over the production and dissemination of which the bourgeoisie, and its subalterns, which include the personnel of all major agencies of political socialization considered in the widest sense, can somehow exert a concerted, deliberate, and sustained control. For the instrument of ideological indoctrination includes all 'institutions which are the purveyors of ideology', that is 'parties, churches, pressure groups, the mass media, education and so on'.[40] In the last analysis, then, what the manipulation assumption entails is the idea of a class actor which however numerous and differentiated in its membership, manages to exercise control over the consciousness and volition of another potential class actor, yet even more numerous, and at least as heterogenous in composition.

The decisive problem then becomes that of demonstrating and explaining the nature of this intentionality and concertedness which characterizes the class actor that is purportedly engaged in a process of 'massive indoctrination'. Here, what is of chief concern to indoctrination theorists is the way in which the ruling class achieves control over the 'distribution' of ideas; they are less interested in how control is exercised over the 'production' of ideas, or ideological innovation.[41] Moreover, when it comes to attempting to show that the ruling class and its agencies exert a conscious and concerted control over the dissemination of values and beliefs, the demonstration is usually indirect, and involves not only argument by assertion but also the conflation of instances drawn from different societies at different historical stages—a method that leads to a rather undiscriminating portrayal of

[40] R. Miliband, 'Reply to Nicos Poulantzas', in Blackburn (ed.), *Ideology and Social Science*, p. 261.

[41] In the latter respect, what is most evident about the bourgeoisie is, first, that, in comparison with the ruling classes of most historical, and of most other contemporary non-capitalist, societies, it appears to have been singularly inept in establishing direct control over ideological innovations that threaten its own system of beliefs; and secondly, connected with this, that the beliefs legitimating its own position are, to a high degree, exploitable. These facts are recognized by many Marxists, and a favourite device for dealing with them is the notion of 'relative autonomy', which, as will be seen below, is either a disingenuous displacement of the problem of manipulation or else a Marxist version of 'functionalist' equilibrium theory.

ideological indoctrination in 'capitalist society' in general. The overall aim is to show that, by virtue of their privileged social backgrounds and shared ideological assumptions, or simply out of self-interest in the face of various sanctions that can be brought to bear on them, and because of the biases built into the procedures for their appointment and promotion, the many different personnel making up the collective enterprises of ideological indoctrination in a capitalist society do act with the unitary resolve that the manipulation assumption requires.

While the several pieces of evidence entering into this kind of argument vary very much in their representativeness and relevance, they do, taken together, suggest that the manipulation hypothesis is at least plausible and that to reject it out of hand would be naïve. At the same time, the argument is not helped by the method of conflation,[42] whereby a patchwork of at best circumstantial evidence[43] serves to support an abstract model of a ruling class whose control over the mental environment is so complete as to be unshakeable. Short of the highly improbable event of successful socialist revolution, it is hard to think of how such a theory could be disconfirmed.

V

The problem of validation is even more acute in the case of those theories which abandon the straightforward manipulation assumption in favour of a more sophisticated version of the indoctrination thesis.[44] Their principal feature is the concept of 'relative auton-

---

[42] For a trenchant critique of this method, see S. E. Finer, 'The Political Power of Private Capital', *Sociological Review*, 3 (1955).

[43] And not always circumstantial. Take, for example, Miliband's observations on the attitudes of 'those who are actually responsible for the contents of the mass media', those who make the 'formidable enterprise of conservative indoctrination . . . immeasurably more formidable'. The 'most numerous group' (including 'producers, editors, journalists, writers, commentators, directors, playwrights, etc.') are people 'whose political commitments are fairly blurred, and who wish to avoid trouble' (*The State in Capitalist Society*, p. 325). This may or may not be true. The point is that, in making this assertion about the group that is perhaps most crucially placed in the entire system of indoctrination, the author appeals not to evidence, but to the impressions of the reader.

[44] This shift is also discernible in the detailed arguments of Miliband's predominantly 'manipulative' thesis, as for instance ibid. 239 ff., where he refers to the 'much broader, more general and diffuse degree of "political socialisation", such as the not necessarily deliberate but none the less effective indoctrination of pupils by school teachers.

omy', which neatly disposes of one of the most awkward facts facing the manipulation hypothesis: namely, that in advanced capitalist societies the various agencies that are supposedly engaged in ideological indoctrination enjoy a remarkable freedom from direct control by the ruling class, however this is conceived of. The interpretation that is then placed on this fact is that the very autonomy of ideological institutions makes their power of indoctrination all the more effective. If these agencies were seen to be subject to ruling-class control, then their legitimating function would be correspondingly diminished. At first sight, this formulation of the problem would appear simply to be a rather disingenuous way of sidestepping the central issue of the manipulation assumption, since it immediately raises the question of how the autonomy of these institutions is kept within the necessary 'relative' bounds; that is, how they in fact continue to serve the ideological interests of the capitalist class.

It is at this point that the break with the strict manipulation assumption occurs and that there takes place a slippage towards a quasi-functionalist Marxism, which is more characteristic of some versions of the theory of hegemony to be considered below. The argument involves abandoning two assumptions that seem to be fairly central to the manipulation hypothesis. The first is that ideological domination means the indoctrination of the proletariat with explicit political ideologies which directly serve the interests of the capitalist class, such as beliefs about the virtues of the free enterprise system. This assumption is replaced by the less stringent one that all that is needed is the construction and fostering of a much wider and diffuse consensus, which, by transcending party politics, at the same time defines their reasonable and realistic limits. This is very similar to Durkheim's distinction between 'social thought' and 'government consciousness'. And just as he said that not everything in the contract is contractual, this interpretation of ideology emphasizes that not everything in politics is partisan. The second assumption that is dispensed with is that of the deliberate or conscious intent of the purveyors of consensus-building beliefs. The ideological agents of capitalism do not need to receive direct instructions from the ruling class or to be sanctioned by it for derelictions of duty. To perform their work it is sufficient that they share certain sub-political ground rules, universes of discourse, implicit understandings, or routine interpretations of what is commonly acceptable. It is assumed that they do have these 'domain assumptions', which serve to maintain the capitalist social order, and that they regard them as the only reasonable and natural way of interpreting events and of organizing the experience of those subject to their influence. Therefore, not necessarily consciously, they help to set the acceptable limits of public discourse and ensure that conflicts remain within the bounds of a fairly wide consensus, but one that is nevertheless ultimately supportive of the *status quo*. Finally, in performing this function, it is not so much that the agents of capital impose their own sincerely held beliefs upon their audiences as that they articulate and refine the inchoate sub-political assumptions which the masses themselves already tend to accept, even though they may run counter to their own everyday experiences.[45]

Given these assumptions, it is no longer possible to refer to ideological indoctrination in the sense hitherto considered. Ruling beliefs are located much more in what Mannheim called the 'general' as opposed to the 'particular' level of ideology. As a result, the correction of working-class 'ignorance' becomes an inordinately more difficult task. Lenin's 'all-embracing political arraignments' can purchase no ready hold on a proletarian consciousness so cognitively impaired as this theory suggests. The ideological machinery of capitalism grinds out every last trace of working-class grit. The interests of the proletariat are as inexorably system-confined and system-determined as those Marx ascribed to the capitalist. But, whereas the capitalist was a personification of an economic category, the proletariat now appears as the incarnation of an ideological one. This is functionalism with a vengeance. Even in normative functionalism sources of social disorder and system disequilibrium are to be found in such contingencies as the failure of socialization and insupportably conflicting role expectations. But in this type of Marxist functionalism there is nothing comparable,[46] and there is consequently no

---

[45] This type of argument is advanced with considerable force but little supportive evidence by S. Hall. 'Culture, the Media and the "Ideological Effect"', in J. Curran, M. Gurevitch, and J. Woollacott (eds.), *Mass Communication and Society* (London, 1977).

[46] In all this, there appears to be insufficient appreciation of the fact that many of the norms that the working class supposedly unthinkingly takes for granted (broadly speaking, those having to do with what Parsons calls 'universalistic

reason to suppose that the deep structure of ideological domination would not be proof against the worst capitalist crisis.

It is also notable that the displacement of manipulation to the subliminal level virtually immunizes the theory against falsification.[47] In this respect at least the cruder versions of the indoctrination thesis have a certain virtue. Moreover, it is all too clear that a main reason for replacing the latter with the concept of a much more diffuse and systemic ideological domination has not simply to do with recently influential notions of the 'relative autonomy' of ideological agencies. It has principally to do with the fact that there is now a considerable body of evidence which shows that attempts at overt indoctrination are much less efficacious than the assumptions of manipulation, monopoly, and ignorance would suggest. As a result, the significance of the question of whether the ruling class seeks or possesses a monopoly of the means of indoctrination becomes entirely secondary to that of whether the means usually thought of as ensuring the 'ideological enslavement' of the masses do actually have this result. There are two kinds of facts that cast doubt on this key assumption. First, a considerable amount of evidence relating to lower- and working-class attitudes suggests a very imperfect degree of socialization into and acceptance of 'dominant' beliefs; certainly not to the extent required by the indoctrination thesis.[48] Secondly, evidence of a more direct and specific kind is provided by research into the effects of the mass media. In every exposition of the indoctrination thesis, control over mass communications is seen as

---

achievement' principles and those relating to 'bourgeois democratic' values) would in some not too different form also be the 'domain' assumptions of a socialist society compatible with the exigencies of modern industrialism and the moral convictions of many leading political theorists of Western Marxism.

[47] See, e.g., J. Westergaard, 'Power, Class and the Media', in Curran *et al.*, *Mass Communication and Society*, p. 111: 'The frameworks of perception which people bring to their viewing, listening and reading—codes with which they decode media messages—come from somewhere, are formed at some time and are liable to be reformed over time. The problem defies solution by empirical measurement. But it is hardly conceivable that the long-term exposure to the media themselves has no significant part to play among the sources for those predispositions by which people make sense both of the world and, in turn, of the particular interpretations of the world on offer from the media.'

[48] See, e.g., Mann, 'The Social Cohesion of Liberal Democracy', and N. Abercrombie, S. Hill, and B. S. Turner, *The Dominant Ideology Thesis* (London, 1980), esp. pp. 140–50.

an extremely influential means of shaping, and indeed changing, political and social attitudes. In fact, generally the opposite has been shown to be the case.[49] This research also shows that 'consumption' of the mass media is generally highly 'selective' and 'reinforcing' (meaning that people listening to and viewing political propaganda assimilate that which fits in with their pre-existing dispositions and slough off that which does not), and that the way in which people interpret these messages is heavily determined by the structure of inter-personal relationships, principally by the so-called 'opinion leaders' of their immediate social milieux.

That these findings have done much to weaken the straight-forward thesis of ideological indoctrination, there can be little doubt. Miliband, once a major exponent of it, now frankly admits that in Marxist literature there has been 'an overstatement of the ideological predominance of the "ruling class", or of the effective-ness of their predominance'.[50] But, since the research in question has been mainly concerned with working-class attitudes to party political programmes or with more general attitudes towards social inequality, it does not really touch upon the position occupied by theorists of 'domain assumptions'. The argument that capitalist ideological domination is effective in preventing the emergence of a revolutionary class consciousness because it operates through a deep structure of tacitly accepted rules makes it very difficult to disprove. The fundamental weakness of this position, however, is

---

[49] As Curran *et al*, 'Editorial Introduction', in *Mass Communication and Society*, p. 3, puts it: 'Most academic students of the media were first attracted to the subject by the belief that the mass media constitute a powerful and important source of influence; they spend most of their working lives apparently discovering that it is not.' The classic study is J. T. Klapper, *The Effects of Mass Communica-tions* (Glencoe, Ill., 1960). See also D. McQuail, 'The Influence and Effects of Mass Media', in Curran *et al.*, *Mass Communication and Society* (London, 1979), ch. 3, and E. Katz, 'Platforms and Windows: Broadcasting's Role in Election Campaigns', in D. McQuail (ed.), *The Sociology of Mass Communications* (London, 1973).

[50] Miliband, *Marxism and Politics*, p. 53. This represents a major qualification of the thesis advanced in his earlier work, *The State in Capitalist Society*. There Miliband does very occasionally note that the agencies of ideological indoctrination may not always deliver the goods. But his general conclusion is somewhat at odds with the statement quoted in the text above and with his further reference to 'the dearth of sustained Marxist work analysing the means and messages purveyed in the cultural output for mass consumption in, say, the thirty odd years since the end of World War II—not to speak of the virtual absence of such work in the years preceding it'.

one that it shares with the less sophisticated indoctrination theory. This is that the touchstone of false consciousness or the power of bourgeois ideology is full-blown revolutionary consciousness. In the end, therefore, irrespective of whether false consciousness is interpreted as acceptance of the dominant ideology or of the domain assumptions that underpin it, only the eruption of revolutionary consciousness on a mass scale could count as decisive evidence of the failure of indoctrination. Finally, if the influence of the dominant ideology is assumed to be so powerful and pervasive that it is virtually a condition of action in capitalist society, then the theory of indoctrination is incapable of explaining variations in class consciousness and class action within and between these societies.[51] Indeed, its chief effect is to demote the significance of such variability. To the extent that this is the case, it becomes an overgeneralized theory of order, basically not dissimilar to Durkheim's model of social integration. Variations in class consciousness cannot be connected with differences in dominant values and beliefs, because such beliefs all serve a common purpose of inducing false consciousness, and are therefore functionally equivalent. As a result, imperfections in solidarity or indoctrination can only be explained by some kind of ideologically uncontaminated 'utilitarian' interest.

[51] Any theory attributing proletarian passivity to the indoctrinating power of bourgeois ideology can surely cope least easily of all with the fact that the most notable recent example of spontaneous, widespread, working-class revolt, *Solidarity*, occurred in a state socialist society, whose rulers possessed means of ideological indoctrination which were at least not inferior to any at the disposal of the capitalist class of any contemporary Western country. The explanation of this social movement is naturally complex, but its major structural determinant is undoubtedly the imbrication of economic and political power; a structure that has the capacity to escalate economic discontent (often the focus of other kinds of grievance) to the level of polity-threatening conflict with a facility that far exceeds Marx's and Lenin's expectations of the course of revolutionary practice in the capitalist societies of their day.

14.

FETISHISM

I

Compared with the dominant-ideology thesis, the theory of commodity fetishism identifies a much more specific obstacle to the development of revolutionary consciousness and gives even greater emphasis to the cognitive aspect of the socially stabilizing function of ideology. But, unlike the former, it does not entail any notion of ruling-class manipulation of proletarian consciousness; fetishism is purely a system effect, the product of capitalist production and exchange relations themselves. Although Marx deals with the concept of commodity fetishism only briefly and schematically, and does not relate it to his analysis of the conditions promoting and hindering class formation, it is plainly one major element—and some would say the major element—of his theory of alienation. 'What Marx here terms the Fetishism of the World of Commodities', writes Korsch, 'is only a scientific expression for the same thing that he had described earlier, in his Hegel–Feuerbach period, as human self-alientation.'[1] Again, a more recent proponent of the idea argues that 'in place of a concept of alienation founded on an essentialist anthropology, we have one tied to the historical specificity of forms of domination'.[2] Whether Marx's writings do exhibit a radical discontinuity of this kind is a matter on which the expounders of his doctrine are deeply divided. But it is unnecessary to take a position on this issue in order to identify those characteristics of the theory of commodity fetishism which have the most direct bearing on its relevance as an explanation of the lack of revolutionary class conflict in advanced capitalist societies. And, since it is doubtful whether more recent interpretations add much of substance to Marx's account of the subject, that is the best place to begin.

---

[1] K. Korsch, *Karl Marx* (New York, 1963), 131.
[2] N. Geras, 'Marx and the Critique of Political Economy', in Blackburn (ed.), *Ideology and Social Science*, p. 289.

In the section of *Capital* entitled 'The Fetishism of Commodities and the Secret Thereof', Marx writes that

A commodity is a mysterious thing, simply because in it the social character of men's labour appears to them as an objective character stamped upon the product of that labour; because the relation of the producers to the sum total of their own labour is presented to them as a social relation, existing not between themselves, but between the products of their labour.

Again, he speaks of 'a definite social relation between men, that assumes, in their eyes, the fantastic form of a relation between things'. He then describes the origin of this phenomenon as follows:

As a general rule, articles of utility become commodities, only because they are products of the labour of private individuals or groups of individuals who carry on their work independently of each other. The sum total of the labour of all these private individuals forms the aggregate labour of society. Since the producers do not come into social contact with each other until they exchange their products, the specific social character of each producer's labour does not show itself except in the act of exchange. In other words, the labour of the individual asserts itself as part of the labour of society, only by means of the relations which the act of exchange establishes directly between the products, and indirectly, through them, between the producers. To the latter, therefore, the relations connecting the labour of one individual with that of the rest appear, not as direct social relations between individuals at work, but as what they really are, material relations between persons and social relations between things.

An initial difficulty can readily be overcome. It will be noted that there is an apparent contradiction between the claim that social relations appear as 'the fantastic form of a relation between things' and the claim that social relations appear 'as what they really are, material relations between persons and social relations between things'. Does, then, commodity fetishism refer to an illusion or a reality? The answer is that it refers to both. Commodity fetishism is all too real if one accepts the thesis that, in exchanging their products, producers are subject to impersonal forces over which they have no control. As Marx puts it,

What, first of all, practically concerns producers when they make an exchange, is the question, how much of some other product they get for their own? in what proportions the products are exchangeable? When these proportions have, by custom, attained a certain stability, they appear to result from the nature of the products, so that, for instance, one ton of iron and two ounces of gold appear as naturally to be of equal value as a pound of gold and a pound of iron in spite of their different physical and chemical qualities appear to be of equal weight. The character of having value, when once impressed upon products, obtains fixity only by reason of their acting and reacting upon each other as quantities of value. These quantities vary continuously, independently of the will, foresight and action of the producers. To them, their own social action takes the form of the action of objects, which rule the producers instead of being ruled by them.

Yet, at the same time, this reality is illusory and 'fantastic', partly because people come to regard their subjection to external economic forces as a natural and inevitable condition whereas, in fact, these forces are the product of a specific social system;[3] and partly because individuals involved in these exchange relationships are unaware of the fact, as Marx would have it, that the 'determination of the magnitude of value by labour-time is therefore a secret, hidden under the apparent fluctuations in the relative values of commodities'.[4] It is argued that this becomes of especial significance when the commodity being sold and bought is labour power, since the relationship is 'transformed, in experience, into the mystifying phenomenal form Wages or wage contract' and 'the fact that the wage form has the form of an exchange of equivalents disguises the reality which is that wage labour contains unpaid labour and is the source of surplus value'.[5]

The labour theory of value is integral to the idea of fetishism, not only as revelatory of the exploitation fetishism obscures but also as measure of the only real revolutionary demand: the abolition of the wages system. But the labour theory of value enters only indirectly into the explanation of the effects of fetishism on working-class consciousness and action—principally through its identification of the internal contradictions of capitalist production and the economic conditions to which they give rise. As will be seen shortly, however, the relationship between the

[3] This point is brought out very well by R. Lichtman, 'Marx's Theory of Ideology', *Socialist Revolution*, 5 (1975).

[4] Marx, *Capital*, i. 46.

[5] Mepham, 'The Theory of Ideology in Capital', pp. 148, 154.

theory of fetishism and the theory of system contradiction is highly indefinite. This is partly because the former is presented in much more abstract and general terms than the latter. But it is also due to the fact that there is no well-developed action schema for linking system and social integration. An important consequence of this is that the only means of explaining how the proletariat overcomes a 'fetishized' consciousness is by appeal to an indeterminate notion of revolutionary practice.

If the ways in which fetishism affects attitudes and behaviour lack specification, the theory of how it is generated represents a familiar and easily identifiable social logic. For, despite the Hegelian terminology of its presentation, the conception of the unintended consequences of social action on which the theory rests is a prominent feature of the utilitarian action schema, and of that of classical political economy in particular. Unlike the theory of indoctrination, commodity fetishism does not refer to the way in which one class imposes its beliefs upon another class as a means of rationally achieving its own ends. Fetishism is the unintended, system effect produced by the market-mediated interactions of a plurality of rational egoists, who purportedly come to think of their relations with one another as relations between commodities, whose exchange values appear to possess a life of their own. Individuals are therefore ruled by social forces that have the same properties of externality, constraint, and ineluctability which Durkheim, in his phase of sociological positivism, attributed to social facts in general. It may also be noted that the explanation of the stability of capitalist class relations presented by the theory of fetishism bears more than a passing resemblance to Durkheim's 'hidden theory' of fatalism. Indeed, in the whole social science literature there can be few more notable interpretations of ideological fatalism than fetishism. And since it is so clearly a product of the mode of utilitarian system-theorizing against which Durkheim's entire sociology was a crusade, it is doubly ironic that the idea originated with Marx, the master theorist of disorder, rather than with Durkheim, the master theorist of order. But what in the end identifies fetishism with the utilitarian strand of social theory and, at the same time, differentiates it from the idea of indoctrination, is that it is an emergent property of social interaction, and the source of systematic (as opposed to purely idiosyncratic, random) ignorance among capitalists and proletarians alike. In this, fetishism is more akin to Adam Smith's 'invisible hand' of the market, except that what it points to is not how the market mechanism produces economic equilibrium by meeting the multifarious material wants of individuals but rather how the market mechanism produces social order by generating misconceptions that prevent classes from becoming aware of their antagonistic class interests. And just because commodity fetishism is systemic, unintended, and inscrutable, its effects are held to be much more deeply ideological in their nature than any that could result from the attempts of one class to impose its beliefs on another.

II

Because of the theory's wide-ranging scope and paucity of particular hypotheses, it is difficult to think of the sort of evidence that might be adduced for or against it. But it is at least necessary to ask whether, even on its own terms, the theory of fetishism provides a coherent explanation of the putative domestication of the proletariat in advanced capitalist societies, and of how such an ideologically impaired class can ever achieve a revolutionary consciousness.

The view that commodity fetishism is the key to understanding the relative stability of these societies has continued to be expressed in terms that differ negligibly from Marx's original formulation. In the 1930s Korsch summarized the thesis as follows:

Such high ideals of bourgeois society as that of the free, self-determining individual, freedom and equality of all citizens in the exercise of their political rights, and equality of all in the eyes of the law, are now seen to be nothing but correlative concepts to the Fetishism of the Commodity, drawn from the existing system of exchange . . . Only by representing the real social relations between the classes of the capitalists and wage labourers as an inevitable result of the free and unhampered 'sale' of the commodity 'labour power' to the owner of capital, is it possible in this society to speak of freedom and equality.[6]

Present-day exponents of the idea use almost identical language. For example, Mepham, drawing on the camera-obscura metaphor

---

[6] Korsch, *Karl Marx*, pp. 141–2.

of *The German Ideology*, concludes that 'the "phenomenal" forms of legal equality, freedom of the individual and "a fair day's work"', are all ideological modes of concealing the reality of exploitation, domination, the class struggle, and the need to 'abolish the wages system'.[7] The thesis that civil rights have the sole function of atomizing society and obscuring class relations remains the unqualified premiss of the orthodox theory of fetishism.

The essentially ahistorical character of this argument has not escaped criticism from writers who also believe that some form of fetishism is the core of the Marxian theory of ideology and alienation. For instance, Lichtman, after a lengthy and careful exposition of the concept of commodity fetishism, concludes that Marx's analysis 'is based on a set of assumptions that no longer hold', and that, as a result of changes in capitalist production relations, 'the nature of mystification is altered'. Because 'society is not atomistic in the way which Marx described an earlier stage of capitalism', there is a need to conceptualize ideological effects in a different manner. 'The fetishism of contemporary life proceeds through the control exercised over individuals in the whole range of their social relations, their character formation, and the articulation of their consciousness.' His parting shot is that 'the fetishism of our lives does not express itself predominantly through the independent fluctuations of commodities, but through the alienated power exercised over us by State, bureaucratic corporations, technology, social roles and the repressed functions of our own character'.[8] This is a pretty impressive list, and the author does not elaborate on the details of it. Further lack of confidence in the theory of commodity fetishism is expressed by Mandel, who asserts that 'belief in omnipotence of technology is the specific form of ideology in late capitalism'. But since what he terms the 'fetishism of technology' or 'technical fetishism' appears to be mainly attributable to the 'vast ideological machine created by the ruling class',[9] this version of the theory of fetishism seems more like a reversion to the indoctrination thesis.

---

[7] Mepham, 'The Theory of Ideology in Capital', pp. 153–7.

[8] Lichtman, 'Marx's Theory of Ideology', pp. 74–6.

[9] Mandel, *Late Capitalism*, pp. 500, 506–7. This line of argument is similar to that advanced by Habermas ('Technology and Science as Ideology'), which would seem to rely on Weber, and particularly Mannheim, rather than Marx.

Despite such claims that the theory of commodity fetishism is outdated, the fact remains that there is no equally distinctive theory of Marxian provenance to replace it; at least, not one that locates ideological constraints in the system of capitalist production and exchange relations as such. And, since it is expected that the abolition of these relations will put an end to all fetishism, it would be quite insupportable if a new form of technical or bureaucratic fetishism could be shown to be emerging in just those advanced capitalist societies that have always been regarded as the prime candidates for socialist transformation. At the same time, however, it is difficult to extract from the theory of commodity fetishism any specification of the conditions requisite to unalienated social relations and of how these conditions are prefigured in contemporary capitalism. This problem is magnified by the fact that the experience of state socialist societies offers no grounds for thinking that the 'sum total', 'the aggregate labour of society', can in the foreseeable future be organized in such a way that 'the relations connecting the labour of one individual with that of the rest' are experienced as 'direct social relations between individuals at work'. In this manner, Marx pictures to himself 'a community of free individuals, carrying on their work with the means of production in common, in which the labour power of all the different individuals is consciously applied as the combined labour power of the community'; a society in which 'the social relations of the individual producers, with regard to their labour and to its products, are in this case perfectly simple and intelligible'.[10] In this type of society, fetishism will no longer exist; the relations between individuals at work will be mediated in such a way that their activities are not and do not appear to be subject to forces over which they have no control. Yet, under present conditions, the transformation of an advanced capitalist society into a socialist one would almost certainly mean the replacement of market by bureaucratic co-ordination. It is difficult to see how even the most highly developed form of 'worker control' now imaginable could prevent the overall co-ordination of the 'aggregate labour of society' taking on a reified or fetishistic character.[11] Even at the

---

[10] Marx, *Capital*, i. 50.
[11] See Cutler *et al.*, *Marx's Capital and Capitalism Today*, p. 77: 'Why, however, should we suppose that the social division of labour and the social forms of the

level of the worker-controlled enterprise, the Yugoslavian experience already reveals one dilemma: namely, that the effectiveness with which workers can participate in management varies inversely with the number of workers who are given the opportunity to participate. At the level of relations between enterprises, never mind that of the total economic system, such problems would plainly be compounded. Marx's conception of the 'associated producers, rationally regulating their interchange with Nature, bringing it under their common control, instead of being ruled by it as by the blind forces of Nature'[12] may be a noble ideal; but as a blueprint for expunging all forms of fetishism from a socialist society of any scale and complexity it is also fanciful.

But what is perhaps most remarkable about the theory of fetishism is that it entails a conception of unalienated labour which at the same time is ruled out as a motive of proletarian action. Workers suffering from commodity fetishism are in no fit state to build socialism; indeed, they are unable to conceive of such an objective. This conclusion stands in marked contrast to Marx's view that capitalism was creating conditions requisite to the self-emancipation of the working class. Even the alternative scenario in which the revolutionary party infuses the proletariat with a consciousness of its fundamental socialist interest is hard to reconcile with the implications of the theory of commodity fetishism as it now stands.

The root cause of the problem is that contemporary theorists have been more concerned with elucidating Marx's brief account of fetishism than with examining its relevance to explaining class consciousness and class action in the light of developments in capitalist societies since his day. As a result, the chief implication of the theory of fetishism is that anything short of an outright revolutionary demand for the 'abolition of the wages system' must be counted as an illusory, irrational interest. As an endemic

products of labour do not take on definite forms in socialist and communist societies (forms which are "independent of the will" of the producers?) The social production and the forms of communal decision-making in a communist society will have an objective social existence, the social division of labour will impose itself on individuals through forms of necessity. Why should these social forms not be considered "thinglike" and opposed to persons?'

[12] *Capital*, iii. 820.

source of alienation, it is regarded as an ideological condition which is global and unchanging. Presumably this is why it has been thought unnecessary to identify in any precise manner the ways in which the effects of commodity fetishism are detectable in working-class attitudes and behaviour. As long as capitalism persists, no other validation of the theory is required; it merely has to be repeated.[13]

This stance is all the more peculiar since the advocates of the theory wish to emphasize that, under capitalism, people, and workers in particular, are deluded into thinking that the production relations are somehow natural and inevitable instead of being the product of a particular historical stage. But what is then most striking about their own theory is that it lacks a historical context.[14] Commodity fetishism is the product of a society in which 'the behaviour of men in the social process of production is purely atomic. Hence their relations to each other in production assume a material character independent of their control and conscious individual action'.[15] In capitalist society, behaviour is said to be 'atomic' because the common legal status of capitalists and workers is the institutional framework within which commodity fetishism can operate and conceal the real exploitation underlying the 'exchange of equivalent for equivalent'. In a famous passage Marx describes this form of society as follows:

[13] Anyone familiar with the literature will quickly be aware of the ritualized repetitiveness of the slender argumentation. One example, in 1938: 'From the bourgeois point of view, the individual citizen thinks of "economic" things and forces as something entering into his private world from without' (Korsch, *Karl Marx*, p. 140); and, forty years later, 'The world men and women have constructed confronts its creators as an independent and immutable *datum* before whose brute facticity they can but acquiesce' (D. Sayer, 'Science as Critique: Marx versus Althusser', in J. Mepham and D. H. Ruben (eds.), *Issues in Marxist Philosophy* (Brighton, 1979), iii. 46).

[14] That provided by Marx is also sparse. He introduces the notion of fetishism in the context of commodity production in general, and simply asserts that its 'historical conditions of existence' are most fully met 'when the owner of the means of production and subsistence meets in the market with the free labourer selling his labour power' (*Capital*, i. 148). Why this should be so is not obvious, since the same effect might be thought to be a consequence of exchanges between independent, yet 'atomistically' related, commodity producers in general. And, as Sweezy notes, 'in fact, a high degree of development of commodity production is a necessary precondition of the emergence of capitalism' (*The Theory of Capitalist Development*, p. 56).

[15] Marx, *Capital*, i. 65.

This sphere that we are deserting, within whose boundaries the sale and purchase of labour power goes on, is in fact a very Eden of the innate rights of man. There alone rule Freedom, Equality, Property and Bentham. Freedom, because both buyer and seller of a commodity, say of labour power, are constrained only by their own free will. They contract as free agents, and the agreement they come to is but the form in which they give legal expression to their common will. Equality, because each enters into relation with the other as with a simple owner of commodities, and they exchange equivalent for equivalent. Property, because each disposes only of what is his own. And Bentham, because each looks only to himself. The only force that brings them together and puts them in relation with each other is the selfishness, the gain and the private interests of each.'[16]

The essential point about this system of 'atomic' social relations is that capitalists and workers never confront one another as classes, which is what they really are, but only as individual buyers and sellers of a commodity whose peculiarly productive nature neither of them understands. Yet the way in which capitalist production takes on a progressively socialized character within this framework of institutionalized individualism is the very core of Marx's theory of system contradiction. Did he then imagine that the ideological effect of commodity fetishism would be undisturbed by this change in the nature of capitalist production? The question is probably an idle one, and for two reasons. First of all, Marx did not have a well-worked-out theory of how ideology enters into the dynamics of class conflict. Secondly, he appears to have thought that even in his own day the contradiction between the social nature and the private control of production was already so glaring, and had made the position of the working class so intolerable, that capitalism was ideologically bankrupt. However this may be, the question of the way the development of capitalism undermines its own ideological defences is one that should be of pressing interest to those who attribute such importance to the structural origin of ideology.

But this is not the case. Exponents of the theory of commodity fetishism seem to be so absorbed in trying to explain the endurability of capitalism that they have given little attention to its demise. As a result, there is much to be explained. For example,

---

[16] Ibid. 155.

it is not easy to see how workers could have combined and formed
trade unions at all if they were as completely subject to the
mystifying effects of commodity fetishism as the theory implies.
Their behaviour would have remained, in Marx's term, 'atomic'.
Yet it is all too plain that the phenomenal form of the 'exchange
of equivalents', the ideology of the 'free, self-determining individual', was something that workers were able to see through—at
least to the extent of realizing that they were not in exactly the
same position as their employers when it came to wage determination in a free market for the buying and selling of labour power.
Therefore, although workers were not privy to the secret of
surplus value, they did in some important measure grasp the real
nature of class relations underlying the free-market ideology.
Furthermore, the egalitarian implications of the ideology of free
contract allowed the working class to exploit it as a means of
legitimating the existence of trade unions. Nevertheless, so the
theory of commodity fetishism goes, collective bargaining remains
confined within the limits of the 'wages system'. As Korsch puts
it, 'The common assumptions underlying the fetishistic concept of
an individual, or even of a collective, "bargaining" with regard to
the commodity "labour power" are still derived from the dream-
land of the free and equal individuals united within a self-governed
society.'[17] But, as the socialization of production grows more
pronounced, as the centralization of capital is paralleled by the
centralization of labour, does commodity fetishism carry on its
ideological work indefinitely with undiminished vigour? Is the
theory of fetishism still relevant to situations in which industrial
conflict becomes politicized, in which confrontations between
national confederations of organized labour and capital become
unavoidably and all too evidently 'public' issues? Presumably the
answer must be that the theory applies just as long as these
conflicts, however disruptive and relevatory of class powers they
may be, are limited to the struggle over the mere 'phenomena' of
wages.

But, if this is so, under what conditions can the working class
escape from this ideological bondage? Its chances appear to be
slim, because it is held that 'ideological language does not just
distract attention away from real social relations, nor does it

---

[17] Korsch, *Karl Marx*, p. 134.

explain them away, nor even does it directly deny them. It structurally excludes them from thought.' Indeed, 'the secret of the labour fund (that it is accumulated surplus value) *cannot be thought* within the categories of bourgeois political economy'.[18] Thus if bourgeois intellectuals cannot understand that the 'selling of the commodity labour power is the real relation of exchange which is transformed, in experience, into the mystifying phenomenal form wages or wage contract', then the chances of workers discovering this basic fact about their class situation must be small, if non-existent. Indeed, it cannot be reasonable to suppose that workers' direct knowledge of the reality of their exploitation can ever become a motive for their revolutionary action. 'Exploitation is hidden by the wage form, concealed as an exchange of equivalents,' write Cutler and his colleagues. 'If it is not so represented it cannot, *as a category*, be effective as a cause of the class struggle— and Marx does not make the class struggle dependent on *consciousness* of exploitation.'[19] This, of course, depends very much on which Marx one is talking about. His belief that philosophy and the proletariat can arm themselves with each other's weaponry suggests that a revolutionary proletariat does have the capacity to grasp the hidden nature of its exploitation. And if Marx did not believe that this was a practical possibility, why did he seek to convey the details of capitalist exploitation to the organized working class? After all, one of the simplest expositions of his theory, which concludes with the call for the abolition of the wages system, is *Wages, Price and Profit*, an address to the General Council of the International Working Men's Association in 1865. Moreover, he welcomed the publication of *Capital* in serial form since thereby it would be 'more accessible to the working class, a consideration which to me outweighs everything else'.[20]

Nevertheless, whatever Marx's position might have been, the theory of commodity fetishism as it is now presented puts paid to any self-emancipation of the working classes that is informed by a knowledge of the true cause of their oppression. It is only through its direct experience of the 'anarchy' of capitalist production

[18] Mepham, 'The Theory of Ideology in Capital', pp. 152, 159.
[19] Cutler *et al.*, *Marx's Capital and Capitalism Today*, p. 46 (italics in original).
[20] Quoted by J. M. MaGuire, *Marx's Theory of Politics* (Cambridge, 1978), 162.

relations, most particularly of the economic crises to which they give rise, that the proletariat can acquire a revolutionary consciousness. But at this point the theory of commodity fetishism hands over its most crucial explanatory problem to the theory of revolutionary practice. And here a difficulty arises. The experience provided to the worker by capitalist crises (unemployment, the struggle over the level of wages, and methods for increasing labour productivity) are precisely those that workers must conceive of as natural and ineluctable if the theory of commodity fetishism is correct. In short, commodity fetishism is called upon to explain why revolutionary practice has not led to demands for the abolition of 'the wages system'; and revolutionary practice is then called upon to explain why the selfsame social system that produces commodity fetishism will inevitably lead to its abolition. The precise relationship between these two theories remains obscure. Take, for example, the following passage from Geras, where, after first noting Marx's observation that, if workers and capitalists confronted each other as classes instead of as individuals, 'standards entirely foreign to commodity production' would apply, he then goes on to say that:

The *political struggle of the working class* is an exact duplication. Here, not the analyst, but the organized working class applies 'standards entirely foreign to commodity production'. *It* ceases to consider the relation of the individual capitalist to the individual worker and views them 'in their totality' by actually confronting the capitalist class as a whole. By doing so it penetrates the false appearances of bourgeois ideology. This in no sense invalidates Marx's proposition that workers are inevitably mystified so long as, and to the extent that, they remain trapped within bourgeois relations of production. For, this is so. But the proletariat does not escape these relations of production only on the day of the socialist revolution. It begins to move outside them from the moment it engages in organized political struggle, since the latter involves the adoption of a class position, this criterion entirely foreign to commodity production, and the refusal any longer to think exclusively in terms of relations between individuals.[21]

While this statement recognizes the problem, it does not deal with the crucial issues raised by the theory of commodity fetishism. What are the specific economic and political conditions under which workers can 'penetrate the false appearances of bourgeois

---

[21] Geras, 'Marx and the Critique of Political Economy', p. 303.

ideology'? To what extent does the 'organized political struggle' of the working class involve the 'adoption of a class position' which leads to a confrontation with 'the capitalist class as a whole'? Is not this struggle itself, as some other exponents of the theory would have it, effectively contained within the limits of bouregois ideology?[22]

III

The elaboration of the theory of commodity fetishism in modern Marxism offers little in the way of a convincing explanation of class action. This issue is completely separate from the question of the validity of the labour theory of value, on which the idea of fetishism rests, and which is far from being universally accepted by Marxist economists. Considered purely as a possible explanation of class action, fetishism refers to an all-pervasive system effect; to social relations which are the unintended consequences of the interactions of individual egoists rationally pursuing their immediate ends within the institutional framework of commodity exchange. The points of similarity between the thesis of fetishism and the utilitarian tradition of thought have already been noted. The function that the theory has come to serve within Marxism, however, is such that it tends to swing explanations of class action away from the utilitarian and towards the idealistic pole of the scheme of action. First of all, the epochal ideology that the theory presupposes and purports to explain is attributed such a universal influence that only the abolition of the capitalist mode of production and its replacement by a type of socialist society that does not yet exist (and might be thought impossible of realization in any advanced industrial society) would constitute a decisive test of the theory. From this point of view, fetishistic consciousness looks

---

[22] 'Bourgeois ideology dominates because, within serious limits, it *works*, both cognitively and in practice. It provides intelligibility and is embodied in effective working-class organizations' (Mepham, 'The Theory of Ideology in Capital', p. 167). He concludes by saying that 'Of course this is not an unchanging or unchangeable state of affairs. But just what Marx's theory of the conditions for the production of mystification can teach us about the conditions for the production of knowledge, and for the production of a non-mystifying social reality, are not questions which I have attempted to answer in this paper.' (pp. 168–9)

very much like a version of the emanative *Geist* of historicism,[23] an impression that is reinforced by the fact that there appears to be no conceptual means of relating this phenomenon to the theory of revolutionary practice. The global ideological effect seems, in a most unMarxian manner, to be unaffected by any changes within the capitalist mode of production. At any rate, advocates of the theory of fetishism have offered no systematic analysis of the relation between changes in production and ideology. Such an exercise would involve primarily a specification of the conditions under which commodity fetishism does have the consequences for class action that are claimed for it. This failure to specify the obstacles to the realization in action of beliefs that are held to be spontaneously generated by bourgeois society as such[24] is the main reason why the theory may be said to represent a regression towards an idealistic action schema. In this respect, the argument that commodity fetishism is the ideological product of the material conditions of the capitalist mode of production in general is of small significance. As far as explanations of class action are concerned, the chief problem is not how this supposedly all-pervasive ideology originates but rather the extent to which, and therefore the conditions under which, proletarian action is subject to this constraint. Within the theory of fetishism, these two problems tend to be conflated: it is taken for granted that the explanation of how ideology is generated is also an adequate explanation of how it affects class action.

[23] Considered, that is, within the framework of the possible schemes of social action; see Parsons, *The Structure of Social Action*, p. 478: 'Instead of being treated by and for itself an individual human act or complex of action tended to be interpreted as a mode of expression of a spirit (*Geist*) sharing this quality with multitudinous other acts of the same and other individuals.'

[24] See, e.g., Mepham, 'The Theory of Ideology in Capital', p. 143: 'To say that the bourgeoisie produces ideas is to ignore the conditions that make this possible, to ignore that which determines *which* ideas are thus produced, and to conceal the real nature and origins of ideology. It is not the bourgeois *class* that produces ideas but bourgeois *society*' (italics in original).

15.

HEGEMONY

I

At first sight, Gramsci's concept of hegemony might be seen as a sophisticated version of the indoctrination thesis. But this would be a mistake. While his formulation of it is fragmentary and often opaque, and has required much interpretation, the significance of this version of ideological domination lies chiefly in the extent to which it represents a departure from the basically utilitarian action schema of the theories of fetishism and indoctrination. Compared with the latter, it places much less emphasis on the deliberate ideological manipulation of the proletariat by the ruling class. Political ideologies *per se* are only one aspect of a wider cultural dominance, or 'intellectual-moral bloc'—a system of values and beliefs whose 'prestige' or authority is due mainly to the relatively spontaneous and organic mode of their establishment as ruling ideas. To the extent that hegemony signifies a system of ideological constraint that is unintended or unplanned and yet exerts a widespread influence on social action, it possesses some of the same features as those postulated by the theory of fetishism. But this correspondence is very superficial. Fetishism, no less than indoctrination, refers primarily to cognitive obstacles to proletarian revolutionary consciousness—misconceptions induced by ruling ideology that are supposedly corrigible by a correct, scientific, understanding. By contrast, hegemony refers also to nonrational beliefs, to values and matters of ethics and convention, commitments far less remediable by the same means. And, as more than one commentator has noted, this brings the notion of hegemony into close approximation to Durkheim's concept of the collective conscience. Finally, through the idea of 'contradictory consciousness', Gramsci gave the Marxist theory of ideology a means of avoiding its tendency to regress towards the idealistic action schema by introducing the possibility of a more thorough understanding of the ambivalent orientations of 'the man in the mass'.

For all these reasons, it is readily appreciable why the theory of hegemony should have had such a great appeal to modern Marxism. But the ulterior purpose it serves remains the same as that of all other theories of ideological domination, which is very adequately summarized as follows: 'Gramsci's analysis went much further than any previous Marxist theory to provide an understanding of why the European working class had on the whole failed to develop revolutionary consciousness.'[1] But this might equally serve as a reminder that it is important to distinguish Gramsci's tentative exposition of the concept of hegemony from the ways in which his ideas have been used to advance much less equivocal and far more global interpretations of the role of ideology in determining class action. In the following discussion, as before, the aim is simply to try to identify the general assumptions about social action on which this theory of ideology is based, and to offer some rough evaluation of their implications for explanations of working-class attitudes and behaviour in particular.

It is, therefore, appropriate to begin with the observation that, despite Gramsci's disapproval of bourgeois and Marxist sociology alike, his elaboration of the Leninist theory of ideology has resulted in a cultural Marxism whose master concept closely resembles Durkheim's notion of the collective conscience. The degree of this correpondence is worth establishing before going on to note the important points of divergence. Hegemony is defined as 'The "spontaneous" consent given by the great masses of the population to the general direction imposed on social life by the dominant fundamental group, this consent is "historically" caused by the "prestige" (and consequent confidence) which the dominant group enjoys because of its position and function in the world of production.'[2] Gramsci describes the process of the formation of such an 'intellectual-moral bloc' by reference to the 'degree of homogeneity, of self-awareness and organisation reached by the various social classes'. In the first stage, the 'economic-corporative', professional solidarity comes into being; at a second stage 'a consciousness is reached among all members

    [1] C. Boggs, *Gramsci's Marxism* (London, 1976), 39.
    [2] A. Gramsci, *Selections from the Prison Notebooks*, trans. and ed. Q. Hoare and G. N. Smith (London, 1971), 12.

of a social class of the solidarity of interests'. But both these stages are characterized by cohesion in respect of economic interests; the larger political and ideological framework within which these interests are pursued is not brought into question. This occurs in the third stage in

> which one becomes aware that one's own corporative interests, in their present and future development, transcend the limits of the purely economic class, and can and must become the interests of other subordinate groups too. This is the more purely political phase, and marks the decisive passage from the structure to the sphere of complex superstructures; it is the phase in which previously germinated ideologies become 'party', come into confrontation and conflict, until only one of them, or at least a single combination of them, tends to prevail, to gain the upper hand, to propagate itself throughout society—bringing about not only a unison of economic and political aims but also intellectual and moral unity, posing all the questions around which the struggle rages not on a corporate, but on a 'universal' plane and thus creating the hegemony of a fundamental social group over a series of subordinate groups.[3]

But of what exactly does hegemony consist? One well-known definition has it that it is

> an order in which a certain way of life and thought is dominant, in which one concept of reality is diffused throughout society in all its institutional and private manifestations, informing with its spirit all taste, morality, customs, religious and political principles, and all social relations, particularly in their intellectual and moral connotation.[4]

Again, it is held that hegemony means

> the permeation throughout civil society—including a whole range of structures and activities like trade unions, schools, the churches, and the family—of an entire system of values, attitudes, beliefs, morality, etc., that is in one way or another supportive of the established order and the class interests that dominate it. Hegemony in this sense might be defined as an 'organizing principle', or world-view (or combination of such worldviews), that is diffused by agencies of ideological control and socialization into every area of daily life. To the extent that this prevailing conscious-

---

[3] Ibid. 181–2.

[4] G. A. Williams, 'The Concept of "Egemonia" in the Thought of Antonio Gramsci: Some Notes and Interpretations', *Journal of the History of Ideas*, 21 (1960), 587. Williams has since repudiated the position he took in this article; see his *Proletarian Order*, p. 335. Nevertheless, his definition is widely quoted, and it is not substantially different from those offered by other commentators.

ness is internalized by the broad masses, it becomes part of 'common sense'; as all ruling groups seek to perpetuate their power, wealth and status, they necessarily attempt to popularize their own philosophy, culture, morality, etc., and render them unchallengeable, part of the natural order of things.[5]

Such cultural domination is exercised by ruling, and revolutionary, classes in the sphere of civil society as opposed to the state, which is primarily the sphere of coercive domination. It is associated with 'equilibrium, persuasion, consent and consolidation', and it is 'the "normal" form of social control, force and coercion being dominant only at times of crisis'.[6] In establishing its own hegemony, then, the task of a revolutionary class, and the task especially of its 'organic intellectuals', is nothing less than that of a total cultural renovation.

What is most striking about the concept of hegemony is its similarity to that component of the collective conscience which Durkheim refers to as 'social thought' in contrast to 'government consciousness'. The former, Durkheim writes,

comes from the collective mass of society and is diffused throughout that mass; it is made up of those sentiments, ideals, beliefs, that the society has worked out collectively and with time, and that are strewn in the consciousness of each one. The other is worked out in the special organ called the State or government. The two are closely related. The vaguely diffused sentiments that float about the whole expanse of society affect the decisions made by the State, and, conversely, those decisions made by the State, the ideas expounded in the Chamber, the speeches made there and the measures agreed upon by the ministries, all have an echo in the whole of society and modify the ideas strewn there. Granted that this action and reaction are a reality, there are even so two very different forms of collective psychic life. The one is diffused, the other has a structure and is centralized.[7]

One consequence of this, according to Durkheim, is that, 'when collective ideas and sentiments are obscure or unconscious, when

[5] Boggs, *Gramsci's Marxism*, p. 39.

[6] Williams, 'The Concept of "Egemonia"', p. 591.

[7] Durkheim, *Professional Ethics*, p. 79. Durkheim identifies 'governmental consciousness' with 'civic morals'. It is his concept of the more diffuse form of social consciousness which broadly corresponds to the Gramscian notion of the hegemony of civil society. However, the correspondence is less than exact, because Gramsci includes political parties as organs of civil society, their main function being to procure 'consent'.

they are scattered piecemeal throughout society, they resist any change', whereas in 'that region of the social consciousness that is lucid, which is government consciousness', the collective conscience 'becomes all the more malleable'.[8]

In a similar manner, Gramsci, in differentiating the hegemony of civil society from the sphere of politics *per se*, that is, coercive control, locates the problem of revolutionary consciousness in the region of the superstructure that is most resistant to change. This is recognized in his notion of the 'war of position', a strategy that has to take account of the fact that in the most advanced capitalist societies ' "a civil society" has become a very complex structure and one which is resistant to the catastrophic "incursions" of the immediate economic element (crises, depressions, etc.). The superstructures of civil society are like the trench-systems of modern warfare.'[9] One major consequence of this quasi-Durkheimian formulation is that 'intellectual and moral reform', the creation of a new hegemony, involves what might well be called a sacralization of the class struggle. At many points, Gramsci likens hegemony to religion. 'An important part of the Modern Prince will have to be devoted to the question of intellectual and moral reform, that is to the question of religion or world view.' By religion, he understands a 'unity of faith between a conception of the world and a corresponding norm of conduct', 'a conception of the world which has become a norm of life (since the term norm of life is understood here not in a bookish sense but as being carried out in practical life)'; and from this it follows that 'the majority of mankind are philosophers in so far as they engage in practical activity and in their practical activity (or in their guiding lines of conduct) there is implicitly contained a conception of the world, a philosophy'.[10] It seems fairly clear that Gramsci is here referring to the grounding of values and beliefs in action, and is dealing with the same broad class of phenomena which Durkheim refers to as 'ritual' and Weber as the 'social ethic' of a religion. It is also evident that Gramsci's notion of the construction of an 'intellectual-moral bloc', or the provision of a 'norm of collective action', embraces a wide range of 'philosophical' elements which combine in a complex hierarchy of

[8] Ibid. 87.
[9] A. Gramsci, *Selections from the Prison Notebooks*, p. 235.
[10] Ibid. 132, 326, 344.

different ideological levels.[11] For this reason, the hegemony of the proletariat can only be achieved if it takes on the character of a 'popular religion'; it must in effect be a new Reformation.

Hegemony, then, denotes a state of intellectual and moral domination which is much more complicated than that which is usually implied by the notion of ideological indoctrination. The ultimate values and beliefs which provide a common ground between the world views of intellectuals and the 'common sense' of the masses are to be distinguished from political ideologies in the narrower sense. The elements making up the basic hegemonic principles are not simply reducible to class-based ideologies, and the struggle for hegemony does not take the form of a simple conflict between two clearly articulated class ideologies which stand in total opposition. Furthermore, the establishment of the hegemony of a class does not consist in the successful imposition of its ideology on the rest of society, just because it possesses superior means of indoctrination or because its ideology is 'scientifically' more convincing. In particular, every successful hegemonic class manages to create a system of values and beliefs through which it is able to express the interests of 'popular' movements whose solidarity is based on the sentiments and symbolism of nationality, regionalism, ethnicity, and religion. It is in this sense of a class establishing its dominance by providing the intellectual and moral leadership for the formation of an ideological or historical 'bloc' that Gramsci can compare hegemony to popular religion and speak of its 'nationalization'.[12]

---

[11] Gramsci, *Selections from the Prison Notebooks*, esp. p. 345, where it is said 'The philosophy of an age is not the philosophy of this or that philosopher, of this or that group of intellectuals, of this or that broad section of the popular masses. It is a process of combination of all these elements, which culminates in an overall trend, in which the culmination becomes a norm of collective action . . .' Again, within such a 'bloc', 'the philosophical elements proper can be "distinguished", on all their various levels: as philosophers' philosophy and the conceptions of leading groups (philosophical culture) and as the religions of the great masses. And it can be seen now, at each of these levels, we are dealing with different forms of ideological "combination".'

[12] The distinction between 'class ideology' and the 'hegemonic principle which unifies an ideological system' is made very persuasively by C. Mouffe, 'Hegemony and Ideology in Gramsci', in C. Mouffe (ed.), *Gramsci and Marxist Theory* (London, 1979). She admits that Gramsci nowhere explicitly defines very precisely what is meant by a 'hegemonic principle', but she offers the following account:

'Thus the intellectual and moral direction exercised by a fundamental class in a

II

It is evident that this idea stands at some considerable distance from the view of ideological indoctrination as the means by which the ruling class purposefully exercises its control over the means of intellectual production to secure social order by inculcating in the subject class a false consciousness of its condition. This theme is by no means absent from Gramsci's work, but it is not what distinguishes it. Indeed, the basic rationality assumptions of the utilitarian action schema, upon which the vulgar theory of ideology rests, are brought into question most directly by what Gramsci has to say about the nature of the institutionalization of hegemonic values and beliefs and about the possibilities of the conversion of the masses to socialism.

Perhaps the most important fact which bears upon the chances of the creation of a 'new culture' in which the 'active man of the masses' will share is that his consciousness is 'contradictory', composed of two conflicting elements. In a famous passage, Gramsci writes:

The active man-in-the-mass has a practical activity, but has no theoretical consciousness of his practical activity, which nonetheless involves understanding the world in so far as he transforms it. His theoretical consciousness can indeed be historically in opposition to his activity. One might almost say that he has two theoretical consciousnesses (or one contradictory consciousness): one which is implicit in his activity and which in reality unites him with all his fellow-workers in the practical transformation of the real world; and one, superficially explicit or verbal, which he

---

hegemonic system consists in providing the articulating principle of a common world-view, the value system to which the ideological elements coming from other groups will be articulated in order to form a unified ideological system, that is to say an organic ideology. . . . It is, therefore, by their articulation to an hegemonic principle that the ideological elements acquire their class character which is not intrinsic to them. This explains the fact that they can be 'transformed' by their articulation to another hegemonic principle. Ideological struggle in fact consists of a process of *disarticulation–rearticulation* of given ideological elements in a struggle between two hegemonic principles to appropriate these elements; it does not consist of the confrontation of two already elaborated, closed world-views.' (pp. 193–4)

This idea of the hegemonic principle seems to be close to Mannheim's concept of 'general' ideology and to Parsons's concept of the 'value-science integrate'; see Parsons, *Sociological Theory and Modern Society*, pp. 151 ff.

has inherited from the past and uncritically absorbed. But this verbal conception is not without consequences. It holds together a specific social group, it influences moral conduct and the direction of will, with varying efficacy but often powerfully enough to produce a situation in which the contradictory state of consciousness does not permit of any action, any decision or any choice, and produces a condition of moral and political passivity.[13]

And again:

This contrast between thought and action, that is, the coexistence of two conceptions of the world, one affirmed in words and the other displayed in action, is not simply a product of self-deception . . . It signifies that the social group in question may indeed have its own conception of the world, even if only embryonic; a conception which manifests itself in action, but occasionally and in flashes—when, that is, the group is acting as an organic totality. But this same group has, for reasons of submission and intellectual subordination, adopted a conception which is not its own but is borrowed from another group; and it affirms this conception verbally and believes itself to be following it, because this is the conception which it follows in 'normal' times—that is, when its conduct is not independent and autonomous, but submissive and subordinate.[14]

This idea of contradictory consciousness has come to play a crucial role in some recent influential interpretations of the stability of modern capitalist societies which emphasize the 'pragmatic' acceptance of dominant institutions by the working class. These explanations will be discussed below when an attempt is made to review Gramsci's distinctive contribution to the Marxist theory of class action. For the moment, however, a more general noteworthy feature of the passages just quoted is that they encapsulate a conception of social order which, despite its superficial resemblance to the idea of ethical fatalism, appears to rest on assumptions about the structuring of social action which are hardly distinct from those used by Parsons in stating the practical premiss of 'voluntarism': namely, that 'the structure of interests in a group is a function of both the structure of the realistic situations in which people act and of the "definitions" of those situations which are institutionalized in the society'.[15] In this, Gramsci's

---

[13] Gramsci, *Selections from the Prison Notebooks*, p. 333.
[14] Ibid. 326–7.
[15] Parsons, *Essays in Sociological Theory*, p. 313.

formulation of contradictory consciousness is also distinguishable from the two opposed, but at base equally utilitarian, concepts of proletarian action between which much Marxist theorizing has oscillated. The first is that which sees the actual course of class action purely as the outcome of a realistic appraisal of the costs and benefits of pursuing one course of action rather than another. This is an assumption that is to be found in some accounts of revolutionary practice and is naturally most explicit in contemporary rational-choice Marxism. The other approach is represented by what has been called the 'ignorance' assumption of the theory of ideological indoctrination. Gramsci's position is closer to the latter, but distinct from it in one important respect. This is that the idea of contradictory consciousness introduces into the theory of practice a concept in the absence of which the explanation of social order in terms of ideological indoctrination tends to come near to a quasi-idealistic interpretation. In Gramsci's case this danger is avoided, at least in general terms. The institutionalization of dominant values and beliefs is conceived of as meeting with and being limited by realistic obstacles in the form of the 'practical activity' of that generalized proletarian actor, 'the active man-in-the-mass'. Gramsci's idea of the 'embryonic' consciousness which arises from the people's involvement in the 'practical transformation of the world', and which stands in opposition to their 'verbal' affirmation of dominant values and beliefs, has an obvious affinity with Durkheim's view that the utilitarian or profane life constantly weakens the integrative power of the collective conscience. But 'practical activity' also tends to remain a highly general, residual, category in Gramsci's theory of class action, playing the same role as that of the utilitarian life in Durkheim's theory of social solidarity. And, as will be seen shortly, interpretations of the contemporary working class that are based on the concept of contradictory consciousness are similarly characterized by the assumption of an homogenous class situation.

For the time being, however, it is sufficient to note that, while the variability of contradictory consciousness lacks specification, it can nevertheless serve as a plausible starting-point in explaining why the 'masses' tend generally to give only a passive and superficial 'consent' to dominant institutions, and why the possibility of their conversion to another, alternative hegemonic principle is always latent.[16]

Nevertheless, the creation of a new culture, of a revolutionary consciousness full blown, is, for Gramsci, a task that is much more difficult than that envisaged by Lenin. Ruling-class hegemony cannot be broken simply by 'arraignment' and 'political exposures'. It involves a more fundamental intellectual and moral re-education of the masses. It means 'the diffusion in a critical form of truths already discovered, their "socialization" as it were, and even making them the basis of vital action, an element of co-ordination and intellectual and moral order'.[17] In short, the revolutionary hegemonic project aims to bring about a union of the religiosity of the masses and of intellectuals which the church has failed to do. The power of the Catholic Church, Gramsci argues, has consisted not 'in bringing the "simple people" up to the level of the intellectuals', but in ensuring that 'the higher intellectual stratum does not get separated from the lower'. By contrast

The philosophy of praxis does not tend to leave the 'simple' in their primitive philosophy of common sense, but rather to lead them to a higher conception of life. If it affirms the need for contact between the intellectuals and the simple it is not in order to restrict scientific activity and preserve unity at the low level of the masses, but precisely in order to construct an intellectual-moral bloc which can make politically possible the intellectual progress of the mass and not only of small intellectual groups.[18]

This sounds very much like Lenin's view that the role of a revolutionary party consists of 'lifting' the proletarian movement to the level of its own programme. But there the similarity ends. For the means by which socialist truths can be socialized are not, according to Gramsci, to be found in the straightforward correction of ignorance and error, the exposure of the falsity of

---

[16] These points are admirably spelt out by Femia, 'Hegemony and Consciousness in the Thought of Antonio Gramsci', pp. 33–5.

[17] Gramsci, *The Modern Prince*, p. 60.

[18] Ibid. 66. As Williams puts it: 'It is not a matter of generating a socially effective class consciousness. That is the function of "ideology", a lower form of intellectual activity whose relationship to philosophy, according to Gramsci, is analogous to that of the Catholicism of the masses to the Catholicism of the Church intellectuals' ('The Concept of "Egemonia"', p. 592).

bourgeois ideology, and in the superior scientific world-view of Marxism. In the process of diffusion of new ideas it is not 'the rational and logically coherent form, the exhaustive reasoning which neglects no argument' that is decisive. 'Mass adhesion or non-adhesion to an ideology is the real critical test of the rationality and historicity of modes of thinking.'[19] And, as far as the man of the masses is concerned, 'philosophy can only be experienced as faith'; that is, faith 'in the social group to which he belongs, in so far as in a diffuse way it thinks as he does'. Gramsci's grounds for believing this are as follows:

Imagine the intellectual position of the man of the people: he has formed his opinions, convictions, criteria of discrimination, standards of conduct. Anyone with a superior intellectual formation with a point of view opposed to his own can put forward arguments better than he and really tear him to pieces logically and so on. But should the man of the people change his opinions just because of this? Just because he cannot impose himself in a bout of argument? In that case, he might find himself having to change every day, or every time he meets an ideological adversary who is his intellectual superior . . . The man of the people thinks that so many like-thinking people can't be wrong, not so radically, as the man he is arguing against would like him to believe; he thinks that, while he himself, admittedly, is not able to uphold and develop his arguments as well as the opponent, in his group there is someone who could do this and could certainly argue better than the particular man he has against him; and he remembers, indeed, hearing expounded, discursively, coherently, in a way that left him convinced, the reasons behind his faith.[20]

In this remarkable passage Gramsci anticipates some of the major findings of research into the effects of mass communications: namely, that people's attitudes and standards of conduct are sustained or changed not so much by their exposure to propaganda as by the 'personal influence' of the 'opinion leaders' of their primary groups.[21] It could be said that this 'two-step flow' model of mass communication is the linchpin of Gramsci's conception of the role of the 'organic intellectuals' of the working class.

[19] Gramsci, *Selections from the Prison Notebooks*, p . 341.
[20] Ibid. 338–9. Diffusion, it may be noted, is a process also 'of a substitution of the old conception, and, very often, of combining old and new'.
[21] E. Katz and P. S. Lazarsfeld, *Personal Influence* (Glencoe, Ill., 1956). The significance of primary-group influentials is well understood in communist party organization. See, e.g., Whyte, *Small Groups and Political Rituals in China*, chs. 2, 3.

The crucial function of the latter is determined by the three main considerations entering into his notion of ideological domination. First, under normal circumstances, the position of the ruling class is secured by its ability to engender 'consent' among the masses. This consent is based on the 'verbal affirmation' by the latter of those fundamental hegemonic principles which they are socialized into accepting through their involvement in the institutions of civil society, and especially through their identification with persons whom they regard as authoritative conveyors of a world-view (such as teachers and the clergy). In this respect, Gramsci is forced to the conclusion that 'new conceptions have an extremely unstable position among the popular masses; particularly when they are in contrast with orthodox convictions (which can themselves be new) conforming socially with the general interests of the ruling classes'.[22] But, secondly, the socialization of the working classes into the values and beliefs of the dominant intellectual and moral order is never so complete as to produce more than a contradictory consciousness. Their involvement in practical activity, in the everyday exigencies of the class struggle, engenders the makings of an alternative consciousness. This means that their 'consent' to dominant institutions is usually never more than passive. But at the same time it is difficult to transform practical consciousness into an alternative world-view, or totality, because the dominant ideological principles which the masses take for granted as 'common sense' provide the chief means of organizing their experience. Thirdly, however, the moral convictions and intellectual beliefs of ordinary people are also shaped by the immediate social groups they belong to, and particularly by the leaders that emerge naturally within these groups.

Moral and intellectual reform, or the development of a revolutionary proletarian consciousness, thus depends in an important degree on the creation of 'elites of intellectuals of a new type which arise directly out of the masses, but remain in contact with them'. Gramsci identifies this vanguard particularly as those with technical education. He envisages them working with and seeking to raise the intellectual level of the masses. At the same time they are the subalterns in a 'hierarchy of authority and intellectual competence growing up within them. The culmination of this

[22] Gramsci, *Selections from the Prison Notebooks*, pp. 339–40.

process can be a great individual philosopher. But he must be capable of re-living concretely the demands of the massive ideological community and of understanding that this cannot have the flexibility of movement proper to an individual brain, and must succeed in giving formal elaboration to the collective doctrine in the more relevant fashion, and the one most suited to the modes of a collective thinker.'[23] Their work of articulating mass consciousness goes hand in hand with their critical role of seizing the intellectual high ground.

One of the most important characteristics of any group that is developing towards dominance is its struggle to assimilate and conquer 'ideologically' the traditional intellectuals, but this assimilation and conquest is made quicker and more efficacious the more the group in question succeeds in simultaneously elaborating its own organic intellectuals.[24]

Gramsci does not say much about how the organic intellectuals of the proletariat are likely to emerge, nor does he consider in detail how they are to go about their task of creating a new intellectual-moral bloc among the masses. But from what has been noted already it would seem that this process would have at least two aspects. First, these cadres have to establish themselves and acquire prestige as leaders of the social groups to which workers naturally adhere and in which they have 'faith'. Secondly, they have the goal of articulating into a new world view (i.e. socialism) that aspect of the worker's contradictory consciousness which derives from his practical activity and which intermittently finds expression in those collective actions that Gramsci describes as occasions of 'organic unity' of the class. What is less easy to understand is how Gramsci conceived of the organic intellectuals carrying out their 'conquest' of traditional intellectuals. But this is perhaps an idle pursuit. The fact of the matter is that the working

---

[23] Ibid. 340.

[24] Ibid. 10. The organic intellectuals of the bourgeoisie are 'the industrial technician, the specialist in political economy, the organizers of a new culture, of a new legal system' (p. 5). The organic intellectuals of the landed aristocracy are ecclesiastics (p. 7). 'In the modern world, technical education, closely bound to industrial labour, even at the most primitive and unqualified level, must form the basis of the new type of intellectual' (p. 9). According to the translators and editors of this volume, traditional intellectuals are 'professional intellectuals, literary, scientific and so on, whose position in the interstices of society has a certain inter-class aura about it but derives ultimately from past and present class relations and conceals an attachment to various historical class formations' (p. 3).

class has not so far produced anything resembling this category of intellectuals.[25] From this point of view, Gramsci's strategy, while soundly sociologically based, seems to have underestimated what seem to have turned out to be the even more soundly based observations of a Michels.[26]

Gramsci was not, of course, merely a natural primary group theorist. The conversion of the masses to new beliefs did not depend upon the activities of its organic intellectuals alone. It depends on the state of society as a whole, and especially on its degree of moral cohesion. But socially destabilizing economic crises by themselves were, in his view, insufficient conditions of revolutionary action. 'It may be ruled out that immediate economic crises of themselves produce fundamental historical events; they can simply create a terrain more favourable to the dissemination of certain modes of thought.'[27] What is decisive for intellectual and moral innovation is a state of affairs which is described in almost Durkheimian terms: that is, an 'organic crisis' in which, due to some sudden discontinuity in social life, the hegemony of the ruling class is disturbed and thrown into disequilibrium.

In every country the process is different, although the content is the same. And the content is the crisis of the ruling class's hegemony, which occurs either because the ruling class has failed in some major political undertaking for which it has requested, or forcibly extracted, the consent of the broad masses (war, for example), or because huge masses (especially of peasants and petit-bourgeois intellectuals) have passed suddenly from a state of political passivity to a certain activity, and put forward demands which taken together, albeit not organically formulated,

[25] There can be no better authority to cite than P. Anderson, *Considerations on Western Marxism* (London, 1976), 105: 'The "organic" intellectuals envisaged by Gramsci, generated within the ranks of the proletariat itself, have not yet occupied the structural role in revolutionary socialism that he believed would be theirs.'

[26] For Gramsci's low opinion of Michels's work ('a whole catalogue of tautological generalizations') and of sociology generally, see *Selections from the Prison Notebooks*, pp. 425–30.

[27] Ibid. 184. Nevertheless, economic crises are conducive to class polarization: 'It is almost always the case that a "spontaneous" movement of the subaltern classes is accompanied by a reactionary movement of the right-wing of the dominant class, for concomitant reasons. An economic crisis, for instance, engenders on the one hand discontent among the subaltern classes and spontaneous mass movements, on the other conspiracies among the reactionary groups.' (p. 199)

add up to a revolution. A 'crisis of authority' is spoken of: this is precisely the crisis of hegemony, or general crisis of the State.[28]

Such crises disturb the existing relations of prestige, authority, and power, but what matters is how social groups react, particularly at the ideological level, to these destabilizing forces. After noting that the French Revolution has been explained by reference to both worsening and improving economic conditions, Gramsci writes:

In any case, the rupture of the equilibrium of forces did not occur as the result of direct mechanical causes—ie. the impoverishment of the social group which had an interest in breaking the equilibrium, and which did in fact break it. It occurred in the context of conflicts on a higher plane than the immediate world of the economy; conflicts related to class 'prestige' (future economic interests), and to an inflammation of sentiments of independence, autonomy and power. The specific question of economic hardship or well-being as a cause of new historical realities is a partial aspect of the question of the relations of force, at the various levels. Changes can come about either because a situation of well-being is threatened by the narrow self-interest of a rival class, or because hardship has become intolerable and no force is visible in the old society capable of mitigating it and of re-establishing normality by legal means.[29]

As in the case of anomie, the loss of legitimacy cannot be immediately repaired, and there is an interregnum during which the struggle for power and moral ascendency go hand in hand.

If the ruling class has lost its consensus, i.e. is no longer 'leading' but only 'dominant', exercising coercive force alone, this means precisely that the great masses have become detached from their traditional ideologies, and no longer believe what they used to believe previously, etc. The crisis consists precisely in the fact that the old is dying and the new cannot be born; in this interregnum a great variety of morbid symptoms appear.[30]

There is then surely no exaggeration in Williams's judgement that Gramsci's

description of the decomposition of the old order, and the progressive establishment of a new *egemonia* in a society which is *regolata*, reads like

[28] Ibid. 210.   [29] Ibid. 184.   [30] Ibid. 275–6.

nothing so much as an exposition in Marxist terms of Durkheim's concept of anomie, that state of social disequilibrium in which the hierarchy of values collapses and in which, consequently, there is no regulation.[31]

III

Fragmentary though it is, Gramsci's account of hegemony provides Marxism with the basis of a sophisticated theory of ideology which avoids the positivistic tendencies of the indoctrination thesis. In contrast with the latter, the concept of hegemony places much less emphasis on control over the production and dissemination of ideas as a means by which the ruling class manipulates proletarian consciousness in order to attain its own ends. Ideology comes to stand for a much more complicated system of values and beliefs, whose diffusion throughout the population results in commonsense ways of thinking and taken-for-granted standards of conduct which unite the judgements and cognitions of the masses with the world-view advanced by professional philosophers of different rank. This grounding of values and beliefs occurs in many different ways, but mainly through the socialization into modes of thinking and moral evaluation which pervade all major institutions of civil society. Hegemony, then, is a very different matter from the ideological struggle which takes the form of conflicting systems of political and social ideas, whose purpose is overtly the legitimation or delegitimation of the *status quo*. Although hegemony includes the latter, its ability to create a 'spontaneous', however imperfect, moral and intellectual consensus is not chiefly attributable to such a deliberate ideological manipulation. The major consequence of this shift in emphasis is that ideological domination is no longer understood as an easily identifiable, basically cognitive, obstacle to proletarian revolution. False consciousness cannot be equated with a state of ignorance and error that is readily overcome by the strategy of an 'all-embracing political arraignment' of ruling-class oppression. The very definition of what counts as common sense is in the last resort determined not by reason but by faith; as such it is not readily alterable by exposure to scientific knowledge. Revolutionary ascendancy, or 'moral and intellectual reform', presupposes there-

---

[31] Williams, 'The Concept of "Egemonia"', p. 595.

fore a long and arduous struggle to establish a proletarian hegemony which can compete on equal cultural terms with that of the
ruling class.[32]

It is easy to see why this view of ideology should have such a
powerful appeal to contemporary Marxism, for what it does is to
modify very substantially the vulgar theory of ideological indoctrination, and, consequently, the utilitarian action schema that it
rests on. At the same time, it gives sociological depth to the key
claim of the theory of fetishism: namely, that the effectiveness of
ideology consists in its embodiment in everyday social relations.

Yet the highly general scope of the hegemony thesis is also its
chief weakness. Gramsci provided no more than the outline of a
theory of ideology, whose detailed working out would have to
include among other things a comprehensive reassessment of the
place within the Marxist action schema of those 'moral' or
'traditional' elements which have so far been residual to it and
have usually been relegated to the category of the irrational. The
same point can be put in a slightly different way by saying that to
give the concept of hegemony a cutting edge requires a specification of the conditions under which the various modes of institutionalization of values and beliefs are likely to be more or less
effective in securing social integration. This task has hardly begun.
Gramsci's theory of hegemony has been incorporated into modern
Marxism in such highly generalized terms that explanations of
class action based upon it veer towards a form of cultural
determinism. This tendency is so marked that Gramsci could be
regarded not only as the Durkheim of modern Marxism, but as
having suffered a similar intellectual fate. Just as Durkheim's
concept of the collective conscience allowed his successors to
construct a sociology characterized by an over-integrated view of
society and an over-socialized view of the individual, so Gramsci's
concept of hegemony has enabled many Marxist theorists concerned with explaining the lack of proletarian revolution to
espouse a not too dissimilar and equally questionable view of
global ideological domination. At one point Gramsci suggests that
'it would be interesting to study concretely the forms of cultural

---

[32] Anderson, 'The Antinomies of Antonio Gramsci', appears to differ from
most interpreters in claiming that Gramsci did not believe that the formation of a
new hegemonic bloc was a precondition of proletarian revolution.

organization which keep the ideological world in movement within a given country, and to examine how they function in practice'.[33] This would seem to call for a vast research programme aimed at discovering the extent to which the various institutions through which hegemonic principles are supposedly implanted in the minds of the masses do in fact procure this outcome. But, on the whole, hegemony has been taken not as hypothesis but as fact. In the place of evidence it is not at all unusual to encounter the following kind of assertion:

Modern bourgeois society includes just about everything that Gramsci had in mind, and more . . . Hegemonic values and behaviour patterns extend throughout every sphere of civil society—schools, the media, culture, trade unions, the family, as well as the workplace—and become interwoven into the structural and ideological totality of capitalism. The socialization process through which people internalize these dominant values, and the alienation that results from it, is no less universal.[34]

There is no better way of describing this style of argument, which leads fairly inexorably towards an idealistic solution of the Marxist problem of disorder, than Goldthorpe's condign 'Parsons through the Looking Glass'.[35]

Couched in such general terms, the concept of hegemony as the incarnation in action of a dominant world-view leaves little room for the idea of contradictory consciousness, whose chief significance is to point to the limits of what Gramsci calls 'spontaneous consent', or the conditions that always make for an imperfect institutionalization of values and beliefs. But his reference to these conditions is also very general, going hardly beyond a term such as the 'practical activity' of the 'man in the mass'. That there is no such socially meaningful category of persons would hardly need pointing out were it not for the fact that this hypothetical actor continues to be the principal reference point in subsequent discussions of hegemonic domination. Even Femia, who has presented the most acute sociological interpretation of Gramsci's theory, does not make the necessary descent into particularities when

[33] Gramsci, *Selections from the Prison Notebooks*, p. 342.

[34] Boggs, *Gramsci's Marxism*, p. 121. For a similar statement, see J. Judis, 'The Triumph of Bourgeois Hegemony in the Face of Nothing that Challenges it', *Socialist Revolution*, 1 (1970).

[35] J. H. Goldthorpe, 'Class, Status and Party in Modern Britain', *European Journal of Sociology*, 13 (1972).

citing the results of research into working-class consciousness. He begins unexceptionably by stating that the importance of the concept of contradictory consciousness lies in the fact that it is 'predicated upon the realization that situational or structural constraints can vitiate the causal impact of ideational factors'.[36] He further notes that it is 'difficult to prove that this abstract adherence [to dominant values and beliefs] has substantive implications for action'. Nevertheless, it is possible, so he argues, to see that Gramsci's hypothesis is supported by the findings of many social surveys which have studied a variety of political and social attitudes held by the working class. These data show

that the average man tends to have two levels of normative reference— the abstract and the situational. On the former plane, he expresses a great deal of agreement with the dominant ideology; on the latter he reveals not outright dissensus but nevertheless a diminished level of commitment to the bourgeois ethos, because it is often inapposite to the exigencies of his class position.[37]

In view of these purported findings, Femia then claims that

despite his lack of familiarity with questionnaires and computers, Gramsci comprehended what appear to be the salient features of mass consciousness in those advanced societies where Communist Parties have made no inroads . . . he understood that the average individual's belief system is internally contradictory; yet he also recognized the widespread, if somewhat equivocal acceptance of perceptions and values favourable to the status quo.

Finally, he finds further support for Gramsci's theory in the fact that 'even in ostensibly consensual capitalist societies, the concrete behaviour and responses of the masses provide intimations, however vague, of an alternative world-view'.[38]

What is striking about Femia's argument is that it tends to refer to the working class as if it were an undifferentiated proletarian mass. In this, however, his perspective does not differ greatly from Gramsci's own or from that of other exponents of the concept of contradictory consciousness. But terms such as 'the average man' or 'the concrete behaviour of the masses' belong less to sociology than to what C. Wright Mills called 'abstract

[36] Femia, 'Hegemony and Consciousness in the Thought of Antonio Gramsci', p. 46.   [37] Ibid. 46.   [38] Ibid. 47.

empiricism'. That this should be so is not surprising since the small amount of evidence Femia adduces in favour of his thesis comes almost entirely from surveys of public opinion. Such findings are notoriously difficult to interpret for several reasons. One is that by their very nature they cannot throw any light on the relationship between people's attitudes and the social milieux (as opposed to the basic socio-economic characteristics) that differentiate the population studied. This rules out the possibility of establishing any but the most elementary structural determinants of the variability of beliefs. Mass surveys are also unable to provide information that bears directly on the issue of a putative contradictory consciousness. This is because they usually focus on attitudes to general socio-political issues and do not inquire into whether replies to these abstract questions chime with respondents' understandings and evaluations of their concrete life situations, still less the actual meaning they attach to the former.[39] Above all, there is the danger of inferring properties of individual beliefs from the distributions of attitudes among a collectivity of individuals. For example, the much quoted conclusions of Mann, which have been construed as evidence of the existence of inconsistent beliefs among the working class, have been shown to be invalid, if only because his interpretation of secondary data commits the ecological fallacy.[40] Survey data therefore provide small ground for thinking that there exists an opposition, still less a basic contradiction, between abstract and concrete social con-

[39] When they do, the results are often surprising. For example, in 1973, 74% of a sample of the French electorate (and among the working class 78%) declared in favour of 'a wholesale transformation of French society'. but 'when pressed for particulars, the respondents put highest the need for an overhauling of the tax structure and the energetic prosecution of tax evasions. A better court system ranked second.' The source is H. W. Ehrmann, *Politics in France* (Boston, 1976), 335.

[40] The reference here is to the influential paper by M. H. Mann, 'The Social Cohesion of Liberal Democracy'. Its methodological weaknesses are noted by Marshall in the course of a wide-ranging critique of such studies. See G. Marshall, 'Some Remarks on Working Class Consciousness', in D. Rose (ed.), *Social Stratification and Economic Change* (London, 1988). It should be added that later, and more detailed, analyses of public opinion survey data in the United States— the case on which Mann's argument largely rests—strongly suggest that what he took to be evidence of a 'pragmatic' acceptance of dominant beliefs, or a split consciousness, is instead a reflection of conflicts within the American value system itself. See especially, H. McClosky and J. Zailer, *The American Ethos: Public Attitudes towards Capitalism and Democracy* (London, 1984).

sciousness. This conclusion is reinforced by far more detailed, albeit limited, evidence from in depth interviews which show that the 'average man' has a remarkably coherent set of beliefs; and that eliciting the reasoning that connects them takes inordinately more time than the doorstep or on-street pollster can conceivably afford.[41] That the beliefs of the 'average man' tend to be coherent rather than contradictory is a conclusion that is further strengthened by the work of social historians. For example, studies of the labour aristocracy are a particularly rich source, and have in some cases been directly informed by the theory of hegemony.[42] This body of research shows quite clearly that, to the extent that labour aristocrats adopted bourgeois values, they did so in a highly innovative way which was entirely consistent with their 'practical activity'. As Crossick puts it, 'ideology only moves and survives if it is capable of making apparent sense of the world in which those who share it live. In this light, it is difficult to see how externally imposed ideas can in the long run be successful.'[43] The norm of 'respectability' was thus not a standard that was simply handed down to the labour aristocracy. It was rather a precapitalist standard of behaviour which they adapted to fit the circumstances of their particular class situation and status interests, and which served to express in an entirely coherent fashion radical as well as accommodative attitudes towards the existing social order.

The conclusion must be that contradictory consciousness is not a label that can easily be attached to the proletariat *ex cathedra*.[44] But, shorn of some such concept of how dominant values and beliefs are imperfectly grounded in everyday practice, the theory of hegemony is liable to regress towards the same idealistic interpretation of class action to which other Marxist theories of ideology have always been prone.

[41] The classic study is Robert Lane, *Political Ideology: Why the American Common Man Believes What He Does* (New York, 1962). A recent notable contribution is David Halle, *America's Working Man* (London, 1987).

[42] See especially Gray, *The Labour Aristocracy in Victorian Edinburgh*, and Crossick, *An Artisan Elite in Victorian Society*.

[43] *An Artisan Elite in Victorian Society*, pp. 253–4. See also G. Best, *Mid-Victorian Britain, 1851–70* (London, 1971), ch. 4.

[44] As it tends to be, see, e.g., in Hyman and Brough, *Social Values and Industrial Relations*, pp. 207 ff.

16.

THE PROBLEM OF CLASS ACTION

I

The first major conclusion to be drawn from the foregoing discussion of the three versions of the Marxist theory of ideology is that they all, albeit in different ways, lead to explanations of working-class passivity which are of a far too general scope. In some form or other, ideological factors are attributed such a pervasive influence in the prevention of proletarian revolution that the whole discourse totters on the brink of circularity. For the answer to the question of why the working class does not revolt seems to be that it has a false consciousness of its position due to its subjection to ruling-class ideology; and the answer to the question of what evidence can be deployed to show that the working class is actually in this state of ideological subordination seems to be that the working class lacks a revolutionary consciousness. Naturally, theorists of ideological domination never descend to quite this crass level. But, on the other hand, they seldom rise far above it, relying mostly on plausible, but empirically unsubstantiated, arguments about the effects of ideology on this or that aspect of working-class attitudes and behaviour. Theorists naturally differ in respect of which version of ideological domination they prefer. But occasionally they are quite indiscriminate and pull out all the stops. Consider, for example, the following statement, which seems to attribute ideologically stabilizing effects to all social spheres:

The fundamental form of the Western parliamentary state—the juridical sum of its citizenry—is itself the hub of the ideological apparatuses of capitalism. The ramified complexes of the cultural control systems within civil society—radio, television, cinema, churches, newspapers, political parties—undoubtedly play a critical complementary role in assuring the stability of the class order of capital. So, too, of course, do the distorting prism of market relations and the numbing structure of the labour process within the economy.[1]

This is a clear case of conceptual overkill, but, like each of the theories of the global obstacles to proletarian reason which it embraces, it has its *raison d'être* in the unquestioned postulate of eventual proletarian revolution. If this goal were not prescribed, it would be unnecessary to invent unrestrained explanations of the proletariat's deflection from the pursuit of it. In this regard, modern Marxism merely renews and updates the comprehensive insurance policy that Marx himself took out when, within the space of thirty pages of the first volume of *Capital*, he claims first that 'the advance of capitalist production develops a working class, which by education, tradition, habit, looks upon the conditions of that mode of production as self-evident laws of nature', and, secondly, that 'with this too grows the revolt of the working class, a class always increasing in numbers, and disciplined, united, organized by the very mechanisms of capitalist production itself'. Modern Marxism does not have a basically different arrangement; it just has to pay a much higher theoretical premium.

The result of this, however, is quite serious, for it introduces into the theory of action a chronic instability which is manifested by the tendency to shuttle back and forth between positivistic and idealistic explanations of working-class radicalism and acquiescence. The positivistic action schema makes it possible, for example, to hold to the belief that the next economic crisis will provide the occasion for that leap in consciousness which will fuse the proximate and ultimate ends of the proletariat. At the same time, the idealistic reaction to this utilitarian conspectus can lead to the opposite, pessimistic theory that the working class is sunk in an almost irremediable false consciousness. Depending on which of these two views is preferred, the role of the revolutionary party differs. In the first case, the party serves as little more than a catalyst of the end-shift of the proletariat. In the second case, revolution being a remote eventuality, it is only through a prolonged ideological struggle that the party, in which proletarian reason is momentarily displaced, can hope to convert the working class to socialism. This oscillation between one conception of the

---

[1] Anderson, 'The Antinomies of Antonio Gramsci', p. 29.

condition of the proletariat and the other is perfectly well understandable if the foregoing account of the instability of the Marxist action schema is correct.[2] It is, moreover, not just an abstract theoretical problem; it has practical political consequences. For example, writers referring to the same society at the same point of time can arrive at widely discrepant estimates of the radical potential of the working class, depending on which conception of social action they base their arguments upon.[3]

This kind of theoretical incoherence is not only the outcome of the instability of the Marxist action schema; it is exacerbated by the tendency to attribute to the proletariat *in toto* either a capacity for reasoning which will imminently be actualized in revolutionary action or a susceptibility to ideological indoctrination which there is little prospect of alleviating. In fact, the two problems are one. The abandonment of the concept of a unitary proletarian actor is the major precondition of the removal of the instability of the Marxist action schema; and vice versa. From either direction, the solution of the problem would involve the replacement of global explanations of class consciousness and class action by a much more precise conception of the way in which interests are, as Parsons puts it, 'a function of the realistic situations in which people act and of the "definitions" of those situations which are institutionalised in the society'. By moving towards such a 'voluntaristic' concept of action, Marxism would perhaps only make explicit at the level of its general theory what is normally recognized to be the case by serious Marxist students of particular, historical instances of class formation. It is, of course, unlikely that any such change in theoretical direction would be accompanied by renouncing the belief in the revolutionary capacity of

[2] It is also, of course, a reflection of the division of Marxist theoretical labour; particularly of the gap between the increasing emphasis on ideological constraints in Marxist political sociology and the basically utilitarian framework of Marxist political economy.

[3] In 1969, Miliband could conclude that 'for the foreseeable future at any rate, no formation of the Left will be in a position seriously to place the question of socialism on the agenda of the most advanced capitalist societies' (*The State in Capitalist Society*, pp. 275–6). But only three years later Glynn and Sutcliffe could argue that 'the capitalist crisis is converting the fight for the rights, wages and conditions of workers into a simultaneous fight for a revolutionary strategy inside the labour movement' and that capitalism 'can be dislodged by conscious and organized political action' (*British Capitalism, Workers and the Profits Squeeze*, pp. 208–16).

the working class. But, until proletarian reason manifests itself, it is difficult to believe that Marxist theorists of class action will not sooner or later be constrained to adopt a mode of analysis which, notwithstanding some naturally to-be-expected 'commodity differentiation', does not differ substantially from that of their 'bourgeois' counterparts. In other words, due recognition will have to be given to the fact that the situations in which proletarian rationality operates include not only highly variable 'realistic' conditions but also normative factors which differ importantly in respect of both their content and the extent to which they become internalized conditions of action. Once again, this is not merely an abstract, polemical point. It is one that is a prerequisite of any attempt to understand which sections of the proletariat are more or less subject to 'bourgeois indoctrination' or open to 'socialist initiatives'. The decomposition of the proletarian actor should therefore be the main concern of Marxist class theory.

II

Surprisingly enough, recent Marxist writings on the class structure of capitalist societies show little sign of the theoretical reorientation just referred to; or even of the recognition of the need for it. The writings in question have two chief characteristics. The first is that they reveal a deep controversy over what are the 'correct' Marxist criteria by means of which definitions of the objective 'places' or 'locations' of classes are to be arrived at. The second is that they virtually reject the problem of the relationship between class structure and class consciousness/class conflict, either by trying to legislate it out of existence, or—and in the end this amounts to the same thing—by treating it as highly indeterminate. As things stand, then, there is, on the one hand, much conflict over the concept of class, and, on the other, not much in the way of a theory of class conflict.

As regards the definition of class, the anarchy of Marxist analysis is well exemplified by a comparison of the work of Poulantzas and Wright. Of fundamental importance is their disagreement over the relevance of the distinction between productive and unproductive labour, since this is really the only possible conceptual means of establishing a direct link between the economic theory of system contradiction and the political sociology of class conflict. For Poulantzas, productive labour is the basic 'economic' criterion of the working class. Wright is of the completely opposite persuasion, and for three reasons. The first is that Poulantzas's restriction of the notion of productive labour to productive labour involved in material production is totally at odds with Marx's definition of it. The second is that, for the purposes of defining class boundaries, the concept is deficient because it is extremely difficult to establish where productive labour ends and unproductive labour begins. Thirdly, and perhaps most importantly, Wright holds to the view that 'It is hard to see where a fundamental divergence of economic interests emerges from positions of unproductive and productive labour in capitalist relations of production. Certainly Poulantzas has not demonstrated that a divergence exists.'[4] In this, he has the support of Braverman who writes that 'Although technically distinct . . . the two masses of labour are not otherwise in striking contrast . . . they form a continuous mass of employment which . . . has everything in common.'[5] And, in what is perhaps the most notable study of economic divisions within the working class, the productive/unproductive labour concept plays no major role.[6] In this respect, then, the most elementary notion of what constitutes the economic definition of class is in grave dispute. But this is not the only aspect of Poulantzas's analysis to which Wright takes exception. In what Poulantzas calls the 'ideological' criterion of class determination, that is, the distinction between manual and non-manual labour, the sociologist may perceive some indirect recognition of the significance of status differentiation.[7] For Wright, however, such a distinction is completely unacceptable, because it means abandoning the tenet of 'the primacy of economic relations in the definition of class'.[8] For Poulantzas's third principle of class placement, the 'political', which is basically the distinction between supervisory and non-supervisory labour, Wright has some sympathy, because it approximates his own criterion of class location, which refers to control over what is produced and over how what is produced is produced. He is, however, loath to accept

---

[4] Wright, *Class, Crisis and the State*, p. 50.

[5] Braverman, *Labor and Monopoly Capital*, p. 423.

[6] O'Connor, *The Fiscal Crisis of the State*.

[7] Poulantzas, *Classes in Contemporary Capitalism*, pp. 258–9.

[8] Wright, *Class, Crisis and the State*, p. 51.

the label of 'political' to signify this distinction, which he prefers to regard 'as one aspect of the structural dissociation between economic ownership and possession at the economic level itself'.[9]

To anyone not absorbed in it, this debate might appear as no more than a futile logomarchy. But this would not explain why the definition of classes is such an important issue for contemporary Marxism and why it should give rise to so much conceptual discord. The answer to the first question is that the definition of class is not simply a sociological exercise but a matter of vital political concern. From the latter point of view, the problem of utmost significance is that of the size of the proletariat, a magnitude that can vary dramatically depending on whether, for example, the productive/unproductive labour distinction (and which particular interpretation of it) is deemed relevant to the determination of class boundaries. Wright calculates that the size of the US proletariat more than doubles if it is estimated according to his criteria (all non-supervisory employees) rather than by those of Poulantzas, who defines this class more stringently as productive, non-supervisory, manual labour.[10] In fact, Poulantzas's criteria could reduce the US working class to hardly 20 per cent of the economically active population. And for Wright this is a bitter pill to swallow, because, as he puts it, 'It is hard to imagine a viable socialist movement developing in an advanced capitalist society in which less than one in five people are workers.'[11] This is not to imply, however, that Marxist theorists simply tailor their definitions of classes to suit their political needs. Their conceptual disagreement has a real foundation in the fact that the development of capitalism is associated with the declining numerical importance of manual or blue-collar workers relative to non-manual or white-collar workers. When the latter threaten to outnumber the former, this raises the crucial question of how to conceptualize the class position of a vast number of heterogeneous functions which cannot easily be identified as either capitalist or proletarian. Politically, it is a question of how many of these white-collar workers can be enlisted in the ranks of the proletariat or counted as its immediate allies. But traditional Marxist categor-

---

[9] Ibid. 52.
[10] Ibid. 57, 86.
[11] Wright, 'Contradictory Class Locations', *New Left Review* , 98 (1976), 23.

ies provide no easy answers. The axiom that within any mode of
production there are only two basic class positions and interests
requires substantial qualification. This is achieved, for example,
by Poulantzas's invention of 'political' and 'ideological' criteria of
class determination and, more generally, by the emphasis that is
now placed on 'relations of possession' and not just on 'economic
ownership' (both real and juridical). Through such notions as
'political' criteria, 'relations of possession', and the 'global functions of capital', Marx's observations on 'the transformation of
the actually functioning capitalist into a mere manager' and on
'the double nature' of the 'labour of supervision and
management'[12] have come to acquire a central and systematic
importance in the definition of class structure. As a result, recent
Marxist writings on the class location of white-collar workers
employ concepts that are fairly familiar to 'bourgeois' social
scientists, whose research into the formation of the middle classes
and the structure of industrial bureaucracy has been in part a
reaction to, and a critique of, an earlier phase of relatively crude
Marxist theorizing. And it is not just that these writings use
different terms to describe the same phenomena that have for
some time past been of interest to 'bourgeois' social scientists; it
is also mainly on the basis of the research carried out by the latter
(into such problems as 'white-collar proletarianization' and 'the
separation of ownership and control') that recent contributions to
Marxist class analysis enjoy whatever empirical credibility they
possess. This is, after all, not very surprising, since, while both
groups of scholars are grappling with the same, highly complicated
set of problems, those committed to a Marxist approach are not
only fewer in number but usually less concerned with collecting
new evidence than with establishing which brand of concepts is
most genuinely Marxian in its derivation.

The final point about these discussions of class structure which
needs to be brought out is that the whole exercise of defining class
'places' and 'locations' is of small relevance to the most important
problem of the Marxist theory of action: namely, the explanation
of the end-shift of the proletariat. Indeed, the most striking
feature of the writings under consideration is not that their
treatment of the placement of white-collar workers exhibits such

[12] *Capital*, iii. 436, 383.

a profound conceptual disarray, but rather that they have practically nothing to say about the structure of the core of the working class or proletariat, both of which terms are used interchangeably. While its boundary alters according to the particular definition preferred, the proletariat remains a mysterious entity. Poulantzas is strict in awarding the privilege of proletarian status, but he ends up with a class that is broadly equivalent to the whole of the industrial, manual labour force. Nevertheless, having defined the proletariat to his satisfaction, he finds it unnecessary to investigate its composition. It is as if in his theatre of structural determination the chief actor never takes to the stage but remains hidden in the left wing. Wright is hardly more informative.[13] He states baldly that 'the working class (i.e. non-supervisory, non-autonomous employees) in the United States consists of between 41 and 54 per cent of the economically active population'.[14] This massive aggregate is not subjected to further analysis. It is true that, in considering briefly the relation between class structure and class struggle, he acknowledges that proletarians differ in their 'structural and organizational capacities'. Class structure 'sets limits of variation on the forms of class capacities', that is on 'the ways in which social relations are formed among positions within the class structure'.[15] But this determination is very broad: it means that 'bourgeois positions, for example, cannot be organized into working class trade unions or revolutionary socialist parties'. Nevertheless, the factors accounting for variations in structural capacity within the limits set by the class structure overall might be thought

---

[13] Since these lines were written, Wright has engaged in a thoroughgoing self-critique, which resulted in the rejection of his original analysis of the structure of class positions since it was seen to be based on a bourgeois sociological concept of authority, in favour of a new scheme deriving from rational choice interpretation of the Marxian notion of exploitation (*Classes* (London, 1986)). However, this sudden change in direction does not affect the line of criticism that follows in the text above, which is mainly concerned not with structural analysis as such but with its relevance to the explanation of class action. Nevertheless, what is most striking about Wright's new scheme is that through the idea of 'organizational assets' he identifies, in much the same manner as Max Weber, a form of class structure which is prefigured in capitalist society and then becomes the principal feature of state socialism. For critical comment on this volte-face, see D. Rose and G. Marshall, 'Constructing the (W)right classes', *Sociology*, 20 (1986).

[14] Wright, *Class, Crisis and the State*, p. 87.

[15] Ibid. Wright, *Class, Crisis and the State*, p. 105–6.

to be of central importance to the explanation of working-class action. Wright certainly accepts this in principle. 'Class capacities', he writes, 'constitute one of the most decisive selection determinations of class struggle. The underlying structural capacities of classes and the specific organizational forms shaped by these structural capacities have a tremendous impact on forms of class struggle.'[16] In view of this, his discussion of the factors explaining variations in the structural capacity of the proletariat is surprisingly short and unsystematic. He mentions four by way of illustration: the concentration of workers in large factories and thus the emergence of 'the collective worker'; attempts by capitalists to undermine working-class solidarity through 'the creation of job hierarchies, structures of privileges and promotions'; the degree to which workers are involved in occupational communities; and the extent to which 'ethnic solidarity' reinforces 'the class-based social relations within the community'.[17] This list of factors is *ad hoc* and plainly inadequate for a thoroughgoing study of variations in the structural capacity of the proletariat. Moreover, these social conditions play no part in the definition of the location of the proletariat in the class structure, which rests simply on the two criteria mentioned above (non-supervisory, non-autonomous employees). Why is this? It cannot be that the kind of factors Wright refers to are so heterogeneous that they defy systematic analysis; after all, there is an extensive literature on the subject which shows that this is not the case. Yet for Wright, no less than for Poulantzas, the proletariat remains conceptually inviolate. The only conclusion that can be drawn from this is that the structure of the working class is not a matter of ultimate importance, because the question of whether the proletariat has a fundamental interest in socialism is considered to be just as unproblematic as that of whether it will eventually realize this interest. In the last analysis, then, it is the objective interest ascribed to the working class as a whole which guarantees its potential unity and makes the detailed analysis of its structure otiose. This does not mean that the diversity of the working class and of its immediate interests is not real, but rather that it is somehow less real than the underlying unity of its basic class location and fundamental

---

[16] Wright, *Class, Crisis and the State*, p. 103.   [17] Ibid. 99–100.

interest, which the class struggle will eventually reveal. It is in other words, still the proletariat of *The Holy Family*.

Remarkably enough, Braverman's study is almost equally uninformative when it comes to elucidating the structure of the working class, which is the task he sets himself.[18] His main concern, however, as is indicated by the subtitle of the book, is to document the moral and material impoverishment of the working class, or as he says its 'degradation'. His study must be seen then as the latest version of the alienation thesis, and in pursuing it he takes a fairly broad-ranging view of the structure of the working class. For Braverman, the latter consists in the relationship between three sections of the working class: the traditional blue-collar working class of industrial manual workers; the 'growing working class occupations' of clerical, sales and service workers; and the 'reserve army' of the unemployed (or subemployed). His argument is that the process of capital accumulation results in an increasing moral impoverishment (i.e. loss of control over the labour process) and/or material impoverishment (i.e. relatively low incomes) among the first two sections of the working class, each one of which is roughly equivalent in size. The mechanization of blue-collar work results in its dehumanization and in displacement of industrial labour, most of which is absorbed into the clerical, sales, and service sector of employment, though some of it is jettisoned into the reserve army of labour. Moreover, even though the extraction, and especially the realization, of surplus value leads to an expansion of employment in the clerical, sales, and service sector, these workers are also subject to increasing degradation as a result of the rationalization and mechanization of their work (particularly clerical employees) and the lowering of their incomes through the pressure on the labour market of the reserve army of the unemployed. If this last section of the working class is defined as including the subemployed, then it overlaps very considerably with the employed working class, and especially with the retail and service sector of employment.

Braverman's view of the working class is very much the same as Wright's. Both reject the productive/unproductive labour distinction as a signficant line of intra-class demarcation. Both define the working class as a whole by reference to loss of control over the

---

[18] Braverman, *Labor and Monopoly Capital*, p. 25.

labour process. And, although Braverman's working class appears to have some structure to it in the sense that he distinguishes between factory workers, clerical workers, retail and service workers, this is more apparent than real because he claims that all these sections of the working class are becoming less and less distinct. As he says,

The giant mass of workers who are relatively homogeneous as to lack of developed skill, low pay, and interchangeability of person and function (although heterogenous in such particulars as the site and nature of work they perform) is not limited to offices and factories. Another huge concentration is to be found in the so-called service occupations and in retail trade.[19]

Thus, having set out to investigate the structure of the working class, Braverman ends up with the now familiar picture of a vast proleterian mass. He and Wright reach the same conclusions, but by different methods. For Wright, it is the fundamental, socialist interest he ascribes to the proletariat which secures its unity, despite intra-class differences in structural and organizational capacity and the short-sightedness of its immediate interests. For Braverman, however, the basic common interest of the working class is demonstrated by the fact of its increasing homogeneity and shared degradation.

But has Braverman really demonstrated that the working class has become practically homogeneous in its work and market situation? And are these the only criteria that are relevant to the study of the structure of the working class? As regards the first question, the evidence Braverman adduces in support of his thesis is not very substantial. In his foreword to the book Sweezy observes that 'there is hardly an occupation or any other aspect of the labour process which would not repay a great deal more detailed historical and analytical investigation than are accorded to it in this broad survey'.[20] Broad survey indeed it is. In fact, the greater part of the book is not even a broad survey of the US working class. It is rather a potted history of 'scientific management' and technological innovation based on familiar, secondary sources which in the majority of instances are concerned less with

---

[19] Braverman, *Labor and Monopoly Capital*, p. 359.   [20] Ibid., p. xii.

describing how factory and clerical work is actually organized than with prescribing how it could and should be organized. While Braverman makes good illustrative use of these materials in his account of the 'degradation of work', this does not alter the fact that much of his argument proceeds by conflation and by assuming what has to be shown to be the case; it is, in consequence, highly schematic and tendentious. For example, to the basic question posed by his own thesis of exactly to what degree which sections of the manual and non-manual labour force are subject to the dehumanizing effects of modern technology that he describes so graphically in general terms, Braverman has scarcely the beginnings of a definite answer. More importantly, recent research has shown that his arguments have to be severely qualified if not completely rejected.[21]

Quite apart from this, in so far as the analysis of the situation of the working class is intended to provide a basis for explaining class action, there is no inherent reason why the organization of the work process should be the exclusive focus of attention. If 'what is needed first of all is a picture of the working class as it exists',[22] then this must emerge from a much more detailed study of the way in which what Wright refers to as 'structural capacities' of the working class differ as a result of not only the organization of work but also the interdependence of work and community relationships. This is brought out very well, for example, in a

---

[21] His underestimation of workers' abilities to resist the technological rationalization of their tasks is well documented in S. Wood (ed.), *The Degradation of Work?* (London, 1982). A more decisive rejection of his argument is to be found in the data collected by a recent national survey of the introduction of the new technology in Britain. The conclusion was that

> Our results provided support for those who have argued that the spread of advanced technology would enrich the jobs of workers affected, certainly in comparison with the quality of work under the characteristic systems of production or working for manual workers during the first half of the century. We found little comfort for those on the other side of the debate who have taken the view that the development of automation represents a further stage in the dehumanisation of work. *The generally favourable picture we found of the impact of the new technology upon the content of jobs applied to both manual and office workers.* (W. W. Daniel, *Workplace Industrial Relations and Technical Change* (Policy Studies Institute, Dorset, 1987), 275 (italics in original)).

See also D. Lockwood, 'Postscript' to the 2nd edition of *The Blackcoated Worker* (Oxford, 1989).

[22] Braverman, *Labor and Monopoly Capital*, 27.

book that was published in the same year as Braverman's:
Kornblum's account of the steel-workers in South Chicago.[23]
There, in the late 1960s and early 1970s at least, the working class
did not take on the shape of a vast homogeneous mass. On the
contrary, it was composed of a dense network of primary groups
which both segregated and aggregated workers whose status
differed according to their jobs, ethnicity, and place of residence.
And, as Kornblum shows, this infrastructure of primary groups is
of vital importance to understanding the dynamics of local union
and political organization. More directly relevant to Braverman's
particular thesis is the fact that, in the production process, groups
of workers differed markedly in respect of the status that attached
to different tasks as well as in their autonomy in carrying out these
tasks. Now it might be said that Kornblum presents a picture of
the working class which is atypical, and that in focusing too closely
on the sources of differentiation within the working class he loses
sight of its basic unity. As regards the first point, Kornblum
recognizes that his study cannot be presented as a ' "typical"
working-class community'. But at the same time he holds that
'South Chicago's diverse population of blue collar ethnic groups
and its range of community institutions are representative of a
rather widespread pattern of working-class community organizations in the United States'.[24] In any case, what is regarded as
typical or representative of the working class is a question that
presupposes a systematic analysis of its structure as a whole; and
Marxists such as Braverman, Wright, and Poulantzas have not
provided this. For them, the proletariat is characterized by its
homogeneity; and from this point of view one section of the
working class must be just as typical as another. The second point
raises questions of a similar kind, since, in the absence of a frame
of reference by which it is possible to establish what is of particular
rather than of general significance in the study of the structure of
the working class, on what basis is it possible to decide which
perspective is the more valid: Kornblum's worm's-eye view, which
is veridical within its limited range; or Braverman's bird's-eye
view, which is the favourite vantage-point of the Marxist wishful
thinker?

[23] W. Kornblum, *Blue Collar Community* (Chicago, 1974).
[24] Ibid. 2.

There is, however, one sense in which Braverman's perspective on the working class is insufficiently broad in its scope. This appertains to a point made by MacKenzie, who, after referring to 'Braverman's failure to consider the *uniqueness* of the United States', goes on to argue that 'any analysis of changes in the structure and composition of the American working class should make explicit recognition of the unique as well as the general structural features of that society'.[25] MacKenzie's strictures on Braverman apply with equal force to the conceptionalization of class structure advanced by Wright and Poulantzas, even though Poulantzas's distinctive concern with the 'petty bourgeoisie' might be thought to reflect something especially characteristic of his own society. For they likewise deny the proletariat any national identity; and thus, in possessing neither a structure nor a history, the proletariat truly acquires the nature of a 'universal' class. What is basically at stake here is not so much the uniqueness of this or that society, but rather those aspects of its historical development which can be grasped, through comparative study, in more general terms. Perhaps the most important single point of reference in this respect is the one referred to earlier on: namely, the status structure of civil, political, industrial, and social citizenship. The mode of the civic incorporation of the working class is a factor of major significance in explaining national differences in class formation. But once again this involves reference to a 'moral and historical' element which has no definite place in Marxist theory, and in the writings being discussed this means that the analysis of the status system can play no part in the definition of the position of the working class. The result is that the conceptual sanitation of the proletariat is complete.

This suggests that these modern theories of class structure are still based, at least implicitly, on the classical Marxist action scheme. For, in so far as the definition of class structure is intended to elucidate the variability of the class struggle, it must involve some idea of the constituents of social action. That is, it must take account not only of the means and conditions of action (such as control over the labour process) but also of the determination of the ends of actors and of the standards by which they

[25] G. MacKenzie, 'The Political Economy of the American Working Class', *British Journal of Sociology*, 28 (1977), pp. 250–1.

relate means to ends. It is in the latter respect that the status order plays a central role in both the differentiation and integration of ends and the legitimation of means. It must be repeated that this does not entail the assumption that an actor's status situation is an internalized condition of his action. The extent to which he regards its legitimation of his ends and means as binding is variable and is affected by, among other things, changes in his class situation. On the other hand, the status situation cannot be reduced to the category of external means and conditions which actors relate to in a purely instrumental manner. In Marxism, however, this problem of the institutionalization of status does not arise. Yet just because the concept of status plays no systematic role in its theory of action, the effects of status can only be taken into account either by treating them in an *ad hoc* fashion or by subsuming them under the catch-all concept of ideology. The former tendency is more evident in the work of contemporary class theorists.

For example, when Braverman characterizes loss of control over the labour process as 'degradation', he resorts to some idea of socially invariable and hence completely unproblematic ends akin to Marx's notion of authentic human needs, and it is only by making this assumption that he can infer the potential of working-class revolt from changes in the conditions of class action.[26] But, quite apart from the fact that this conclusion sits uneasily, though familiarly, with his discussion of the 'habituation' of the worker to his alienated conditions of work, Braverman's explanations of both degradation and habituation take no account of the way in which the status system inculcates different levels of expectation of autonomy in work. Once again, this is not to suggest that variations in these expectations provide a sufficient explanation of action; the problem is rather to understand how action is jointly determined by both realistic and normative elements and particularly by the way in which changes in these elements are mutually interdependent. In Wright's work also there are traces of the resort to an arbitrary notion of status. For example, when he writes that 'job hierarchies, structures of privileges and promotions' can operate to 'weaken the social relations among workers

[26] Braverman, *Labor and Monopoly Capital*, pp. 139, 151.

within production',[27] his argument relies on the general assumption that status differentiation can shape ends in a way that is inimical to class solidarity. But there is no reason why effects of this kind should be seen as restricted to 'workers within production'. So what is glimpsed here is but the tip of a conceptual iceberg which could appear anywhere on the chart of class locations. Finally, as was noted above, Poulantzas's treatment of the ideological division between manual and non-manual labour involves a fairly explicit reference to what anyone but a Marxist would term a line of status demarcation. But again, why should status manifest itself only at this level of the class structure, and not, for instance, as Wright suggests, within the working class itself? The answer is that it is the consequence of Poulantzas's decision that the ideological criterion of class relates exclusively to the distinction between manual and non-manual labour. And, to make things worse, it is a decison that has no Marxian warrant.

From this rather lengthy discussion of recent Marxist definitions of class structure three main conclusions can be drawn. The first is that, while the criteria for placing or locating classes are in deep dispute, the one that there is least disagreement about in principle—namely, the significance of 'relations of possession'—raises conceptual and empirical issues of a basically similar kind to those that have occupied the attention of 'bourgeois' social scientists in their studies of the bureaucratization of industrial organization. The second notable feature of Marxist class definition is that the classical conception of the proletariat as a unitary class actor survives intact. The working class retains its essential identity either by the ascription to it of a unifying fundamental interest or by the attempt to demonstrate its homogeneity. Thirdly, by concentrating on the means and conditions of action, these definitions of class structure perpetuate a conception of action whose chief defect has always been its failure to take account of the nature and variability of normative elements in the determination of ends and of the means–ends relationship. At the structural level, the most striking consequence of this omission is the abstraction of class relations from the context of the status system of a society. By ignoring these factors, the class theories of modern Marxism implicitly fall back on a notion of action in which

---

[27] Wright, *Class, Crisis and the State*, 100.

the only significant ends are the given or fundamental interests of class actors, the only norm for relating means to ends is that of rationality, and the only way of explaining deviation from rational action is by reference to ideologically induced ignorance or error.

In raising this last issue, the discussion of the definition of class structure has already engaged with the second main problem it set out to deal with: namely, the question of the relation between class structure on the one hand, and class consciousness and class conflict on the other. It is now time to face this problem directly.

III

Within classical Marxism, the crucial problem of the end-shift of the proletariat centred on the distinction between a class-in-itself and a class-for-itself. This is a distinction between a class that has objectively defined interests by virtue of its position within the class structure and a class that constitutes an ideologically united and politically organized entity which is acting in pursuit of its interests against those of another class. In general, modern Marxism continues to accept this distinction. That is to say, the purpose of the analysis of class structure is to provide an explanation of class consciousness and class conflict. As Wright puts it, 'It is all very well and good to clarify the structure of positions defined by social relations of production and to link these to other positions in the social structure. Marxism, however, is not primarily a theory of class structure: it is above all a theory of class struggle.'[28] How, then, is the relationship between class structure and class conflict understood?

The first approach to this problem which is fairly characteristic of writers whose work is almost exclusively concerned with the definition of classes, is in one way or another to avoid it. Braverman, for example, excludes the analysis of class conflict and class consciousness from his discussion altogether. 'No attempt will be made to deal with the modern working class on the level of its consciousness, organization, or activities. This is a book about the working class *in itself*, not as a class *for itself*. I realize that to many readers it will appear that I have omitted the most urgent part of the subject matter.' He goes on to say it is not

---

[28] Wright, *Class, Crisis and the State*, 97–8.

his purpose 'to deprecate the importance of the study of the state of consciousness of the working class, since it is only through consciousness that a class becomes an actor on the historic stage'. But the only indication he gives of how this study might proceed is by distinguishing between the 'absolute expression' of class consciousness ('a pervasive and durable attitude on the part of a class towards its position in society'), its 'long-term relative expression' ('found in the slowly changing traditions, experiences, education, and organization of the class'), and its 'short-term relative expression' ('a dynamic complex of moods and sentiments affected by circumstances and changing with them, sometimes, in periods of stress and conflict, almost from day to day').[29] Virtually the same position is taken up by Crompton and Gubbay, whose study is almost entirely given over to the analysis of class position. In asking how 'the location in the class structure is reflected in the consciousness of particular groups', their general answer is that there are 'no easy answers: the particular structure of the labour market, the dominant ideology and short-term historical circumstances will all tend to act as intervening variables in the description and explanation of objective location in the class structure and the consciousness, attitudes and behaviour of the groups so located'.[30] This list of intervening variables is presented simply to indicate the complexity of the problem and not as a basis for the systematic analysis of it. And in the section of the book where they attempt to discuss class consciousness in rather more detail, their treatment of it relies on an equally *ad hoc* reference to adventitious 'secondary structural factors' (differentiation of function, bureaucracy, market, and status factors), which, 'far from determining the class structure of contemporary capitalist societies', must nevertheless 'be systematically taken into account in the detailed empirical analysis of the class structure of any particular society'.[31] Finally, Wright, who gives primacy to the study of class struggle, provides no more than a highly schematic account of how such a study might proceed. This involves a distinction between class structure (which defines the potential objectives of the potential actors in the class struggle), class

---

[29] Braverman, *Labor and Monopoly Capital*, pp. 27–30.
[30] Crompton and Gubbay, *Economy and Class Structure*, pp. 97–8 .
[31] Ibid. 196.

formation (which refers to structural and organization capacities of classes), and class struggle itself, conceived as 'the complex social processes which dialectically link class interests to class capacities'.[32] Wright provides brief illustrations of the 'dialectical' relationships between these three elements. But the exposition is merely indicative of how the schema might be applied. Its 'central message' is that

An adequate political understanding of the possibilities and constraints present in a given social formation depends upon showing the ways in which class structure establishes limits on class struggle and class forma- tion, the ways in which class struggle transforms both class structure and class formation, and the ways in which class struggle mediates the relationship between class structure and class formation.[33]

One definition of 'message' given by *The Concise Oxford Dictionary* is a 'prophet's, writer's, preacher's, inspired com- munication'. Until Wright demonstrates how his schema might illuminate the relation between class structure and class struggle in a given social formation, his advocacy of its usefulness for this purpose must be considered as no more than a message in the sense just defined.

The work of Poulantzas belongs in a different category because it begins by attempting to abolish the distinction between a class- in-itself and a class-for-itself. For him, 'classes have existence only in the class struggle', and the latter is not something that is to be treated separately from the analysis of class structure. 'Classes do not firstly exist as such and then only enter into the class struggle.'[34] By this he means that classes are not purely economic- ally determined entities which then become transformed into classes-for-themselves at the political and ideological level of class consciousness and organization. According to Poulantzas, this misleading distinction derives from an Hegelian interpretation of Marx, which he foists on Lukács. The purpose of saddling Lukács with this error and absolving Marx from it is all too transparent and requires no further comment. What is important about Poulantzas's argument is, first, that his rejection of the Hegelian 'problematic' leads to ambiguity in his concepts of the 'political',

[32] Wright, *Class, Crisis and the State*, 102.
[33] Ibid. 108.
[34] Poulantzas, *Classes in Contemporary Capitalism*, 14.

the 'ideological', and the 'class struggle', and, second, that the resolution of this ambiguity results in the resurgence of the 'problematic' he attempts to dispose of.

To say that classes cannot be defined outside the class struggle is all very well in so far as it means that class relations are inherently an arena of class struggle and that this class struggle does not necessarily involve class consciousness and class struggle in the traditional sense of a class-for-itself. Moreoever, there is nothing exceptionable about Poulantzas's argument that class structure is to be defined by reference to 'political' and 'ideological' (as well as economic) criteria as long as it is remembered that these refer to the supervisory and non-manual functions which are focal points of class struggle in the social division of labour. So far, so good. The difficulty arises not from this special meaning of political and ideological class struggle being constitutive of class structure but from the fact that class struggle and class consciousness are empirically variable. Granted that in Poulantzas's terms production relations contain a political and ideological dimension, it is nevertheless the case that this refers to a different order of fact from the political organization and ideology through which the objectively determined interests of a class are expressed or represented at the societal level of the class struggle. Poulantzas is forced to recognize this distinction:

This structural determination of classes, which thus exists only as the class struggle, must, however, be distinguished from class position in each specific conjuncture—the focal point of the always unique historic individuality of a social formation, in other words the concrete situation of the class struggle.[35]

To exemplify this distinction, take, for example, the working class. Its structural place is determined by reference to aspects of class struggle which constitute class structure: that is, by the economic aspect (productive labour), the political aspect (subjection to supervision), and the ideological aspect (manual labour excluded from the 'secret knowledge' of the production process). Its 'class position', however, implies '"class consciousness" and autonomous political organization, i.e. as far as the working class is concerned, a revolutionary proletarian ideology and an autono-

[35] Ibid. 14.

mous party of class struggle, refer to the terrain of class positions and the conjuncture'.[36]

What this means is that there is a latent class struggle and a manifest class struggle. There is the political and ideological class struggle that determines the structure of classes, and there is the political and ideological class struggle which is manifested in the specific forms of class consciousness and political organization of class 'positions' in the 'conjuncture'. In other words, by distinguishing between a structural and a conjunctural class struggle, Poulantzas conjures up in a different form the Hegelian spectre of the class-in-itself/class-for-itself which he set out to exorcize. Moreover, his conception of the relationships between the structural determination of classes and class positions in the conjuncture is no less vague. On the one hand, 'A social class, or fraction or stratum of a class, may take up a class position that does not correspond to its interests, which are defined by the class determination that fixes the horizon of the class's struggle.' Yet, on the other hand, 'structural class determination involves economic, political and ideological class struggle, and these struggles are all expressed in the form of class positions in the conjuncture'.[37] The problem here is basically that, while Poulantzas admits that classes may not take up positions in the conjunctural class struggle that correspond to their interests which are determined by their place in the class structure, this discrepancy can only be explained by a systematic study of the specific political and ideological factors affecting 'the concrete situation of the class struggle'. Since he does not undertake this kind of analysis, it is difficult to disagree with the conclusion of one Marxist critic, who argues that 'Poulantzas's class determination/class position distinction is incoherent and unstable' because the concept of class position in the conjuncture is 'not theorized. It is merely a means of hedging any bets made on the basis of class determination.'[38]

In the present context, however, what is most important about Poulantzas's theory of class structure and class consciousness is that the place, interest, and position of the proletariat appear to

[36] Poulantzas, *Classes in Contemporary Capitalism*, 17.
[37] Ibid. 15–16.
[38] P. Q. Hirst, 'Economic Classes and Politics', in A. Hunt (ed.), *Class and Class Structure* (London, 1977), 133.

be entirely unproblematic. It has already been noted that his definition of the class place of the proletariat is such that it constitutes a clear-cut entity: it is at once economically exploited, politically subjected, and ideologically excluded, i.e. productive, non-supervisory manual labour. Beyond this, Poulantzas has very little to say about the working class. It is excluded from his purview at the outset. But its role in his theory of classes is as crucial as its socialist class 'position' is indisputable. As he says, although 'these essays do not deal directly with the working class, this class is constantly present'; and it is always present as 'the class that is situated beneath the exploitation which the bourgeoisie imposes on the popular masses, and the class to which the leadership of the revolutionary process falls'.[39] It has already been observed that he equates the 'position' of the working class with 'a revolutionary proletarian ideology', and elsewhere he refers to 'The long-term interests of the working class itself, which is the only class that is revolutionary to the end'.[40] Only occasionally is there a glimpse of doubt: for example, 'certain ideological elements specific to the petty bourgeoisie may themselves have their effects on the working class's ideology' and 'this is even the main danger that permanently threatens the working class'.[41] But his basic assumption is that the interests and 'position' of the proletariat are beyond question. 'The class struggle in a social formation takes place within the basic context of a polarization of various classes in relation to the two basic classes, those of the dominant mode of production, whose relationship constitutes the principal contradiction of that formation'.[42] These basic classes are naturally 'the bourgeoisie and the proletariat; the only real class ideologies, in the strong sense of this term, are those of these two basic classes, which are in fundamental political opposition'.[43]

The problem of the relationship between the class place and class position of the proletariat—the problem of its end-shift—is therefore solved by fiat. This 'solution' has most unfortunate consequences for his analysis of the new petty bourgeoisie, a subect to which Poulantzas devotes a great deal of attention. Given his general theory of class struggle, the new petty bourgeoisie can have no real class position of its own that is independent

---

[39] Poulantzas, *Classes in Contemporary Capitalism*, 9.   [40] Ibid. 204.
[41] Ibid. 289.   [42] Ibid. 200.   [43] Ibid. 287.

of 'the bourgeois way and the proletarian (the socialist) way'.[44] Its class place is distinguished from those of the two basic classes by reference to the economic, political, and ideological criteria of class determination; and particularly by its intermediate location in bureaucratic structures of authority. Much of what Poulantzas has to say on this score is sociologically commonplace and derivative: compare, for example, his remarks on 'the stupidity of the bourgeois problematic of social mobility' with his subsequent observations on the significance of mobility chances for the consciousness of the new petty bourgeoisie.[45] It is, however, on the basis of this analysis of the structural place of the new petty bourgeoisie that he seeks to identify its class position. As he says, the 'structural determination of the new petty bourgeoisie in the social division of labour has certain effects on the ideology of its agents, which directly influences its class positions'.[46] The chief features of this ideology, which unites the new and the traditional petty bourgeoisie at the ideological level, are as follows: it is anti-capitalist, reformist, individualistic, and conceives of the state as a neutral arbiter of class interests. But the new petty bourgeoisie is not a homogeneous body. By reference to several broad changes affecting the petty bourgeoisie in general (its feminization, the narrowing of wage differentials between non-manual and manual labour, the rationalization and mechanization of office work, etc.), Poulantzas seeks to identify three 'fractions' of the class which 'display the most favourable objective conditions for a quite specific alliance with the working class and under its leadership'.[47] His discussion of the internal differentiation of the new petty bourgeoisie is much more acute than Braverman's treatment of the subject, and not least because Poulantzas's is empirically and sociologically more discriminating. The result is a novel and challenging Marxist interpretation of class structure which identifies precisely the potential allies of the working class.

But it is at this point that Poulantzas's argument begins to break down. The class position of those 'fractions' of the new petty bourgeoisie whose place in the class structure most closely approximates that of the proletariat depends ultimately on the strategy of the latter class. It is not to be assumed that 'an objective

[44] Poulantzas, *Classes in Contemporary Capitalism*, 297.
[45] Ibid. 33, 280, 284.   [46] Ibid. 287.   [47] Ibid. 314.

proletarian polarization of class determination must necessarily lead in time to a polarization of class positions'.[48] In fact,

the objective polarization which, together with current transformations, marks the class determination of these petty-bourgeois fractions, has not till now been accompanied by a polarization of their class positions. In other words, no alliance has yet materialized between the major sections of these fractions and the working class, based on the specific objectives of a socialist revolution.

Whether this alliance takes place depends entirely on 'the strategy of the working class and its organizations of class struggle'.[49] In the last analysis, then, everything depends on the proletariat, the class actor to whom he assigns a 'socialist position' *ex cathedra*— but only when one reaches the penultimate page of his book. There Poulantzas admits that the problem of how the working class can attempt to establish its 'hegemony' over the proletarianized 'fractions' of the new petty bourgeoisie presupposes a study of the working class that he has not even begun to make.

For this [he writes], it would have been necessary, among other things, to undertake a study of the history and experience of the workers' and international revolutionary movement in this respect—of its organizations, of its theories, and the changes in them, on the question of the revolutionary process, of organization (party and trade unions) and of alliances, and finally to understand in more detail the significance of social-democratic ideology and social-democratic tendencies, and their real basis.[50]

In other words, it would be necessary to consider how working-class consciousness is formed not only by its economic, political, and ideological place in the class structure but also by the specific political organizations and ideologies which represent its objective interest. Most importantly, the latter would involve a comparative study of the formation of the working class which took account of 'the unique historical individuality of a social formation' and the cumulative effect on the political organization of the working class of the outcomes of successive 'concrete situations of the class struggle'.

In conclusion, then, whatever the merits of Poulantzas's analysis of the class place of the bourgeoisie and the petty bourgeoisie, his

[48] Ibid. 334.   [49] Ibid. 333–4.   [50] Ibid. 335.

theory of social classes provides no systematic explanation of class action and does not even begin to deal with the chronic and intractable problem of the end-shift of the proletariat. His belated recognition that the study of specific working-class organizations and their ideologies is essential to an understanding of the way in which the interest of the proletariat is represented in the concrete, conjunctural class struggle introduces a quite abrupt and damaging qualification of his general thesis that the relation between the structural place and the position of the proletariat is unproblematic: that the 'long-term interests' of the working class ensure that it is 'the only class that is revolutionary to the end'. Like most of his fellow theorists of class structure, Poulantzas holds to a fundamentalist conception of the proletariat. Absolutely basic to this idea is the assumption that the proletariat has an objective, long-run, interest in socialism. The action of the class may deviate from the pursuit of this interest because of a variety of particular social and economic circumstances which influence the course of the concrete class struggle. But, given that its socialist interest is known to be the only 'reasonable' end that it can pursue, deviations from this goal must be misrepresentations of its interest and are explicable finally in terms of ignorance or error. This is brought out nicely in Poulantzas's interpretation of the rise of fascism, a conjuncture in which neither social democracy nor communism served the interest of the working class: the former was an 'ideological state apparatus' whose role was 'to mislead the masses and hold back the revolution', while the latter was itself misled by its 'incorrect strategy' based on the theory of social fascism.[51]

The demolition of this whole orthodox framework is the aim of the last version of Marxist class theory to be considered here. Its most forceful exponent is Hirst. The crux of his argument is that Marxism is forced to choose between some form of economism, which conceives of the political and ideological struggle as ultimately the expression or representation of class interests that are objectively given by the economic structure, and what he calls 'necessary non-correspondence', which means that there are no such objective interests, but only the interests that are constituted by specific political and ideological forces. Classes as such do not

[51] N. Poulantzas, *Fascism and Dictatorship* (London, 1974), pp. 147–65.

have interests and are not actors, and the basic misconception of economism is its assumption that the real actors in the class struggle, namely political organizations in a broad sense, must necessarily, in the long run, represent objective class interests. Economism is held to be deficient because the divergence of political representation and objective class interest is historically all too apparent. One solution of this problem is to accord the political with a 'relative autonomy', a device which is, in effect, identical with Poulantzas's notion of class position in the conjuncture. But this is merely a sophisticated, but none the less theoretically unstable, version of economism. 'Once any degree of autonomous action is accorded to political forces as a means of representation *vis-à-vis* classes of economic agents, then there is no necessary correspondence between the forces that appear in the political (and what they "represent") and economic classes.'[52] Given the idea of relative autonomy, there can be no guarantee that the political means of representation can be constrained in such a way that they do represent class interests, unless the relativeness of the autonomy is restricted by some kind of 'last instance' clause. But the latter means a reversion of economism: 'It asserts the primacy of the economy while affirming that politics and ideology cannot simply be reduced to its effects.'[53] Moreover, like economism in general, it can provide no satisfactory theory of the 'specificity of the political'. This has already been shown to be a major weakness of Poulantzas's theory of classes, in which the conjunctural class struggle finally emerges as a zone of particularity and contingency. At best, the systematization of the relative autonomy of the political results in a functionalist form of economism, typified by the concept of 'ideological state apparatuses'.[54]

Hirst and his colleagues realize that in rejecting the concept of objective class interest and in espousing the idea of necessary non-correspondence they adopt a position that 'shatters the classical conception of classes'.[55] If their argument is accepted—and it is a

[52] Hirst, 'Economic Classes and Politics', p. 130.
[53] Cutler *et al.*, *Marx's Capital and Capitalism Today*, pp. 235–6.
[54] Ibid. 200–2; Hirst, 'Economic Classes and Politics', pp. 131–2.
[55] Cutler *et al.*, *Marx's Capital and Capitalism Today*, p. 236. It also allows them to conclude, by a startling reference to empirical evidence, that 'The USA is an excellent example of a situation where the conditions of wage-labour and the levels of wages are determined, *inter alia*, by the conflict of workers' and employers' representatives but without the intervention of any significant socialist forces' (p. 242).

very cogent one—then many of the most intractable problems of
the Marxist theory of class action just disappear. But what of
Marxism remains? Their broadest statement of intent is that the

connections between social relations, institutions and practices must be
conceived of not in terms of any relations of determination, 'in the last
instance' or otherwise, but rather in terms of conditions of existence. This
means that while specific social relations and practices always presuppose
definite social conditions of existence they neither secure these conditions
through their own action nor do they determine the form in which they
will be secured. Thus, while a set of relations of production can be shown
to have definite legal, political and cultural conditions of existence these
conditions are in no way determined by the action of the economy.[56]

What this seems to imply then is replacing the quasi-Parsonian
functionalism of Althusser[57] with a form of Marxism that begins
where Weber left off.[58]

[56] Cutler *et al.*, *Marx's Capital and Capitalism Today*, p. 314.

[57] The similarity between Parsons's later system of normative functionalism and
the covert functionalism of Althusserian Marxism (Cutler *et al.*, *Marx's Capital
and Capitalism Today*, pp. 201–2), is, on the surface, fairly obvious. Even though
the latter cannot stand comparison with the former in terms of analytical
development, there is, nevertheless, a striking correspondence between Parsons's
concept of the 'cybernetic hierarchy' of action, in which values have the 'ultimately
determining' role, and Althusser's notion of a social totality, which is composed of
'relative autonomous' levels or instances, and which obtains its structural unity
through 'determination in the last instance' by the 'economy' of which of the levels
plays the 'dominant' role. Marxism has been transformed into a more clearly
functionalist form by Habermas (*Legitimation Crisis*), who makes free use of terms
such as 'functional necessities' and 'functional equivalents' and concentrates on
certain substantive problems which have long been of central interest to sociological functionalism and 'political systems' theory. Although his work is highly
tentative and schematic, its most novel feature is the discussion of 'legitimation'
and 'motivation' crises. What Habermas does not seem to appreciate, however, is
how closely his general approach to this problem resembles Parsons's theory of
'power deflation'.

[58] The rejection of the idea of ascribed or objectively given class interests in
favour of the idea of their constitution through historically specific modes of
political, ideological, and ultimately linguistic representations has now gone so far
that the proponents of this view risk excommunication on the ground that theirs is
a Marxism in which 'there are no such things as material interests but only
discursively constituted *ideas* about them', and in which 'society itself is constituted
by ideology and discourse. There remain no social relations or identities; there are
only fields of discursivity' (E. M. Wood, *The Retreat From Class* (London, 1986),
58, 61). One notable essay in this genre—G. Stedman Jones's interpretation of the
rise and fall of Chartism (in *Languages of Class* (Cambridge, 1983))—attributes
such decisive importance to the ideology of pre-capitalist political radicalism in
providing the nascent working class with its 'vocabulary of grievance' that it reads

IV

Contemporary Marxist theories of social class are in a poor state. There are no doubt other reasons why this is the case than those advanced above. Nevertheless, it might be useful to finish by considering the latter from a wider perspective. In doing so, it is necessary briefly to return to those fundamental themes which by now have been stated and restated in so many previous contexts that the reader may understandably be weary of hearing of them yet again and hope to find relief in the concluding chapter. It is, however, important to recognize that a major reason for so much attention having been devoted to the analysis of class structure and so little to that of class formation is the persistence within Marxism of a basically utilitarian action schema. One reason why the latter should have been so predominant is that it is fundamental to the economic theory of capitalist development, which is by far the most powerfully developed branch of the subject. Furthermore, in seeking to demonstrate that the proletariat has an objective, scientifically guaranteed interest in socialism, Marxist economic theory has provided the terms of reference for the analysis of social integration. It has set the 'norm' against which the rationality of proletarian action must be measured. This, together with the assumption that the proletariat possesses a power of reason commensurate with the task of realizing its fundamental interest, has meant that, from the outset, explanations of conflict and order have taken on a characteristically utilitarian form. The standard of rationality is the major reference point for understanding how capitalists and proletarians adapt their means to their respectively given, intra-systemic, ends, just as the higher-order rationality of reason is indispensable to explaining the end-shift of the proletariat. Finally, in the absence of a clear distinction between action that is simply irrational, and nonrational action oriented to the alternative standard of ultimate values, there is no other way of accounting for ostensible lapses from rationality and reason save by recourse to some version of the classical utilitarian notions of ignorance and error.

---

like nothing less than exemplary proof of Weber's thesis that ideas 'have, like switchmen, determined the tracks along which action has been pushed by the dynamic of interest'.

This theory of action has two basic defects. First, it precludes systematic analysis of the factors determining the extent to which the values and norms defining the legitimate ends and means of actors become internalized conditions of action. The whole problem of the institutionalization of values is inadmissible. Most crucially, this denies Marxism an adequate conception of the status order, the primary focus of the integration of the ends of class actors. The tendency to dismiss both hierarchical and egalitarian aspects of status as ideological reflections of the class structure is not only far too crude to grasp the complicated ways in which the legitimation of status relationships is both contingent upon, and constitutive of, class interests; it is also symptomatic of the second major defect. In so far as normative elements enter into Marxist explanations of action, they do so either in an implicit, *ad hoc* way, or, as is more usually the case, through their incorporation into the general category of ideology. This is to be expected. By according the standard of rationality such a central place in its explanatory system, and by collapsing the distinction between irrational and nonrational action, Marxism is constrained to lump together as ideologically determined all kinds of apparently irrational behaviour. The concept of 'ideological state apparatuses' is only the most egregious example of this. Ideology thus serves an analytical function analogous to that performed by the concepts of ignorance and error in utilitarian theorizing. Even though it locates the sources of irrationality in society rather than in the individual, the theory of ideology has been formulated at a highly abstract level which befits its chief purpose of providing global explanations of social order. Indeed, in the course of its promotion to account for the absence of proletarian revolution in the most advanced capitalist societies, its conceptual scope has widened to cover ever more disparate phenomena, including not only systems of beliefs and values, but most major social institutions and corporate groups, all of which are seen in some way to be performing ideological functions. At the same time, the precise manner in which, and therefore the effectiveness with which, ideological factors enter into the determination of social action has remained extremely problematic. For these reasons, ideology comes close to being a residual category, resort to which has the theoretically destabilizing effect of introducing into the basic, strongly positivistic, framework of Marxism a type of explanation that approaches the opposite pole of the idealistic scheme of action.

These inherent defects of the theory may help to explain why contemporary studies of class concentrate so heavily on the analysis of class structure and avoid the problem of class action. But this is putting the cart before the horse, because the identification of significant structural factors presupposes an explicit and well-founded theory of action. This is most strikingly evident in the way these studies deal, or rather fail to deal, with the composition of the working class. By reducing to the very minimum the elements that define the basic conditions of the proletarian class situation, it is then discovered that the working class still possesses the homogeneity and potential solidarity requisite to the attainment of its ultimate interest in socialism. But the question of how, under these conditions, the working class will act to realize its final goal, receives hardly any serious attention. To provide an adequate answer would require nothing less than the reconstitution of the classical Marxist theory of action. But far from attending to this task, contemporary class theorists appear to have no clear concept of action whatsoever. So now it is no longer just the case that explanations of the relationship between class structure and class struggle are bound to be unstable and contradictory: the relationship is completely indeterminate.

CONCLUSION

I

The principal aim of this study of Durkheimian and Marxist explanations of conflict and order has been to show that, while the two bodies of theory rest on fundamentally opposed ideas of social structure and social action, both have to draw on auxiliary hypotheses which are to a high degree complementary—the residual categories of the one theory proving to be those that are analytically central in the other. At the risk of making the basic line of argument appear more formal, categorical, and symmetrical than it really is, it may be summarized as follows.

1. Each body of theory has a dominant concept of structure which is the key to the understanding of society as a totality, and therefore to explanations of order and disorder. In the Durkheimian case, the notion of social or moral classification occupies this crucial role. In Marxism, the corresponding structural concept is naturally that of production relations. Broadly speaking, the one theory concentrates attention on the socially integrative structure of status, and the other on a socially divisive structure of class.

2. Each theory possesses a more or less well articulated action schema. In Durkheimian sociology, this is closely related to the dominant concept of structure. It takes the form of a radical repudiation of the utilitarian model of action, and places decisive emphasis on the systematic importance of normative elements in the structuring of social action. While less clear-cut, the Marxist action schema has, in contrast, strong utilitarian underpinnings. This is most evident in 'economic' explanations of system contradiction; but it is also discernible in 'sociological' explanations of class polarization.

3. While the major structural concepts of the two theories are antithetical, they are also complementary in the sense that the concept that has analytical priority in the one theory is, generally speaking, the residual concept of structure in the other. For

summary purposes, these residual concepts may be identified by the part played by 'utilitarian' factors in the Durkheimian model, and by 'moral' or 'traditional' elements in the Marxist one.

4. Each theory generates a distinctive problem of disorder, for the solution of which its dominant concept of structure and its basic action schema are inadequate. In Durkheimian sociology this problem centres on the explanation of anomic declassification. It is revealed in the unstable relationship between solidarity and anomie, the first entailing an alternative and unaccountable problem of schismatic disorder, and the second a hidden theory of fatalistic order. Given the Durkheimian notion of normative structure, the theory of anomic declassification is untenable, and schismatic disorder is inexplicable. Within Marxist theory, the chronic problem of disorder is the lack of schismatic disorder or revolutionary class polarization, and has its locus in what has been called the problem of the proletarian end-shift.

5. Neither theory can resolve its problem of disorder without an *ad hoc* resort to its residual concept of structure, which, in turn, necessarily destabilizes the basic action schema. In the Durkheimian case, this explanatory move is relatively crude and analytically inchoate. It principally involves the introduction of an extraneous, quasi-structural element, namely, sudden changes in 'the distribution of men and things' or in 'power and wealth'. The *deus ex machina* in any Durkheimian explanation of disorder is always that unruly and shapeless character, 'the economic life'. At the level of social action, there is occasional acknowledgement of the fact that ends are determined by resources as well as by normative constraints; but the stability of the basic action schema is preserved at the cost of denying systematic recognition of this fact. The action schema remains unregeneratively anti-positivist. Correspondingly, in the Durkheimian mode, there can be no definite conception, save in normative terms, of the structure, still less of the dynamics, of the 'profane', the 'utilitarian', or the 'economic' realm of activity, which is the primary origin of forces making for anomic deregulation.

In Marxism, the promotion of the residual category is ostensibly an expedient of a rather more sophisticated kind. But in fact it consists mainly of highly generalized explanations of the lack of revolutionary class polarization in terms of some form of global ideological domination. Except in the case of the primitive, and now not much favoured, 'indoctrination' thesis, which represents an extension of the underlying utilitarian concept of action, the resort to theories of systemic ideological effects introduces a high degree of instability into the Marxist action schema, swinging it between the sociological poles of positivism and idealism. Moreover, reliance on such a highly generalized category of ideology is the chief obstacle to a thoroughgoing analysis of the institutionalization of values and beliefs, which is a direct counterpart to the failure of Durkheimian sociology to provide a systematic account of economic life in its realistic as well as its normative aspects. To the extent that Marxist historians and sociologists do engage in detail with this issue, the results of their work generally only serve to emphasize the analytical gap between the concepts they fashion and those purveyed by theorists of ideological domination who seek some more abstract, uncomplicated, and unconditioned solution of the problem of disorder. Though nowhere near as amorphous as the Durkheimian notion of the socially disruptive nature of the economic life, the pervasive and structurally undifferentiated effect attributed to the power of ideology testifies all too clearly to the residual character of this category in Marxist macrosociology. It is essentially a means of avoiding all the paramount problems about the nature and variability of consensus that have been the major stumbling blocks within the Durkheimian tradition; and it has prevented Marxist theoreticians from arriving at a close and considered understanding of the operation of the status system of a society, which is indispensable to any adequate analysis of the formation of class interest.

6. Finally, there is an important point of convergence between the two bodies of theory which is most generally connected with the fact that both identify what may be broadly referred to as the dynamics of social stratification as the main subject-matter of the sociological analysis of order and conflict. While Durkheimian sociology is founded on the importance of the integrative function of a common value system, and more particularly of a social or status classification, the theory of anomie leads inexorably towards a conception of class structure, however inchoate this may be. Similarly, within Marxism, attempts to account for the lack of class polarization point to an equally imperative need to complement a purely class analysis with one that takes account of the ways in which interests are shaped by the status order, considered

not only as a system of legal rights but also as a mode of moral evaluation that enters continuously into the regulation of social conduct in practically every sphere. This argument can be advanced only tentatively since in both cases the tendencies referred to are no more than implicit. The fact that Marxism has made little headway in attending to the interrelations of class and status, mainly because of its reliance on untested theories of ideological domination, is just as evident as the fact that Durkheimian and normative functionalist sociology has avoided the same issues because its conceptualization of status stratification has not been matched by any comparably detailed treatment of the determinants and operation of the class system. Nevertheless, it is a major claim of the present work that from both viewpoints the study of the structure and dynamics of class and status emerges as the distinctive task of the sociology of order and disorder.[1]

7. This conclusion is strengthened by a convergence of a more specific kind: namely, that both bodies of theory seek the chief source of disorder in a structural incongruity or contradiction which can most appropriately be understood as a state in which the system of class relationships becomes incompatible with the system of status relationships. In the Durkheimian case, anomic disorder is clearly the outcome of insupportable strains placed on the social classification or status system by some sudden and widespread redistribution of resources, which, in the last analysis, is tantamount to a fundamental alteration in class structure. While this may not be the only interpretation that can be put on his idea of anomie, it is the only one that affords the basis for extracting from his work any coherent theory of disorder. The Marxist theory of disorder also rests basically on the kindred concept of contradiction. At one level of analysis, contradiction refers to system effects that are only hinted at in the vaguest terms in Durkheim's discussion of the anomic dysfunctionalities, or 'abnormalities', of the division of labour in societies whose normal form of solidarity is what he terms 'organic'. Yet in Marxism these system contradictions pose a threat to social order only in so far

---

[1] Which in turn many social theorists would regard as the distinctive aim of sociology as such. See, e.g., Cohen, *Modern Social Theory*, ch. 2, and J. C. Alexander, *Theoretical Logic in Sociology*, i. *Positivism, Presuppositions and Current Controversies*.

as they generate class conflict. The 'forces' of increasingly socialized production, which become incompatible with private appropriation, do not exert their influence save through human agency; and this incompatibility therefore must be understood as expressing itself in the form of conflicts arising from the actualization of latent class powers and interests which lead eventually to a widespread and radical challenging of the institutional structure that legitimates control over resources and the allocation of rewards. Considered in its widest ramifications, this structure is more or less equivalent to Durkheim's idea of 'the social classification of men and things'; that is, a status system whose legal and customary definitions of entitlement and worth serve to regulate a range of social interaction which encompasses, but extends beyond, production relations in the narrow economic sense. This equivalence is more evident with the tendency of modern Marxism to treat the reproduction of relations of production as a more general social process, involving political and, especially, ideological constraints on class formation.

II

It is hoped that the austerity of the theses just stated is compensated for by the detail of the particular arguments that have led up to them. But where these claims themselves lead, the kind of sociological enquiry they imply, are questions that require some further comment. Most especially, the conclusion that Durkheimian and Marxist theories of disorder rest on assumptions that are in important respects complementary might be taken to suggest that some synthesis of the two theories is called for, if not overdue. Before attending to this issue, however, it is necessary to emphasize the limited scope of the present work, since this is indispensable to a proper evaluation of the results arrived at so far.

To begin with it has been confined to an examination of how the problem of disorder arises and is resolved within the two bodies of social theory that are generally regarded as having had the greatest influence on the study of social conflict and social integration. Inevitably, at various points, reference has been made to the work of other writers who belong directly to neither camp. But the fact remains that the discussion has been limited to a critical appraisal of a fairly narrow range of topics within Durkheimian and Marxist social theory; and as such it has not attempted to present a balanced exposition of either body of thought. Moreover, while it can be claimed that the topics selected do have a central bearing on the study of order and conflict, it is at the same time clear that they offer less than a comprehensive analysis of the subject. One important reason for this is that neither theory is able to deal adequately with those empirically important instances of conflict between groups divided from one another by such ascriptive solidarities as ethnicity, territoriality, and language.[2]

But the more fundamental qualification that must be made about the claims of the present work is that it has dealt with the problem of disorder from the viewpoint of social rather than system integration. Whereas social integration refers to the more or less orderly or conflicting relationships between the actors of a society, system integration refers to the more or less functional or contradictory relationships between its institutional subsystems.[3] Although this distinction is somewhat artificial, it has empirical as well as analytical significance. For at any particular point of time, and indeed over long periods of time, a society may be riven by acute social conflicts even though its basic institutional system remains intact and is stably reproduced in the course of the resolution of such conflicts: traditional Chinese society exhibits just this pattern. Conversely, system dysfunctions, such as economic crises, are by no means always accompanied by widespread socially destabilizing conflict, as is shown by the experience of the more mature capitalist democracies during the inter-war depression.

If this is a valid distinction, it means that the problem of social integration, whose limits have been treated above as solidarity and schism, and more specifically as ritualized status and class war, cannot be fully understand without taking account of the

---

[2] For an elaboration of this point as it relates to Marxist theory, see Parkin, *Marxism and Class Theory*, ch. 3, and D. Lockwood, 'Race, Conflict and Plural Society', in S. Zubaida, *Race and Racialism* (London, 1970).

[3] See Appendix; also Parkin, 'System Contradiction and Political Transformation'; and esp. N. Mouzelis, 'System and Social Integration: Some Reflections on a Fundamental Distinction', *British Journal of Sociology*, 25 (1974), and his *Back to Sociological Theory: Bridging the Micro-Macro Gap* (London, 1991).

ways in which changes in both the normative and realistic conditions of action are usually the unintended consequences, or
system effects, of the interrelations of a society's economic,
political, and religious subsystems. The degree to which status
stratification or class division is the predominant form of structured social inequality is always of decisive importance in mediating the consequences for social order of systemic dysfunctions or
contradictions. Nevertheless, in concentrating on the problem of
social integration, the foregoing discussion has treated the latter
as 'given' or exogenous. Certain broad classes of system effects,
such as the disruptiveness of rapid economic change or the
availability of exploitable values and beliefs, have been introduced
only from the point of view of how they are likely to impinge
upon the structure of status and class relationships. In the case of
Durkheimian theory proper this approach poses no particular
difficulty, since his writings portray the relationship between
system and social integration in very general even rudimentary
terms.[4] Marxism, on the other hand, lays claim to be the only
unified social science in which these two fundamental aspects of
social order and disorder are coherently related in a general
theory of society. This, however, is much more of a promise than
a reality, since, as the previous extended discussion of the subject
has shown, the links that can be established between the workings
of the economic (not to mention the ideological) system and class
formation turn out to be meagre and imprecise.[5] This is, however,
a criticism that requires an important qualification, which is that,
whatever its failings, Marxist theory remains unique in seeking to

---

[4] This charge cannot be levelled against Parsons's later sociology, which is like
a Russian doll, a society's functional subsystems revealing their own subsystems in
turn, all of which are interrelated through highly complex and sometimes factitious
'boundary exchanges'. However, this scheme has served mainly as a conceptual
map, and has been much less influential than the model of society presented in the
chief work of his middle period, *The Social System*.

[5] The most obvious example of this is that the distinction between productive
and unproductive labour—indispensable to orthodox interpretations of capitalist
system dynamics—is largely irrelevant to explanations of working-class action.
The fact that there exist intriguing accounts of the relationship between structural
contradiction and social conflict in particular capitalist societies—such as T. Nairn's
The Breakup of Britain (London, 1981)—does not gainsay the general argument,
since the most compelling studies of this kind attest less to the power of any
abstractly formulated law of capitalist development than to the author's grasp of
unique historical developments.

establish a coherent relationship between system and social integration. In this respect at least, its model of society still presents a formidable challenge to 'bourgeois' social science.[6]

III

With these qualifications in mind, it is possible to return to the main line of argument that prompted them: namely, that, since Durkheimian and Marxist explanations of order and disorder rest on assumptions about structure and action that are in important respects complementary, there is a need for and the possibility of some kind of sociological synthesis which builds upon their respective strengths and remedies their respective deficiences. While several writers have attempted this task, there must be doubts about the profitability of such ventures. First of all, it is arguable that Durkheimian and Marxist conceptions of society and human nature are so divergent as to be irreconcilable, except in the most abstract and barren terms; and that more might be gained from pursuing the opposite course of explicating and comparing the competing claims of the two bodies of theory in those instances where they appear to offer explanations of the same broad issues: for example, whether the discontents of industrial civilization are more adequately understood in terms of alienation or anomie.[7] Certainly, attempts at synthesis have not been very impressive, either in redefining the macro-social problems inherited from these two traditions of social theory, or in

[6] By contrast with Marxist economic and social theory, the division between neo-classical economics and the other social sciences is even more pronounced. The utilitarian action assumptions of modern economic theory became much more explicit and uncompromising as a result of the marginalist revolution, which bought great precision by abstracting the economy from its social and political context. This break with classical political economy was decisive for the subsequent definition of the form and scope of sociological thought, especially through the writings of Max Weber. See, above all, S. Clarke, *Marx, Marginalism and Modern Sociology* (London, 1982). The dissociation of economics from the other social sciences has also been facilitated by the fact that statistical macro-economic data on which theories of system equilibrium can gain some purchase are incomparably more readily available than macro-sociological data that have a bearing on societal order and consensus.

[7] For the former strategy, see e.g. P. van den Berghe, 'Dialectic and Functionalism', *American Sociological Review*, 28 (1963), and P. Sztompka, *System and Function* (New York, 1974); for the latter, Lukes, *Essays in Social Theory*, ch. 4, 'Alienation and Anomie'.

providing more specific kinds of hypothesis which could compete, as foci of research, with those advanced by practitioners of Durkheimian and Marxist sociology. Much the same can be said of the alternative objective of seeking not to supersede, but rather perpetuate and accentuate conceptual oppositions that are held to represent the basic contributions of Marxist *contra* Durkheimian theory. The dichotomous terminology of this debate has become enshrined in textbook distinctions such as 'values' versus 'power', 'consensus' versus 'conflict' models of society, and, at base, 'socialized' versus 'rational' man. But all of this has resulted in little more than the ritualized polemics of a metasociological stalemate.[8] Thus the first reason for resisting the conclusion that the insights of Durkheimian and Marxist sociology can be advantageously either neutrally amalgamated or systematically contrasted is that neither programme has proved a particularly rich source of substantive sociological problems which are as intriguing or compelling as those arising from the two original theoretical traditions.

The second reason for eschewing both these solutions is that for the purposes of social research it is unnecessary to seek either a synthesis or an opposition of the two bodies of theory because, in practice, their conceptual divergence becomes progressively less apparent the more concrete the problem either theory is called upon to explain. Whether their provenance be Durkheimian or Marxist, ideas amenable to sociological investigation can be formulated convincingly only by means of assumptions about the structuring of social action that are virutally indistinguishable. The particular as well as the general grounds for making this claim have been adduced in many contexts throughout the present work, and further evidence in support of it will be provided below. In this respect at least, then, the distinction between Durkheimian and Marxist sociology is much less marked.

Nevertheless, the two theories do entail quite distinct ways of thinking about the structure of social systems, and attempts to synthesize or contrast these conceptions are not so inconsiderable that they can be dismissed without further comment. The former aim is of particular interest: partly because it represents serious

---

[8] See Cohen, *Modern Social Theory*, esp. chs. 2 and 9; for a more recent and elaborate statement, Alexander, *Theoretical Logic in Sociology*, i, ch. 2.

efforts to overcome the limitations of the two major theoretical traditions which the present work has attested to; and partly because it seeks to provide sociology with the kind of unifying conceptual scheme for which it has always hungered—albeit more out of a search for a symbolic centre than from any exigent need to bring together the manifold and substantial accomplishments through which the subject has made its mark.

IV

At first sight, the attempt to synthesize the basic structural concepts of Durkheimian and Marxist sociology would seem to be a very different afffair from that which seeks to exploit and accentuate their opposition. In the former, there is the search for a sociological lexicon that can unite the competing vocabularies of 'power' and 'values'. In the latter, the very possibility of such a *lingua franca* is resolutely denied by those who seek to oppose a 'conflict' to a 'consensus' model of society. Yet, despite this divergence of aim, both endeavours had a common starting point in Parsons's attempt to integrate into a single conceptual scheme the two irreducible elements of the situation of action which he called the 'normative' and the 'realistic'. The means of achieving this was his concept of 'voluntarism', which quite properly occupies the middle ground between the equally untenable extremes of sociological idealism and positivism.[9] However, his attempt to construct a theory of social systems that took account of actors' creative adaptation to realistic as well as normative conditions was far from successful. Indeed, the emergence of a conflict, in contradistinction to a consensus, model of society was a direct reaction to the fact that the voluntaristic conception of action which Parsons had argued for so powerfully in *The Structure of Social Action* had been lost sight of by the time he came to write *The Social System*, the key work of normative functionalism. It

[9] It will be remembered that the main reference points are: the 'idealistic' schema, in which action is seen as the effortless, unconditional actualization of the actor's beliefs or values, or of some world view of which he is the bearer; the 'radical positivistic' position, in which action is explained by hereditary or environmental conditions; and the 'utilitarian' version of positivism in which the only significant standard governing action is scientific rationality in the choice of means to realize ends.

was dissatisfaction with this aspect of his social-system theorizing which also provided the occasion for the formulation of those conceptual schemes that aimed to correct his over-emphasis on the significance of normative constraints by giving due recognition to kinds of materialistic factors predominant in, but not peculiar to, Marxist theory.

What proved to be particularly controversial, then, was not Parsons's identification of the elements of social action—and the types of social theory that could be derived from them—but rather his ideas about the structuring of systems of social action. His arguments in favour of the voluntaristic theory of action were compelling and unexceptionable. Few were disposed to argue with its major practical premiss that 'the structure of interests in a group is a function both of the realistic situations in which people act and of the "definitions" of those situations which are institutionalized in the society'. For the most part, even those who favoured a return to some kind of rational-choice theorizing acknowledged the force of Parsons's critique of the utilitarian action schema. Nevertheless, it was Parsons's tendency to demote the importance of instrumental action, and his focus on the normative structure of social systems, which gave rise to the sharpest criticism. Some concentrated their fire on his neglect of those aspects of the structuring of social action that he had termed the realistic, most particularly, those that took the form of power relationships. This was complemented by criticisms of the way in which Parsons's revision of his original 'voluntaristic' action schema had come to place much greater emphasis on the stabilization of social interaction through the internalization of values and norms, such that conformity with them became an in-built moral need. They were most nicely summed up in Dennis Wrong's phrase 'the oversocialized concept of man'.

On the whole, however, these criticisms did not entail a complete rejection of Parsons's theory of social systems. Their purpose was rather to seek to reconstitute it by giving equal weight to the realistic elements to be found in his original, voluntaristic, theory of action. As Rex put it:

What we want is a theory which finds a place for both normatively oriented action and action which can be understood as governed by something like scientific knowledge of the relation between means and ends. We also need to recognize that some of the ends which actors in our system pursue may be random ends from the point of view of the system or actually in conflict with it. If there is an actual conflict of ends, the behaviour of actors towards one another may not be determined by shared norms but by the success which each has in compelling the other to act in accordance with his interests. Power then becomes a crucial variable in the study of social systems.[10]

Giddens offered a similar prescription: 'We must assert that power extends as deeply into the roots of social life as do values and norms: if all social relationships involve normative elements, so also do all social relationships contain power differentials. A general theory of social systems must begin from the interdependency of norms and power.'[11]

Such programmatic statements can give little cause for quarrel. But how is it possible to conceptualize the relationship between norms and power? One familiar method is to treat norms as a form of power; in particular, to treat the award and withdrawal of status as normative power. Ever since Hobbes spoke of 'Riches, honour, command and other forms of power', some conception of status has been part of this sociological trinity, as in Weber's 'class, status and party' (forms of 'the distribution of power in a community') or Etzioni's typology of utilitarian, normative, and coercive organizations.[12] Here then is a well-tried conceptual strait-jacket in which the unruly notion of power has been long and deservedly restrained.[13]

Nevertheless, reducing status to normative power poses intractable difficulties when it comes to accounting for social integration. These hinge on the distinction it is necessary to make between status as a personal resource and status as a social institution or

---

[10] J. Rex, *Key Problems in Sociological Theory* (London, 1961), 112.

[11] Giddens, '"Power" in Recent Writings of Talcott Parsons', p. 268.

[12] A. Etzioni, *Complex Organizations* (New York, 1961). See also W. G. Runciman, 'Class, Status and Power?', in J. A. Jackson (ed.), *Social Stratification* (Cambridge, 1968), and the rejoinder to this article by G. K. Ingham, 'Social Stratification: Individual Attributes and Social Relationships', *Sociology*, 4 (1970).

[13] Otherwise it tends to become a kind of social structural *Doppelgänger*—as in Steven Lukes's 'third' dimension of power, in which A may be said to exercise power over B if the unintended consequences of A's actions damage B's objective interests even though B may be unaware that he has such interests. See his *Power: A Radical View* (London, 1974).

system of social relations, since the existence of the latter is a precondition of the effective use of the former. It is, then, one thing to say that people may use their personal status or prestige as a means of attaining their ends; it is quite a different matter to say that the system itself is simply a form of power, a device created and overseen by one group to attain its ends against the opposition of another group. Even ideological indoctrination theorists have not gone that far. Yet the reduction of status to normative power leads inexorably to this conclusion. The same point can be made from a slightly different angle. If the ability to award and withdraw status or prestige is understood as a form of power, then the problem of the relationship between norms and power is neatly resolved; but only at the cost of resurrecting the problem of social order. If people seek status because it is a kind of power, a means of gaining a variety of other ends, then it belongs to the category of what Parsons calls intermediate ends or generalized means. But the struggle to acquire such inherently scarce and versatile resources is what creates the problem of order in the first place. Therefore, to treat status simply as a means by which actors seek to attain their idiosyncratic ends directs attention to its socially deregulating effects and away from the integrative function of the status system as a whole, which is that of defining the ends and means appropriate to different kinds of actors according to some ultimate standard of value. But if status is reduced to normative power, then this function must also belong to the same category; in other words, the institutionalization of status has to be understood as yet another kind of power; a complex but nevertheless deliberately created means of securing some particular end.

A reversion to this sort of unmistakably utilitarian action schema was not the manifest intention of those who argued that Parsons's model of society lacked an adequate concept of power and that his solution of the Hobbesian problem of order gave undue emphasis to normative factors. However, the programmatic claims noted above—commonly advanced by writers of a left-Weberian persuasion—hardly amounted to an alternative theory of social integration and conflict. Both conceptually and in empirical application, the normative functionalism of Parsons and his associates was much more detailed and comprehensive than anything in the way of a sociology that his critics could counterpose to it.[14] Until it could be shown in which precise respects the former was deficient, and how a comparably extensive analysis of power could either complement or compete with it, the promise of a counter-theory was simply placed on the agenda.

V

Marxism was the main alternative, but its claim to be a general theory of society was not impressive. Its assumptions about social action seemed in turn simplistic and obscure. Most importantly, its conception of social power had succumbed to Weber's argument that the separation of the worker from the means of production is just a special case of a more general form of bureaucratic domination. However, Weber was not a sociological systematizer; at any rate not of the Parsonian ilk. His methodological individualism precluded thinking about societies as systems in that way.

But this was exactly the challenge that faced Parsons's sociological critics: his social system theorizing had raised the analytical stakes so high that they had no option but to formulate conceptual schemes of equal generality. He had, after all, attempted nothing less than a solution of the problem of order in society. Therefore, those who thought that his theory paid insufficient attention to the role of power in social life, but was sufficiently important to take issue with on its own terms, were forced to formulate equally abstract conceptual schemes. Some thought that Parsons's emphasis on normative integration should be balanced by giving due weight to power; others that this bias was too great to be corrected by anything less than a counter-theory.

Prominent among the latter were Dahrendorf and Rex, who opposed a conflict or coercion model of society to the Parsonian consensus or integration model.[15] Although the conflict model was considered to be an alternative framework for the analysis of conflict and order (according to Dahrendorf, it could exist side by

---

[14] Quite apart from Parsons's work, there was nothing comparable to that of his school, such as Williams, *American Society*, or M. J. Levy, *The Family Revolution in Modern China* (Cambridge, Mass., 1949), to take only two examples of the genre.

[15] R. Dahrendorf, *Class and Class Conflict in Industrial Society* (Stanford, Calif., 1959); Rex, *Key Problems in Sociological Theory*.

side with its rival, each one being useful for different purposes), this proved to be a rather drastic, baby-out-with-the-bathwater, solution. It replaced the normative functionalist scheme with an equally one-sided one, in which the problem of order, or conflict, was reduced essentially to the balance of power between conflicting groups or classes. Either by conceptual fiat, or in practice, this approach avoided the crucial question of how the interdependency of norms and power enters into explanations of order and disorder. Just as normative functionalism made genuflections to the importance of power and conflict, so too the coercion or conflict theorists paid lip-service to the importance of values and consensus. But in both cases, these qualifications were of minor significance in the kinds of explanations put forward.

In the case of conflict theory, the result was a more or less explicit adoption of a utilitarian concept of action for the purpose of explaining social conflict, which in turn was understood as structured by unequal power relations. It would seem that conceptual schemes that are tailor-made to account for social conflict have been characterized by a marked tendency to lay emphasis on instrumental, as opposed to norm-governed, action, and on the coercive, as opposed to the consensual, nature of social relationships, and on explanations of conflict (and to a large extent social order) in terms of the balance of power between groups constituted by these relationships. Since conflict theory was seen as a necessary corrective to the model of society provided by normative functionalism, and designed to explain conflict rather than order, the result was that normative elements played no real part in explanations of the generation of interests or in the conflict to which they gave rise. As Rex was well aware, this necessarily meant the adoption of a fairly thoroughgoing utilitarian action schema in which common values have to be explained variously as the product of successful ruling-class indoctrination, as a means necessary to continue ideological struggles, as negotiated outcomes of class compromise or truce in situations where there is a power balance between conflict groups, or finally as a component of class solidarity.[16] Such a conflict model of society is justified by

---

[16] On the first point, a more or less unqualified indoctrination thesis runs throughout Rex's account, ibid. 103–35. On the second, for example: 'Even where conflict is total, there are nearly always common traditions to which appeal can be

arguing that the normative functionalist model of '"complete integration" or "institutionalization"' is inadequate for the analysis of 'modern industrial societies and plural societies brought into being by culture contacts'. At the same time, it is recognized that 'as a specialized study of one analytically separate element of social systems it has real value'.[17] But if this is so, and if 'What we need is a theory which finds a place for both normatively oriented action and action which can be understood as governed by something like scientific knowledge of the relation between means and ends', why then is there a need for a special conflict model of society?

The same sort of problem arises in Dahrendorf's 'coercion' model, which is again presented as a theory with especial relevance to the understanding of conflict in industrial society. Nevertheless, while not claiming to be a general theory of social conflict, the 'coercion' model of society is formulated in sufficiently abstract terms for Dahrendorf to argue that the prospect of its combination with an 'integration' model of society is highly remote.[18] At first sight, the key term, 'coercion', might be taken to imply that the problem of how values and power are interrelated in the determination of social action and class interests is resolved by an exclusive concentration on power. But in fact the conceptual linchpin of the coercion model is not power, but authority; and authority is defined conventionally as legitimate power,[19] with the added twist that authority is always an inherently coercive relationship, involving a latent zero-sum power antagonism between superordinates and subordinates, which is in turn the basis of the

---

made . . . but the sole reason for the survival of the common tradition may be that it is necessary for the conduct of the ideological battle' (p. 114). And on the third: 'We should also allow for the fact that certain acts might be related to group ends not as the scientifically appropriate means but as appropriate in terms of what we called "ritual rules" of the group' and 'that these actions [contribute] to group solidarity' (p. 113).

[17] Ibid. 114.

[18] Dahrendorf, *Class and Class Conflict*, pp. 165, 169, 164.

[19] 'The important difference between power and authority consists in the fact that whereas power is essentially tied to the personality of individuals, authority is always associated with social positions or roles . . . It is another way of putting this difference if we say—as does Max Weber—that while power is merely a factual relation, authority is a legitimate relation of domination and subjection. In this sense, authority can be described as legitimate power.' (p. 166).

formation of conflict groups. Dahrendorf argues that the coercive face of authority requires emphasis because it is absent in the normative functionalist concept of power which Parsons identifies with the the mobilization of resources for the 'attainment of goals for which a general "public" commitment has been made, or may be made'.[20] Nevertheless, the costs of trying to have one theory for the explanation of social order and another for the explanation of social conflict are considerable. In Dahrendorf's scheme, the principal drawback is that the whole complex problem of legiti-mation (entailed by his definition of authority) plays no systematic part in the explanation of how conflict groups are formed within structures of authority.[21] But such conflict and the interests entering into it are inevitably a function of the perceived legiti-macy of the exercise of authority, that is, its conformity with recognized norms, and, in the last analysis, of the extent of consensus on values from which specific acts and structures of authority seek their validation.

As a result, the exclusive concentration on the coercive nature of authority relationships precludes systematic study of the inter-dependence of values and power in the formation of group interests. Dahrendorf's solution of this problem is to sidestep it by ascribing 'latent' and mutually conflicting interests to the actors who occupy superordinate and subordinate roles in all systems of authority. This not only entails a reversion to the givenness of ends, which is a chief characteristic of utilitarian theorizing, but reintroduces the cognate Marxist idea of objective interest, which is one of the most questionable assumptions of the very theory that Dahrendorf aims to supersede.[22]

---

[20] T. Parsons, *Structure and Process in Modern Societies* (New York, 1960), 221.

[21] That is, as set out in Dahrendorf, *Class and Class Conflict*, pp. 157–205. The only reference to what might be thought to be value elements is in connection with the conditions under which the 'latent' interests of conflict groups become 'manifest'. 'Either there must be a person or circle of persons who take on themselves the tasks of articulation and codification [of values], or, alternatively, an "ideology", a system of ideas, must be available which in a given case is capable of serving as a program or charter of groups.' But 'Ideologies do not create conflict groups or cause conflict groups to emerge. Yet they are indispensable as obstetri-cians of conflict groups, and in this sense as an intervening variable' (pp. 185–6). The fact that normative elements do appear to have considerable explanatory significance in his subsequent discussion of particular forms of conflict merely signifies their residual nature within the general explanatory scheme.

[22] 'The occupants of positions of domination and the occupants of positions of

Thus, in general, conflict models of society represent an over-reaction to normative functionalism, based very largely on a Weberian generalization of Marxism, but lacking the latter's most distinctive feature: namely, the connection it seeks to establish between system contradictions on the one hand, and, on the other, the social conflicts centering on the emergence of new *de facto* power relations within existing structures of institutionalized authority.[23]

VI

The difficulties encountered in attempts to counterpose a conflict or coercion model of society to that of normative functionalism are also recognizable in those alternative schemes that aim to integrate the two approaches by introducing the idea of a dual structure: normative and non-normative.[24] While commendable in its general purpose, the weakness of this strategy of synthesis is that it operates with such a highly abstract, and essentially residual, notion of non-normative factors that their relationship

---

subjection hold, by virtue of these positions, certain interests which are contrary in substance and direction'; again, 'the substance of socially structured "objective" interests can be described only in highly formal terms; they are interests in the maintenance or modification of a *status quo*'; and 'The individual who assumes a position in an association finds these role interests with his position'. Dahrendorf, *Class and Class Conflict*, pp. 174–8.

[23] See Appendix, 'Social Integration and System Integration', esp. n. 7.

[24] A basis for which can be found in Parsons and Shils, *Towards a General Theory of Action*, pt. 2. 'Values, Motives and Systems of Action'. A scheme similar to theirs is presented by A. Giddens, *Studies in Social and Political Theory* (London, 1977), esp. pp. 117–18. His idea of 'structuration' gives greater prominence to the creative role of social actors, reminding us that individuals are not only the products but also the producers of society. This emphasis is embodied in his definition of structure as the outcome of 'generative rules and resources that are both applied in and constituted out of action'. But his key concepts of resources and rules are very similar to the terms used by Parsons and Shils. For Giddens, resources are 'possessions—material or otherwise—actors are able to bring to bear to facilitate the achievement of their purposes in the course of social interaction: that therefore serve as a medium for the use of power'. This corresponds closely to Parsons's and Shils's concept of 'facilities'. Under the heading of 'rules', Giddens distinguishes the semantic from the moral ('any sort of rule generating evaluation of acts as "right" or "wrong"'). But Parsons's and Shils's classification remains the more exhaustive since it includes actors' orientations towards not only cognitive and evaluative, but expressive, or appreciative, standards.

with the normative or institutional order remains obscure and
structurally unanchored. In this respect, they resemble the categories of the profane or utilitarian sphere in Durkheim's schema.
Two examples of this problem will serve to indicate its nature.

Chalmers Johnson finds the main precondition of revolutions to
be what he calls a lack of 'synchronization of the value structure
and the environment'.[25] Although his analysis maintains a fairly
consistent distinction between values, which belong to what normative functionalists would call the cultural system, and norms,
which are a structural property of social systems, the meaning of
the concept of 'environment' is vague and fluctuating. The most
explicit account of it is as follows:

A system of action has for its setting a complex social, economic and
political environment (i.e., an economic geography and the presence of
other, often hostile, social systems). The values of the system are, so to
speak, addressed to this 'environment' and they can either facilitate or
retard attempts to exploit or adapt to it . . . the influence of the
environment—the 'substratum' of social action, or the tangible facts of
life which the value structure explains and makes intelligible—must be
considered on a par with that of the value system in any analysis of the
determinants of a particular social system.[26]

At another point, the environment is equated broadly with the
'division of labour', and, in the list of the internal and external
sources of change in the 'pattern of adaptation to the environment', technological innovations are the ones most frequently
mentioned.[27] What Johnson appears to have in mind in using the
concept of environment are all the various ways in which scarce
resources are deployed to meet a whole range of functional
exigencies with which any society is faced. It seems to refer to
societal adaptation in a very general sense and not to any definite
set of social relationships. What is achieved by its use, therefore,
is merely the transposition to the level of social systems of the
equally general idea of means and conditions as properties of the
situation of action. Johnson does not, as he claims, provide a
'model of the social system that synthesizes the coercion theory
and the value theory of social integration',[28] because his concept
of the environment, which he contrasts with that of 'value struc-

---

[25] Chalmers Johnson, *Revolutionary Change*, p. 56.
[26] Ibid. 35.   [27] Ibid. 38, 69.   [28] Ibid. 39.

ture' or 'value system', refers basically to social functions and not to any kind of structure that is at all comparable to institutions, that is a set of norms defining role obligations and hence social relationships. Because norms define what actors expect, and have a right to expect, of one another at the concrete level of social interaction, they may be said to be the structural expression of the values and beliefs. But in what kinds of structures does functional adaptation to the environment manifest itself? Since Johnson offers no clear answer to this question, his thesis that 'social disequilibration' is due to a lack of 'value-environmental synchronization' remains a highly abstract formula which yields no concept of the structure of social systems as detailed as that of the normative functionalist model which his own aims to incorporate and supersede.

A scheme very similar to Johnson's is constructed by Béteille, who distinguishes between 'existential and normative' systems, whose interrelationship is considered crucial for the understanding of order and conflict. 'When the two are broadly consistent with each other, I would characterize the society as harmonic; and when they are sharply at variance, I would describe it as disharmonic.'[29] Like Johnson, Béteille wishes to identify a non-normative aspect of social systems in contrast with the normative order and his conception of the latter is more or less the same as that presented by normative functionalists. Regularities in behaviour, he writes,

> can be studied in themselves, but they become more easily intelligible when we view them in relation to certain rules of behaviour which exist, in a sense, independently of the regularities. The rules themselves do not fully account for every item of behaviour in a particular sphere, for there are many deviations from them. On the other hand, the behaviour as such would appear mechanical and devoid of meaning unless it were related to the appropriate rules. These rules or norms have in their turn to be viewed in relation to the broader values of the society as a whole.[30]

It is this normative order then that stands in a more or less disharmonic relation to what he refers to variously as 'conditions of existence', 'existential order', and the 'existential system'. More

---

[29] A. Béteille, *Harmonic and Disharmonic Social Systems* (Sydney 1971), 11.
[30] Ibid. 12.

particularly he wishes to draw attention to 'inequalities in the conditions of existence', and goes on to say that

the most conspicuous among them, in an agrarian society, are inequalities in the ownership, control and use of land. The grading of occupations and the distribution of income are also important aspects of the objective structure of inequality. Together with these we must consider the distribution of power and authority which derive from established institutional structures.[31]

This is not a little confusing. Authority deriving from established institutional structures might be thought to belong at least as much to the normative as to the existential order; the same might apply to the grading of occupations, in so far as this is one manifestation of status stratification. On the other hand, the distribution of income is as it stands merely a statistical term, a non-relational aspect of inequality unlike that of the ownership and control and use of land, although this again conflates the normative and factual relations of production. It is difficult to see how from a collation of such disparities there can be extracted a coherent concept of non-normative structure, which the idea of harmonic and disharmonic social systems requires.

The main conclusion that emerges from this brief survey of the two main types of post-Parsonian theorizing is that they exhibit a by now familiar opposition. In conflict theory there is a fairly clear conceptualization of power relationships, but the treatment of normative factors tends to regress towards a utilitarian mode of theorizing. By contrast, in attempts at synthesis the concept of normative structure is well articulated, but its relationship to the non-normative remains obscure, due to the vague and fluctuating definition of the latter.

VII

Whatever their shortcomings, these attempts at synthesis and contestation do raise important general issues that have a close bearing on one of the major themes of the present work—which is that the congruity between class and status relationships emerges as a central point of reference for the analysis of order

---

[31] A. Béteille, *Harmonic and Disharmonic Social Systems*, p. 13.

and conflict in both Durkheimian and Marxist sociology. In particular, the most important implication of the idea of the incongruity between power and status relationships is that the material and moral resources which are at any one time embodied in, or appropriated by, structures of institutionalized authority never exhaust the full range of potentially exploitable resources. Of wide sociological currency, the notion of exploitablity finds various formulations. For Johnson, it refers to the cultural and technological environment of a society or one of its subsystems. As he puts it: 'Endogenous sources of value change consist primarily of internal "innovations" which affect the value structure much as technological innovations affect adaptation to the environment.'[32] Poggi makes much the same point when he writes that

the engine of the historical process (in so far as it lends itself to sociological analysis) is the pressure exercised by groups upon the existent constraints on modes of human feeling and experience, a pressure mostly exercised in the name of suppressed interests, heretical values, unmobilized resources, unsanctioned visions, previously untested devices.[33]

In the context of his analysis of historical bureaucratic societies, Eisenstadt provides a useful term for describing these diverse elements when he refers to 'free-floating' resources, that is, 'manpower, economic resources, political support, and cultural identifications—not embedded within or committed beforehand to any primary ascriptive–particularistic groups'; resources that constitute a 'reservoir of generalized power in the society, not embedded in such groups, that could be used by different groups for varying goals'.[34] These free-floating resources provide means of creating new social practices, of actualizing social relationships already latent in existing structures of authority and status. The idea of the exploitability of free-floating resources is as basic to Marx's view of social change and conflict generated by new production relations taking shape within the prevailing property relations as it is to Durkheim's theory of anomic declassification in which changes in the 'distribution of men and things' deregulate the status order, which then accommodates these emergent power

---

[32] Johnson, *Revolutionary Change*, p. 65.
[33] G. Poggi, *Calvinism and the Capitalist Spirit* (London, 1983), 37.
[34] S. N. Eisenstadt, *The Political Systems of Empires* (Glencoe, Ill., 1963), 27.

relations through a process of reclassification. Moreover, to think of values and power as resources or potentialities in the environment of a social system—resources that are always only partially actualized in the social relationships defining its structure and boundaries—implies least of all the opposition of ideal to material factors. For example, if power is understood in its most narrow and concretely materialistic sense as control over means of coercion, it is not difficult to understand how military power relations may undergo dramatic and sudden change as a result of technological innovation. 'With the invention of a new instrument of warfare, firearms,' writes Marx, 'the whole internal organization of the army necessarily changed; the relationships within which individuals can constitute an army and act as an army were transformed and the relations of different armies to one another also changed.'[35] But it is not the case that new technologies bring about organizational changes in an institutional vacuum or have nothing to do with morale. The military ascendency of the Swiss pikeman also had something to do with kinship and community solidarities, not to mention deviant, democratic, attitudes towards the correct rules of feudal combat. Moral as well as material resources determine how armies, like any other corporate groups, are constituted and confront one another.

The ways in which, and the extent to which, free-floating resources are generated and appropriated in different types of society is a problem of system rather than social integration, and one that is naturally highly complex.[36] What can be said, however, is that for the most part, free-floating resources are not random in occurrence; indeed they are chiefly the consequences of system contradictions, which produce not only patterns of deviant motivation, deriving from a sense of relative deprivation or social injustice, but also the conditions—especially those favourable to innovations in beliefs—under which such latent discontent can be

[35] Marx, *Selected Works*, i. 82.

[36] Three recent works that seem likely to set the agenda for this subject are M. Mann, *The Sources of Social Power*, i (Cambridge, 1986), W. G. Runciman, *A Treatise on Social Theory*, ii (Cambridge, 1989), and N. Mouzelis, *On the Construction of Social Orders: Post-Marxist Alternatives* (London, 1991). For a thoroughgoing analysis of what have been referred to above as free-floating ideological resources and ideological exploitation, see M. S. Archer, *Culture and Agency: The Place of Culture in Social Theory* (Cambridge, 1989).

mobilized in the promotion of new social practices.[37] Of most general significance in this connection is the fact that all institutions contain in some degree zones of normative ambiguity which not only normally encourage the questioning of existing structures of authority and status but sometimes contribute to their subversion and reconstitution to accommodate changes in power relations. In conflict at what has been called the frontier of control,[38] the existence of normative ambiguity facilitates the weakening of authority and the legitimation of new powers, as well as being in its own right a direct cause of a sense of injustice or relative deprivation. So, whether moral resources are thought of as potentialities available in the wider cultural environment of social systems, or as generated by their own institutions, such ideal factors are just as real and efficacious in the modification or transformation of authority and status as are material factors— with which they are anyway so closely combined in social action as to make the distinction quite artificial.

VIII

Attempts at synthesis and contestation have produced thin results if gauged by the direct influence of these conceptual schemes on the course of empirical research. The apperceptions of practical sociologists seem to have been little affected by either type of metasociological discourse. Most research relating to the wider issues of social order and conflict has continued to be informed by middle-range hypotheses of a distinctly more partisan provenance; that is to say by ideas stemming from Durkheimian and Marxist modes of theorizing. Moreover, the best work of this kind shows that writers whose research is shaped by these opposing theoretical viewpoints can nevertheless often arrive at explanations that reveal a degree of conceptual convergence which is far more impressive than anything to be found in abstract schemes such as those just discussed. This is another reason for thinking that the search for grand theory, whether by way of synthesis or contesta-

[37] An example, that of the 'feudalizing' tendencies of agrarian bureaucratic polities, is sketched out in the Appendix.

[38] A term coined by the industrial sociologist, C. L. Goodrich, *The Frontier of Control* (New York, 1920), but which has since acquired a much wider currency than its original usage.

tion, may be misdirected. The proof of this point would require another volume, and at this stage an additional illustration of it adds nothing of consequence to the arguments presented in the present one. Nevertheless, an example will at least serve to indicate the extent to which explanatory convergence is possible.

Chinoy's research into how automobile workers in Detroit, in the 1950s, managed to reconcile their experience of small chances of upward occupational mobility with the ideal of the 'American dream' of success offers an interpretation of the formation of their aspirations which, in its form, differs very little from Gray's account of how the aristocracy of labour in nineteenth-century Edinburgh accommodated their interests to the Victorian ideal of 'Respectability'.[39] These two pieces of research are very different in their theoretical orientation, Chinoy's belonging to mainstream US sociology and displaying the influence of Merton's revision of Durkheimian anomie theory, whereas Gray's is quite evidently Marxist in inspiration, and Gramscian in particular. Despite this, both are exemplary demonstrations of the way in which interests are the outcome—via the creative response of the actors—of both the realistic situations in which people find themselves and the norms defining those situations. In both cases, the exploitability of the dominant value and belief system is a crucial element of the explanation. Chinoy shows how the 'chronology' of workers' aspirations is marked by a gradual redefinition of success, a process in which the American dream is not abandoned but transmuted, so that, for instance, the acquisition of consumer goods becomes a substitute for occupational mobility. In a similar fashion, Gray shows how the Victorian artisanate, while sharing with bourgeois strata the norm of respectability, accommodated this ambiguous ideal to the reality of its changing work situation, managing to find room for beliefs in collectivism and mutual aid within what was traditionally an individualistic ethic. In both these works, then, aspirations and behaviour are interpreted neither as merely a reflection of the economic, class situation nor as a passive acceptance of dominant values and beliefs. They are understood rather as the rational adaptation of values and beliefs to realistic conditions; and in turn as innovations in the definition of class

---

[39] Chinoy, *Automobile Workers and the American Dream*, and Gray, *The Labour Aristocracy in Victorian Edinburgh*.

situation and thereby of class interest. In Parsonian terms, both explanations are voluntaristic.

While this example of explanatory convergence is remarkable, its implications are not unequivocal. One instance is obviously insufficient to prove that the logic of actual research will generally guarantee such an outcome, and in this particular case it certainly cannot be concluded that sound sociology needs no theoretical schooling. Moreover, it would no doubt be just as easy to come up with an instance of an equally notable divergence in interpretation. But what does seem certain is that explanations become more divergent as they cease to deal with specific situations or courses of social action, such as those just referred to, and take on the form of generalized theories of societal integration.

The reasons for this are not difficult to understand. When it comes to explaining not the attitudes and behaviour of some particular group, but the sources of order and conflict in the wider society, the claims of opposing general theories are far less easily reconcilable. At this level, the rivalry between schools of thought is exacerbated because the integrity of entire theoretical systems is at stake; not to mention the philosophical, moral, and political beliefs of their protaganists. At the same time, these kinds of conflicting claims and interpretations are empirically much harder to adjudicate. Even in the case of a great many middle-range theories, such as those on which the discussion of the main body of this work has concentrated, there is all too often no adequate means of deciding between alternative interpretations, which can anyway usually be salvaged by means of auxiliary hypotheses.

That more and better evidence is needed is a perennial cry. But this presupposes the elucidation of theories that appear susceptible of disproof and most especially of their underlying assumptions about the structuring of social action. In Durkheimian and Marxist sociology, however, these assumptions are not always sufficiently well defined; they are often highly ambiguous; sometimes they are residual; and conceptual escape routes are usually available. Simply because working hypotheses are in this fashion so contingently related to the general theories from which they supposedly derive, the attempt to clarify and test the former cannot be expected to amount to anything like a decisive confirmation or rejection of the latter.

For this reason alone, the present work has not aimed to replace the dense problematics of Durkheimian and Marxist theory by yet another conceptual compromise that resolves their differences by dissolving their substance. It has rather sought to demonstrate that what appear to be two quite fundamentally opposed theories of society do nevertheless sometimes yield—and more often imply—fairly specific explanations of order and conflict that exhibit significant points of convergence because of the complementarity of their core and peripheral concepts of the structuring of social action. Therefore, the book will have served its main purpose if it has helped to show that these rival bodies of theory share a common set of problems whose sociological clarification also requires very similar basic assumptions.

APPENDIX

Social Integration and System Integration

I

The term 'social change' will be taken to mean a change in the institutional structure of a social system; more particularly, a transformation of the core institutional order of a society such that we can speak of a change in type of society. I do not believe that it is necessary to reach agreement on what is meant by the 'core institutional order' of a society or on how a typology of societies is to be differentiated before there can be meaningful discussion of how the process of change takes place. That is, unless there is some a priori commitment to a 'dominant factor' theory of social change; in which case the wrangle about whether change has 'really' taken place can be endless.

The main purpose of this chapter is to discuss some of the implications of recent criticisms of functionalism, especially those which have a bearing on how social change is internally generated in a society. The thesis is that, in concentrating their fire on a special, albeit prominent, version of functionalism ('normative functionalism'), critics have become over involved with what may be called the problems of 'social integration'. As a result, they have tended to ignore what is just as relevant to their central interests in conflict and social change, namely, the problem of 'system integration'. And here the perspective of general functionalism would still seem to be the most useful instrument.

In a recent article, Kingsley Davis[1] has proposed such a catholic definition of functionalism as to make it virtually indistinguishable from the most basic presuppositions of contemporary sociology. This is all very comforting. But if by functionalism nothing more were meant than seeing society as a system of interdependent parts, and an aversion to 'reductionism', then most of those who have been engaged in criticism of functionalism would be proselytized overnight. How many would accept the attendant ideas, such as that of 'functional requisites', is more debatable, and would probably depend on how they were interpreted. Again, exactly what elements are included as 'parts' of a social system, and the exact implications of the idea of 'interdependence' itself, are obviously areas of potential disagreement.[2]

---

[1] K. Davis, 'The Myth of Functional Analysis as a Special Method in Sociology and Anthropology', *American Sociological Review*, 24 (1959).

[2] A. W. Gouldner, 'Reciprocity and Autonomy in Functional Theory', in L. Gross (ed.), *Symposium on Sociological Theory* (New York, 1959).

But, omitting these considerations, surely the 'general' functionalist standpoint which Davis has restated must be distinguished from its more specific and controversial form. Davis avoids mentioning precisely those characteristics which are now widely associated with, though not logically entailed by, a functionalist orientation: first, the emphatic role attributed to 'common value elements' in the integration of social action; and, second, the unwarranted assumption that the study of social stability must precede the analysis of social change. Both these predispositions, but especially the first, typify what we wish to speak of from now on as normative functionalism.[3]

Before going on to examine the position to which we are led by the critics of normative functionalism, one further distinction is relevant to the subsequent argument. It is the wholly artificial one between 'social integration' and 'system integration'. Whereas the problem of social integration focuses attention upon the orderly or conflictful relationships between the *actors*, the problem of system integration focuses on the orderly or conflictful relationships between the *parts*, of a social system.

It may be said at once that the connection between these two aspects of integration is neatly made by normative functionalism. The logic is simple. Since the only systematically differentiated parts of a society are its institutional patterns, the only source of social disorder arising from system disorder is that which takes the form of role conflict stemming from incompatible institutional patterns. If, however, it is held that such institutional patterns do not exhaust the general relevant 'parts' of a social system, then this particular articulation of system and social integration is only one way of relating the phenomena of 'deviance' and 'conflict' to the operation of the system as a functioning entity. To this point we shall return later. For the moment, what needs stressing is that the critics of normative functionalism have devoted their critique entirely to the way in which this theory handles the problem of social integration; and particularly to the ambiguities of the concept of 'institution'.

II

The leading exponent of the general functionalist school, Robert K. Merton, has already drawn attention to the static connotation of the term

---

[3] Gouldner quite properly points out that this tendency has amounted to what is in fact 'implicit factor-theorizing': 'Although the methodological position of the earlier functionalists commonly affirmed an amorphous interdependence of parts within a social system, it does not follow that the specific empirical analysis in which they engaged actually utilized this principle. In particular, the classic contributions, from Comte to Parsons, have gone out of their way to stress the significance of 'shared value elements' in maintaining the equilibrium of social systems.' ('Reciprocity and Autonomy in Functional Theory', 265.)

institution: 'It is not enough', he writes, 'to refer to the "institutions" as though they were all uniformly supported by all groups and strata in the society. Unless systematic consideration is given to the *degree* of support of particular "institutions" by *specific* groups we shall overlook the important place of power in society.'[4] The major criticism of normative functionalism which has frequently been made is that it treats insitutions primarily as moral entities, without rigorously exploring the interplay between norms and power that is universally present in major institutional contexts. This weakness has been seized upon by such writers as Dahrendorf and Rex.[5] Their basic theses are sufficiently similar to be treated jointly. For the sake of convenience, their ideas may be called 'conflict theory'.

The conflict theorists have pointed out first that norms and power must be considered as general alternative modes of 'institutionalizing' social relationships. To quote Rex:

We have also to recognize that some of the ends which the actors in our system pursue may be random ends from the point of view of the system or actually in conflict with it. If there is an actual conflict of ends, the behaviour of actors towards one another may not be determined by shared norms but by the success which each has in compelling the other to act in accordance with his interests. Power then becomes a crucial variable in the study of social systems.[6]

Second, potential conflicts of interests are seen as endemic in all social systems which 'institutionalize' power relationships,[7] because power (authority) over others is the most general form of 'scarce resource' and one that is inherent in society itself. 'The distribution of authority in associations', writes Dahrendorf, 'is the ultimate "cause" of the formation

---

[4] Merton, *Social Theory and Social Structure*, p. 122.

[5] Dahrendorf, *Class and Class Conflict in Industrial Society*, and Rex, *Key Problems of Sociological Theory*.

[6] Ibid. 112.

[7] Briefly, to define authority as institutionalized power is to beg exactly the question that Merton raises, if the line between authority and power is drawn in terms of the presence or absence of a claim to legitimacy, not in terms of the sentiments of those (principally) over whom authority is exercised. Perhaps the most general consideration which makes the 'deinstitutionalization' of authority an ever-present possibility is the fact that, whereas the legitimacy of authority tends to take the form of general principles, acts of authority are always specific; and they are always more specific than derived rules of authority, no matter how well developed the latter. Thus, the 'exploitable' ambiguity surrounding the derivation and interpretation of the legitimacy of specific acts means that authority is never given, but is always contingent upon its exercise. It is precisely with such conflicts arising within the interstices of institutionalized power that 'conflict theory' is concerned; and not simply with the more unusual approximations to 'unstructured' power conflicts.

of conflict groups.'[8] Thus, if potential conflicts of interest between those who exercise authority and those over whom authority is exercised are a 'normal' feature of social organization, the deinstitutionalization of power, and the use of power to maintain institutions, are ever present possibilities. In any realistic and dynamic view of institutionalization, the role of power, both in the generation and control of conflict, is of prime concern.

At first sight, it would seem that the image of society constructed by normative functionalism has given rise to counter-arguments which bring us round full circle to the polemical starting-point of modern sociology, namely, the debate on social contract. But fortunately both normative functionalists and conflict theorists are not prepared to recognize as a real issue the Greenian dichotomy of 'Will' versus 'Force'.[9] The themes of norms–consensus–order, and power–alienation–conflict are not regarded as viable sociological alternatives.[10]

It is, therefore, a little surprising to find that both Dahrendorf and Rex consider it necessary to develop their antitheses to normative functionalism in a *systematic* form. These take the shape, respectively, of a 'coercion theory of society' and a 'conflict model of society'.[11] For this strategy they give reasons which are even more surprising. The first is that they both feel their 'models' or 'frames of reference' are specially suited to certain problem areas in sociology, particularly to the study of industrial socie-

[8] Dahrendorf, *Class and Class Conflict*, p. 172.

[9] T. H. Green, *Principles of Political Obligation* (London, 1906).

[10] At any rate, in formal terms. For instance, Parsons: 'I do not think it is useful to postulate a deep dichotomy between theories which give importance to beliefs and values on the one hand, to allegedly "realistic" interests, e.g., economic, on the other. Beliefs and values are actualized, partially and imperfectly, in realistic situations of social interaction and the outcomes are always codetermined by the values and realistic exigencies; conversely what on concrete levels are called "interests" are by no means independent of the values which have been institutionalized in the relevant groups.' (Parsons, *Structure and Process in Modern Society*, p. 173.) See also Dahrendorf, *Class and Class Conflict*, pp. 159, 163, and Rex, *Key Problems of Sociological Theory*, p. 112. But, while there is formal agreement on this point, both the normative functionalists and the conflict theorists fail to explore in any rigorous way the interrelationships of 'normative' and 'realistic' elements of social systems.

[11] Both authors state their propositions in summary form (Dahrendorf, *Class and Class Conflict*, pp. 236–40; Rex, *Key Problems in Sociological Theory*, pp. 129–31, 195). Their premises are very similar: 'Every society displays at every point dissensus and conflict; social conflict is ubiquitous' (Dahrendorf, p. 162); 'Instead of being organized around a consensus of values, social systems may be thought of as involving conflict situations at central points' (Rex, p. 129). The major disagreement between the two would seem to be how far, *in fact*, lines of social conflict overlap (see Rex, pp. 117–18).

ties.[12] And, second, Dahrendorf feels that the unification of the 'integration theory' (normative functionalism) and the 'coercion theory' is unlikely and probably impossible.[13]

Neither of these reasons is very compelling. You cannot assert that society is unthinkable as either a purely moral or a purely coercive entity, and then suggest that a vocabulary built around one or the other of these unthinkable premises is necessary because some societies are manifestly more orderly or conflictful than others. To be sure, the degree to which power enters into social relationships is a factor indispensable for the understanding of both the 'imperfection' of consensus and the propensity to conflict. But even in situations where power is very evident and conflict endemic, it is doubtful whether the phenomena of conflict can be adequately grasped without incorporating into conflict theory many of the concepts and propositions concerning the dynamic properties of value systems (or ideologies) which have been developed, or taken over, by normative functionalism. For, given the power structure, the nature of the value system is of signal importance for the genesis, intensity, and direction of potential conflict. Particularly crucial is the way in which it structures the levels of aspiration of different social strata. It may, of its own accord, create aspirations which generate demands for change, or add fuel to the fire of conflicting material interests. It may be sufficiently open and ambiguous to be exploited simultaneously by different conflict groups; or, contrariwise, be capable of absorbing counter-ideologies within itself. Or, sudden change in the relative material positions of different groups may result in widespread conflict as a consequence of what Durkheim calls 'moral declassification'. It could, therefore, be argued that even the analysis of that facet of social integration to which Dahrendorf and Rex consider their theories to be especially relevant— namely, social conflict—requires nothing less than a systematic extension of their framework to take explicitly into account the variable properties of value systems that have been the focus of normative functionalism.[14] To the extent that this is done, their conflict theory ceases to be a 'special' approach. That status is reserved for the unmodified version of normative funcationalism.

Finally, both normative functionalism and conflict theory quite

---

[12] Dahrendorf, *Class and Class Conflict*, pp. 161–4; Rex, *Key Problems in Sociological Theory*, pp. 112, 114.

[13] Dahrendorf, *Class and Class Conflict*, p. 164.

[14] To take an actual example, compare the explicit use of the idea of the 'exploitability' of the common value system by Parsons (*The Social System*, pp. 293, 355) in accounting for the intensification of 'deviance' with the implicit reference to such an idea by Rex (*Key Problems in Sociological Theory*, p. 125) in discussing class conflict.

obviously utilize many sociological concepts which are the property of neither the one perspective nor the other for the solution of their respective problems. Witness only Dahrendorf's extensive use of the concept of 'multiple group relationships' to account for the variability of class conflict in a way that is not at all dissimilar from the way it is used, for example, by Williams.[15] Surely it is in the active use of precisely such common concepts and propositions, rather than in procuring an agreed definition of 'institution' or 'society', that the desired unification of which Dahrendorf is so sceptical is constantly being achieved. In actual fact, the divergence between what he calls 'integration theory' and 'coercion theory' is much more evident in defining problems than in solving them.

Why, then, the concentration on the development of alternative conceptual schemes in which the ideas of power and conflict play a central role? Partly because the recognition given by normative functionalism to the arguments put forward along these lines has so far amounted to nothing more than lip-service. More fundamentally, perhaps, it is because, in seeing equilibrium analysis combined in normative functionalism with a focus on shared value elements, Dahrendorf and Rex, with their manifest interest in social change, have as a consequence sought the key to this problem in the area of power and conflict. If this is so, how far do the conflict theorists take us in the analysis of social change?

Dahrendorf and Rex assert that social change is a result of the shifting balance of power between conflict groups.[16] Now, while social change is very frequently associated with conflict, the reverse does not necessarily hold. Conflict may be both endemic and intense in a social system without causing any basic structural change. Why does some conflict result in change while other conflict does not? Conflict theory would have to answer that this is decided by the variable factors affecting the power balance between groups. Here we reach the analytical limits of conflict theory. As a reaction to normative functionalism it is entirely confined to the problem of social integration. What is missing is the system-integration focus of general functionalism, which, by contrast with normative functionalism, involves no prior commitment to the study of system stability.[17]

[15] Dahrendorf, *Class and Class Conflict*, pp. 213–18, and Williams, *American Society*, pp. 560–1.

[16] Dahrendorf, *Class and Class Conflict*, pp. 231–6; Rex, *Key Problems of Sociological Theory*, p. 196.

[17] I may refer here once more to the excellent essay by Gouldner ('Reciprocity and Autonomy in Functional Theory'), and especially to his idea of the 'functional autonomy' of parts. This concept provides an obvious link between social and system integration. He explicitly points out that 'the concept of the differential functional autonomy of parts directs attention to the need to distinguish between parts having a greater or lesser vested interest in system maintenance', and that

This is exceedingly interesting, because both Dahrendorf and Rex arrive at their respective positions through a generalization of Marx. Yet it is precisely Marx who clearly differentiates social and system integration. The propensity to class antagonism (social integration aspect) is generally a function of the character of production relationships (e.g. possibilities of intra-class identification and communication). But the dynamics of class antagonisms are clearly related to the progressively growing 'contradictions' of the economic system. One might almost say that the 'conflict' which in Marxian theory is decisive for change is not the *power* conflict arising from the relationships in the productive system, but the *system* conflict arising from 'contradictions' between 'property institutions' and the 'forces of production'. Though definitely linked, these two aspects of integration are not only analytically separable, but also, because of the time element involved, factually distinguishable. Thus it is perfectly possible, according to this theory, to say that at any particular point of time a society has a high degree of social integration (e.g. relative absence of class conflict) and yet has a low degree of system integration (mounting excess productive capacity).

Further interest attaches to the fact that the idea of structural contradictions is central to the general functionalist view of change:

The key concept bridging the gap between statics and dynamics in functional theory is that of strain, tension, contradiction, or discrepancy between the component elements of social and cultural structure. Such strains may be dysfunctional for the social system in its then existing form; they may also be instrumental in leading to changes in that system. When social mechanisms for controlling them are operating effectively, these strains are kept within such bounds as to limit change of social structure.[18]

The vital question is, of course: what are the 'component elements' of social systems which give rise to strain, tension, or contradiction? General functionalism, as I understand it, does not attempt to formulate an answer to this question.[19]

It is, by contrast, in normative functionalism that institutional patterns emerge as the only generally identified and systematically differentiated

---

'not only efforts to change the system, but also those directed at *maintaining* it are likely to entail conflict and resistance' as a result of differential functional autonomy. What I find a little ambiguous, however, is his use of the term 'parts' of a system: at one stage they seem to mean structural aspects (e.g. ecological conditions); at another, actual groups (the French bourgeoisie). The 'parts' which may become functionally autonomous are surely *groups*; the 'parts' whose interplay conditions their functional autonomy are the *structural* elements of the system. I hope this will become clear in the subsequent argument.

[18] Merton, *Social Theory and Social Structure*, p. 122.
[19] Gouldner, 'Reciprocity and Antonomy in Functional Theory', pp. 244–8.

components of a social system between which there can be conflict and resultant strain. Since social systems are differentiated only along the institutional axis, there can be no place for the kind of contradictions which Marx envisaged, contradictions which are obviously relevant to the problem focus of conflict theory. We may ask, therefore, does the Marxian view contain the elements of a more general sociological formulation?

III

Criticism of the Marxian interpretation of society and social change has focused on the meaning and importance attributed to the 'material mode of production'. Sometimes, this has been simply and erroneously interpreted as technology. Yet it is quite obvious that in the Marxian schema technological change is not regarded as the prime mover, but as a force which operates interdependently with the productive relations of the society, that is, the prevailing organization of property and labour. The inclusion of productive relationships in the concept 'mode of production' lays the theory open to the criticism that the degree of differentiation and independence of such relationships from other social structures in the same society varies very considerably; and that, in particular, the saliency of the economic system under capitalism is not at all characteristic of most historical societies, in which the mode of political organization heavily conditioned the structure and potential change of productive relationships.[20] Marxian theory has not, for fairly obvious reasons, been overmuch concerned to rebut such criticism of its basic sociological assumptions. Given its premises about the general long-run decisiveness of the economic order for social change, it has quite logically confined its discussion of system integration to the *internal* dynamics of the mode of production itself—to the economic theory of the contradiction between 'forces of production' (technological potential) and the 'relations of production' (property institutions).[21]

While this narrowing down of the problem of system integration is highly questionable, the idea of a contradiction between the material conditions of production and the productive institutions of the economic system has a more general relevance that should not be ignored.

First, contradiction implies that the material means of production (e.g. industrial technology) favour a set of potential social relationships (social-

---

[20] See, especially, M. Weber, *Economy and Society*, 1044–51.

[21] See, e.g., P. A. Baran, *The Political Economy of Growth* (New York, 1957) and Sweezy, *The Theory of Capitalist Development*. For the difficulty of locating the 'crisis mechanism' of feudalism, see M. H. Dobb (ed.), *The Transition from Feudalism to Capitalism: A Symposium* (Patna, India, 1957).

ist ownership) which constitutes a threat to the existing social relationships institutionalized in the property system (private ownership). Now, whatever reservations one may have about the specific linkage of industrial production with socialist property relationships, there is nothing metaphysical about the general notion of social relationships being somehow implicit in a given set of material conditions. Material conditions most obviously include the technological means of control over the physical and social environment and the skills associated with these means. They include not only the material means of production, but also what Weber frequently refers to as the material means of organization and violence. Such material conditions must surely be included as a variable in any calculus of system intergration, since it is clear that they may facilitate the development of 'deviant' social relationships which run counter to the dominant institutional patterns of the system. Michels's study of oligarchical tendencies is only the classic example.

Second, according to Marx, the actualization of these potential counter-relationships is determined by the success with which those with vested interests in the existing order are able to resolve the functional incompatibility between the material means of production and the property framework. In the capitalist case, this incompatibility arises from the inability of private property institutions to accommodate the productive capacity of the industrial system. The focal point of strain is 'overproduction'. The argument, of course, goes further than this. The theory of the 'crisis mechanism' not only postulates dysfunctionality but attempts to demonstrate how the internal contradictions of the mode of production are endogenously intensified to the point of system breakdown by the inherent development of productive forces. This mechanism, most fully elaborated in the case of capitalist societies, is the conveyor belt which moves a society from one stage of its historical evolution to the next. But, in order to use the idea of a functional incompatibility between the dominant institutional order of a social system and its material base, it is not necessary to assume that the system must inevitably break down or that it must inevitably be succeeded by another system of a given type.[22]

We now have a view of system integration, particularly relevant to conflict theory, which may be summed up as follows:

1. One generally conceivable source of tension and possible change in a social system is that which arises from a 'lack of fit' between its core institutional order and its material substructure.

2. The material substructure in such a case facilitates the development

---

[22] See the instructive remarks of R. Coulborn, *Feudalism in History* (Princeton, NJ, 1956), 254–69.

of social relationships which, if actualized, would directly threaten the existing institutional order.

3. The system will be characterized by a typical form of 'strain' arising from the functional incompatibility between its institutional order and material base.

4. The actualization of the latent social relationships of the system will depend on the success with which groups having vested interests in the maintenance of the institutional order are able to cope with the dysfunctional tendency of the system in the face of particular exigencies.

5. If these exigencies lead to an intensification of the functional incompatibility of the system, and if compensating measures by vested interest groups lead (unintentionally) to a further actualization of the potential social relationships of the system, a vicious circle of social disintegration and change of the institutional order is under way. If, on the other hand, compensating measures are effective, the institutional order will remain intact, but the focal point of strain will continue to be evident so long as the functional incompatibility of the system persists.

These propositions do not limit the analysis of system integration to the productive system of a society. Nor do they imply a differentiation of types of societies primarily in terms of their modes of production. Such problems cannot be settled a priori. Consequently, the 'dominant' or 'core' institutional orders may vary from one type of society to another; and the identification of such institutional orders would seem to be first and foremost a way of defining what is meant by saying that a society has changed.[23] There are, however, certain problems which arise when the concepts of 'dominant' institutional order and material base are applied to social systems. It may make sense to apply such a distinction to some particular subsystem of a society or to some particular type of corporate group; is it equally relevant, in the case of a society, to regard, for example, the productive system as a 'material base' from the point of view of the 'dominant' political system, even though the productive system manifestly includes institutional elements? In so far as the predominant concern is with the way in which the material preconditions of a certain type of political action are, or are not, to be found in a given economic order, there would appear to be good reason for answering this question in the affirmative.[24] Such an answer would, of course, in no way

---

[23] Thus differences of opinion about the endurance of Western feudal society depend very largely on whether the military, the political, or the economic aspect of this institutional complex is singled out as the 'core' order; see O. Hintze, 'Wesen und Verbreitung des Feudalismus', *Staat und Verfassung* (Leipzig, 1941).

[24] What else does Weber imply when he writes: 'It is clear, therefore, that the disintegration of the Roman Empire was the inevitable political consequence of a basic economic development: the gradual disappearance of commerce and the

prejudice the further explanation of how such a *given* economic order came about; the problem of the 'causes' of the type of system instability under consideration is, anyway, a quite separate issue. It should also be noted that the degree of institutional differentiation of economic and political structures varies very considerably. In cases where the relations of production and the relations of political power are not institutionally very distinct, and especially where the relations of production are institutionalized to a considerable extent around political goals, it would seem reasonable to regard the economic order much more directly as a 'material base' of the 'dominant' political institutions. A brief reference to Weber's discussion of patrimonialism may serve to illustrate these points as well as the propositions previously advanced.

Although Weber's concept of patrimonialism, and especially that of patrimonial bureaucracy, refers primarily to a type of political structure, it is clear from his remarks that this structure might well be regarded as the 'core' institutional order of the society and as a major point of reference for societal change. Moreover, Weber's analysis of the material preconditions of bureaucratization clearly indicates the nature of the functional problems facing societies of the patrimonial bureaucratic type. These centre on the relationship between the institution of bureaucracy and the material substructure of a subsistence economy. After setting out the general rule that 'A certain measure of a developed money economy is the normal precondition for the unchanged and continued existence, if not for the establishment, of pure bureaucratic administration,' Weber goes on to note that historical cases of 'distinctly developed and quantitatively large bureaucracies' may be found which 'to a very great extent, partly even predominantly, have rested upon compensation of the officials in kind'. This he explains by arguing that, 'even though the full development of a money economy is not an indispensable precondition for bureaucratization, bureaucracy as a permanent structure is knit to the one presupposition of a constant income for maintaining it', and that 'a stable system of *taxation* is the precondition for the permanent existence of bureaucratic administration'. But again: 'For well-known and general reasons, only a fully developed money economy offers a secure basis for such a taxation system.'[25]

The strategic functional problem, then, is one of maintaining a taxation system that can effectively meet the material needs of a bureaucracy in

---

expansion of a barter economy. Essentially this disintegration simply meant that the monetarized administrative system and political superstructure of the Empire disappeared, for they were no longer adapted to the infrastructure of a natural economy.' *The Agrarian Sociology of Ancient Civilizations*, trans. R. I. Frank (London, 1976), 408.

[25] *From Max Weber*, pp. 205–9.

the context of a subsistence, or near-subsistence, economy. The central-izing goal of bureaucratic institutions is constantly liable to sabotage by the potential social relationship structure of the subsistence economy which favours the decentralization and 'feudalization' of power relation-ships.[26] As Weber himself says: 'According to all historical experience, without a money economy the bureaucratic structure can hardly avoid undergoing substantial internal changes, or, indeed, turning into another type of structure.'[27] The relationship between bureaucracy and taxation is a highly interdependent one. The efficiency of the bureaucracy depends upon the effectiveness of its taxation system; and the effectiveness of the taxation system depends on the efficiency of the bureaucratic apparatus. Thus, for whatever reason, any increase in the bureaucratic load or decrease in taxation capacity may generate a vicious circle of decentrali-zation of power. Indeed, it might be argued that the 'taxation' crisis of patrimonial bureaucracy is essentially analogous to the 'production' crisis of capitalism. At any rate, the focal point of strain in this type of society is taxation capacity relative to bureaucratic needs.

This strategic functional problem sets the stage for the characteristic conflicts of interest that arise between the bureaucratic centre, the officialdom, landed magnates, and peasantry. The points of tension are those which represent an actualization of the potential for 'feudalization': the tendency of officials to appropriate the economic and political resources of the office; the struggle of large landowners to gain immunity from taxation and/or usurp fiscal and political functions; and the local relationships of economic and political dependency into which the peas-antry are forced in seeking protection against the tax burden of the bureaucratic centre. These centrifugal tendencies may be seen as both a cause and a consequence of the possible failure of mechanisms for maintaining effective taxation capacity and central control. The outcome of such struggles, and the success with which the functional problem is solved by the bureaucratic centre, is, of course, decided in each historical case by the particular circumstances facing the patrimonial bureaucracy. These may vary very considerably; but whether they make for stability or breakdown or bureaucratic institutions, all societies of this type may be studied from the point of view of their common contradiction.[28]

[26] The logic of this is succinctly argued by Bloch, *Feudal Society*, p. 68, and L. M. Hartman, *The Early Medieval State* (London, 1960), 19.

[27] *From Max Weber*, p. 205.

[28] On the particular conditions favouring the stability of patrimonial bureaucracy in Egypt and China, see Weber, *Economy and Society*, ii, ch. 12. The most famous instance of breakdown, that of the later Roman Empire, is a case where the 'defence mechanisms' introduced by the bureaucracy (aptly described by Lot as the 'regime of castes') intensified the trend towards subsistence economy and actualized the potential for 'feudal' relationships. See Weber, *The Agrarian*

Another example of a not too dissimilar kind is that of the functional tensions arising from the relationship between the totalitarian political system and the industrial economy of the Soviet Union. It is noteworthy in this connection that many who would deny the relevance of the idea of 'internal contradictions' to capitalist societies have only too readily exaggerated the incompatibility of industrialism and the institutions of a one-party state. Be this as it may, it would seem that the type of contradiction envisaged here is one which those having an interest in the dominant political institution have thus far successfully controlled, but which nevertheless is likely to remain as a focal point of strain and potential change. It arises from the tendency of an industrial mode of production to create latent interest groups of a class character. This tendency must be 'dysfunctional' for a totalitarian political system, one precondition of which is a 'classless' society, i.e. an absence of bases of potential social organization outside the party bureaucracy.

Such a contradiction could manifest itself either by such latent interest groups striving for an autonomous corporate existence (which seems unlikely given the nature of party control) or by their subversion of the party organization from within. Of such groups, associated with industrialization, the least potentially threatening is that of worker opposition. Using Weber's typology of class formation, worker protest hardly advanced beyond the stage of 'mass reactions of a class character' (labour turnover and so on) in the early phase of Soviet industrialization; and, while disruptive to the economy, it was not allowed to develop into a more politically dangerous 'societal' action. More of a threat from this point of view, however—and this is the element of truth in Burnham's otherwise extravagant thesis of a 'managerial revolution'—is the so-called 'Soviet bourgeoisie': the functionally important quasi-group of predominantly industrial bureaucrats which has emerged as a result of rapid industrialization.[29]

The focal point of strain for the totalitarian political system is not simply that this latent class tends to develop vested interests in its position and privileges, but that it has an organizational capacity and cohesiveness that could form the basis of a political opposition. And, given the nature

---

Sociology of Ancient Civilizations, Part IV; F. Lot, *La Fin du Monde Antique et le debut du Moyen Âge* (Paris, 1951); M. Bloch, 'The Rise of Dependent Cultivation and Seignorial Institutions', and G. Ostrogorsky, 'Agrarian Conditions in the Byzantine Empire in the Middle Ages' (both in J. H. Clapham and E. Power (eds.), *The Cambridge Economic History*, i (Cambridge, 1942)). The general problem of 'feudalizing' tendencies in patrimonial bureaucratic societies is discussed in R. Coulborn, *Feudalism in History* (Princeton, NJ, 1956), and S. N. Eisenstadt, 'Political Struggle in Bureaucratic Societies', *World Politics*, 9 (1956).
[29] Feldmesser, 'Equality and Inequality under Khrushchev'.

of the political system, such an interest group would be most likely to take the form initially of cliques within the party bureaucracy. Therefore, the strategic functional problem of the dominant institutional order, from this point of .view, is that of maintaining the control of the party bureaucracy over the industrial bureaucracy, and more especially of securing the party against infiltration by vested interest groups of the managerial élite (which includes insulating the latter from any wider support in the society). Most fundamentally, the party must develop means by which it can systematically 'de-classify' the lines of stratification and interest-group formation that have their basis in the industrial substructure. At the same time, however (and here arises the point of system tension), such declassification must not undermine the conditions of industrial efficiency.

IV

The foregoing examples have been all too sketchy, but perhaps they may serve the purpose of illustrating the viewpoint advanced in the main body of the chapter. It has not been the intention to claim that this perspective is the only possible way to approach the problem of social change, still less to imply that there is anything other than a polemical advantage to be gained by focusing on system integration *as opposed* to social integration. What has been suggested, however, may be summed up as follows:

1. The propensity to social change arising from the functional incompatibility between an institutional order and its material base has been ignored by normative functionalists because of their concentration on the moral aspects of social integration.

2. It has been equally ignored by conflict theorists, who, in concentrating on the weakness of the normative functionalist approach to social integration, have failed to relate their interest in social change to the problem of system integration.

BIBLIOGRAPHY

ABEGG, E., *Der Messiasglaube in Indien und Iran* (Leipzig, 1928).

ABERCROMBIE, N., and TURNER, B. S. 'The Dominant Ideology Thesis', *British Journal of Sociology*, 29 (1978).

—— HILL, S., and TURNER, B. S., *The Dominant Ideology Thesis* (London, 1980).

ABERLE, D., 'A Note on Relative Deprivation as Applied to Millenarian and other Cult Movements', in S. L. Thrupp (ed.), *Millenial Dreams in Action* (The Hague, 1962).

ABRAMOWITZ, A. I., 'The United States: Political Culture Under Stress', in G. A. Almond and S. Verba (eds.), *The Civic Culture Revisited* (Boston, 1980).

ALEXANDER, J. C., *Theoretical Logic in Sociology* (4 vols.; London, 1982).

ALMOND, G. A., and VERBA, S., *The Civic Culture* (Princeton, NJ, 1963).

—— —— (eds.), *The Civic Culture Revisited* (Boston, 1980).

ANDERSON, P., *Lineages of the Absolutist State* (London, 1974).

—— 'The Antinomies of Antonio Gramsci', *New Left Review*, 100 (1976).

—— *Considerations on Western Marxism* (London, 1976).

ARCHER, M. S., *Culture and Agency* (Cambridge, 1988).

ARGYRIS, C., *Personality and Organization* (New York, 1957).

AVINERI, S., *The Social and Political Thought of Karl Marx* (Cambridge, 1970).

BAILEY, F. G., *Caste and the Economic Frontier* (Manchester, 1957).

BAKKE, E. W., *Citizens without Work* (New Haven, Conn., 1940).

BALAZS, E., *Chinese Civilization and Bureaucracy* (New Haven, Conn., 1964).

BALIBAR, E., 'The Basic Concepts of Historical Materialism', in L. Althusser and E. Balibar (eds.), *Reading Capital* (London, 1972).

BARAN, P. A., *Political Economy of Growth* (New York, 1952).

—— and SWEEZY, P. M., *Monopoly Capital* (New York, 1966).

BARBALET, J. M., *Citizenship: Rights, Struggle and Class Inequality* (Milton Keynes, 1988).

BARBER, B., *Social Stratification* (New York, 1957).

BARBER, E. G., *The Bourgeoisie in Eighteenth-century France* (Princeton, NJ, 1955).

BARKIN, S. (ed.), *Worker Militancy and its Consequences, 1965–75* (New York, 1975).

BARNES, S. H., KAASE, M., *et al.* (eds.), *Political Action: Mass Participation in Five Western Democracies* (Beverly Hills, Calif., 1979).

BARRY, B., *Sociologists, Economists and Democracy* (London, 1970).

BENDIX, R., *Max Weber: An Intellectual Portrait* (New York, 1960).

—— 'The Lower Classes and the "Democratic Revolution"', *Industrial Relations*, 1 (1961).

—— *Nation Building and Citizenship* (New York, 1964).

BERGER, P. L., 'Charisma, Religious Innovation and the Israelite Prophecy', *American Sociological Review*, 28 (1963).

BERREMAN, G. D., 'Caste in India and the United States', *American Journal of Sociology*, 64 (1960).

BERTRAND, C. L. (ed.), *Revolutionary Situations in Europe, 1917–1922* (Quebec, 1977).

BEST, G., *Mid-Victorian Britain, 1851–70* (London, 1971).

BÉTEILLE, A., *Caste, Class and Power* (Berkeley, Calif., 1965).

—— *Castes Old and New* (Bombay, 1969).

—— *Harmonic and Disharmonic Social Systems* (Sydney, 1971).

BIRNBAUM, N., 'Conflicting Interpretations of the Rise of Capitalism: Marx and Weber', *British Journal of Sociology*, 4 (1953).

BLACKBURN, R., 'The New Capitalism', in R. Blackburn (ed.), *Ideology and Social Science* (London, 1975).

BLAU, P. M., *Exchange and Power in Social Life* (New York, 1964).

BLAUNER, R., *Alienation and Freedom: The Factory Worker and his Industry* (Chicago, 1964).

BLICKLE, P., *The Revolution of 1525: The Peasants' War from a New Perspective* (London, 1985).

BLOCH, M., 'The Rise of Dependent Cultivation and Seignorial Institutions', in J. H. Clapham and E. Power (eds.), *The Cambridge Economic History*, i (Cambridge, 1942).

—— *Feudal Society*, trans. L. A. Manyion (London, 1961).

BOARDMAN, E. P., 'Millenary Aspects of the Taiping Rebellion, 1851–64', *Comparative Studies in Society and History*, Supplement II (1962).

BOBER, M. M., *Karl Marx's Interpretation of History* (New York, 1948).

BOGGS, C., *Gramsci's Marxism* (London, 1976).

BOTTOMORE, T. B. (ed.), *Karl Marx* (Oxford, 1973).

—— *Marxist Sociology* (London, 1975).

BRAVERMAN, H., *Labor and Monopoly Capital* (New York, 1974).

BROWDER, E., *Marx and America: A Study of the Doctrine of Impoverishment* (London, 1959).

BUCHANAN, A., 'Revolutionary Motivation and Rationality', *Philosophy and Public Affairs*, 9 (1980).

BURAWOY, M., *Manufacturing Consent* (Chicago, 1979).

—— 'The Politics of Production and the Production of Politics', in

Maurice Zeitlin (ed.), *Political Power and social Theory*, i (Greenwich, Conn., 1980).

BURRIDGE, K., *New Heaven, New Earth* (Oxford, 1971).

CALHOUN, C. J., 'The Radicalism of Tradition', *American Journal of Sociology*, 88 (1983).

CHESNEAUX, J., *Peasant Revolts in China, 1840–1949* (London, 1973).

CHINOY, E., *Automobile Workers and the American Dream* (New York, 1955).

CLARK, M., *The Revolution that Failed* (New Haven, Conn., 1977).

CLARKE, S., *Marx, Marginalism and Modern Sociology* (London, 1982).

CLARKE, T., and CLEMENTS, L. (eds.), *Trade Unions under Capitalism* (London, 1977).

CLEGG, H., *Trade Unionism under Collective Bargaining* (London, 1976).

CLEMENTS, L., 'Reference Groups and Trade Union Consciousness', in T. Clarke and L. Clements (eds.), *Trade Unions under Capitalism* (London, 1977).

CLINARD, M. B. (ed.), *Anomie and Deviant Behaviour* (Glencoe, Ill., 1964).

CLOWARD, R. A., and OHLIN, L. E., *Delinquency and Opportunity* (London, 1961).

COHEN, G. A., 'On Some Criticisms of Historical Materialism', *Proceedings of the Aristotelian Society*, Supplement (1970).

—— *Karl Marx's Theory of History: A Defence* (Oxford, 1978).

COHEN, P. S., *Modern Social Theory* (London, 1968).

CONVERSE, P. E., 'The Nature of Belief Systems in Mass Publics', in D. Apter (ed.), *Ideology and Discontent* (New York, 1964).

COULBORN, R., *Feudalism in History* (Princeton, NJ, 1956).

CROMPTON, R., and GUBBAY, J., *Economy and Class Structure* (London, 1977).

CROSSICK, G., 'The Labour Aristocracy and its Values', *Victorian Studies*, 19 (1976).

—— *An Artisan Elite in Victorian Society: Kentish Town London, 1840–1880* (London, 1978).

CROUCH, C., 'The Drive for Equality: Experience of Incomes Policy in Britain', in L. L. Lindberg *et al* (eds.), *Stress and Contradiction in Modern Capitalism* (Lexington, Mass., 1975).

—— and PIZZORNO, A. (eds.), *The Resurgence of Class Conflict in Western Europe since 1968* (London, 1978).

—— 'The State, Capital and Liberal Democracy', in C. Crouch (ed.), *State and Economy in Contemporary Capitalism* (London, 1979).

CURRAN, J., GUREVITCH, M., and WOOLLACOTT, J. (eds.), *Mass Communication and Society* (London, 1979).

CUTLER, A., HINDESS, B., HIRST, P., and HUSSAIN, A., *Marx's Capital and Capitalism Today* (London, 1977), i.

DAHRENDORF, R., *Class and Class Conflict in Industrial Society* (Stanford, Calif., 1959).

DANIEL, W. W., *Workplace Industrial Relations and Technical Change* (Policy Studies Institute, Dorset, 1987).

DAVIES, J. C., 'Towards a Theory of Revolution', *American Sociological Review*, 27 (1962).

DAVIS, K., 'The Myth of Functional Analysis as a Special Method in Sociology and Anthropology', *American Sociological Review*, 24 (1959).

DAVIS, M., 'Why the U.S. Working Class is Different', *New Left Review*, 123 (1980).

DAWE, A., 'Theories of Action', in T. Bottomore and R. Nisbet (eds.), *A History of Sociological Analysis* (London, 1979).

DAWLEY, A., *Class and Community: The Industrial Revolution in Lynn*, (Cambridge, Mass., 1976).

DE GRAZIA, S., *The Political Community: A Study of Anomie* (Chicago, 1948).

DE KNIGHT, A. and J. (eds.), *Caste and Race: Comparative Approaches* (London, 1967).

DE MAN, H., *The Psychology of Socialism* (London, 1928).

DOBB, M. H. (ed.), *The Transition from Feudalism to Capitalism* (Patna, 1957).

DOHRENWEND, B., 'Egoism, Altruism, Anomie and Fatalism', *American Sociological Review*, 24 (1959).

DRECKMEIER, C. A., *Kingship and Community in Early India* (Stanford, Calif., 1962).

DUMONT, L., *Homo Hierarchicus: The Caste System and its Implications* (London, 1970).

DURKHEIM, E., *The Division of Labour in Society*, trans. W. D. Halls (London, 1984).

—— *Suicide*, trans. and ed. J. A. Spaulding and G. Simpson (London, 1952).

—— *Sociology and Philosophy*, trans. D. F. Peacock, with an introduction by J. G. Peristiany (London, 1953).

—— *Professional Ethics and Civic Morals*, trans. C. Brookfield (London, 1957).

—— *Moral Education*, trans. E. K. Wilson and H. Schnurer, foreword by P. Fauconnet, ed., with an introduction, by E. K. Wilson (New York, 1961).

—— *Socialism*, ed. A. W. Gouldner (London, 1962).

DURKHEIM, E., and MAUSS, M., *Primitive Classification*, trans. and ed. R. Needham (London, 1963).

—— —— *The Elementary Forms of the Religious Life*, trans. E. K. Wilson and H. Schnurer (London, 1964).

—— —— *Selected Writings*, ed. A. Giddens (Cambridge, 1972).

EHRMANN, H. W., *Politics in France* (Boston, 1976).

EISENSTADT, S. N., 'Political Struggle in Bureaucratic Societies', *World Politics*, 9 (1956).

—— *The Political Systems of Empires* (London, 1963).

—— 'Institutionalization and Change', *American Sociological Review*, 29 (1964).

ELDER, J. W., 'Fatalism in India', *Anthropological Quarterly*, 39 (1966).

—— 'Political Attitudes', in D. E. Smith (ed.), *South Asian Politics and Religion* (New York, 1969).

ELLIS, D. P., 'The Hobbesian Problem of Order: A Critical Appraisal of the Normative Solution', *American Sociological Review*, 36 (1971).

ELSTER, J., *Logic and Society* (Chichester, 1978).

—— *Making Sense of Marx* (Cambridge, 1985).

—— *The Cement of Society* (Cambridge, 1989).

ENGELS, F., *The Peasant War in Germany* (Moscow, 1956).

ENTHOVEN, R. E., 'Lingayats', *Encyclopaedia of Religion and Ethics*, viii (New York, 1915).

ERIKSON, R., and ÅBERG, R., *Welfare in Transition: A Survey of Living Conditions in Sweden, 1968–1981* (Oxford, 1987).

ESPING-ANDEREN , G., and KORPI, W., 'Social Policy as Class Politics in Post-War Capitalism: Scandinavia, Austria and Germany', in J. H. Goldthorpe (ed.), *Order and Conflict in Contemporary Capitalism* (Oxford, 1984).

ETZIONI, A., *Complex Organizations* (New York, 1961).

EVANS-PRITCHARD, E. E., *Theories of Primitive Religion* (Oxford, 1965).

FEIERABEND, I. K., 'Social Change and Political Violence: Cross National Patterns', in H. D. Graham and T. R. Gurr (eds.), *The History of Violence in America* (New York, 1969).

FELDMESSER, R. A., 'Equality and Inequality under Khrushchev', *Problems of Communism*, 9 (1960).

FEMIA, J., 'Hegemony and Consciousness in Thought of Antonio Gramsci', *Political Studies*, 23 (1975).

FINER, S. E., 'The Political Power of Private Capital', *Sociological Review*, 3 (1955).

FINLEY, M. I., *The Ancient Economy* (London, 1975).

FONER, E., 'Why is there no socialism in the United States?', *History Workshop*, 17 (1984).

FORD, F. L., *Robe and Sword: The Regrouping of the French Aristocracy after Louis XIV* (New York, 1965).

FROMM, E., *Beyond the Chains of Illusion* (New York, 1962).

GALLACHER, W. M., and CAMPBELL, J. R., 'Direct Action', in Clarke and Clements (eds.), *Trade Unions under Capitalism*.

GALLIE, D., *In Search of the New Working Class: Automation and Social Integration within the Capitalist Enterprise* (Cambridge, 1978).

—— *Social Inequality and Class Radicalism in France and Britain* (Cambridge, 1983).

—— 'Social Radicalism in the French and British Working Classes: Some Points of Comparison', *British Journal of Sociology*, 30 (1979).

GANS, H. J., 'Poverty and Culture: Some Basic Questions about Methods of Studying Life-styles of the Poor', in P. Townsend (ed.), *The Concept of Poverty* (London, 1970).

GARRATY, J. A., *Unemployment in History* (New York, 1978).

GEARY, D., 'Identifying Militancy: The Assessment of Working Class Attitudes towards State and Society', in R. J. Evans (ed.), *The German Working Class, 1888–1933* (London, 1982).

—— *European Labour Protest, 1848–1939* (London, 1981).

GERAS, N., 'Marx and the Critique of Political Economy', in R. Blackburn (ed.), *Ideology and Social Science* (London, 1975).

GERMANI, G., 'Social and Political Consequences of Mobility', in N. J. Smelser and S. M. Lipset (eds.), *Social Structure and Mobility in Economic Development* (London, 1966).

GIDDENS, A., '"Power" in the Recent Writings of Talcott Parsons', *Sociology*, 2 (1968).

—— *Capitalism and Modern Social Theory* (Cambridge, 1971).

—— *Emile Durkheim: Selected Writings* (Cambridge, 1972).

—— *The Class Structure of the Advanced Societies* (London, 1973).

—— *Studies in Social and Political Theory* (London, 1977).

GINZBERG, E., *The Unemployed* (New York, 1943).

GLYN, A., and SUTCLIFFE, B., *British Capitalism, Workers and the Profits Squeeze* (Harmondsworth, 1972).

GOLDTHORPE, J. H., 'L'Image des classes chez les travailleurs manuels aises', *Revue française de sociologie*, 11 (1970).

—— 'The Current Inflation: Towards a Sociological Account', in F. Hirsch and J. H. Goldthorpe (eds.), *The Political Economy of Inflation* (London, 1978).

—— 'Class, Status and Party in Modern Britain', *European Journal of Sociology*, 13 (1972).

GOODRICH, C. L., *The Frontier of Control* (New York, 1920).

GORZ, A., *Strategy for Labor* (Boston, 1964).

—— *Farewell to the Working Class* (London, 1982).

GOUGH, I., *The Political Economy of the Welfare State* (London, 1981).

GOULDNER, A. W., 'Some Observations on Systematic Theory, 1945–55', in H. L. Zetterberg (ed.), *Sociology in the United States of America* (Paris, 1956).

—— 'Reciprocity and Autonomy in Functional Theory', in L. Gross (ed.), *Symposium on Sociological Theory* (New York, 1959).

—— *The Coming Crisis of Western Sociology* (London, 1970).

GRAMSCI, A., *Selections from the Prison Notebooks*, trans. and ed. Q. Hoare and G. N. Smith (London, 1971).

GRAY, R. Q., 'Styles of Life, the "Labour Aristocracy" and Class Relations in Later Nineteenth Century Edinburgh', *International Review of Social History*, 18 (1973).

—— *The Labour Aristocracy in Victorian Edinburgh* (Oxford, 1976).

GREEN, T. H., *Principles of Political Obligation* (London, 1906).

GREENSLADE, S. L., *Schism in the Early Church* (London, 1953).

GURR, T. R., *Why Men Rebel* (Princeton, NJ, 1970).

—— 'A Comparative Study of Civil Strife', in H. D. Graham and T. R. Gurr, *The History of Violence in America* (New York, 1969).

HABERMAS, J., 'Technology and Science as Ideology', in his *Towards a Rational Society* (London, 1971).

—— *Legitimation Crisis* (London, 1976).

HABIB, I., *The Agrarian Structure of the Mughal State* (Bombay, 1963).

HALEVY, E., *The Growth of Philosophic Radicalism* (Boston, 1955).

HALL, S., 'Culture, the Media and the "Ideological Effect"', in J. Curran, M. Gurevitch, and J. Woollacott (eds.), *Mass Communication and Society* (London, 1977).

HALLE, D., *America's Working Man* (London, 1987).

HAMMOND, T. T., *Lenin on Trade Unions and Revolution, 1893–1917* (New York, 1957).

HAMPSON, N., *A Social History of the French Revolution* (London, 1966).

HART III, G. L., *The Poems of Ancient Tamil* (Berkeley, Calif., 1975).

—— 'The Theory of Reincarnation among the Tamils', in W. D. O'Flaherty (ed.), *Karma and Rebirth in Classical Indian Tradition* (Berkeley, Calif., 1980).

HARTMANN, L. M., *The Early Medieval State* (London, 1960).

HEATH, A., *Rational Choice and Social Exchange* (Cambridge, 1976).

HELLER, A., *The Theory of Need in Marx* (London, 1976).

HILTON, R., *Bond Men Made Free* (London, 1973).

—— *The English Peasantry in the Later Middle Ages* (Oxford, 1975).

HINDESS, B., and HIRST, P. Q., *Pre-capitalist Modes of Production* (London, 1975).

HINTZE, O., 'Wesen und Verbreitung des Feudalismus', *Staat und Verfassung* (Leipzig, 1941).

HIRST, Paul Q., 'Economic Classes and Politics', in A. Hunt (ed.), *Class and Class Structure* (London, 1977).

HOBBES, T., *Leviathan*, ed. M. Oakeshott (Oxford, n.d.).

HOBSBAWM, E. J., *Social Bandits and Primitive Rebels* (London, 1959).

—— 'Introduction' to K. Marx, *Precapitalist Economic Formations* (London, 1964).

—— 'Inventing Traditions', in E. J. Hobsbawm and T. Ranger (eds.), *The Invention of Tradition* (Cambridge, 1983).

HUSBANDS, C. T., editorial Introduction to W. Sombart, *Why is there no socialism in the United States?* (London, 1976).

HUTTON, J. H., *Caste in India* (Cambridge, 1940).

HYMAN, H. H., 'The Value Systems of Different Classes', in R. Bendix and S. M. Lipset (eds.), *Class, Status and Power* (Glencoe, Ill., 1953).

HYMAN, R., *Marxism and the Sociology of Trade Unionism* (London, 1971).

—— and Brough, I., *Social Values and Industrial Relations* (London, 1975).

INGHAM, G. K., 'Social Stratification: Individual Attributes and Social Relationships', *Sociology*, 4 (1970).

JAHODA, M., LAZARSFELD, P., AND ZEISEL, H., *Marienthal* (London, 1972).

JOHNSON, B. D., 'Durkheim's One Cause of Suicide', *American Sociological Review*, 30 (1965).

JOHNSON, Carol, 'Reformism and Commodity Fetishism', *New Left Review*, 119 (1980).

JOHNSON, Chalmers, *Revolutionary Change* (Boston, 1966).

JOHNSON, H., *Sociology* (London, 1961).

JOYCE, P., *Work, Society and Politics: The Culture of the Factory in Later Victorian England* (Brighton, 1980).

JUDIS, J., 'The Triumph of Bourgeois Hegemony in the Face of Nothing that Challenges it', *Socialist Revolution*, 1 (1970).

KATZ, E., 'Platforms and Windows: Broadcasting's Role in Election Campaigns', in D. McQuail (ed.), *The Sociology of Mass Communications* (London, 1973).

—— and LAZARSFELD, P. S., *Personal Influence* (Glencoe, Ill., 1956).

KAVANAGH, D., 'Political Culture in Great Britain: The Decline of Civic Culture', in G. A. Almond and S. Verba (eds.), *The Civic Culture Revisited* (Boston, 1980).

KERR, C., and SIEGEL, A., 'The Inter-industry Propensity to Strike: An International Comparison', in A. Kornhauser, R. Dubin, A. M. Ross (eds.) *Industrial Conflict* (New York, 1954).

KEYES, C. F., and DANIEL, E. V. (eds.), *Karma: An Anthropological Inquiry* (Berkeley, Calif., 1983).

KLAPPER, J. T., *The Effects of Mass Communications* (Glencoe, Ill., 1960).

KLEHR, H., 'Marxist Theory in Search of America', *Journal of Politics*, 35 (1973).

KORNBLUM, W., *Blue Collar Community* (Chicago, 1974).

KORPI, W., 'Conflict, Power and Relative Deprivation', *American Political Science Review*, 68 (1974).

—— *The Democratic Class Struggle* (London, 1983).

KORSCH, K., *Karl Marx* (New York, 1963).

KOTHARI, R., *Politics in India* (Boston, 1970).

KUPER, L., *Race, Class and Power* (London, 1974).

—— 'Conflict and the Plural Society', in L. Kuper and M. G. Smith (eds.), *Pluralism in Africa* (Berkeley, Calif., 1971).

LACLAU, E., *Politics and Ideology in Marxist Theory* (London, 1979).

LANE, C., *The Rites of the Rulers: Ritual in Industrial Society, The Soviet Case* (Cambridge, 1981).

LANE, D., and O'DELL, F., *The Soviet Industrial Worker* (Oxford, 1978).

LANE, R., *Political Ideology: Why the American Common Man Believes what he does* (New York, 1962).

LANNOY, R., *The Speaking Tree* (Oxford, 1971).

LASLETT, J. H. M., and LIPSET, S. M. (eds.), *Failure of a Dream? Essays in the History of American Socialism* (Garden City, NY, 1974).

LATTIMORE, O., *The Inner Asian Frontiers of China* (New York, 1940).

LEFEBVRE, H., *The Sociology of Marx* (London, 1968).

LEFF. G., *The Tyranny of Concepts* (London, 1969).

LENIN, V. I., *What Is To Be Done?*, trans. and ed. S. V. and P. Utechin (London, 1970).

—— *Selected Works*, i (Moscow, 1950); ii (Moscow, 1947).

LENSKI, G. E., 'Status Crystallization: A Non-Vertical Dimension of Social Status', *American Sociological Review*, 19 (1954).

—— 'Status Inconsistency and the Vote', *American Sociological Review*, 32 (1967).

LEVENSON, J. R., *Confucian China and its Modern Fate*, ii (London, 1964).

LEVY, M. J., *The Family Revolution in Modern China* (Cambridge, Mass., 1949).

LICHTMAN, R., 'Marx's Theory of Ideology', *Socialist Revolution*, 5 (1975).

LINDBERG, L. L., ASFORD, R., CROUCH, C. and OFFE, C., (eds.), *Stress and Contradiction in Modern Capitalism* (Lexington, Mass., 1975).

LINDSAY, A. D., *Karl Marx's Capital: An Introductory Essay* (London, 1925).

LIPJHART, A., *The Politics of Accommodation* (Berkeley, Calif., 1968).

LIPSET, S. M., *Political Man* (London, 1960).

LIPSET, S. M., and ROKKAN, S., (eds.), *Party Systems and Voter Alignments* (New York, 1967).

LOCKWOOD, D., 'Some Remarks on "The Social System"', *British Journal of Sociology*, 7 (1956).

—— 'Social Integration and System Integration', in G. K. Zollschan and W. Hirsch (eds.), *Explorations in Social Change* (New York, 1964).

—— 'Race, Conflict and Plural Society', in S. Zubaida (ed.), *Race and Racialism* (London, 1970).

—— 'The Weakest Link in the Chain? Some Comments on the Marxist Theory of Action', in I. H. and R. L. Simpson (eds.), *Research in the Sociology of Work*, i (Greenwich, Conn., 1981).

—— 'Schichtung in der Staatsbuergergesellschaft', in B. Giesen and H. Haferkamp (eds.), *Soziologie der sozialen Ungleichheit* (Opladen, 1987).

LOT, F., *La Fin du Monde Antique et le debut du Moyen Âge* (Paris, 1951).

LOW-BEER, J. R., *Protest and Participation: The New Working Class in Italy* (Cambridge, 1978).

LOZOVSKY, A., *Marx and the Trade Unions* (London, 1935).

LUCAS, E., *Zwei formen von Radicalismus in der deutschen Arbeiterbewegung* (Frankfurt, 1976).

LUKÁCS, G., *History and Class Consciousness* (London, 1971).

LUKES, S., *Emile Durkheim: His Life and Work* (London, 1973).

—— 'Durkheim's "Individualism and the Intellectuals"', *Political Studies*, 17 (1969).

—— 'Political Ritual and Social Integration', *Sociology*, 9 (1975).

—— 'Socialism and Equality', in L. Kolakowski and S. Hampshire (eds.), *The Socialist Idea* (London, 1977).

—— *Essays in Social Theory* (London, 1977).

—— *Power: A Radical View* (London, 1974).

MCCLOSKY, H., and ZALLER, J., *The American Ethos: Public Attitudes toward Capitalism and Democracy* (London, 1984).

MCCORMACK, W., 'Lingayats as a Sect', *Journal of the Royal Anthropological Institute*, 93 (1963).

MACFIE, A. L., *The Individual and Society: Papers on Adam Smith* (London, 1967).

MACHONIN, P., 'Social Stratification in Contemporary Czechoslovakia', *American Journal of Sociology*, 75 (1970).

MACKENZIE, G., 'The Political Economy of the American Working Class', *British Journal of Sociology*, 28 (1977).

MCLELLAN, D., *The Thought of Karl Marx: An Introduction* (London, 1971).

—— *Marx's Grundrisse* (St Albans, 1973).

MacPherson, *The Political Theory of Possessive Individualism* (Oxford, 1977).

McQuail, D. (ed.), *The Sociology of Mass Communications* (London, 1973).

—— 'The Influence and Effects of Mass Media', in J. Curran *et al* (eds.), *Mass Communications and Society* (London, 1979).

Maguire, J. M.. *Marx's Theory of Politics* (Cambridge, 1978).

Malalgoda, K., 'Millennialism in Relation to Buddhism', *Comparative Studies in Society and History*, 12 (1970).

Malewski, A., 'The Degree of Status Incongruence and its Effects', in R. Bendix and S. M. Lipset (eds.), *Class, Status and Power* (London, 1967).

Mallet, S., *The New Working Class* (Nottingham, 1975).

Mandel, E., *Late Capitalism* (London, 1978).

—— 'Revolutionary Strategy in Europe', *New Left Review*, 100 (1976).

—— *The Marxist Theory of Alienation* (New York, 1973).

Mann, M. H., 'The Social Cohesion of Liberal Democracy', *American Sociological Review*, 35 (1970).

—— *Consciousness and Action among the Western Working Class* (London, 1973).

—— *The Sources of Social Power* (Cambridge, 1986).

Mannheim, K., *Ideology and Utopia* (London, 1952).

Marriott, M., 'Little Communities in an Indigenous Civilization', in M. Marriott (ed.), *Village India* (Chicago, 1955).

Marsh, R. M., *The Mandarins* (New York, 1961).

Marshall, G., *Presbyteries and Profits* (Oxford, 1981).

—— 'Some Remarks on the Study of Working Class Consciousness', in D. Rose (ed.), *Social Stratification and Economic Change* (London, 1988).

Marshall, T. H., *Citizenship and Social Class* (Cambridge, 1950).

Martynow, A., 'Die Theorie des Beweglichen Gleichgewichts der Gesellschaft und die Wechselbeziehungen zwischen Gesellschaft und Milieu', *Unter Dem Banner Des Marxismus*, 4 (1930).

—— 'Kritik an Bucharins Idendifikation der Produktivkraefte mit der Produktionstechnik', in *Der Marxismus*, i (Munich, 1963).

Marx, K., *Selected Writings in Sociology and Social Philosophy*, ed. T. B. Bottomore and M. Rubel (London, 1956).

—— *Early Writings*, ed. T. B. Bottomore (New York, 1963).

—— *Capital*, i (London, 1906); iii (London, 1972).

—— *Grundrisse*, trans. with a foreword by M. Nicolaus (Harmondsworth, 1973).

—— and Engels, F., *The German Ideology* (London, 1940).

—— —— *Selected Works*, i (Moscow, 1950); ii (Moscow, 1949).

MARX, K., and ENGELS, F., *Basic Writings in Politics and Philosophy*, ed. L. Feuer (New York, 1959).

—— —— *Marx and Engels on Religion*, ed. R. Niebuhr (New York, 1964)'.

—— —— *Articles on Britain* (Moscow, 1971).

MASARYK, T. G., *Der Selbstsmord als Sociale Massenerscheinung der modernen Civilisation* (Vienna, 1881).

MASLOW, A. H., *Motivation and Personality* (New York, 1954).

MATTHEWS, M., *Privilege in the Soviet Union* (London, 1978).

MAWSON, A. R., 'Durkheim and Contemporary Social Pathology', *British Journal of Sociology*, 21 (1970).

MEPHAM, J., 'The Theory of Ideology in Capital', in J. Mepham and D. H. Ruben (eds.), *Issues in Marxist Philosophy* (Brighton, 1979).

MERTON, R. K., *Social Theory and Social Structure* (Glencoe, Ill., 1957).

MESZAROS, I., *Marx's Theory of Alienation* (London, 1970).

—— 'Contingent and Necessary Class Consciousness', in I. Meszaros (ed.), *Aspects of History and Class Consciousness* (London, 1971).

MICHAEL, F., *The Taiping Rebellion* (Seattle, 1966).

MICHELS, R., *Political Parties* (Glencoe, Ill., 1949).

MILIBAND, R., *The State in Capitalist Society* (London, 1969).

—— 'Reply to Nicos Poulantzas', in R. Blackburn (ed.), *Ideology and Social Science* (London, 1975).

—— *Marxism and Politics* (London, 1977).

MILLS, C. W., *White Collar* (Oxford, 1951).

MITCHELL, W., *Sociological Analysis and Politics: The Theories of Talcott Parsons* (Englewood Cliffs, NJ, 1967).

MOORE, B., *The Social Origins of Dictatorship and Democracy* (Boston, 1966).

—— *Injustice: The Social Bases of Obedience and Revolt* (London, 1978).

MOORHOUSE, H. F., 'The Marxist Theory of the Labour Aristocracy', *Social History*, 3 (1978).

MOSCA, G., *The Ruling Class* (New York, 1939).

MOUFFE, C., 'Hegemony and Ideology in Gramsci', in C. Mouffe (ed.), *Gramsci and Marxist Theory* (London, 1979).

MOUZELIS, N., 'System and Social Integration: Some Reflections on a Fundamental Distinction', *British Journal of Sociology*, 25 (1974).

—— *Back to Sociological Theory: Bridging the Micro-Macro Gap* (London, 1991).

—— *On the Construction of Social Orders: Post-Marxist Alternatives* (London, 1991).

NAIRN, T., 'The English Working Class', in R. Blackburn (ed.), *Ideology and Social Science* (London, 1975).

—— *The Breakup of Britain* (London, 1981).

NICOLAUS, M., 'The Unknown Marx', in C. Oglesby (ed.), *New Left Reader* (New York, 1969).

NIE, N., and ANDERSEN, K., 'Mass Belief Systems Revisited', *Journal of Politics*, 36 (1974).

NOCK, A. D., *Conversion* (Oxford, 1933).

NOLAN, M., *Social Democracy and Society: Working Class Radicalism in Düsseldorf, 1890–1920* (Bonn, 1974).

NORDLINGER, E. A., *Conflict Regulation in Divided Societies* (Cambridge, Mass., 1972).

OAKESHOTT, M., 'The Moral Life in the Writings of Thomas Hobbes', in M. Oakeshott, *Hobbes on Civil Association* (Oxford, 1975).

OBEYESEKERE, G., 'Theodicy, Sin and Salvation in a Sociology of Buddhism', in E. R. Leach (ed.), *Dialectic in Practical Religion* (Cambridge, 1968).

O'CONNOR, J., *The Fiscal Crisis of the State* (London, 1973).

—— *The Meaning of Crisis* (Oxford, 1987).

OLLMAN, B., *Alienation: Marx's Concept of Man in Capitalist Society* (Cambridge, 1971).

—— 'Towards Class Consciousness Next Time: Marx and the Working Class', *Politics and Society*, 3 (1972).

OLSEN, M. E., 'Durkheim's Two Concepts of Anomie', *Sociological Quarterly*, 6 (1965).

OLSON, M., 'Rapid Growth as a Destabilizing Force', *Journal of Economic History*, 23 (1963).

—— *The Logic of Collective Action* (New York, 1968).

OLSSON, A. S., *The Swedish Wage Negotiation System* (Uppsala, 1989).

O'MALLEY, L. S. S., *Popular Hinduism: The Religion of the Masses* (Cambridge, 1935).

OSTROGORSKY, G., 'Agrarian Conditions in the Byzantine Empire in the Middle Ages', in J. H. Clapham and E. Power (eds.), *The Cambridge Economic History*, i (Cambridge, 1942).

OZMENT, E., *The Reformation and the Cities: The Appeal of Protestantism to Sixteenth-Century Germany and Switzerland* (New Haven, Conn., 1975).

PARKIN, F., 'System Contradiction and Political Transformation', *European Journal of Sociology*, 13 (1972).

—— *Marxism and Class Theory: A Bourgeois Critique* (London, 1979).

PARSONS, T., 'The Place of Ultimate Values in Sociological Theory', *International Journal of Ethics*, 45 (1935).

—— *The Structure of Social Action* (New York, 1937).

—— 'An Analytical Approach to the Theory of Social Stratification', in his *Essays in Sociological Theory: Pure and Applied* (Glencoe, Ill., 1949).

PARSONS, T., *The Social System* (London, 1952).
—— *Structure and Process in Modern Societies* (New York, 1960).
—— *Societies: Evolutionary and Comparative Perspectives* (Englewood Cliffs, NJ, 1966).
—— 'Durkheim's Contribution to the Theory of Integration of Social Systems', in his *Sociological Theory and Modern Society* (London, 1967).
—— 'Full Citizenship for the Negro American?' in his *Sociological Theory and Modern Society* (London, 1967).
—— 'An Approach to the Sociology of Knowledge', in his *Sociological Theory and Modern Society* (New York, 1967).
—— and SHILS, E. A. (eds.), *Towards a General Theory of Action* (Cambridge, Mass., 1951).
—— —— NAEGELE, K. D., and PITTS, J. R. (eds.), *Theories of Society* (New York, 1961).
—— and SMELSER, N. J., *Economy and Society* (New York, 1956).
PARTRIDGE, P. H., *Consent and Consensus* (London, 1971).
PLAMENATZ , J., *Man and Society*, ii (London, 1969).
PLOWMAN, D. E. G., MINCHINTON, W. E., and STACEY, M., 'Local Social Status in England and Wales', *Sociological Review*, 10 (1962).
POGGI, G., *Images of Society* (Stanford, Calif., 1972).
—— *Calvinism and the Capitalist Spirit* (London, 1983).
POLE, J. R., *The Pursuit of Equality in American History* (Berkeley, Calif., 1978).
POSTAN, M. M., *The Medieval Economy and Society* (Harmondsworth, 1975).
POULANTZAS, N., *Political Power and Social Classes* (London, 1973).
—— *Fascism and Dictatorship* (London, 1974).
—— *Classes in Contemporary Capitalism* (London, 1978).
PRZEWORSKI, A., *Capitalism and Social Democracy* (Cambridge, 1986).
—— 'Material Interests, Class Compromise and the Transition to Socialism', *Politics and Society*, 10 (1980)
—— 'Marxism and Rational Choice', *Politics and Society*, 14 (1985).
PURCELL, V., *The Boxer Uprising* (Cambridge, 1963).
RAMANUJAN, A. K. (ed.), *Speaking of Siva* (London, 1973).
RAMMSTEDT, O., *Sekte und Soziale Bewegung: Soziologische Analyze der Täufer in Münster* (Cologne, 1966).
RAO, M. S. A., *Tradition, Rationality and Change* (Bombay, 1972).
RENNER, K., *The Institutions of Private Law and their Social Functions*, ed. with an introduction by O. Kahn-Freund (London, 1949).
REX, J., *Key Problems in Sociological Theory* (London, 1961).
ROBBINS, L., *The Nature and Significance of Economic Science* (London, 1948).

ROBERTSON SMITH, W., *The Religion of the Semites* (New York, 1956).

ROCK, P., *Deviant Behaviour* (London, 1973).

ROGERS, E. M., *Modernization among Peasants* (New York, 1969).

ROSE, D., and MARSHALL, G., 'Constructing the (W)right Classes', *Sociology*, 20 (1986).

ROSENBERG, H., *Bureaucracy, Aristocracy and Autocracy* (Cambridge, Mass., 1958).

ROSS, A. M., and HARTMAN, P. T., *Changing Patterns of Industrial Conflict* (New York, 1960).

RUNCIMAN, W. G., 'Class, Status and Power?', in J. A. Jackson (ed.), *Social Stratification* (Cambridge, 1968).

—— *Relative Deprivation and Social Justice* (London, 1972).

—— *A Treatise on Social Theory*, ii (Cambridge, 1989).

RYDER, A. J., *The German Revolution of 1918* (Cambridge, 1967).

SARIOLA, S., 'Fatalism and Anomie: Components of Rural–Urban Differences', *Kansas Journal of Sociology*, 1 (1965).

SAYER, D., 'Science as Critique: Marx versus Althusser', in J. Mepham and D. H. Ruben (eds.), *Issues in Marxist Philosophy*, iii (Brighton, 1979).

SCASE, R., *Social Democracy in Capitalist Society: Working Class Politics in Britain and Sweden* (London, 1977).

SCHELER, M., *Ressentiment*, trans. W. W. Holdheim, with an introduction by L. A. Coser (Glencoe, Ill., 1961).

SCHONFIELD, W. R., 'The Classical Marxist Conception of Democracy', *Review of Politics*, 33 (1971).

SCHULLER, T., *Democracy at Work* (Oxford, 1985).

SCHUMPETER, J. A., 'Social Classes in an Ethnically Homogeneous Environment', in his *Imperialism and Social Classes* (Oxford, 1951).

SCOTT, J., *The Upper Classes* (London, 1982).

SCOTT, J. F. 'The Changing Foundations of the Parsonian Action Scheme', *American Sociological Review*, 28 (1963).

SELIGER, M., *The Marxist Conception of Ideology* (Cambridge, 1977).

SEN, A. K., 'Rational Fools: A Critique of the Behavioural Foundations of Economic Theory', in F. H. Hahn and R. Hollis (eds.), *Philosophy and Economic Theory* (Oxford, 1979).

SENNETT, R., and COBB, J., *The Hidden Injuries of Class* (Cambridge, 1972).

SHAW, W. H., *Marx's Theory of History* (London, 1978).

SHILS, E. A., 'Order, Charisma and Status', *American Sociological Review*, 30 (1965).

—— *Centre and Periphery: Essays in Macrosociology* (Chicago, 1975).

SHIN, V. Y. C., *The Taiping Ideology: Its Sources, Interpretations and Influence* (Seattle, 1972).

SHORTER, E., and TILLY, C., *Strikes in France, 1830–1968* (Cambridge, 1974).

SILVERBERG, J. (ed.), *Social Mobility in the Caste System in India* (The Hague, 1968).

SINGER, M., review of Max Weber, *The Religion of India*, *American Anthropologist*, 63 (1961), 143–50.

SMELSER, N. J., *Theory of Collective Behaviour* (London, 1962).

SRINIVAS, M. N., *Social Change in Modern India* (Berkeley, Calif., 1966).

STEDMAN JONES, G., *Languages of Class* (Cambridge, 1983).

STEVENSON, J., and COOK, C., *The Slump That Never Was* (London, 1979).

STEVENSON, S., *The Heart of Jainism* (New Delhi, 1915; repr. 1970).

STONE, L., *The Causes of the English Revolution, 1529–1642* (London, 1972).

SWANSON, G., *Religion and Regime* (Ann Arbor, Mich., 1967).

SWEEZY, P. M., *The Theory of Capitalist Development* (London, 1949).

SWINGEWOOD, A., *Marx and Modern Social Theory* (London, 1975).

SYKES, G., *A Society of Captives* (Princeton, NJ, 1958).

SZTOMPKA, P., *System and Function* (New York, 1974).

TALMON, Y., 'Pursuit of the Millenium', *European Journal of Sociology*, 3 (1962).

TAMPKE, J., *Ruhr and Revolution* (London, 1979).

TENG, S. Y., *The Taiping Rebellion and the Western Powers* (Oxford, 1971).

THAPAR, R., *A History of India*, i (Harmondsworth, 1974).

THERBORN, G., 'The Rule of Capital and the Rise of Democracy', *New Left Review*, 103 (1977).

THOMAS, K., *Religion and the Decline of Magic* (London, 1971).

THOMPSON, E. P., *The Poverty of Theory* (London, 1978).

TITMUS, R., *Social Policy* (London, 1974).

TOURAINE, A., *La Conscience ouvrière* (Paris, 1966).

TUMIN, S. M., *Social Class and Social Change in Puerto Rico* (Princeton, NJ, 1961).

URRY, J., *Reference Groups and the Theory of Revolution* (London, 1973).

VAN DEN BERGHE, P., *South Africa: A Study in Conflict* (Berkeley, Calif. 1970).

—— 'Dialectic and Functionalism', *American Sociological Review*, 28 (1963).

VAN PARIJS, P., 'Sociology as General Economics', *European Journal of Sociology*, 22 (1981).

VASQUEZ, A. S., *The Philosophy of Praxis* (London, 1977).

VERBA, S., and LEHMAN, K., 'Unemployment, Class Consciousness and Radical Politics: What Didn't Happen in the Thirties', *Journal of Politics*, 39 (1977).

VESTER, M., *Die Entstehung des Proletariats als Lernprozess: Die Entstehung antikapitalistischer Theorie und Praxis in England, 1792–1848* (Frankfurt, 1970).

WAKEMAN, F., 'Rebellion and Revolution: The Study of Popular Movements in Chinese History', *Journal of Asian Studies*, 36 (1977).

WEBER, M., *The Theory of Social and Economic Organization*, ed. T. Parsons (London, 1947).

—— *From Max Weber: Essays in Sociology*, ed. H. H. Gerth and C. W. Mills (London, 1948).

—— *The Religion of China*, trans. and ed. H. H. Gerth (Glencoe, Ill., 1951).

—— *The Religion of India*, trans. and ed. H. H. Gerth and D. Martindale (Glencoe, Ill., 1958).

—— *The Sociology of Religion*, trans. and ed. E. Fischoff (London, 1965).

—— *Economy and Society*, ed. G. Roth and C. Wittich (Berkeley, Calif., 1968).

—— *The Agrarian Sociology of Ancient Civilizations*, trans. R. I. Frank (London, 1976).

—— 'Anticritical Last Word on *The Spirit of Capitalism*', trans. with an introduction by W. M. Davis, *American Journal of Sociology*, 83 (1978).

WESOTOWSKI, W., and STOMCZYNSKI, K., 'Reduction of Social Inequalities and Status Inconsistency', in *Social Structure: Polish Sociology* (Wroctaw, 1977).

WESTERGAARD, J., 'Power, Class and the Media', in J. Curran *et al.*, (eds.), *Mass Communications and Society* (London, 1977).

—— and RESLER H., *Class in a Capitalist Society* (London, 1975).

WHYTE, M. K., *Small Groups and Political Rituals in China* (Berkeley, Calif., 1974).

WILLIAMS, G. A., 'The Concept of "Egemonia" in the Thought of Antonio Gramsci: Some Notes and Interpretations', *Journal of the History of Ideas*, 21 (1960).

—— *Proletarian Order* (London, 1975).

WILLIAMS, R., *American Society: A Sociological Interpretation* (New York, 1960).

—— 'The Idea of Relative Deprivation', in L. Coser (ed.), *The Idea of Social Structure: Papers in Honor of Robert K. Merton* (New York, 1975).

WOLF, E. R., *Peasant Wars of the Twentieth Century* (London, 1971).

WOLPE, H., 'Some Problems Concerning Revolutionary Consciousness', *Socialist Register* (1970).

WOOD, E. M., *The Retreat from Class* (London, 1986).

WOOD, S. (ed.), *The Degradation of Work?* (London, 1986).

WOOTTON, B., *The Social Foundations of Wage Policy* (London, 1955).

WRIGHT, E. O., 'Contradictory Class Locations', *New Left Review*, 98 (1976).

—— *Class, Crisis and the State* (London, 1978).

—— *Classes* (London, 1986).

WRONG, D., 'The Oversocialized Conception of Man in Modern Sociology', *American Sociological Review*, 26 (1961).

YANG, C. K., *Religion in Chinese Society* (Berkeley, Calif., 1961).

YINGER, M., *Religion, Society and the Individual* (New York, 1957).

ZAEHNER, R. C., *Hinduism* (London, 1972).

INDEX

indoctrination thesis:
  basic assumptions of 292–3
  sophisticated version of 300–5

normative functionalism 7–16,
    42–3, 384–7, 399–401

problem of disorder:
  in Durkheimian sociology ix–x,
    3–4, 17–20, 152–7
  in Marxist sociology x–xii,
    166–71, 268–9, 279–80,
    369–71
production relations:
  and anti-system 171–2, 183–4,
    189–92, 393–5, 406–8
  and forces of production 186–9
  and legal relations 178–83
  see also system contradiction

rationality:
  differential class rationality
    203, 235, 293–4
  rational versus non-rational
    action 14–15, 209–10, 232–5
  and revolutionary practice
    236–8, 271–5, 330–1
  versus ignorance and error
    100, 209, 309–10, 316–18
  versus reason 8, 203, 207–8
  see also ritual; utilitarian theory
    of action
rebellion (versus revolution)
    58–61, 111
residual categories 235 n.
  in Durkheimian theory 19,
    64–6, 78–80, 95–7, 114,
    145–6, 152–5, 373
  in Marxist theory 210, 215–18,
    249–50, 255–6, 337, 355–7,
    373–4
  see also egoism; status;
    utilitarian factors
ritual:
  as archetype of non-rational
    action 170, 210
  and revolutionary practice
    248–50
  socially integrative function
    23–5
  and stability of caste system
    53–8

versus ritualization 46–50
  see also hyper-ritual

schism:
  as class polarization 107, 161,
    163–5
  defined xi, 17 n.
  as limiting case of disorder
    17–18, 32–3, 107–13
  structural versus ideological
    polarization 163–6
  see also class conflict; sect
sect 26–8, 31, 109, 132–3, 290
solidarity:
  consensual versus ascriptive 6,
    377
  contractual versus organic
    80–2
  defined 10–11, 28, 45, 96, 154
  see also anomie; schism
status:
  and charisma 84–5
  dereliction and abrogation 126
  as embodiment of values 76–7,
    87–8, 92–3
  interactional versus
    attributional 86
  and power 83, 93–4, 173–8,
    216–17, 383–5
  and social comparisons 88–9,
    216–17, 254–5, 264–5
  'social hierarchy/classification'
    65, 70, 76–8, 91–2, 109–11
  see also citizenship; incongruity
    of power and status
system contradiction 183–5, 188,
    192–8, 377–9, 405–12
  and class action 192–4, 308–9,
    315–16, 334–6
  and the 'collective worker'
    189, 191–2
  see also production relations

utilitarian factors:
  and fatalism 39–42
  and impoverishment/affluence
    213–18
  'power and wealth'/the
    distribution of 'men and
    things'/the 'economic life'
    24–5, 29, 64, 70–1, 95–7,
    114–15, 139–40, 153–5